COLLECTOR'S
ENCYCLOPEDIA OF

Metlox Potteries

IDENTIFICATION
AND VALUES

CARL GIBBS JR.

COLLECTOR BOOKS
A Division of Schroeder Publishing Co., Inc.

Searching for a Publisher?

We are always looking for knowledgeable people considered to be experts within their fields. If you feel that there is a real need for a book on your collectible subject and have a large comprehensive collection, contact Collector Books.

On the Cover:

California Provincial coffee pot, $115 – 125; California Freeform water pitcher, $210 – 230; Mouse Mobile cookie jar, $175 – 200; Angelfish vase from Romanelli's Modern Masterpieces, $75 – 90; Sculptured Grape teapot, $100 – 110; Lotus dinner plate, $12 – 13; Lotus mug, $20 – 22; and Bambi with Butterfly Walt Disney figurine, $225 – 250.

Cover design by Sherry Kraus
Book design by Terri Stalions

Additional copies of this book may be ordered from:
Collector Books
P.O. Box 3009
Paducah, Kentucky 42002-3009

or

Carl Gibbs, Jr.
P.O. Box 131584
Houston, TX 77219-1584

@$24.95. Add $2.00 for postage and handling.
Copyright: Carl Gibbs, Jr., 1995

Printed by IMAGE GRAPHICS, INC., Paducah, Kentucky

Contents

Introduction and Acknowledgments

My acquaintance with Metlox Potteries began quite inadvertently in January, 1990, at a 1950s resale shop in Houston, Texas. The previous summer, engrossed with the finer decor and design of that period, I had begun a purchasing spree that progressed from 1950s furniture to art pottery to dinnerware, especially hand-painted dinnerware. I was fascinated with an unmarked item, a wonderfully lopsided, abstract W-shape with a meandering, almost hypnotic, black and gray primitive design on a textured white background. I immediately rejected the proprietor's assertion that it was a large ashtray and proceeded to try to discover the manufacturer's name and the possibility of other items with the same pattern. Four months passed before I could positively identify it as the twin vegetable of Metlox's California Aztec dinnerware pattern. While searching in vain for a complete pattern listing, I purchased every piece of Aztec I could find, along with countless other dinnerware patterns by Metlox and other companies.

In retrospect, my evolution from collecting to selling dinnerware through the mail to running The California Connection Dinnerware Shop seems almost inevitable. The most rewarding aspects of this vocation/avocation have been the continual discovery of new patterns and the process of learning about them. More than any other pottery, Metlox intrigued me with its quality, diversity, and imaginative designs.

The idea for a book about Metlox Potteries began as I collected copies of company brochure material from various sources. I showed these to noted author Ann Kerr during her visit to Houston. Aware of the growing interest in Southern California pottery, she strongly suggested that I write a book. At first I intended to self-publish a small book covering only the 20 or so major dinnerware patterns. I contacted authority Jack Chipman with the hope of acquiring lists and information concerning several popular 1950s patterns for which I had little material. Mr. Chipman informed me that he possessed a large amount of Metlox literature which he would share with me if I would write a comprehensive book including all of the dinnerware patterns and artware lines. Since the length and expense of such a large book precluded self-publication, both he and Mrs. Kerr recommended that I submit a proposal to Collector Books, America's pre-eminent publisher of antique and collectibles books. The publisher's immediate approval was a further source of inspiration. The support of owners Bill Schroeder and Bill Schroeder, Jr., and especially the assistance of editor Lisa Stroup have been gratefully appreciated.

I have been blessed with a wealth of Metlox brochure materials that provided the extensive listings in the text. Mr. Chipman's literature was augmented with copies of Metlox publications on file for research use at the Manhattan Beach Historical Society's Museum at Polliwog Park in Manhattan Beach, California. This material, supplied by Society members Keith Robinson and Judy Scott, was donated by Melinda Avery as part of a permanent Metlox exhibit housed at the museum. Company employees supplied additional leaflets, brochures, and archive photographs that added to the completeness of the lists.

Personal interviews with Metlox employees provided an extremely in-depth look at the inner workings of the company. My sincere thanks to Bob Allen, Mel Shaw, Melinda Avery, Vincent Martinez, Frank Irwin, Bob Chandler, Dan Baird, Ted Ball, Doug Bothwell, and Gene Friedman who generously offered information, recollections, and knowledge of production techniques and industry practices that greatly enhanced the accuracy and informativeness of the text.

Experts who have been extremely helpful with specific topics include Joyce and Fred Roerig (the cookie jars), David R. Smith and Margaret Adamic of the Walt Disney Archives (the Disney figurines), Stan Pawlowski (the Disney figurines), Maxine Nelson (the Vernonware Division), Jan Dennis (the early history of Metlox Potteries and Manhattan Beach), Harvey Duke (the Prouty years), and, of course, Jack Chipman. As interested collectors and dealers learned of the project, they too offered brochure material, information, and item photographs. These many individuals are listed at the end of the book along with a directory of contributing mail-order dealers who regularly stock Metlox items.

Several others deserve special thanks. Houston-based editor Cynthia Dresden assisted me with typing and proofreading the lengthy manuscript and corrected any flagrant abuses of the English language. I sincerely appreciate all of her suggestions and advice. My business partner Juan Fernandez helped me with the extensive photography. His expertise, sharp eyes, and critical judgment were invaluable. Thanks also to Barbara and Tom Gibbs, Jr., my aunt and late uncle, who graciously offered their hospitality during my visits to Southern California, and my parents, Mr. and Mrs. Carl Gibbs, Sr., who helped whenever and however they could.

This book was a labor of love on my part. Coming at a time when collector interest in Metlox is growing rapidly, I hope that readers will find the book extremely informative in their appreciation of Metlox's immensely varied contribution to American pottery.

Metlox Potteries:
A Historical Perspective

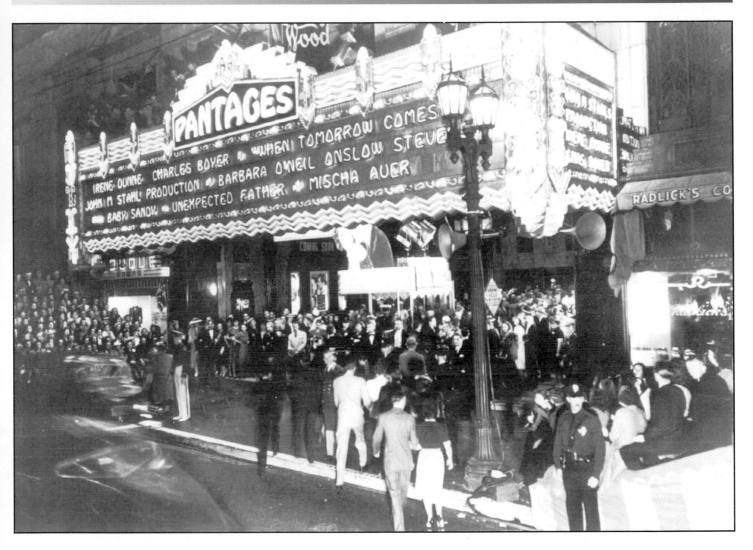

The famous outdoor ceramic sign produced by Metlox for the Pantages Theater in Hollywood. Metlox archive photo.

Metlox Potteries is now recognized as one of the foremost manufacturers of American ceramic dinnerware and artware. Several features of its history are quite unique. In operation from 1927 to 1989, its longevity as a successful pottery is exceptional. Ownership stayed under the control of only two families, the Proutys and the Shaws. For what was essentially a small business operating and producing in a small factory, the quality and quantity of its varied output is truly impressive.

The Prouty Years

Michigan-born T. C. Prouty and his son Willis, the first owners of Metlox, were primarily inventors who were credited with over 70 patented

inventions. Many of their early inventions were designed and manufactured for government use during and after World War I and included tachometers, speedometers, altimeters, and oxygen gas equipment.

In 1919 the Proutys settled in Hermosa Beach, California, where they became interested in ceramic tile production. After experimenting with the clays found in the region and determining the superiority of talc from the Death Valley area, in 1920 they patented a tile body formulated with talc as the primary ingredient. This move was followed by the creation of Proutyline Products Company in 1921 to sell their inventions and produce architectural tiles. A two-story tile factory, at 719 Pier Avenue in Hermosa Beach, was constructed in 1922. The following year they installed a patented tunnel kiln featuring the innovative use of setters rather than saggers to increase efficiency. Wall and floor tiles, both plain and decorative, were marketed as Hermosa Tile until the factory was sold to the American Encaustic Tiling Company of Ohio in 1926.

In 1927 the Proutys created Metlox Manufacturing Company as a division of their Proutyline Products Company. The name Metlox was a contraction of the phrase "metal oxide." Metlox began operations on June 3, 1927, in a newly constructed facility, the West Coast's first electrically welded steel building, located at 1200 Morningside Drive in downtown Manhattan Beach, California. The plant occupied an approximately four-acre tract on the corner of Manhattan Beach Boulevard and Morningside Drive, a few blocks away from the Pacific Ocean. The Proutys purchased the northern half of the site. The southern half was leased from the Santa Fe Railway Company which retained ownership throughout Metlox's existence. This arrangement was ideal for the new company. With the Santa Fe tracks nearby, a spur was constructed on the company grounds which allowed the easy shipment of raw materials into the plant and products out. At this time Manhattan Beach was a small beach resort community rather isolated from downtown Los Angeles and the other industrialized coastal towns. The residents considered the factory an economic

Evan K. Shaw

godsend since it provided jobs for local inhabitants and tax money for the city. As the reputation of the company grew nationally, the name recognition of the city was also enchanced.

At first, Metlox specialized in the production of outdoor ceramic advertising signs with letters molded in five varied styles. These huge signs, impervious to weather conditions, served as insulated bases for decorative neon tubing, thereby allowing them to function at night as well as day. Well-known examples are the Metlox signs for the Pantages Theater in Hollywood, the Pathe Studios in Culver City, and the Warner Brothers Theater in Huntington Park. Despite the deepening of the Great Depression, initially the Proutys' new business endeavor prospered as the popularity of movies led to the construction of new theaters that needed outdoor signs. The factory expanded in the summer of 1930 and by 1932 had contracts in 11 western states. In time, however, the demand dwindled and many purchasers who ordered signs on credit reneged on payments.

After T. C. Prouty died in 1931, Willis became Metlox's guiding force. Realizing that the focus of the company's production had to change and cognizant of the growing popularity of J. A. Bauer Pottery's new solid color tableware and kitchenware, Willis decided to adapt the facilities for dinnerware production. After favorable consumer response to its first dinnerware pattern, California Pottery in 1932, Metlox followed with "200" Series (aka Poppy Trail) in 1934, Mission Bell in 1935, Pintoria c. 1937, and Yorkshire in 1937 — all solid color dinnerware each with a different design shape. Metlox expanded into artware in 1938. When sculptor Carl Romanelli joined Metlox as an artware designer, his Modern Masterpieces and Metlox Miniatures lines provided the highpoint of the Prouty years.

Dinnerware and artware production completely stopped when the United States entered World War II. Metlox supported the war effort by manufacturing shell casings, machine parts, nuts, and bolts. After the war a brief attempt to market toys made from the surplus metal did little to alleviate Metlox's burden of a reported $10,000 a month loss. After deciding to resume full-scale dinnerware production, Metlox introduced its first hand-decorated embossed pattern, Camellia, which seemed to mark a new direction for the company. Prouty's influence, however, ceased when he sold Metlox to Evan K. Shaw in 1946.

Evan K. Shaw

Evan K. Shaw's rise from very enterprising but small-scale young businessman to highly prosperous entrepreneur epitomized a success story often repeated in Southern California in the late 1930s and 1940s. Due to the rapid population growth and economic development of the region, small fortunes could be made handily if one's business instincts were sound and one's speculations and judgments were accurate.

Shaw's industrious nature was evident even in his younger years. Born in Pennsylvania in 1909 as one of six children and raised in Ridgefield Park, New Jersey, he assumed responsibility as the head of the family after the early deaths of his father and oldest brother. His excellence in athletics, especially football and track, won him a scholarship to William and Mary College in Virginia. He enrolled in the Univeristy of Southern California after an unsuccessful attempt to make the 1932 Olympic track team brought him to the area. At USC he served as the captain of the polo team. There he met Jean Hessell who became his wife in 1936, and with whom he raised four children.

In the late 1930s Shaw was introduced to the ceramics business when he accepted a position in a small dinnerware company owned by Toby Anguish. There his chief duty was to purchase the seconds and closeouts of various Southern California potteries. These sets were then sold to movie theaters to use as giveaways between the "A" and "B" features on theater gift nights. This job familiarized him with the business and most of the potteries in the area, including Vernon Kilns where he developed a close relationship with the company's president, Faye Bennison.

Seeing how pottery-oriented Southern California had become and realizing the business opportunities available in ceramics, Shaw decided to establish his own distributorship, the Evan K. Shaw Company. Shaw rented a showroom in the Brack Shops Building located at 527 West 7th Street in downtown Los Angeles. At this point he became what was known in trade jargon as a "jobber" — a businessman who owns a sales organization, sends himself or a salesman to various factories to purchase large amounts of products at very substantial discounts, stocks the items in his own warehouse, and then sells them to retail outlets under his company's name. Jobbers were especially indispensable to small ceramics businesses who utilized the jobber instead of salaried sales representatives to sell their wares.

As a jobber, Shaw became associated with Brad Keeler, who was just beginning his popular bird figurine line, and modeler Frank Irwin's family, who rented space in Keeler's small studio in Glendale. During this period it was common practice for small potteries to rent a workspace and, more importantly, the use of the kiln in a larger pottery. Shaw's expanding business soon led to his purchase of American Pottery, a manufacturer of terra cotta gardenware and brick, located on Washington Boulevard in east Los Angeles. Brad Keeler immediately leased 5,000 square feet of workspace at Shaw's new facility. The Irwin family also joined Shaw at American Pottery.

Shaw's new company received a welcome boost when Vernon Kilns transferred its Walt Disney Figurine contract to American Pottery on July 22, 1942. This was only the first instance in which Shaw's association with Faye Bennison was beneficial. The Disney Figurine line became Shaw's major product at American Pottery. Frank Irwin mod-

eled the figurines and Brad Keeler assisted with the glazing and firing. American Pottery thrived until it was destroyed by fire in 1946. Suddenly Shaw no longer had a factory. Keeler relocated his business to a new facility at 2936 Delay Drive in Los Angeles. Fortuitously, Shaw learned that Willis Prouty wished to sell Metlox Potteries. In a transaction finalized on November 8, 1946, Shaw purchased Metlox with the insurance money from the fire.

Metlox — The Beginning of the Shaw Years

With the acquisition of a much larger facility, Shaw was faced with several important choices. In every instance, his acute business sense and accurate perceptions guided his judgments. His first decisions concerned the style and type of product Metlox would offer. It is commonly believed that Shaw purchased Metlox primarily to continue his profitable Disney Figurine Line. Although this was a factor, his true intentions were much grander. He hoped to establish Metlox as America's foremost dinnerware manufacturer. With foreign imports severely limited by the decimation of European and Japanese factories during World War II and with the changing lifestyles of post-World War II America, the climate seemed right to introduce new styles of dinnerware design. Ironically, Shaw's avowed preference was the traditional, fancy dinnerware of Spode and other English companies. Influential importer Paul Straub counseled and almost convinced Shaw to imitate this style. Surveying the successful products of his major Southern Californian competitors — Franciscan Ceramics' embossed patterns, Vernon Kilns' English-style transfer prints, and J. A. Bauer's solid color lines — Shaw judged that Metlox should develop its own design style. Aware of the moderate success of Prouty's Camellia, Shaw chose hand-decorated dinnerware as the company's specialty.

Metlox's reputation would be built on the production of hand-painted dinnerware. Patterns generally were released on company shapes that offered a large variety of open stock items. Starter sets were priced economically. The real profits came from the wonderful assortment of open stock items that were sold separately. Since hand-decorated patterns in general were more expensive to produce, Metlox's products usually retailed at higher prices than those of its competitors.

Of major importance was Shaw's decision to hire Bob Allen and Mel Shaw as his art directors in 1946. Without question Metlox would never have attained its stature and success without the innovative and imaginative designs of this talented team. Both men came to Metlox from backgrounds in the animation business. They developed a close personal friendship which dated from 1933, the year they both became cartoon artists at Harman-Ising Productions. In 1937 Bob

Allen helped to start MGM's new cartoon studio while Mel Shaw worked on *Fantasia* and *Bambi* for Walt Disney Studios. Their association was renewed during the war when Shaw joined Allen in the making of service films at Hugh Harman Productions. In 1946 they formed their own design firm, Allen-Shaw Associates, working as toy designers for Plakie Toys, Inc. and as commercial and residential architectural designers. A little known fact is that they created the Howdy Doody puppet design in 1949, which was patented as design number 156,687 in their names on January 3, 1950. Before joining Metlox they worked briefly for a small ceramics company named Helen's Ware which introduced them to pottery designing. Such backgrounds certainly influenced their free, uninhibited approach to dinnerware design. They also had a keen, instinctive sense of which designs were technically possible in the ceramic medium. As part of their agreement with Shaw, they were allowed to work as designers for other individuals or companies exclusive of ceramics manufacturers. Their office was never located in the Metlox plant.

Fortunately for Metlox and Evan K. Shaw, Allen and Shaw's first pattern, the 1946 streamlined, hand-decorated California Ivy, was an unqualified success, reflecting the public's eagerness for a new dinnerware design approach. Shaw decided to continue to

Design sketch by Allen and Shaw, dated 4/11/51, that includes the California Provincial dinnerware coffee pot.

Designers Bob Allen and Mel Shaw (far left and far right respectively) discuss the modeling of the California Provincial dinnerware coffee pot with Bernie Hassenstab (center). Metlox archive photo.

One of Allen and Shaw's first design drawings for Metlox that shows four possible design shapes for the California Ivy dinnerware cup.

market Metlox's dinnerware under the trade name "Poppytrail." Prouty had originally adopted this name, referring to California's colorful state flower, in 1936 because it suggested the varicolored selection of solid-tone dinnerware Metlox produced at that time. Very pleased with consumers' acceptance of Allen and Shaw's fresh designs, Evan K. Shaw allowed the team almost complete creative freedom to style distinctive dinnerware patterns and shapes that became trend-setters. During the 1950s the immensely popular early American shapes of the Provincial dinnerware patterns were followed by the modernistic designs featured in the patterns of the Navajo, Confetti, and Freeform shapes. At the same time quality artware lines were developed in the company's Poppytrail Artware Division.

In the late 1940s, Evan K. Shaw began to organize one of the best sales staffs in the industry. Shortly after purchasing Metlox, he met Sam Haspel, a dinnerware representative, when they happened to be seated next to each other in a Dallas, Texas, restaurant. Each was surprised to learn of the other's occupation. Haspel, whose organization S. M. Haspel & Son had offices with Gene Friedman in Dallas, and Joe Friedman in Memphis, Tennessee, agreed to represent Metlox's products. S. M. Haspel & Son and Shaw's Evan K. Shaw Company became the cornerstones of Metlox's national sales organization. As an added benefit of their association, Haspel arranged for Shaw to sell Metlox's large remaining inventory of Prouty products to two compa-

nies in Louisville, Kentucky, thereby acquiring needed capital for Shaw's new company. In 1957 Ted Ball became Metlox's Poppytrail Division sales manager. His aggressive leadership helped greatly to promote the impressive sales of the company during the late 1950s and the 1960s.

The Vernonware Division

In 1958, Evan K. Shaw and Metlox profited once again from Shaw's close friendship with Faye Bennison. Suddenly and quite unexpectedly, Bennison decided to close Vernon Kilns. Although foreign competition and rising labor costs figured in his decision, reportedly he was just tired of the hassles of the ceramics business. Bennison allowed Shaw to purchase from Vernon Kilns the right to use the well-known trade name "Vernonware" on Metlox products and the molds, blocks, and cases of selected dinnerware patterns and shapes including Vernon's English-style San Fernando shape on which Shaw produced patterns with a design style more akin to his personal tastes. Shaw immediately created Metlox's Vernonware Division. By establishing a second sales division within the company, Shaw hoped to reinvigorate a Poppytrail Division sales staff that he felt had become too complacent with its own success. Employees relate that he also wanted Metlox to emulate the organization of his ideal company, the General Motors Corporation, and its structure of competing divisions.

The Vernonware Division had its own sales staff, budget, and selection of dinnerware patterns. With very few exceptions, each Poppytrail Division or Vernonware Division sales representative could represent only the patterns of his division. Retail outlets, therefore, had to deal with two separate sales staffs — a procedure most did not find objectionable at first. Shaw truly believed that this arrangement was healthy for the company. Although he always considered the Poppytrail Division first in importance and the Vernonware Division second, he treated both sales forces fairly. New dinnerware patterns, including the choice ones, were evenly divided between the two divisions and in time the Vernonware Division's pattern selection equalled that of the Poppytrail Division.

Initially the Vernonware Division floundered. Its first new patterns had disappointing sales as did the Vernon Kilns' patterns it continued to offer. This situation improved when Metlox began to release patterns on Allen and Shaw's redesign of the San Fernando shape that became very popular. An important addition to the division's sales staff was Doug Bothwell, a former sales vice president for Vernon Kilns, who Shaw hired to head the division in 1960. Bothwell's first duty was to convince Vernon Kilns' old sales staff to join Metlox's Vernonware Division. The division began to prosper under this experienced staff's expertise. Its strongest regions were Texas, the Midwest, and the South.

The two-division concept worked well until the late 1970s when Metlox's sales diminished drastically. Retail outlets began to object to the inconvenient procedure of having to deal with two sales staffs. Finally, around 1980 Metlox merged the two divisions and reduced the entire sales staff.

The 1960s

The 1960s marked the height of Metlox's productivity and prosperity. Profits continued to rise with the introduction of the best-selling sculptured patterns and the steady sales of the Provincial patterns. At this time Metlox had over 5,000 accounts including a multitude of speciality stores and all of the major department stores except Sears, Roebuck & Co. and J. C. Penney. Metlox's hand-decorated style was immensely popular. Its only real domestic competitor was Franciscan Ceramics.

As the company grew during the 1950s, Evan K. Shaw hired additional designers, artists, technicians, and stylists who brought their expertise, creativity, and talents into the company. The following important individuals worked in various smaller sections of one large department called the Research, Design, and Development Department (RD & D), headed by art directors Allen and Shaw.

1. *John Johnson* — Metlox's glaze genius; began working for the company in 1939 under Prouty; credited with over 80,000 different formulas, many of which were truly innovative.

2. *Frank Irwin* — model development supervisor; worked for Shaw at American Pottery and Metlox; an expert in modeling the detailed, intricate Metlox designs.

3. *Bob Chandler* — talented assistant modeler to Irwin; his tremendous engineering skills were instrumental in converting the factory from a labor-intensive hand operation to a nearly completely automated process.

4. *Dan Baird* — design manager; directed the entire operation of the RD & D; responsible for the quality of each product from its inception to its finish.

5. *Helen McIntosh* — originally hired as a color specialist; worked for Walt Disney Studios before joining Metlox; created many of Metlox's cookie jars along with other artware items.

6. *Vincent Martinez* — originally hired as a lab technician; his artistic talents led to his transfer to the RD & D where he became a chief modeler and designer; plant manager from 1988 – 89.

7. *Helen Slater* — hired specifically to design the Poppets and Toppets lines.

8. *Phyllis Ord* — modeler of various artware lines and cookie jars.

9. *Doris Cafazza* — head of the decorating department.

10. *Rick Reingold* — trained in the Delft factories in Holland; hired for his expertise in hand painting and decorating techniques.

11. *George Newsome* — came from Vernon Kilns; designed and developed Vernonware Division patterns.

12. *John Karrash* — studio potter hired for a short time to develop hand-thrown shapes which became important in the 1970s.

13. *Jane Ellis* — stylist knowledgeable in cookware and tableware designs.

14. *Benito Sanchez* — trained in Spain; assistant designer.

15. *Mary Louise Baird* — product display specialist.

The most unusual characteristic of the workings of the RD & D from the mid-1950s through the 1960s was that Evan K. Shaw gradually

Aerial photograph of Metlox Potteries.

came to exercise complete, almost dictatorial, control over the department rather than to delegate some, even minor, decision-making responsibilities. Related to this was Shaw's practice of assigning the various stages of a project's development in a one-step-at-a-time fashion to the different sections within the RD & D. Dinnerware and artware items, therefore, received input from the various sections separately, with Shaw making all of the final decisions. Allen and Shaw began to feel they were art advisors rather than art directors.

Certainly Shaw's chief attributes were his astute knowledge and comprehension of the dinnerware business and his uncanny ability to know which designs and shapes were right for the market and when. He constantly studied decorating and furnishing trends and always considered the advice and recommendations of his design staff, sales representatives, and buyers. Designing, however was not his strongest point. Metlox's design process might have worked smoother and better had he allowed his staff more creative freedom. Occasionally his changes and alterations of the staff's original designs and/or color selections were detrimental to a dinnerware pattern's or an artware item's success.

His compartmentalization of the RD & D also had its drawbacks. Shaw's perfectionist attitude and control tended to slow the advance of each project through the various divisions within the RD & D. Although many times the result was an improved finished product, it drastically delayed the arrival of new items in retail outlets. Dan Baird was instrumental in hastening the RD & D process when he became the manager of the department. This entire setup changed slowly as sales started to decline in the early 1970s and Metlox began to feel the pressures of competition from foreign companies. Shaw was forced to relinquish more and more of his control as he became progressively more engrossed with the increasing economic troubles of the company.

The Changes of the 1970s

The early 1970s marked the beginning of a gradual decline for the company. The primary reason was that Metlox's specialty — hand-decorated dinnerware patterns with a generous selection of open stock items — began to be unpopular with the American consumer. The hurried, sometimes frantic, pace of the typical American family's lifestyle created a more utilitarian attitudes towards dinnerware. Simpler, smaller, less expensive dinnerware sets that required little extra care in daily use became favored. Buyers for the retailers did not help the situation as they strongly objected to stocking large sets with separate accessories. For the first time Metlox was forced to compete and struggle in the marketplace on an almost equal footing with the products of foreign companies, especially Japanese companies.

The following quote appeared in the Metlox company newsletter, "The Poppytrail Kiln Run."

Comments Evan Shaw, Metlox president: "The threat of Japanese competition is serious, but eastern manufacturers have been harder hit than our company. Metlox is much better off than many of our competitors because the Japanese have so far not been able to achieve our quality of ware or imitate our type of patterns successfully.

Japan, as our ally...must of course become strong enough to stand alone. However the Administration's present policy is favoring Japan by inviting disaster to American industry. Quota limitations would solve the problem if applied immediately so that Japanese expansion can be spread more reasonably over a number of fields and kept within economic bounds in each."

This insightful quote appeared in the August 1952 newsletter. Shaw's fears were later realized as one by one American potteries succumbed to Japanese competition and closed. With its "most favored nation" trade status, its extremely cheap labor force, and the absence of restrictive U. S. tariffs on Japanese imports, Japan was able to undersell American pottery companies who faced continually rising labor and production costs. Although the Japanese industries as a whole can not be faulted for seizing the opportunities of an advantageous trade situation, American pottery companies were understandably bitter about the inordinate amount of copycatting and cutthroat underpricing — often conducted with the support of major U. S. department stores — that accelerated their eventual downfall. To its credit, Metlox was one of the last potteries to close.

Metlox's work force, which at its peak numbered over 500 employees — including 70 hand-decorators working three shifts daily — was gradually cut back. Many retailers began to drop Metlox products as the demand for them diminished. Metlox attempted to appeal to changing customer tastes by emphasizing the production of gourmet and contemporary styled studio pottery lines over sculptured and elegant patterns.

In the mid-1970s some of the company's key employees retired or accepted positions with other companies. Modeler Frank Irwin left first, followed by Bob Allen who retired in 1974. Mel Shaw decided to return to his career as an animator, and has worked recently on Walt Disney's *Beauty and the Beast* and *The Lion King*. The sales staffs were hard hit too with the departures of Ted Ball and Doug Bothwell.

Shaw, against the advice of many in the industry, decided to return to the solid color lines of the Prouty years. In the late 1970s, the elegant Lotus and contemporary Colorstax proved to be very successful and helped to sustain the company economically.

The most pivotal event for the company was the death of Evan K. Shaw in 1980. Metlox lost its leader, the dominant, driving force that held the company together. His death signaled the beginning of the end.

The Struggles of the 1980s

Melinda Avery, Shaw's daughter and successor, believes that, in retrospect, Metlox probably should have closed immediately after the death of her father, thereby avoiding the continual economic turmoil and struggles of the 1980s. If it had, however, Metlox would never have created and produced the wonderful dinnerware patterns, cookie jars, and giftware groups of its last decade. It is truly commendable that, under ever worsening, depressing economic conditions, the remaining design staff — including Vincent Martinez, Helen McIntosh, and Bob Chandler — remained loyal to the company by upholding Metlox's standards of high quality and innovation.

The fierce rivalry in the ceramics business, intensified by the entry of many other foreign countries as well as Japan, rapidly eroded Metlox's economic viability. The buyers for retail outlets, who actually determined which products were offered in stores, deserted Metlox in large numbers. One powerful Japanese manufacturer demanded that retailers either stock only a large selection of its dinnerware patterns or none at all, thus forcing Metlox and other companies out of many stores. Consumers, who now preferred very inexpensive complete sets in one box that could be cheaply replaced when damaged, were no longer interested in open stock accessories. Metlox's successes, including Colorstax, were immediately copied. These ceramic "plagiarisms" were then retailed at prices much lower than Metlox's. To remain competitive, Metlox was forced to keep prices at a lower profit margin despite a reduced volume in sales.

At the same time, production costs continued to rise. One of Metlox's largest expenses was the natural gas it took to fire the kiln. Increasing government regulations added additional costs. The facility itself began to deteriorate and repairs were deferred while relocation was being considered.

In the meantime, the character of Manhattan Beach had changed. The small coastal resort community that once welcomed Metlox as a boost for its economy now regarded it as an eyesore. The town had experienced an explosion in its popularity and the real estate value of its beachfront property. There was not much affection for a noisy, dirty factory.

Metlox appeared to make a comeback in 1988 with the introduction of Pescado, Holstein Herd, and California Harvest. These patterns, conceived by Melinda Avery, were very well received in the industry and by consumers. However, the wave of optimism soon subsided. Unable to survive the economic setbacks of the last decade, Metlox shut its doors in May of 1989. Of the five big potteries located in the Los Angeles area — Metlox Potteries, J. A. Bauer Pottery, Vernon Kilns, Franciscan Ceramics, and Pacific Clay Products — Metlox was the last to cease pottery operations. Regretfully, its close marked the end of a significant era in the history of American pottery.

Markings

Metlox's customary practice was to design a new marking for almost every dinnerware pattern. During the Prouty years, a pattern's in-mold mark was incised on most items in the pattern. In the Shaw years, usually an elaborate ink-stamped mark, including the pattern's name, was created that appeared on the dinner plate. Other items in the pattern were stamped with a simpler company/division identification.

Artware of the Prouty and Shaw years also had many markings. Prouty preferred in-mold marks while Shaw used ink-stamps. Paper labels were used for longer periods of time and were changed infrequently. Several artware lines had a unique label.

The following is a sampling of these markings. The markings of important artware lines are discussed in the appropriate chapters.

The Prouty Years

Dinnerware patterns used the following in-mold marks.

California
POTTERY

(1)

"*poppy trail*"
BY METLOX

(2)

"*Poppy trail*"
MADE IN
CALIFORNIA
U.S.A.

(3)

Mission Bell
California

(4)

Items in Romanelli's Modern Masterpieces and other artware lines frequently used variations of these two marks.

Designed
by C. Romanelli

1814

METLOX
MADE IN USA

(5)

"*Poppy trail*"
BY METLOX
P746
MADE IN USA

(6)

These three paper labels were common. Two were developed for the Miniatures line.

The Famous
"*Poppytrail*"
POTTERY
BY
METLOX

(7)

Miniatures
by METLOX
MANHATTAN BEACH
CALIFORNIA

(8)

Miniatures
by METLOX
MANHATTAN BEACH
CALIFORNIA

(9)

The Shaw Years

These representative ink-stamp marks appeared on dinner plates.

(10)

(11)

(12)

(13)

(14)

(15)

Other items in most dinnerware patterns used an ink-stamped identification of their division.

This ink-stamp or a variation of it was commonly used on artware, especially cookie jars and canisters.

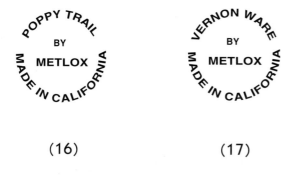

(16)

(17)

(18)

Two paper labels were often used on artware items.

A paper label was designed specifically for the Walt Disney Figurine line with the character's name in the center.

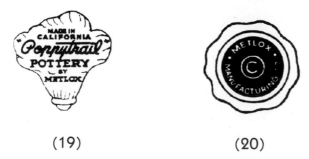

(19)

(20)

(21)

Dinnerware Patterns

Despite a long, established tradition of quality artware production, the primary emphasis and foremost priority of Metlox Potteries was always the manufacture of ceramic dinnerware. The introduction of dinnerware lines in 1932 by Willis Prouty saved the company during the Great Depression. Dinnerware manufacture, curtailed when the company switched to defense-related work to support the war effort, resumed immediately after World War II. Evan K. Shaw, after purchasing Metlox in 1946 and modernizing the facility, began to expand the number of dinnerware patterns, production output, and retail markets. Although he recognized the importance of a strong, active artware division, Shaw realized that the financial success of his company was dependent on the popularity of its dinnerware. He enhanced Metlox's reputation by focusing on the production of hand-crafted, hand-decorated dinnerware patterns which became the company's specialty.

Three Main Divisions

Metlox's dinnerware patterns are divided into three groups — the Prouty Years (1932 – 1946), the Poppytrail Division (1946 – 1989), and the Vernonware Division (1958 – 1980). The classification of every pattern into one of these three groups has been followed explicitly in this book.

Under Evan K. Shaw's direction, the Poppytrail and Vernonware Divisions existed as separate entities, each with its own assortment of patterns and group of assigned pattern numbers — P 001 – P 599 for the Poppytrail Division and V 601 – V 999 for the Vernonware Division. This system skipped the even-hundred numbers (100, 200, 300, etc.) because they were numbers from the Prouty years. When the Vernonware Division was dissolved in the early 1980s, the separation of patterns by division was formally abandoned. The designation "Metlox Dinnerware," beginning with the introduction of Colorstax in 1978, was adopted for all patterns introduced after the early 1980's. These patterns are included in the Poppytrail Division group because they were assigned Poppytrail pattern numbers.

Classification by Shape

The Poppytrail and Vernonware sections of this book are divided into chapters that each focus on one of Metlox's design shapes. This organization by shape, rather than alphabetization or pattern number, was chosen to further classify and relate the numerous patterns, thereby imparting a better, more coherent understanding of the company's design process.

During the Evan K. Shaw years, various dinnerware shapes were created. A group of patterns was released on each shape. A shape consisted of basic place setting items plus a varying number of additional pieces all designed to complement each other stylistically. Each shape group was assigned to either the Poppytrail or the Vernonware Division and was produced concurrently with other shape groups. Some shapes were designed either as a large or as a small complete set with few, if any, items added later. Other shapes evolved from a small original set into a larger one with many later additions. Occasionally some of the items in a shape were redesigned to vary the overall look of the set. The original shape and the redesigned shape still included identical items and shared the same design concept and style. Sometimes, only the cup and/or flatware were altered while the other items were unchanged.

Each chapter follows this basic outline. A discussion of the shape is followed by a leaflet or brochure photograph of the items produced on the shape, itemized lists of the shape's patterns with current values, and a descriptive company blurb and/or a photograph of each of the shape's individual patterns. A shape's name and all pertinent information about its creation and development were obtained from interviews with Metlox designers and modelers.

Itemized Lists

Metlox pattern leaflets, brochures, and master price lists provided itemized lists of each dinnerware pattern's set composition. A large quantity of this material was obtained from various sources for comparison. Fortunately, from 1946 until the company's close, Metlox had printed an extremely large amount of this material. A pattern leaflet was routinely included in each starter set to allow the purchaser to know which items were offered. Brochures and master price lists were distributed to retail outlets. These materials were accurate and current. Company employees emphatically concurred that an item was produced if it was listed in these sources.

In this book, the itemized list for each pattern is a compilation of its separate listings in the various source materials. A standard Metlox practice, especially for the best-selling patterns, was to delete items that were not selling well and to add new items to entice purchasers. Therefore, to obtain a complete, accurate pattern list, all of the source materials were compared. To illustrate, for P 190 California Provincial 16 different lists were checked. This is an extreme example; however, for a majority of the patterns, at least three lists were compared for each pattern.

An additional problem was that there were items, designed on an experimental or limited basis, that were never included in company publications. This was especially true of the Poppytrail patterns from 1946 through the mid-1950s. An awareness of these pieces came from

company employees, collectors, dealers, and archive company photos. The production of each of these items was verified by company designers and/or modelers before it was included in an itemized list.

Metlox did not always release all of a shape's patterns with the same set composition. In fact, Evan K. Shaw typically and deliberately varied patterns' composition according to projected sales potential or established popularity. This complicated the listing of a shape's patterns together in order to avoid unnecessary duplication. The solution was to combine all patterns with a similar set composition — i.e. the larger sets, the redesigned sets, and the smaller sets — and list each group separately. For each group, first a core list of items common to all of the patterns is given. This is followed by an individual listing of the additional items available for each separate pattern.

An item shape photograph of a representative pattern is reprinted before most of the lists. These leaflet photographs include all or most of the listed items with item numbers for easier identification. The items are not always shown proportionally in the photos.

The number, name, description, and measurement of each item is taken directly from the company materials. Prouty originated Metlox's item numbering system. Each item was assigned a two-digit number — i.e. 00 for a cup, 02 for a saucer, 03 for a bread and butter plate, etc. The item numbers ranged from 00 – 99 and combined with three-digit pattern numbers (discussed earlier) to allow easy identification of both the item and the pattern together. Shaw adopted this system with some later modifications. From 1946 to 1965 the same two-digit item numbers were used with four-digit pattern numbers. Metlox was obliged to convert to three-digit item numbers (010 for a cup, 020 for a saucer, 030 for a bread and butter plate, etc.) when the company switched to a separated three-digit pattern numbering system in 1965. Both the two-digit and the three-digit systems are used in the itemized lists, depending on which system was used in the item shape photograph and whether the pattern was released well before 1965 or shortly thereafter. For several pattern groups with lengthy production runs both systems are given. The item numbers are listed in numerical order, facilitating their identification in the item shape photograph and providing a continuity to the listing since each item number denotes the same item in every pattern. The few exceptions are accounted for in the lists.

All item names are those used by Metlox. Metlox sometimes changed the name, but not the number, of an item in later brochure material — i.e. the lug soup to individual soup server, the chop plate to buffet server, the water pitcher to large pitcher, and the milk pitcher to medium pitcher. In all instances, the item's shape and intended use are quite obvious from its name. The item shape photograph should clarify any questions.

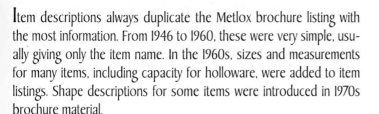

Item descriptions always duplicate the Metlox brochure listing with the most information. From 1946 to 1960, these were very simple, usually giving only the item name. In the 1960s, sizes and measurements for many items, including capacity for holloware, were added to item listings. Shape descriptions for some items were introduced in 1970s brochure material.

Measurements were given for only a few items in 1950s company materials. Although measurements for most items were added in the 1960s, these usually were inexact, rounded figures. Company lists from the 1970s gave very accurate measurements to the ¼" and ⅛". These are used if a pattern was still in production or released during the 1970s. For patterns discontinued before the 1970s, the most accurate measurement, if known, is included in the item listing. Collectors should be aware that variances in production molds and shrinkage during firing may cause slight measurement discrepancies.

Pattern Descriptions

Whenever it was included in a pattern leaflet, Metlox's description is quoted. Written in a slick, sales-pitch style that utilized unorthodox punctuation, capitalization, and grammar, these blurbs provide informative descriptions of the patterns as well as entertaining reading. If these were unavailable, usually a photograph is given to identify the pattern.

Pricing

In the past several years, Metlox dinnerware as a whole has undergone a rather dramatic increase in value as noted at antique and collectible shows, in resale and replacement shops, and in trade publications. Many patterns, such as the popular Provincial patterns, California Ivy, the four Freeform patterns, and all of the sculptured sets have rather consistent, established pricing nationwide. Other patterns sell well in the Midwest and the South, where Metlox had its biggest accounts. The lesser-known patterns, of which there are many, presently have little resale value unless the owner is seeking replacements or additions. A few patterns, produced in the last ten years of Metlox's existence, are becoming very collectible. Among these are Lotus, Colorstax, Pescado, and Holstein Herd. All these factors have been considered in the pricing, which attempts to distinguish between the popular and the less desirable patterns. It will be interesting to see which among many fascinating patterns will emerge

Evan K. Shaw's Guide Posts for Successful Dinnerware Patterns

The following text is quoted from a 1974 *Poppytrail Dealer Information Booklet.* It expounds Shaw's credo for creating a successful dinnerware pattern. According to company designers, the credo was posted in the design department meeting room, where each new pattern's merit was evaluated in strict accordance with the eight points.

...Mr. Evan K. Shaw...always believed that there was a market for colorful, beautiful dinnerware and accessories.

To achieve this beauty, styling and quality the following principles were set as guide posts:

1. An idea or story behind a design that had merit.
2. Integrity in design and color rightness.
3. Beauty and creative inspiration to the end that design mass and line are balanced.
4. Function and utility detailed to use, needs, capacities and sizes.
5. Adherence to details.
6. The total finished product must stand the test of "Is it best for the consumer, the store, the buyer, the sales person, our salesmen and the factory?"
7. Life — Does it have the "plus" look, life, movement and lift?

8. Love — a. Does it reflect the artist's love for his work?
   b. Will it enhance a person's home?

Mr. Shaw set forth to perpetuate these thoughts and to instill the goals in the people who worked with him.

Standards have been established and each pattern, each piece of ware created and manufactured is examined and tested for conformity to this creed.

Naturally this meant securing the top designers, the best quality control talent, modelers, decorators, shapers, glaze technicians and kiln men to achieve the desired result.

With these eight points as inspiration the result has been creative leadership, and that is why Poppytrail patterns have long life and continued salability.

The Manufacturing Process of Poppytrail and Vernonware Dinnerware

This excellent, extremely detailed description of the manufacturing process of Metlox dinnerware appeared in company promotional literature, date unknown. It is quoted in its entirety so that readers can better understand and fully appreciate the complex production of Metlox dinnerware.

When raw materials are shipped to our plant for use in the making of earthenware-fine dinnerware, our control laboratory goes into action, giving these materials a complete testing. One test measures the grain-size of the clays, another washes them through very fine screens to check for any foreign matter which might be present and which would cause spots on a finished piece. Special mixes of the materials are made up so they may be tested for proper weight, for absorption and for warpage. Only after all of the tests show satisfactory results are materials used as ingredients in the "body" of our dinnerware.

Before production can begin on any item it must be brought through the Development Department. First the artists make drawings which are given to the modelers. The modelers make the piece in soft clay and from these first clay models the various molds needed for experimental purposes are made. When the artists and designers feel the piece is exactly as it should be for production the model is sent to the Mold Shop where the mother mold and production molds are made.

At Metlox we use clays from Kentucky, Tennessee, England and some of our materials can be obtained in California. These clays are mixed, by special formula, with water in a huge vat and are blended or stirred by large paddles. Some of this mixture will be used in liquid form and some will be used in damp, more-or-less solid form. The liquid clay, or "slip," goes directly from the large blending vats to a storage tank where more ingredients are added before it is pumped to the casters' benches. The rest of the liquid is pumped to a filter press, where the water and air bubbles are removed before the clay, now called "mud" is stored in a mud cellar for an aging period. When it has aged enough, usually two or three weeks, it is put through the Pug Mill where water is added, the rest of the air removed, and it is turned out in long, round strips called "pugs." This solid clay is used on the different kinds of jiggers—the electrified brother of the old potter's wheel. A piece of clay is placed on a mold — for a platter, a plate, or a bowl — is pounded flat by a heavy "claw," and is then placed on the spinning jigger machine. The jiggerman brings down a lever with a blade attached that carves the clay into the proper shape inside the mold; he removes the extra clay from the edges with a wire trimmer. The piece, still in the mold, is then placed on a continuous belt that runs through a gas drier which hardens the clay enough so that the piece may be removed from the mold.

The liquid clay is poured by casters into molds for the harder-to-make pieces — like sugar bowls and cream pitchers. After the mold has been allowed to stand for thirty minutes to an hour, enough clay has adhered or set up along the sides of the mold to form the piece. The caster turns the mold upside down and lets the extra "slip" run out. This mold is made in sections and is held together with rubber clamps, so the caster may, by removing the rubber clamps, simply move the mold away from the cream pitcher or sugar bowl. It looks dark gray and is now called "green ware." After these pieces are dried on gas-heated racks they are moved to long, narrow ovens or bisque kilns, where they are loaded in cars on the "train" which moves continuously through the kiln. These kilns are fired with gas, and the temperatures are carefully regulated with electronic controls. The gas burners are at the center of the kiln so that the ware is brought up to temperature gradually and is cooled gradually. The green ware is soaked to a temperature of 2,150 degrees for 44 hours; when it is unloaded it is very hard and white and is called "bisque." The bisque pieces are inspected very closely for flaws before being transferred to the Decorating and Spraying Departments.

In the Decorating Department underglaze ceramic colors are used for hand painting decorations. The decorator is a skilled artist applying the various ceramic colors with a brush as though she were doing an original painting. After decorating, the pieces are taken to the Spray Department for glazing. The glazes are mixed, again by special formula, including such ingredients as titanium, litharge, zinc, oxide, silica, etc. The ingredients are placed in huge "Ball Mills" and are blended for eight to 24 hours. The finished glazes are applied to the bisque ware in several ways — by dipping, in hand-spray booths, and on an automatic spraying machine. The pieces are loaded on "setters" or "pins," this time riding the kiln train for 24 hours, at a temperature of about 1,900 degrees. At the end of this kiln the ware is graded, the setter pin marks gound (sic) off, and sent immediately to the Shipping Room for packing and shipping to all parts of the United States and the world. All decorations are under-glaze and are therefore guaranteed against detergents in the dish-washer, against fading, marring or washing off. Products of Metlox Potteries are durable, ovenproof, and chip resistant. They represent fine dinnerware from California.

List of Patterns

A comprehensive list of Metlox's known dinnerware patterns follows on pages 22 – 24. The patterns are arranged in numerical order by company-assigned pattern number. In most cases, the year the pattern was introduced is included with the pattern name and number. Every attempt was made to verify the accuracy of these release dates. In some cases an approximate date was the only one obtainable. For a few patterns this date was not verifiable.

This master list was derived from several different sources. Keith Robinson, past president of the Manhattan Beach Historical Society, provided an extensive pattern list compiled from 1946 – 79 pattern production records — referred to as the "Metlox files" in the text — that were stored at the factory. Despite obvious missing patterns and pattern numbers in these files, this list proved very valuable as a checklist.

Lois Lehner's *Lehner's Encyclopedia of U. S. Marks on Pottery, Porcelain & Clay* contained a large list, provided by Metlox, of discontinued patterns with pattern numbers. Brochures, pattern leaflets, and master price lists yielded several missing names and numbers. During interviews with company employees, lesser-known patterns were identified.

On first consideration, the list presents a bewildering, haphazard assignment of pattern numbers with inconsistent correlation between the numerical order of the pattern numbers and the chronology of the release dates. A detailed explanation of the development of Metlox's pattern numbering system may help to explain some of the confusion.

Prouty established the original numbering system which assigned each pattern a three-digit even-hundred number (100, 200, 300, 400, and 500). Even hundreds were chosen because they combined easily with a smaller two-digit number —

ranging from 00 through 99 — assigned to each dinnerware item. The combined number represented the pattern name and the item name together. For example, 500 was the pattern number for Yorkshire and 19 was the item number for the creamer. The combined number 519 indicated a Yorkshire creamer.

After Shaw's purchase of Metlox, the company adopted Prouty's system with several alterations. Prouty's three-digit even-hundred numbers were discontinued. Pattern numbers were changed to even-thousand/hundred numbers (P 1100, P 1200, P 1300, etc.) which still combined with the two-digit item numbers while substantially increasing the total of possible pattern numbers. Numbers P 1100 – P 5900 were assigned to the Poppytrail Division and numbers V 6100 – V 9900 to the Vernonware Division. This system was adequate until the early 1960s when all of the available Poppytrail numbers had been assigned. At first, new patterns were given the number of a discontinued pattern which accounts for some numbers having two pattern names. Since the number of new patterns continued to grow, the company realized this was a temporary measure only.

In 1967, the final pattern numbering system was instituted. Pattern numbers were changed to three-digit numbers and separated from item numbers. Therefore, all the numbers between 001 and 999 (except the even-hundred Prouty numbers) could be used. This dramatically increased the total of usable pattern numbers. This is the system used in the master list since it allows all of the patterns to be included. Although many patterns follow a fairly chronological order, others appear to be randomly assigned and out of sequence. Company employees, too, have been at a loss to explain completely the rationale of Metlox's numbering system.

California Ivy
PD170 Page 2 (1946)

California Provincial
PD190 Page 3 (1950)

Homestead Provincial
PD140 Page 2 (1952)

Red Rooster (decorated)
PD390 Page 4 (1955)

Woodland Gold
PD560 Page 6 (1959)

True Blue
VD930 Page 17 (1959)

Antique Grape
PD250 Page 7 (1964)

Sculptured Daisy
PD270 Page 8 (1964)

Sculptured Zinnia
PD310 Page 8 (1964)

Vintage Pink
PD260 Page 9 (1965)

Della Robbia
VD780 Page 19 (1965)

Vernon Rose
VD790 Page 19 (1965)

Bandero
PD571 Page 10 (1969)

Vernon Florence
VD781 Page 19 (1969)

Wild Poppy
PD579 Page 11 (1972)

Vernon Nasturtium
VD921 Page 21 (1972)

Cinnamon
VD639 Page 21 (1973)

Sculptured Berry
PD181 Page 11 (1973)

Geranium
PD002 Page 13 (1976)

Mesa
VD601 Page 23 (1976)

Moulin Rouge
PD003 Page 13 (1976)

Old Cathay
VD604 Page 23 (1976)

Flower Basket
VD605 Page 24 (1976)

Primary Red
PD008 Page 14 (1977)

Gigi
VD655 Page 26 (1978)

Primary Blue Daisies
PD022 Page 14 (1978)

Primary Red Daisies
PD024 Page 14 (1978)

Primary Yellow
PD025 Page 14 (1978)

Primary Yellow Daisies
PD026 Page 14 (1978)

Autumn Berry
PD027 Page 11 (1978)

Mt. Whitney
VD657 Page 27 (1978)

Colorbands
Page 28 (1979)
Sand
MD044
Chocolate
MD045
Terra Cotta
MD046
Forest Green
MD047
Fern Green
MD048
Midnight Blue
MD049
Sky Blue
MD050
Yellow
MD051

Rattan
VD658 Page 27 (1979)

Quail Ridge
PD052 Page 16 (1979)

Colorful assortment of active dinnerware patterns produced in 1979.

Provincial Fruit
PD490 Page 5 (1960)

Vineyard
VD950 Page 17 (1960)

Autumn Leaves
VD970 Page 18 (1960)

California Strawberry
PD590 Page 6 (1961)

Fruit Basket
VD980 Page 18 (1961)

Sculptured Grape
PD240 Page 7 (1963)

Vernon Antiqua
VD770 Page 20 (1966)

San Fernando
VD920 Page 20 (1966)

Colonial Garden
PD161 Page 9 (1967)

Golden Garden
PD163 Page 9 (1967)

La Mancha Gold
PD165 Page 10 (1968)

La Mancha Green
PD167 Page 10 (1968)

Vernon Bouquet
VD642 Page 22 (1974)

Matilija
PD582 Page 11 (1974)

Grape Arbor
PD241 Page 9 (1975)

Antique Blue
VD647 Page 22 (1975)

California Whitestone
PD591 Page 12 (1975)

California Brownstone
PD001 Page 12 (1976)

Primary Blue
PD010 Page 14 (1977)

Strawflower
PD013 Page 15 (1977)

Calico
PD014 Page 15 (1977)

Monterey
VD633 Page 24 (1977)

Hermosa Collection-Uno
VD651 Page 25 (1978)

Hermosa Collection-Mucho
VD654 Page 25 (1978)

Colorstax
Page 28 (1978)

White
MD036

Sand
MD028

Chocolate
MD029

Terra Cotta
MD030

Forest Green
MD031

Fern Green
MD032

Midnight Blue
MD033

Sky Blue
MD034

Yellow
MD035

Happy Days
VD656 Page 26 (1976)

Spring Garland
VD661 Page 28 (1979)

Lotus
Page 16 (1979)

White
PD150

Sand
PD151

Chocolate
PD152

Yellow
PD153

Apricot
PD154

Grey
PD156

Plum
PD157

Blue
PD158

Green
PD159

Cranberry
PD162

Photo of active dinnerware patterns from a 1979 company brochure.

Poppytrail

P 001	California Brownstone (aka Coco Blanc), 1976	
P 002	Geranium, 1976	
P 003	Moulin Rouge (aka Tiffany Blue), 1976	
P 004	Sandflower, 1976	
P 005	Pomegranate, 1976	
P 006	Tiffany (aka Tiffany Green), 1976	
P 007	Tiffany Yellow, 1976	
P 008	Primary Red, 1977	
P 010	Primary Blue, 1977	
P 012	Provincial Whitestone, 1977	

California Naturals Group

P 013	Strawflower, 1977
P 014	Calico, 1977
P 015	Macramé, 1977
P 016	Wildflower, 1977
P 017	William, 1977

P 018	Iris, 1978
P 020	Rhythm, 1978
P 021	Blues, 1978
P 022	Primary Blue Daisies, 1978
P 023	Marguerite, 1978
P 024	Primary Red Daisies, 1978
P 025	Primary Yellow, 1978
P 026	Primary Yellow Daisies, 1978
P 027	Autumn Berry, 1978
P 028	Colorstax Sand, 1978
P 029	Colorstax Chocolate, 1978
P 030	Colorstax Terra Cotta, 1978
P 031	Colorstax Forest Green, 1978
P 032	Colorstax Fern Green, 1978
P 033	Colorstax Midnight Blue, 1978
P 034	Colorstax Sky Blue, 1978
P 035	Colorstax Yellow, 1978
P 036	Colorstax White, 1978
P 038	Federated Yellow
P 039	Federated Fern Green
P 040	Federated Forest Green
P 041	Federated White
P 042	Federated Light Blue
P 044	Colorbands Sand, 1979
P 045	Colorbands Chocolate, 1979
P 046	Colorbands Terra Cotta, 1979
P 047	Colorbands Forest Green, 1979
P 048	Colorbands Fern Green, 1979

P 049	Colorbands Midnight Blue, 1979
P 050	Colorbands Sky Blue, 1979
P 051	Colorbands Yellow, 1979
—	Colorbands Cranberry
—	Colorbands Aqua
P 052	Quail Ridge, 1979

Botanical Collection

P 053	Silver Dollar, 1979
P 054	Dill, 1979
P 055	Eucalyptus, 1979
P 056	Bottle Brush, 1979

P 053	Sorrento, 1980
P 054	American Heritage, 1980
P 054	American Heritage (Gourmet Set), early 1980s
P 056	Lavender Blue, 1980
P 061	Colorstax Cranberry
P 063	Colorstax Aqua
P 064	Colorstax Plum, 1980
P 065	Colorstax Apricot, 1980
P 066	Colorstax Black, 1980
P 073	Colorstax Rose, early 1980s
P 074	Colorstax Jade, early 1980s
P 075	Colorstax Lilac, early 1980s
P 076	Colorstax Canary, early 1980s
P 079	Marigold, 1980
P 080	Colorstax Brick, 1984
P 081	Colorstax Camel, 1984
P 082	Colorstax Evergreen, 1984
P 083	Colorstax Pewter, 1984
P 084	Colorstax Pumpkin, 1984
P 085	Colorstax Silver, 1984
P 086	Colorstax Wheat, 1984
P 088	Colorstax French Blue

California Spatterware

P 089	Sky Blue, 1987
P 090	Cranberry, 1987
P 093	Black, 1987
P 094	Midnight Blue, 1987

P 095	Holstein Herd, 1988

Galaxy (Second Series)

P 095	Delphinium Blue, 1988
P 096	Garden Green, 1988
P 097	Orange, 1988
P 098	Yellow, 1988

100	California Pottery, 1932

P 120	Provincial Blue, 1950
P 130	Mayan Necklace, 1964
P 140	Homestead Provincial, 1950
P 145	Chantilly Blue, early 1980s
P 146	Lotus White, 1974
P 146	Memories, early 1980s
P 147	Lotus Yellow, 1974
P 148	Lotus Lime, 1974
P 149	Lotus Pink, 1974
P 150	Fleur-de-lis, 1964
P 150	Lotus White, 1979
P 151	Lotus Sand, 1979
P 152	Lotus Chocolate, 1979
P 153	Lotus Yellow, 1979
P 154	Lotus Apricot, 1979
P 155	Lotus Black, 1979
P 156	Lotus Grey, 1979
P 157	Lotus Plum, 1979
P 158	Lotus Blue, 1979
P 159	Lotus Green, 1979
P 160	California Apple, 1949
P 161	Colonial Garden, 1967
P 162	Lotus Cranberry, 1979
P 163	Golden Garden, 1967
P 164	Tradition White, 1967
P 165	La Mancha Gold, 1968
P 166	Flair Pink, 1968
P 166	La Mancha Parchment, 1968
P 166	Lotus Aqua
P 167	La Mancha Green, 1968
P 168	La Mancha White, 1971
P 169	Flair Parrot Green, 1968
P 170	California Ivy, 1946
P 175	Lotus Rose
P 177	Tapestry, 1975
P 178	Lotus Jade
P 179	Lotus Lilac
P 180	California Fruit, 1949
P 181	Sculptured Berry, 1973
P 182	Lotus Canary
P 183	Lotus Brick, 1984
P 184	Lotus Camel, 1984
P 185	Lotus Concord (Decorated)
P 186	Lotus Wisteria (Decorated)
P 187	Lotus Fuchsia (Decorated)
P 188	Lotus Honeysuckle (Decorated)
P 189	Lotus Chocolate, 1984

P 190   California Provincial, 1950
P 191   Lotus Evergreen, 1984
P 192   Lotus Midnight Blue, 1984
P 193   Lotus Pewter, 1984
P 194   Lotus Pumpkin, 1984
P 195   Lotus Silver, 1984
P 196   Lotus Wheat, 1984

200   "200" Series
      (aka Poppy Trail), 1934
P 210   Monte Carlo
P 220   California Peach Blossom, 1952
P 230   Shoreline, 1953
      Deep Sea Green
      Driftwood Brown
      Horizon Blue
      Seafoam White
      Surf Chartreuse
      Wet Sand Beige
P 240   Sculptured Grape, 1963
P 241   Grape Arbor, 1975
P 241   Sonoma, 1988
P 242   Mission, 1988
P 250   California Golden Blossom,
      c.1953
P 250   Antique Grape, 1964
P 260   Indian Summer, 1953
P 260   Vintage Pink, 1965
P 270   Central Park, 1953
P 270   Sculptured Daisy, 1964
P 271   Oh' Susanna, 1975
1942 Series
      P 272   Aqua, 1985
      P 275   Canary, 1985
      P 283   Rose, 1985
      P 286   Sky Blue, 1985
P 280   Country Side
P 290   Happy Time

300   Mission Bell, 1935
P 310   California Freeform, 1954
P 310   Sculptured Zinnia, 1964
P 311   Floralace, 1975
P 320   California Mobile, 1954
Impression Series
      P 320   White, 1971
      P 321   Yellow, 1971
      P 322   Orange, 1971
      P 323   Green, 1971
P 330   California Aztec, 1955

P 340   California Contempora, 1955
P 350   Street Scene, 1956
P 350   Blueberry Provincial, 1962
P 360   Solid Colors
      (probably Modern)
P 360   Provincial Flower, 1962
P 370   Mardi Gras, 1955
      Red
      Black
      White
P 370   Cape Cod, 1961
Traditions Series
      P 371   Apricot, 1985
      P 372   Aqua, 1985
      P 375   Canary, 1985
      P 380   Lilac, 1985
      P 383   Rose, 1985
      P 386   Sky Blue, 1985
      P 387   White, 1985
P 380   Colonial Heritage, 1956
P 380   Rooster Bleu, 1966
P 390   Red Rooster (Decorated),
      1955
P 391   Red Rooster (Red), 1956

400   Pintoria, c.1937
P 410   Palm Springs, 1962
P 420   California Del Rey, 1955
P 430   California Confetti, 1955
P 430   Golden Scroll, 1962
P 440   California Tempo Series
      P 441   Walnut with Sky Blue,
            1960
      P 442   Walnut with Yellow
            Gold, 1960
      P 443   Walnut with Beige, 1960
      P 444   Walnut with Terra Cotta,
            1960
      P 445   Walnut with Olive
            Green, 1960
      P 446   Walnut with White, 1960
P 450   California Geranium, 1958
P 460   Luau, 1959
P 470   Navajo, 1956
Galaxy (First Series)
      P 473   Black, 1985
      P 481   Midnight Blue, 1985
      P 483   Rose, 1985
      P 486   Sky Blue, 1985
      P 487   White, 1985

P 488   Yellow, 1985
P 480   Jamestown, 1957
P 490   Provincial Fruit, 1960

500   Yorkshire, 1937
P 510   Golden Fruit, 1961
P 520   Pepper Tree, 1957
P 530   Painted Desert, 1960
P 540   California Palm, 1958
P 550   Provincial Rose, 1958
P 560   Woodland Gold, 1959
P 561   Gold Dahlia, 1968
P 562   Blue Dahlia, 1969
P 570   California Rose, 1959
P 570   Indigo, 1969
P 571   Bandero, 1969
P 572   Carmel, 1969
P 573   San Clemente La Casa
      Brown, 1970
P 574   San Clemente Spanish
      Yellow, 1970
P 575   Marina, 1970
P 576   San Clemente Laguna Blue,
      1970
P 577   Flamenco Red, 1971
P 578   Medallion Red, 1971
P 580   Tropicana, 1960
P 580   Mission Verde, 1966
P 581   Wild Poppy, 1972
P 583   Matilija (aka White Poppy),
      1974
P 585   Mission Gold, 1966
P 586   California Orchard, 1973
P 590   California Strawberry, 1961
P 591   California Whitestone, 1975
P 592   Fashion Plate Red, 1976
P 593   Fashion Plate Yellow, 1976
P 594   Fashion Plate Green, 1976
P 595   Fashion Plate Blue, 1976

Other Poppytrail Patterns
—   California Harvest, 1988
—   Camellia, 1946
—   Pescado, 1988
—   Wicker Strawberry, c.1982
—   Wicker White, c. 1982
—   Winter Berry, c. 1986
—   Winter Scene

Vernonware

V 601   Mesa, 1976
V 602   Brookside, 1976
V 603   Cinnamon Green, 1976
V 604   Old Cathay, 1976
V 605   Flower Basket, 1976
V 606   Classic Blue, 1977
V 609   Classic Wheat, 1977
V 610   Accents, 1961
V 615   Reflection Coral, 1977
V 617   Reflection Blue, 1977
V 619   Painted Desert, 1977
V 620   Sierra Flower, 1962
V 620   Petalburst, 1968
V 621   Golden Amber, 1968
V 622   La Jolla, 1969
V 623   Margarita, 1969
V 624   Vernon Gaiety, 1970
V 625   Vernon Tulips (aka Vernon
        Tulip Time), 1971
V 626   Vernon Calypso, 1971
V 627   White Rose, 1977
V 628   Vernon Pacific Blue, 1971
V 630   Sun 'n Sand, 1962
V 631   Vernon Pueblo, 1972
California Collection
   V 633   Monterey, 1977
   V 634   Big Sur, 1978
   V 635   Catalina, 1978
   V 636   Capistrano, 1978
V 637   Cognac, 1978

V 640   Blue Zinnias, 1963
V 641   Cinnamon, 1973
V 642   Vernon Bouquet, 1974
V 643   Lemon Tree, 1975
V 644   Lime Tree, 1975
V 648   Antique Blue, 1975
Hermosa Collection
   V 651   Uno, 1978
   V 652   Dos, 1978
   V 653   Tres, 1978
   V 654   Mucho, 1978
V 655   Gigi, 1978
V 656   Happy Days, 1978
V 657   Mount Whitney, 1978
V 658   Rattan, 1979
V 660   Italian Delight, 1979
V 661   Spring Garland, 1979
V 664   Meadow, 1980
V 665   Sherwood, 1979
V 666   Morning Glory, 1980
V 668   Marissa, 1980
V 670   Classic Flower, 1964
V 680   Classic Antique, 1963
V 690   Classic Roma, 1964
V 710   Butterscotch, 1960
Town and Country Series
   V 720   Nutmeg Brown, 1961
   V 730   Clover Green, 1961
   V 740   Larkspur Blue, 1961
   V 750   Buttercup Yellow, 1961

V 760   Springtime, 1961
V 760   Blue Bird, early 1980s
V 761   Country Floral, early 1980s
V 762   Chesapeake, early 1980s
V 770   Vernon Antiqua, 1966
V 780   Vernon Della Robbia, 1965
V 781   Vernon Florence, 1969
V 790   Vernon Rose, 1965
V 810   Tickled Pink, 1958
V 820   Heavenly Days, 1958
V 830   Anytime, 1958
V 840   Tisket-A-Tasket
V 850   Sherwood, 1958
V 860   Fancy Free
V 870   Rose-A-Day, 1958
V 880   Year 'Round, 1958
V 910   Castile, 1964
V 920   San Fernando, 1966
V 921   Vernon Nasturtium, 1972
V 930   True Blue, 1959
V 940   Pink Lady, 1960
V 941   Laura, early 1980s
V 950   Vineyard, 1960
V 960   Patrician White, 1959
V 970   Autumn Leaves, 1960
V 980   Fruit Basket, 1961
V 981   Blue Fascination, 1967
V 982   Caprice, 1967

Skipped numbers do not indicate a missing pattern name. Numbers 100 and 300 are believed to be California Pottery and Mission Bell respectively. According to the Metlox files, P 166 Flair Pink, P 166 La Mancha Parchment, P 169 Flair Parrot Green, P 585 Mission Gold, and V 622 La Jolla were never released. Information was unobtainable from any source concerning the Federated patterns P 038 – P 042, P 177 Tapestry, P 210 Monte Carlo, P 360 Solid Colors (probably Modern), V 615 Reflection Coral, V 617 Reflection Blue, V 665 Sherwood (different from V 850 Sherwood, a Metlox/Vernon Kilns pattern), and V 860 Fancy Free. Modern was definitely released. The other patterns may not have been produced. A pattern number was not available for Camellia, Wicker Strawberry, Wicker White, Winter Berry, and Winter Scene.

Dinnerware Decoration

Metlox used four types of dinnerware decoration as follows: hand-painted rubber-stamped designs, hand-painted sculptured designs, solid colors, and decals.

The rubber stamp process, although not invented by Metlox, was adapted so successfully by the company that it became the most commonly used method. After the pattern was designed on paper in all its different sizes, proportions, and versions, a rubber stamp company made imprints of each design separately on flexible sheet rubber. Each rubber sheet was molded and shaped to follow the contours — either flat or curved — of a given

Metlox Potteries booth at the July 1988 California Gift Show. This impressive display won the blue ribbon for best booth and product design.

item. This rubber stamp was glued to a sponge (shaped flat, convex, or concave) for added pliancy. The sponge was cemented onto a permanent block to provide support. These stamps were very durable, allowing Metlox to use them repeatedly by hand or automation. After the design was ink-stamped onto a bisque item, hand decorators filled in the outlines of the design with the appropriate pattern

Front and back of a coaster dated July 19, 1969. A limited number of these coasters were produced to be given as favors at a company party for sales representatives. The design was patterned after decorative tiles in Evan K. Shaw's home.

colors. The advantages of this process were that it worked on all surface contours and it furnished an identical pattern on each item.

Hand-painted sculptured designs became a Metlox specialty. During the 1940s Franciscan Ceramics popularized bas-relief with smoothly embossed patterns such as Apple, Desert Rose, and Ivy. Metlox's sculpting carried the process several degrees further with more sharply defined contrasts. The objects in a design were juxtaposed closely together with the minutiae of each outlined by increasing the depth of the carving. An intensified three-dimensional effect was created by the interplay of varying depths against one another. The decorator's paint settled mostly in the pronounced crevices of the designs, enhancing the illusion of added height and depth. The overall impression was that of a realistic design carved with a sculptor's chisel. The modeling of sculptured designs, achieved by the expertise of Frank Irwin and Bob Chandler, was extremely difficult, tedious, and time consuming. The extent and amount of carving varied from one sculptured pattern to another depending on the design. A few patterns, such as Camellia, were embossed rather than sculptured designs.

Ironically, solid color patterns were the economic mainstay of the company during the early Prouty years of the 1930s through the mid-

1940s and the final ten years of the 1980s. Until 1946 all Metlox patterns were exclusively solid color, reflecting the popularity of solids at that time. Evan K. Shaw's fondness for solid color patterns prompted the occasional manufacture of solid-tone patterns, none of which were particularly successful until Colorstax and Lotus in the late 1970s. Solids were either painted with a spray gun or dipped into a paint vat, then sealed with a gloss or matte glaze.

Metlox used decal decorations sparingly. After each greenware item was fired, it was then glazed. A thick coat of shellac was applied to prevent dust from settling on the glaze and to allow easier handling. The decal was then placed on the shellacked surface. The second firing began at a low temperature to disintegrate the layer of shellac and allow the decals to gradually become a part of the glaze. As the kiln temperature was increased, the glaze and decal fused together permanently. Central Park and Indian Summer, Metlox's first decal patterns, were released in 1953. After their commercial failure Metlox avoided decal patterns until the release of Wild Poppy in 1972 and Matili-ja in 1974, two very successful patterns. Decals were then used on a limited number of patterns from the mid-1970s through the early 1980s.

The large Metlox Potteries tile sign is all that remains of the factory in Manhattan Beach.

Prouty Dinnerware

100 California Pottery (1932)
200 "200" Series (aka Poppy Trail) (1934)
300 Mission Bell (1935)
400 Pintoria (c. 1937)
500 Yorkshire (1937)
— Camellia (1946)

In 1932 Metlox produced its first dinnerware pattern in hopes of revitalizing the company's stagnant economic situation. After founding the company in 1927, T. C. Prouty successfully specialized in the production of outdoor ceramic signs. When orders for this unusual product sharply declined with the deepening of the Great Depression, Willis Prouty, who became the director of the company after the death of his father in 1931, realized that the survival of Metlox depended on the manufacture of a different type of product. The younger Prouty, along with others in the Southern California tile and pottery business, had noted the great success of J. A. Bauer's innovative solid color dinnerware lines. First introduced in 1931, these brightly colored tablewares and kitchenwares were ideally suited for the area's outdoor, casual lifestyle and its emphasis on patio dining. Deciding to capitalize on the popular appeal of these wares, Willis converted the plant to dinnerware production. Five solid color dinnerware lines were created before World War II. Camellia, released in 1946, was Metlox's first hand-decorated pattern, an experiment which Evan K. Shaw, after purchasing the company in the same year, developed into the company's specialty. By this time Prouty's solid color lines had already established Metlox nationally as a leading manufacturer of fine quality earthenware.

The dinnerware patterns, as well as the artware lines, of the Prouty years are difficult to document due to the lack of both printed brochure material and employee accounts of operations during the 1930s and early 1940s. The detailed listings for the "200" Series (aka Poppy Trail), Pintoria, and Yorkshire were obtained from a comprehensive Poppy Trail dinnerware and artware booklet, dated January 1, 1942, and a one-page dinnerware leaflet from the late 1930s, reprinted in Jo Cunningham's *The Collector's Encyclopedia of American Din-*

nerware. Since item photographs were printed with item numbers only, the appropriate item names were determined with assistance from noted authority Jack Chipman. Although listings for California Pottery, Mission Bell, and Camellia were unavailable, the reader can safely assume that they included the standard dinnerware items of the other lines. The designer of these five lines is unknown and could have been Willis Prouty himself. It certainly was not famed sculptor Carl Romanelli who designed the outstanding Metlox artware lines of the late 1930s and early 1940s. Additional information was gathered from advertising and trade articles of the period.

Prouty's initial venture was 100 California Pottery, a modest line composed of place setting items plus a few standard serving pieces. Introduced in 1932, it featured a simple raised ridge styling and, imitative of Bauer, offered a variety of vivid solid colors with a gloss glaze. The name "California" — "POTTERY" was incised on the backside of many items. This in-mold marking did not include the company name "Metlox."

This pattern was followed in 1934 by 200 Poppy Trail, an extensive line of dinnerware, beverageware, and kitchenware. The official company designation, appearing in brochure material, was "200" Series. The common name Poppy Trail, mentioned in advertising material and adopted by collectors, was taken from its markings "'Poppy trail'" — "BY METLOX" and "'Poppy trail'" — "MADE IN" — "CALIFORNIA" — "U.S.A." Originally spelled as two words, "Poppy trail" became a company trade name in 1936.

Willis Prouty's inspiration for the name Poppy Trail was a book about California wildflowers entitled *California Poppy Trails* by Evelyn White. Prouty wished to relate the brilliant colors of the state's wildflowers to those of his new dinnerware pattern. Initially offered only in blue, red-orange, rose, and green, during an eight-year production run Poppy Trail's palette was gradually increased to a spectrum of 15 solid colors, including eight vivid colors with a gloss glaze (turquoise blue, old rose, canary yellow, delphinium blue, poppy orange, sea green, cream, and rust) and seven pastel colors with a satin glaze (powder blue, petal pink, satin ivory, satin turquoise, pastel yellow, peach, and opaline green).

Poppy Trail evolved into a huge line. The dinnerware offered rim-style and coupe-shaped plates, four kinds of cups and saucers, four different salt and pepper sets, and two sugar and creamer styles. A noteworthy feature was the inclusion of a large variety of beverage-ware (two teapots, two coffee carafes, two coffee pots, various pitchers, a tumbler, a mug, and the Tom & Jerry bowl and cup). Individual beverage items were grouped in various combinations and merchandised as beverage sets and as luncheon sets that included a chop plate. Kitchenware items included a four-piece range set, grease jar, and handled batter bowl.

The #750 four-piece mixing bowl set, and the #75 five-piece and #77 six-piece mixing bowl sets, although marketed separately, were intended for use with Poppy Trail. The #750 set presented a fluted, single band styling in probably all or most of Poppy Trail's 15 colors. The #75 and #77 mixing bowl sets were produced as a rainbow assortment. Each size came only in its own separate color of rose, green, yellow, white, orange, or blue. The number of the bowl and the name "METLOX" were incised on the backside of each bowl.

The exact history of 300 Mission Bell is uncertain. This solid pastel, satin matte dinnerware and kitchenware line, displaying a simple border rope design, was manufactured exclusively for Sears, Roebuck and Company from 1935 – 38. The markings "Mission Bell" — "California" or "Mission" — the item number — "USA" — "Bell" were incised on most items without a reference to the name "Metlox." Lois Lehner's *Lehner's Encyclopedia of U. S. Marks on Pottery, Porcelain & Clay* discusses the registration of a "MISSION" — "BELL" mark, designated for pottery (especially various dinnerware items), in 1939 by the May Department Stores. If this line was Metlox's Mission Bell, its marketing rights were transferred from Sears to the May Department Stores. This reasoning is supported by Shaw employees' assertion that the May Department Stores carried a Prouty dinnerware line in the early 1940s. To confuse the issue further, trade articles from the 1930s mentioned a Metlox dinnerware line with a rope border produced in six deep colors and three soft pastels that most likely was Mission Bell. This would suggest that Metlox also distributed Mission Bell nationwide. The "Mission Bell" — "California" marking also appeared on a number of Metlox artware items.

400 Pintoria presented the most distinctive dinnerware styling of the Prouty years. Patterned after an English Staffordshire geometric design, this small luncheon set, consisting of only nine items, was produced briefly from circa 1937 – 1939. The flatware and bowls were straight-sided rectangular shapes with a wide, flat border created by an inner circular depression for food. Pintoria was produced in six vivid colors with a gloss glaze — delphinium blue, old rose, canary yellow, turquoise blue, poppy orange, and rust. The in-mold marking "Pintoria" — "BY METLOX" was used. It has become the most collectible, valued Prouty line due to its scarcity and unique design.

Introduced in 1937, 500 Yorkshire was characterized by a swirled design on the wide rim of plates, platters, and most bowls and on the exterior of holloware and serving items. Although not quite as large a line as the "200" Series, it also offered a varied assortment of items. It is presumed that Yorkshire was produced only in the seven pastel colors of the "200" Series. Production of all five solid color lines was interrupted when Metlox adapted the factory for defense-related work during World War II.

Camellia, released in 1946, represented a new approach to dinnerware design. Influenced by the success of Franciscan Ceramic's embossed Apple and Desert Rose patterns, Metlox produced Camellia as a hand-decorated set with a camellia border design in smooth bas-relief on a cream white background. Two color variations were offered. A brown border version featured pink camellias and shaded medium-to-light green leaves on a brown branch. The olive border set presented pink camellias with yellow centers and dark green leaves on an olive green branch. Camellia-shaped finials added a decorative touch. An underglaze ink backstamp including "Camellia by METLOX" was used in several versions. Since Camellia quickly became quite popular, one can only speculate whether or not Prouty might have continued this new styling. Shortly after Camellia's release, Evan K. Shaw purchased the company.

Pricing for California Pottery and Mission Bell follows that of "200" Series items. Camellia values are the same as Metlox's popular sculptured patterns. The high values for Pintoria indicate its rarity. A special thanks to Jack Chipman for assisting in the pricing which is reflective of the Southern California collector's market.

California Pottery: 7⅜" salad plates.

200 "200" Series Dinnerware (aka Poppy Trail)

200	Cup, curved handle	$10 – 12
201	Cup, angular handle	$15 – 18
202	Saucer	$3 – 4
201-D	Demitasse Cup	$22 – 25
202-D	Demitasse Saucer	$6 – 8
200-J	Jumbo Cup	$22 – 25
202-J	Jumbo Saucer	$6 – 8
203	Bread & Butter, rim	$8 – 10
204	Salad Plate, rim	$10 – 12
205	Luncheon Plate, rim	$12 – 14
206	Dinner Plate, rim	$15 – 18
207	Rim Soup Bowl	$25 – 28
209-9½	Individual Soup Bowl & Lid, double handle	$40 – 45
211	Sherbet	$20 – 22
212	Soup/Cereal Bowl	$12 – 15
213	Butter & Lid	$50 – 55
214	Vegetable Bowl, oval	$28 – 30
214½	Vegetable Bowl, oval	$30 – 32
215	Vegetable Bowl, rnd.	$28 – 30
216	Platter, med., 11½"	$25 – 30
217	Platter, lg., 13¾"	$30 – 35
218	Sugar & Lid, double handled	$22 – 25
218½	Sugar, open, single raised handle	$18 – 20
219	Creamer	$18 – 20
219½	Creamer, raised handle	$15 – 18
220	Jam Jar & Lid	$45 – 50
221	Fruit Bowl	$10 – 12
222	Salad Bowl, individual	$15 – 18
223	Gravy/Sauce Boat	$22 – 25
223-C	Celery Dish	$20 – 25
224	Custard	$18 – 20
224-M	Mustard & Lid	$45 – 50
225	Deep Bowl/Pudding Bowl	$22 – 25
226	Relish Dish, sm., single handle	$25 – 30
226-A	Relish Dish, lg., double handle	$30 – 35
227	3-Part Grill Plate	$20 – 22
228	Bread & Butter, coupe	$10 – 12
228½	Salad Plate, coupe	$12 – 15
229	Dinner Plate, coupe, 10"	$15 – 18
229½	Chop Plate, 12"	$20 – 25
230	Chop Plate, 14"	$25 – 30
231	Chop Plate, 17"	$35 – 40
232	Salad Bowl/Console Bowl	$35 – 40
233-S	Salt, S-shaped	$10 – 12
233-P	Pepper, P-shaped	$10 – 12
234	Salt, footed	$10 – 12
234½	Pepper, footed	$10 – 12
234-A	Salt, jug-shaped, handled	$10 – 12
234-B	Pepper, jug-shaped, handled	$10 – 12
234-S	Salt, horizontal ribs	$12 – 15
234-P	Pepper, horizontal ribs	$12 – 15
235-T	Tumbler, smooth-sided	$15 – 18
235-H	Tumbler Handle, clip-on	$4 – 5
236-M	Mug, ribbed	$15 – 18
236½	Mug Handle, clip-on	$5 – 6
237-L	Pitcher, lg., ice-lip	$45 – 50
238-8½	Coffee Carafe & Lid, ball-shaped	$30 – 35
238-A	Coffee Carafe, no lid, ribbed	$35 – 40
240-243	Range Set	
	Salt	$25 – 35
	Pepper	$25 – 35
	Sugar	$25 – 35
	Flour	$25 – 35
244	Grease Jar & Lid	$40 – 45
245	Pitcher, ball-shaped, footed, spout on top	$35 – 40
247	Pitcher Lid	$10 – 15
248–250	Matching Pitcher Set	
248	Large	$30 – 35
249	Medium	$25 – 30
250	Small	$20 – 25
251	Small Pitcher	$18 – 20
253	Coffee Pot & Lid, footed	$50 – 55
254	Tom & Jerry Bowl & Lid	$90 – 100
255	Tom & Jerry Cup	$15 – 18
257	Pitcher, ice-lip, horizontal ribs	$60 – 65
265	Coaster	$10 – 12
266	Teapot Stand/Hot Plate	$22 – 25
10	Teapot & Lid	$40 – 45
11	Demitasse Teapot & Lid	$50 – 55
78	Batter Bowl, handled	$35 – 40
901-C	Batter Pitcher & Lid	$45 – 50
902-C	Syrup Pitcher & Lid	$30 – 35

Additional Items

—	Pitcher, ball-shaped, ice-lip, spout on side.	$60 – 65
—	Cookie Jar & Lid (Tom & Jerry Bowl & Lid without lettering)	$115 – 125
—	Coffee Pot & Lid, ribbed top half, narrower pedestal-like lower half	$60 – 65

"200" Series (aka Poppy Trail): Tom & Jerry bowl and cups.

"200" Series (aka Poppy Trail): No. 238 coffee carafe and lid.

"200" Series (aka Poppy Trail): coasters.

Mission Bell: 8¼" soup bowl.

Pintoria: serving plate, luncheon plates, bread and butter plate, and cup and saucer.

DINNERWARE ✩ BEVERAGEWARE ✩ KITCHENWARE

● *Pintoria* COLORS: Gloss Glazes, Vivid Colors: Delphinium Blue, Old Rose, Canary Yellow, Turquoise Blue, Poppy Orange and Rust.

"200" Series (aka Poppy Trail) and Pintoria patterns from a c. 1939 brochure.

Pintoria: luncheon plate, saucer, fruit bowls, and cups and saucers.

400 Pintoria

400	Cup	$50 – 60
402	Saucer	$25 – 30
403	Bread & Butter	$30 – 40
405	Luncheon Plate	$50 – 60
415	Serving Bowl	$90 –100
418	Sugar, open	$80 – 90
419	Creamer	$80 – 90
421	Fruit Bowl	$40 – 50
429	Serving Plate	$80 – 90

COLORS: Gloss Glazes, Vivid Colors: Delphinium Blue, Old Rose, Canary Yellow, Turquoise Blue, Poppy Orange and Rust.
Satin Glazes, Pastel Colors: Opaline Green, Powder Blue, Petal Pink, Pastel Yellow, Satin Turquoise, Peach and Satin Ivory.

Yorkshire pattern, from a c. 1939 brochure.

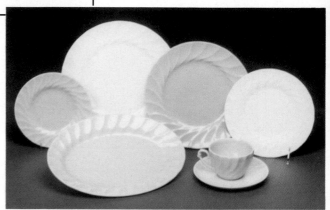

Yorkshire: bread and butter plate, dinner plate, luncheon plate, salad plate, medium platter, and cup and saucer.

500 Yorkshire

No.	Item	Price	No.	Item	Price
500	Cup	$10 – 12	522	Sauce Boat	$20 – 25
502	Saucer	$3 – 4	523	Gravy with Attached Plate	$30 – 35
500-D	Demitasse Cup	$22 – 25	524	Celery Dish	$20 – 25
502-D	Demitasse Saucer	$6 – 8	526	5-Part Handled Relish	$50 – 55
503	Bread & Butter	$8 – 10	527	3-Part Condiment, handled	$35 – 40
504	Salad Plate	$10 – 12	530	Chop Plate	$30 – 35
505	Luncheon Plate	$12 – 14	532	Console Bowl	$40 – 45
506	Dinner Plate	$15 – 18	533	Salad Bowl	$45 – 50
509–9½	Cream Soup	$40 – 45	534-A	Salt, jug-shaped, handled	$10 – 12
510	Cream Soup Saucer (if different from no. 502)	$10 – 12	534-B	Pepper, jug-shaped, handled	$10 – 12
511	Sherbet	$20 – 22	535	Tumbler, sm.	$15 – 18
512	Soup/Cereal Bowl	$12 – 15	235-H	Tumbler Handle, clip-on	$4 – 5
513	Butter & Lid	$50 – 55	536	Tumbler, lg.	$20 – 25
514	Vegetable Bowl, oval	$28 – 30	537-L	Pitcher, lg.	$40 – 45
514½	Vegetable Bowl, oval	$30 – 32	538-8½	Coffee Carafe & Lid	$35 – 40
515	Vegetable Bowl, rnd.	$28 – 30	539	Coffee Pot & Lid, sm.	$40 – 45
516	Platter, med., 11"	$25 – 30	540	Coffee Pot & Lid, lg.	$50 – 55
517	Platter, lg., 13 ¾"	$30 – 35	551	Ashtray	$18 – 20
518	Sugar, open, double handle	$20 – 22	569	Teapot & Lid, sm.	$65 – 70
519	Creamer	$18 – 20	570	Teapot & Lid, lg.	$50 – 55
520	Double Egg Cup	$25 – 30	580	Tall Handled Shaker, footed	$15 – 18
521	Fruit Bowl	$10 – 12	581	Candle Holder	$20 – 25

Mixing Bowls

70	Very Small	$8 – 10
71	Small	$12 – 15
72	Medium	$18 – 20
73	Large	$20 – 25
74	Extra Large	$30 – 35
75	5-Piece Set (70 – 74)	
76	Jumbo	$45 – 55
77	6-Piece Set (70 – 74, 76)	
750	4-Piece Set (711 – 714)	
711	Small	$8 – 10
712	Medium	$12 – 15
713	Large	$18 – 20
714	Extra Large	$20 – 25

Mixing Bowls: No. 74 extra large and No. 70 very small.

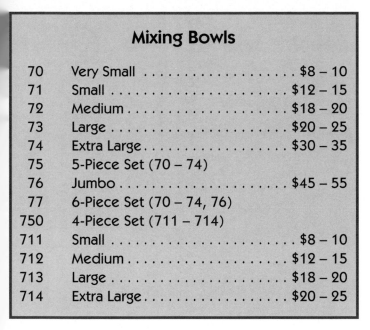

Camellia (brown trim): dinner plate, bread and butter plate, and cup and saucer.

Camellia (brown trim): chop plate, creamer, and sugar and lid.

Yorkshire: Two-handled open sugar.
Mission Bell: two-handled open sugar.
"200" Series (aka Poppy Trail): handled, jug-shaped pepper shaker.

Camellia (green trim): dinner plate, bread and butter plate, fruit bowl, sugar and lid, and creamer.

Poppytrail
Division

Three sizes of Poppytrail dealer signs: large, 6 x 8½"; medium, 5¾ x 7¾"; and small, 5¼ x 7¼".

Ivy Shape

P 170 California Ivy (1946)
P 160 California Apple (1949)
P 180 California Fruit (1949)

California Ivy introduced Metlox's refreshing, different approach to dinnerware design under the leadership of Evan K. Shaw. It was the first of many successful patterns created on distinctive shapes by Shaw's talented design team of Bob Allen and Mel Shaw. The inspiration for California Ivy and the beginning of Allen and Shaw's collaboration with Evan K. Shaw started with a chance meeting in the Brack Shops Building, where Shaw's distributorship, the Evan K. Shaw Company, was located. The newly formed team of Allen and Shaw went there hoping to persuade a manufacturer to hire them as designers. Although neither man was aware of the other's occupation, Evan K. Shaw immediately recognized Mel Shaw as his frequent opponent on the polo field in matches when Evan played for the Warner Brothers team and Mel for the Riviera Country Club team.

After the initial surprise of meeting one another in such unlikely surroundings, Mel Shaw explained their purpose for being there. Evan K. Shaw remarked that, needing designers for his recently acquired dinnerware company (Metlox), he had even contemplated approaching famed designer Raymond Loewy whose creations were considered the ultimate in contemporary design at that time. Shaw agreed to allow the team to submit some designs for his consideration. As they left the building, Allen and Shaw inquired what types of designs Shaw wished. "Streamline it like that," Shaw jokingly responded as he pointed to a new Loewy Studebaker parked nearby. Allen and Shaw proceeded to do just that, creating the innovative California Ivy styling that shocked a dinnerware establishment accustomed to the fancy, fussy, ornate primness of English and European designs. The buying public reacted also, making the California Ivy pattern an instantaneous success.

The appealing unpretentiousness of California Ivy was achieved by the incorporation of coupe shapes for the flatware, simple bowl designs, and straightforward, streamlined contours for the serving pieces. Brown vine handles and finials added a decorative touch to the overall design. This unassuming styling highlighted the curving dark green ivy vine pattern on a pure white background. Evan K. Shaw allowed the designers complete creative freedom with their first design — something he would never do again — and they responded by exceeding his expectations. Bob Allen designed most of the shapes while Mel Shaw created the ivy

35

pattern and the vine handle concept. Mel Shaw developed the rubber stamp design process which ink-stamped the pattern outline onto an item before hand decoration. This was extremely important since it became the primary decorating method for most Metlox patterns. Mel Shaw also conceived the stylus etching technique whereby the hand decorators realistically created the veins of the ivy leaves by scratching through the paint to the white bisque below.

The success of California Ivy led to the creation of the complementary California Ivy Artware line which decorated the ivy pattern on vases, centerpiece bowls, planters, and other artware items. Gracie Allen became the spokesperson for the pattern, with a photograph captioned "Gracie Allen enjoys her California Ivy at home" included on pattern leaflets. No other Metlox pattern surpassed the lengthy production run of California Ivy, which was listed as an active limited production pattern as late as 1984.

California Ivy's popularity inspired two other patterns on the Ivy shape, California Apple and California Fruit. Although both offered the same assortment of items as California Ivy, neither pattern was very successful. California Apple displayed an apple branch design on

every item. California Fruit was more inventive, presenting six different fruits, each on a different item so that the entire table setting, rather than a single item, represented the entire cornucopia. Mel Shaw created the pattern designs for both sets.

The importance of the Ivy shape — and especially the California Ivy pattern — was paramount. California Ivy initiated the hand-decorated style that became Metlox's trademark. Its sales boosted the financial status of Shaw's struggling new company. Perhaps most importantly, it began the close association between the adventuresome entrepreneur Evan K. Shaw and his imaginative, uninhibited design team, a working relationship which would produce the wonderful shapes and patterns of the 1950s and 60s.

California Ivy
As Modern as you wish...yet perfectly at home with your provincial pieces. It adds romantic interest to your table setting. California Ivy gives your dining room that "fresh-as-Spring" personality!

California Ivy: 1948 brochure.

P 170 California Ivy

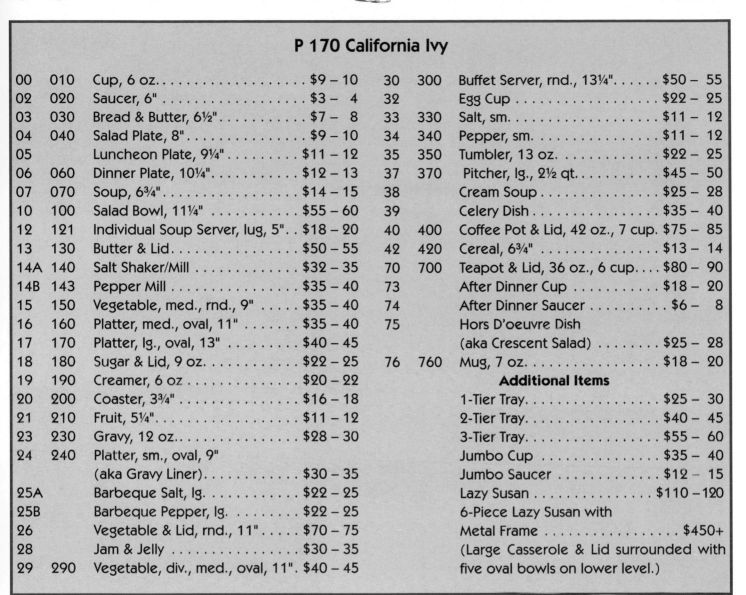

00	010	Cup, 6 oz.	$9 – 10
02	020	Saucer, 6"	$3 – 4
03	030	Bread & Butter, 6½"	$7 – 8
04	040	Salad Plate, 8"	$9 – 10
05		Luncheon Plate, 9¼"	$11 – 12
06	060	Dinner Plate, 10¼"	$12 – 13
07	070	Soup, 6¾"	$14 – 15
10	100	Salad Bowl, 11¼"	$55 – 60
12	121	Individual Soup Server, lug, 5"	$18 – 20
13	130	Butter & Lid	$50 – 55
14A	140	Salt Shaker/Mill	$32 – 35
14B	143	Pepper Mill	$35 – 40
15	150	Vegetable, med., rnd., 9"	$35 – 40
16	160	Platter, med., oval, 11"	$35 – 40
17	170	Platter, lg., oval, 13"	$40 – 45
18	180	Sugar & Lid, 9 oz.	$22 – 25
19	190	Creamer, 6 oz	$20 – 22
20	200	Coaster, 3¾"	$16 – 18
21	210	Fruit, 5¼"	$11 – 12
23	230	Gravy, 12 oz.	$28 – 30
24	240	Platter, sm., oval, 9" (aka Gravy Liner)	$30 – 35
25A		Barbeque Salt, lg.	$22 – 25
25B		Barbeque Pepper, lg.	$22 – 25
26		Vegetable & Lid, rnd., 11"	$70 – 75
28		Jam & Jelly	$30 – 35
29	290	Vegetable, div., med., oval, 11"	$40 – 45
30	300	Buffet Server, rnd., 13¼"	$50 – 55
32		Egg Cup	$22 – 25
33	330	Salt, sm.	$11 – 12
34	340	Pepper, sm.	$11 – 12
35	350	Tumbler, 13 oz.	$22 – 25
37	370	Pitcher, lg., 2½ qt.	$45 – 50
38		Cream Soup	$25 – 28
39		Celery Dish	$35 – 40
40	400	Coffee Pot & Lid, 42 oz., 7 cup.	$75 – 85
42	420	Cereal, 6¾"	$13 – 14
70	700	Teapot & Lid, 36 oz., 6 cup	$80 – 90
73		After Dinner Cup	$18 – 20
74		After Dinner Saucer	$6 – 8
75		Hors D'oeuvre Dish (aka Crescent Salad)	$25 – 28
76	760	Mug, 7 oz.	$18 – 20

Additional Items

1-Tier Tray	$25 – 30
2-Tier Tray	$40 – 45
3-Tier Tray	$55 – 60
Jumbo Cup	$35 – 40
Jumbo Saucer	$12 – 15
Lazy Susan	$110 – 120
6-Piece Lazy Susan with Metal Frame	$450+

(Large Casserole & Lid surrounded with five oval bowls on lower level.)

California Ivy: 1968 brochure.

California Ivy: cup and saucer and rare jumbo cup and saucer.

California Ivy: vegetable and lid and divided vegetable.

California Ivy: dinner plate, coffee pot and lid, sugar and lid, and creamer.

California Ivy: tumbler, bread and butter plate, and butter and lid.

California Ivy: cup and saucer, luncheon plate, salt and pepper, and jam and jelly.

California Apple: Metlox archive photo.

California Fruit: small platter and salt and pepper.

Provincial Shape

Provincial Blue

Poppytrail DINNERWARE

hand decorated under glaze . . . from California

The Provincial Shape continued Metlox's fresh, different approach to dinnerware design. One of the company's most original creations, the Provincial shape was inspired by Early American wood, tin, pewter, basket, and pottery dinnerware models. Many unique items directly copied colonial designs. Other pieces imitated the styling of the originals in details such as the use of handles on standard items usually without them, basket weave exteriors, and the addition of rivets on holloware reminiscent of antique Tole Ware. Figural hen and rooster items added personality to the set. The incorporation of artware items as an integral part of the dinnerware patterns enhanced the decorative effect of the colorful designs. The emphasis on unusual accessories continued throughout the 1950s with the two- and five-piece cruet sets, the pipkin set (a ceramic wall holder with hanging funnel, strainer, and measuring cup), lazy susan, four-piece canister set, and other additions. The shape's appealing designs, released when Early American furnishings were becoming very fashionable, certainly captured the imagination and fancy of many American households. Even Donna Reed's TV kitchen was decorated with Provincial accessories.

The original suggestion that led to the creation of the shape came from a buyer from Barker Brothers, a Los Angeles department store closely associated with Metlox and Evan K. Shaw. During a tour of the plant, the buyer advised Shaw that a provincial rooster pattern might coordinate very well with the Early American furniture reproductions becoming very popular during the late 1940s. When approached with the idea by Evan K. Shaw, Allen and Shaw decided immediately to design item shapes after colonial examples. Allen and Shaw's penchant for authenticity affected every aspect of the designs. They made an exhaustive study of examples shown in art and design books and displayed in museums such as the Metropolitan Art Museum in New York City and the National Gallery in Washington, D.C. Their research included the study of Early American art styles and home decoration as well as dinnerware.

Bob Allen, in close collaboration with Mel Shaw, created most of the shapes. The basket weave exterior decorating several items was his idea. Bernie Hassenstab, later joined by Frank Irwin and Bob Chandler, expertly modeled Allen's explicit paper drawings into plaster shapes for the master molds. Mel Shaw contributed the captivating pattern designs — the sprightly, strutting rooster of California Provincial, and the rustic farm scenes, featuring a colonial couple, of Homestead Provincial and Provincial Blue. Allen's border designs — a continuous wavy line with dots on California Provincial and a repetitive, stylized tulip pattern on Homestead Provincial and Provincial Blue — were common Early American decorative patterns. Favorite eighteenth century colors — dark red, forest green, and leaf green for Homestead Provincial; maroon, forest green, and straw yellow for California Provincial; and a deep blue for Provincial Blue — were appropriate color choices. John Johnson developed a textured maple glaze for California Provincial and Homestead Provincial, and a blue textured glaze for Provincial Blue that further imparted a feeling of antique charm.

The inclusion of wood and metal parts in conjunction with some of the ceramic items was a special design feature from Allen and Shaw. Melco, a company owned by Evan K. Shaw's friend Mel David, produced these additions. A metal frame held the casseroles of the no. 60 – 61 lazy susan, while a metal warmer with a ceramic candle holder supported the kettle casserole and the coffee carafe. The kettle casserole also sported a metal handle. Elaborate wood bases were used for the two-piece and five-piece cruet sets and the no. 79 lazy susan. The coffee carafe had a wood handle with a metal attachment band. The salad fork & spoon were each wood with a ceramic handle. Especially noteworthy were the wood lids with a ceramic finial of the four-piece canister set and cookie jar. These usually fit loosely because they were designed slightly smaller than the ceramic canisters to compensate for any shrinkage of the canister clay body during firing.

Provincial began as a small set of 26 items. As the pattern's popularity increased, it evolved into an extremely large group with many accessory items. The table (right) traces the development of the shape from 1949 to 1980. Eleven representative leaflets and master price lists spanning this time period are duplicated in chronological order. By comparing which items were included or excluded during particular years, collectors can trace approximately the introduction and deletion of individual items. The table includes only those items listed in company brochure material. Additional rare and experimental pieces are discussed later. All listed items were produced in California Provincial, Homestead Provincial, and Provincial Blue.

ITEM #	ITEM	|	PRICE LIST PER CATALOGUE DATES									
		1949	1950	1953	1957	1959	1961	1967	1972	1974	1979	1980
CD	CUP	$1.00	$1.10	$1.10	$1.50	$1.75	$2.25	$2.50	$3.50	$4.15	$6.50	$7.50
O2	SAUCER	0.75	0.85	0.90	0.85	0.95	1.25	1.40	1.90	2.25	4.50	5.50
O3	BREAD & BUTTER	0.85	0.90	0.95	1.15	1.25	1.60	1.90	2.50	3.15	4.95	6.00
O4	SALAD PLATE	1.20	1.35	1.40	1.65	1.75	2.10	2.35	2.95	3.50	6.50	7.50
O5	LUNCHEON PLATE	1.40	1.60	1.70	1.80							
O6	DINNER PLATE	1.75	1.85	2.00	2.00	2.25	2.75	2.95	3.95	4.75	7.95	9.00
O7	SOUP	1.20	1.35	1.40	1.75	1.95	2.35	2.75	3.50	4.25	7.25	8.00
10	SALAD BOWL	3.75	4.50	4.75	5.95	6.95	7.95	8.95	10.95	13.50	25.50	
13 (50)	HEN ON NEST	3.50	3.95	4.20	4.95	5.50	6.95	7.95	10.95	13.50	18.50	
15	VEGETABLE	2.00	2.00	2.10	3.25	3.50	3.75	3.95	4.50	5.25	10.25	17.00
17	OVAL PLATTER, LG	3.75	4.25	4.50	4.95	4.95	5.25	5.50	7.95	9.50	14.95	24.00
18	SUGAR	2.25	2.50	2.65	3.75	3.95	4.25	4.95	6.95	8.25	11.25	19.00
19	CREAMER	1.75	2.00	2.10	2.50	2.95	3.25	3.95	4.95	5.95	8.95	15.00
20	COASTER	0.80	0.90	0.95	0.85	1.00	1.10	1.50	1.95	2.35	4.25	
21	FRUIT	0.85	0.90	0.95	1.15	1.25	1.60	1.90	2.50	3.15	5.25	7.00
23	GRAVY	3.50	3.95	4.20	4.50	4.75	4.95	5.75	7.50	9.50	15.95	23.00
26	COVERED VEGETABLE	5.00	5.00	5.25	6.25	6.50	7.95	9.95	11.95	14.50	26.50	
31	CHOP PLATE	3.00	3.50	3.70	4.50	4.75	4.95	5.95	7.95	9.50	15.95	
33	SALT	1.10	1.25	1.30	1.50	1.60	1.75	2.25	2.75	3.50	5.25	7.50
34	PEPPER	1.10	1.25	1.30	1.45	1.60	1.75	2.25	2.75	3.50	5.25	7.50
36	CANDLEHOLDER	1.50	1.75	1.85								
40	COFFEE POT	7.50	7.50	7.95	8.95	9.50	10.95	11.95	14.95	18.95	27.50	40.00
41	JAM & MUSTARD	3.00	3.00	3.15	3.50							
71	BREAD DISH	5.00	5.00	5.25	5.95	6.95	7.95	8.95	12.50	15.50	21.00	
72	MUG WITH LID	2.50	3.00	3.15								
72	MUG WITHOUT LID	1.75	1.95	2.00	2.95	3.25	3.95	4.95	5.50	6.50	9.95	
12	LUG SOUP		1.95	2.00	2.50	2.60	2.95	3.50	4.25	5.25	7.95	
14A	SALT SHAKER		3.00	3.15	4.00	4.00	4.95	4.95				
14B	PEPPER MILL		4.95	5.25	5.95	6.95	6.95	6.95				
29	DIVIDED VEGETABLE		5.00	5.25	6.95	7.95	8.95	9.95	12.50	15.50	19.25	27.50
43	MILK PITCHER		3.50	3.70	4.95	5.50	6.95	7.95	9.95	12.25	16.50	
70	TEAPOT & LID		7.50	7.95	8.95	9.50	10.95	11.95	14.95	18.50	26.50	38.00
80	CIGARETTE BOX		2.75	2.90								
81	MATCH BOX		4.00	4.25	5.00							
82	SPICE BOX PLANTER		4.50	4.75								
83	DOWER CHEST		6.50	6.90								
84	SPRINKLING CAN		4.00	4.25	4.95							
85	STEEPLE CLOCK		5.00	5.25								
27	BASKET VEGETABLE				2.25	3.50	3.75	4.25	5.50	6.75	8.25	13.50
44-47	CANISTER SET (4 PIECE)				24.95	24.95	24.95	29.95	34.95	44.95	55.95	79.95
44	FLOUR CANISTER				10.00	10.95	10.95	12.50	11.95	14.95	18.25	26.00
45	SUGAR CANISTER				7.50	8.50	8.50	10.00	10.00	12.00	14.95	21.00
46	COFFEE CANISTER				5.00	6.00	6.00	7.00	7.00	9.50	11.75	18.00
47	TEA CANISTER				3.95	5.50	5.50	6.00	6.00	8.50	11.00	15.00
46-31	3-TIER TRAY				9.95	9.95						
48-49	SOUP TUREEN/LADLE				24.95	24.95						
51-54	CRUET SET (5 PIECE)				19.95	19.95	19.95	22.95	27.95	34.95	42.75	
60	CHICKEN COVERED CASS.				9.95	10.95	11.95	12.95	14.95	17.95	22.50	33.50
60-61	LAZY SUSAN (WIRE)				27.50							
86	SALT BOX				7.95	7.95						
16	OVAL PLATTER, MED.				3.25	3.75	3.95	4.50	5.95	7.50	13.50	21.00
22A-B	FORK & SPOON SET					3.95	3.95	4.50	5.00	6.00	7.50	11.50
32	EGG CUP					2.25	2.25	2.75	3.95	3.95	4.75	7.75
37	WATER PITCHER					8.95	8.95	10.95	12.95	14.95	18.25	22.95
50 (13)	BUTTER				4.95	5.50	5.95	7.95	9.95	12.25	15.95	25.00
51-51	CRUET SET (2 PC)				12.95	12.95	15.95	17.95	19.95	24.50		
55	COOKIE JAR					10.95	10.95	12.50	11.95	14.95	18.25	26.00
56-59	PIPKIN SET					14.95						
67	KETTLE CASSEROLE					12.45	12.95	13.95	14.95	17.95	22.50	35.50
67W	KETTLE CAS. WARMER					1.50	2.00	2.50	3.00	5.00		
68	COFFEE CARAFE					9.45	10.95	10.95	11.95	14.95	18.25	28.95
68W	COFFEE CAR. WARMER					1.50	2.00	2.00	3.00	4.50		
76	COCOA MUG				2.00	2.50	2.75	3.50	3.95	4.75	7.50	9.00
78	TURKEY PLATTER					19.95	19.95	19.95				
93	HEN ON NEST SALT					1.75	2.00	2.25	2.75	3.75	4.50	7.50
94	ROOSTER PEPPER					2.25	2.50	2.50	3.95	4.50	5.50	7.50
90	ASHTRAY (6")					2.00	2.25	2.50	3.25	3.95	4.95	7.50
91	ASHTRAY (8")					3.00	3.25	3.50	4.50	4.95	6.00	11.25
92	ASHTRAY (10")					4.50	4.95	4.95				
95	ASHTRAY (12")					6.00						
96	ASHTRAY (4")					1.50	1.75	1.75	1.95	2.75	3.50	4.95
25	OVAL PLATTER, EX.LG.						8.95	8.95	8.95	14.95	18.25	29.50
42	CEREAL					1.95	2.35	2.65	3.25	3.85	6.95	8.00
79	LAZY SUSAN (WOOD)						14.95	17.95	19.95	27.95	34.95	
88	PITCHER (1 PINT)					4.50	4.95	6.50	6.95	8.50	13.75	
08	SMALL VEGETABLE						3.75	4.95	5.50	6.95	9.25	
35	TUMBLER							3.25	3.50	4.25	4.95	7.25
98	3 DIV. SERVER							9.95				

Table tracing the development of the Provincial Shape from 1949 to 1980.

Provincial Blue was dropped as an active pattern after 1968. By 1979 Homestead Provincial was a limited production pattern consisting of 19 items while California Provincial continued production of the 51 pieces listed in the table. A December 1, 1980 price list reduced Homestead Provincial to 13 basic items and California Provincial to 21. Homestead Provincial was discontinued on December 31, 1981, and California Provincial shortly thereafter.

Some interesting information about the shape is apparent from this table. The decorative artware items appeared very early in the line as did such unique items as the jam and mustard, bread dish, hen on nest, and tankard mug with lid. No additions were introduced after 1961. From 1959 to 1979 the item selection remained relatively constant. Items listed only once or twice should be considered rare. The suggested retail prices indicate gradual increases from 1950 – 1967, then steeper, more dramatic increases from 1967 – 1980.

A number of Provincial items never appeared in company leaflets. Some of these were produced in limited quantities for only a brief period. Others were experimental items which, after poor test-marketing results, were never mass produced. The 14" figural rooster water pitcher, an impressive piece with the rooster's open beak serving as the spout, was deemed impractical because of its weight and awkwardness. Along with the three-tier tray with maple finish divider listed in leaflets, Metlox also offered trays with one, two, or three plates and a metal loop handle divider. Three sizes of flower pots were created. The largest was 6½" tall, the smallest, 4¾" tall, and the medium probably about 5½" tall. The large mug appeared with a long spout similar to the teapot. A small version of the medium three-divided server, a handled square divided dish, and a snack or hostess plate — square with a stick handle and cup-well indent — were designed. A four-piece hanging wall set included a planter, water tank, and two candle holders with fitted metal parts. Frank Irwin states that planters were created by dividing serving pieces such as the teapot in half during the greenware stage and adding a ceramic back. A report of three sizes of window box planters could not be verified by company employees. Although it appeared once in an early 1950s brochure, special mention must be given to the no. 60 – 61 lazy susan. This outstanding design was a circular wrought-iron stand with partitions to hold the large chicken covered casserole surrounded on a lower level by five smaller hen on nest casseroles. This item was produced in two versions — one with, and one without, lids on the hen on nest casseroles. All of the above mentioned items are rare and considered very valuable by collectors.

Other companies, both domestic and Japanese, tried to capitalize on the popularity of the Provincial patterns by merchandising accessory and go-along items featuring poor imitations of Mel Shaw's original rooster and farm couple designs. These included glassware sets,

metal trays, wooden kitchen accessories, and tablecloth and napkin sets. Metlox, which produced only ceramic items, never commissioned, sanctioned, or marketed any of these items. Furthermore, lamps and clocks made with Provincial pieces were created by jobbers or small independent companies, never Metlox.

The immediate and sustained popularity of the first three Provincial patterns fostered the creation of others. Apropos of what became become a characteristic Evan K. Shaw practice, these patterns included alterations and redesigns as well as pattern variations.

P 390 Red Rooster presented Mel Shaw's rooster design in shades of red, yellow, dark charcoal brown, and touches of leaf green on an off-white nontextured background. The pattern did not include a border design. Dark charcoal edges, handles, and finials enhanced the aged effect with smoky highlighting. Red Rooster was specifically created to showcase John Johnson's newly developed selenium "live-coal" red glaze. Red was always a very difficult color to duplicate under the glaze on pottery. Johnson's ingenious solution was to develop an on-glaze red with selenium added. This allowed the color to move slightly during firing and to fuse with the clear glaze. After the once-fired bisque item was hand-decorated with all colors except red, it was sprayed with a thicker than usual coat of a special milky glaze concocted by Johnson. Normally, glazes were opaque before firing; Johnson's new glaze was semi-translucent and thus allowed the decorators to see the rooster pattern. After the selenium red was appropriately applied, the item was fired a second time, permanently sealing both the red glaze and the clear glaze.

Red Rooster was released initially as an entirely decorated pattern. However, as the popularity of the red color increased, certain items were introduced in solid red also. Later these items plus additional ones were produced only in red. These solid pieces, assigned the separate pattern number P 391, appeared as follows in brochure material.

1959: 22 items either red or decorated: cup, lug soup, salt shaker/mill, pepper mill, sugar, creamer, coaster, salad fork and spoon set (red only), gravy, basket vegetable, divided vegetable, salt, pepper, coffee pot, milk pitcher, butter, 2-piece cruet set, 5-piece cruet set, teapot, bread server, mug, and cocoa mug.

1961: 28 items either red or decorated — additions: salad bowl, tumbler (red only), coffee carafe, 4", 6", and 8" ashtrays.

1964: 38 items in red only — additions: egg cup, water pitcher, four-piece canister set, cookie jar, kettle casserole, one-pint pitcher, and 10" ashtray.

1968: 39 items in red only — additions: small vegetable and small divided vegetable. The 10" ashtray was discontinued.

The cup was always offered in red and decorated versions. The salad fork and spoon set, tumbler, small vegetable, and small divided vegetable were only produced in red.

From its release in 1955, the item selection of Red Rooster duplicated that of the first three Provincial patterns as listed in the above table. All item shapes were unchanged except for the larger, straight-sided, redesigned cup. In 1968, Red Rooster added the small divided vegetable and small 9½" oval platter, two items never produced in the first patterns. Since brochure information before 1959 was unavailable for verification purposes, uncertainty remains concerning the production of Provincial shape items deleted before 1955 as well as the unlisted, experimental pieces discussed earlier. Company employees believe that most of these items were produced in Red Rooster.

In time, the popularity of Red Rooster rivaled the success of California Provincial. Finally, reduced to a limited production pattern of 21 items in 1980, it was discontinued along with California Provincial shortly after 1981. The proud rooster certainly had served its creators well.

The instantaneous success of Red Rooster led to the creation of Colonial Heritage which decorated Homestead Provincial's farm couple and scenes in hues of red, leaf green, and dark charcoal brown on an off-white background. Charcoal highlighting was again used on edges, handles, and finials, and a variety of 22 items were offered in both decorated and solid red versions. Item selection paralleled that of Red Rooster. Colonial Heritage never attained the success of Red Rooster and was discontinued after 1962.

Happy Time, the creation of folk artist Gisella Loeffler, was released on the Provincial shape shortly after Red Rooster and Colonial Heritage. Loeffler owned a studio in Taos, New Mexico, where she specialized in quaint, decorative drawings featuring children. Unfamiliar with pottery techniques and uncomfortable with designing on curved surfaces, she preferred the medium of opaque paint on colored or toned paper. After Evan K. Shaw became fascinated with her work's

charming naivete during a visit to New Mexico, he invited her to Manhattan Beach to design a new dinnerware pattern. The Provincial shape was chosen for the pattern even though the childlike scenes were of a folk rather than a provincial style. Shaw had great hopes for Happy Time and issued it as a large line accompanied by aggressive promotion. He was bitterly disappointed when it was not a commercial success. Loeffler left the company, blaming the pattern's failure on Shaw's adamant insistence on a white background with bright yellow trim instead of Loeffler's color backgrounds to contrast the multicolored designs. Perhaps the timing of Happy Time's release was merely premature since it is now becoming a very collectible Metlox pattern. Even though brochure material was unobtainable, company employees believe that most of the Provincial items produced circa 1957 were also available in Happy Time.

Country Side was seemingly doomed to fail even before its release. Sears, Roebuck and Company hired Metlox to produce a provincial pattern featuring farm scenes by Mel Shaw similar to Homestead Provincial. The basic color scheme and textured maple background were also the same. A repetitive leaf design with red dots served as the border. Country Side was offered as a small pattern consisting of only basic Provincial items. Problems with Sears surfaced almost immediately. Displeased with the pattern and doubtful of its success, Sears wanted Metlox to warehouse a large inventory of the pattern without a guarantee to purchase it. Metlox employees believe Sears really desired the exclusive right to merchandise the extremely popular Homestead Provincial and California Provincial patterns which it wanted to purchase at greatly reduced bulk rates. Evan K. Shaw balked at these suggestions, terminating the company's involvement with Sears and discontinuing the pattern after a limited run. This was unfortunate because Country Side was a delightful pattern reflecting the charming simplicity of Homestead Provincial. Country Side was backstamped with Sears' "Harmony House" logo and name above the pattern name "COUNTRY SIDE" and "MADE IN CALIFORNIA."

Winter Scene — named by Bob Allen in lieu of an official company title — was a seasonal pattern marketed for the Thanksgiving/Christmas holidays. Consisting of only the Provincial turkey platter and dinner plate, it displayed a very detailed, hand-decorated scene — a horse-drawn wagon carrying two people with a mill house, barn, and farmhouse in the wintry background — in the Currier & Ives tradition by Mel Shaw. The turkey platter was white with the wide basket weave rim trimmed in gold. Cup and saucer sets may have been offered to complete the place setting.

Provincial Blue: cup and saucer and salad plate.

Mealtime contentment is yours...

POPPYTRAIL

Provincial Blue

DINNERWARE
for Modern Home Makers

Poppytrail
Made in California

The American Style in Dinnerware

Write For Free Folder

A postcard or letter will bring you a colorful, descriptive folder—and the name of your nearest Poppytrail dealer. If you wish to purchase by mail, write to us and we will arrange to have your nearest dealer make the shipment.

PHOTOGRAPH COURTESY B. ALTMAN & CO. NEW YORK

Modern in Design
Antique in Flavor

The charm of Provincial Blue lies in the shapes, which are similar to Colonial Classics created in the 1700's of tin, pewter, pottery, and wood. Note the cleverly simulated "rivets." Provincial Blue captures the Early American appreciation for blue—and its ability to create a pleasing, harmonious, mealtime atmosphere.
Art direction by Allen-Shaw.

Easily Yours...

Buy the "bargain" Starter Set, consisting of 16 pieces— 4 each cups, saucers, bread and butters, and large dinner plates —for only $12.95. As time goes on, add other pieces to your set from open stock.

METLOX MANUFACTURING CO.
Manhattan Beach, California

Provincial Blue: magazine ad.

Provincial Blue
Modern in Design . . . Antique in Flavor
The charm of Provincial Blue lies in the shapes, which are similar to Colonial Classics created in the 1700's of tin, pewter, pottery, and wood. Note the cleverly simulated "rivets." Provincial Blue captures the Early American appreciation for blue — and its ability to create a pleasing, harmonious, mealtime atmosphere.

Provincial Blue: 1961 brochure.

Provincial Blue: 1961 brochure.

Provincial Blue: very rare four-piece wall set (water tank, candle holders, and planter).

Provincial Blue: vegetable bowl, fruit bowl, lug soup bowl, and soup bowl.

Homestead Provincial: three-divided server.

Homestead Provincial: cookie jar and lid and 6⅜" medium ashtray.

Homestead Provincial: steeple clock and spice box planter.

Homestead Provincial: dower chest and jam and mustard.

Homestead Provincial

A Touch of History with a Modern Accent

The current trend in interior decoration is toward the casual with Ranch House dominating in many localities. This pattern was created to fit in with this trend, as well as with Early American, Provincial, English Farmhouse, Cape Cod, Swedish — and Modern. Designed by Allen & Shaw, Homestead Provincial is based upon Early American folk art, and its charm comes from the fact that the shapes are similar to those created in pottery, tin, pewter and wood. The warm, maple glaze gives it the charming, authentic feeling of age. It has the beautiful deep red and rich greens used so much in the folk art of Colonial America.

Homestead Provincial: large platter.

Homestead Provincial: 1950 brochure.

California Provincial: very rare six-piece lazy susan with metal frame.

California Provincial: medium pitcher (milk pitcher).

California Provincial: hen on nest and chicken covered casserole.

California Provincial: bread and butter plate and pepper mill.

California Provincial: kettle casserole and lid.

California Provincial
Antique Flavor...Modern Design!
Fanciful Provincial Dinnerware in early day Pilgrim motif! Style your table of today with authentic designs that date back to Plymouth Rock! Against a background of maple, the strutting rooster is done in maroon and Provincial tones of leaf green and straw yellow. The border is decorated in green and coffee brown...Created to fit in with practically all types of home decoration from Early American or Provincial, English Farmhouse, Cape Cod, Swedish, Victorian, French Provincial, Ranch House — all the way to informal, Modern, patio use. Designed under the art direction of Allen & Shaw, California Provincial's charm comes from the fact that the shapes are similar to those created in pottery, tin, and wood by Early American craftsmen.

California Provincial: medium platter and lug soup bowl.

California Provincial: candle holder, chop plate, and teapot and lid.

California Provincial: four-piece canister set.

California Provincial: salt and pepper, dinner plate, and large mug.

California Provincial: three-tier tray with maple finish divider.

California Provincial: creamer, coffee carafe and warmer, and sugar and lid.

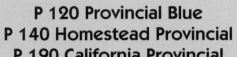

P 120 Provincial Blue
P 140 Homestead Provincial
P 190 California Provincial

00	010	Cup, 6 oz..................	$12 – 13
02	020	Saucer, 6⅛"...............	$4 – 5
03	030	Bread & Butter, 6⅜"........	$9 – 10
04	040	Salad Plate, 7½"..........	$12 – 14
05		Luncheon Plate, 9"........	$18 – 20
06	060	Dinner Plate, 10"..........	$15 – 18
07	070	Soup, 8".................	$22 – 25
08	080	Vegetable, sm., rnd., 7⅛"...	$40 – 45
10	100	Salad Bowl, 11⅛".........	$80 – 85
12	121	Individual Soup Server, lug, 5" (aka Lug Soup).....	$22 – 25
13	500	Hen on Nest.............	$95 – 100
14A	140	Salt Shaker/Mill...........	$40 – 45
14B	143	Pepper Mill..............	$45 – 50
15	150	Vegetable, med., rnd., 10"....	$50 – 55
16	160	Platter, med., oval, 11"......	$40 – 45
17	170	Platter, lg., oval, 13½"......	$50 – 55
18	180	Sugar & Lid, 8 oz.........	$30 – 35
19	190	Creamer, 6 oz.	$25 – 30
20	200	Coaster, 3¾"............	$20 – 22
21	210	Fruit, 6".................	$14 – 16
22A-B	220	Salad Fork & Spoon Set	$60 – 65
23	230	Gravy, 1 pt..............	$40 – 45
25	250	Platter, ex. lg., oval, 16"....	$80 – 85
26	260	Vegetable & Lid, med., rnd., 1 qt., 10"	$90 – 100
27	270	Vegetable, basket design, rnd., 8⅛"................	$45 – 50
29	290	Vegetable, div., med., rect., 12".	$60 – 65
31	300	Buffet Server, rnd., 12¼" (aka Chop Plate).........	$70 – 75
32	320	Egg Cup	$28 – 30
33	330	Salt....................	$14 – 15
34	340	Pepper	$14 – 15
35	350	Tumbler, 11 oz...........	$32 – 35
36		Candle Holder	$40 – 45
37	370	Pitcher, lg., 2¼ qt. (aka Water Pitcher)...........	$80 – 85
40	400	Coffee Pot & Lid, 42 oz., 7 cup.	$115 – 125
41		Jam & Mustard	$60 – 65
42	420	Cereal, 7¼"..............	$16 – 18
43	430	Pitcher, med., 1 qt. (aka Milk Pitcher)...........	$60 – 65
44	440	Flour Canister & Lid........	$80 – 85
45	450	Sugar Canister & Lid	$70 – 75
46	460	Coffee Canister & Lid	$60 – 65
47	470	Tea Canister & Lid........	$50 – 55
46-31		3-Tier Tray, maple finish divider	$90 – 100
48		Soup Tureen & Lid	$325 – 350
49		Soup Tureen Ladle	$40 – 45
50	130	Butter & Lid	$65 – 70
51-51	519	Cruet Set, 2-piece, complete...	$100 – 110
	510	Cruet Oil & Lid, 7 oz.	$35 – 38
	515	Cruet Vinegar & Lid, 7 oz....	$35 – 38
	518	Cruet Wood Base for 2-Piece Set...............	$28 – 30
51-54	549	Cruet Set, 5-piece, complete ..	$165 – 180
	510	Cruet Oil & Lid, 7 oz.	$35 – 38
	515	Cruet Vinegar & Lid, 7 oz. ..	$35 – 38
	520	Cruet Mustard & Lid, 4 oz. ...	$28 – 30
	530	Cruet Salt	$20 – 22
	540	Cruet Pepper	$20 – 22
	548	Cruet Wood Base for 5-Piece Set...............	$28 – 30
55	550	Cookie Jar & Lid..........	$90 – 95
56-59		Pipkin Set	$185 – 195
60	600	Casserole & Lid, chicken cover, 1 qt. 10 oz.	$135 – 145
60-61		Lazy Susan, wire frame a. w/out small casserole lids	$500+
		b. with small casserole lids	$850+
67	670	Kettle Casserole & Lid, 2 qt. 12 oz.	$115 – 125
67W	675	Kettle Casserole Warmer, med., metal	$30 – 35
68	680	Coffee Carafe & Lid, 44 oz., 7 cup	$125 – 135
68W	684	Coffee Carafe Warmer, sm., metal...............	$30 – 35
70	700	Teapot & Lid, 42 oz., 7 cup...	$115 – 125
71	710	Bread Server, 9½"........	$65 – 70
72		Mug with Lid, lg., 1 pt......	$50 – 55
72	720	Mug, no lid, lg., 1 pt.......	$32 – 35
76	760	Mug, 8 oz. (aka Cocoa)	$22 – 25
78		Turkey Platter, 22½"......	$200 – 225

(continued)

79 799 (790)	Lazy Susan Set, 7-piece, complete	$190 – 200
	791	Lazy Susan End Dish (2)	$32 – 35
	792	Lazy Susan Side Dish (2)	$32 – 35
	795	Lazy Susan Wood Base (1)	$28 – 30
	500	Hen on Nest	$95 – 100
80	Cigarette Box	$90 – 95
81	Match Box	$80 – 85
82	Spice Box Planter	$75 – 80
83	Dower Chest	$95 – 100
84	Sprinkling Can	$90 – 95
85	Steeple Clock	$90 – 95
86	Salt Box	$115 – 125
88	880	Pitcher, sm., 1½ pt.	$45 – 50
90	900	Ashtray, med., 6⅜"	$22 – 25
91	910	Ashtray, lg., 8¼"	$28 – 30
92	Ashtray, 10"	$35 – 40
93	930	Hen on Nest Salt	$28 – 30
94	940	Rooster Pepper	$28 – 30
95	Ashtray, 12"	$40 – 45
96	890	Ashtray, sm., 4½"	$18 – 20
98	3-Divided Server, med., 13¼"	$115 – 125

Red Rooster: sugar and lid, creamer, large platter, and coffee pot and lid.

Red Rooster: two-tier tray with metal divider.

Red Rooster: five-piece cruet set.

Red Rooster: 4½" ashtray, extra large platter, and teapot and lid.

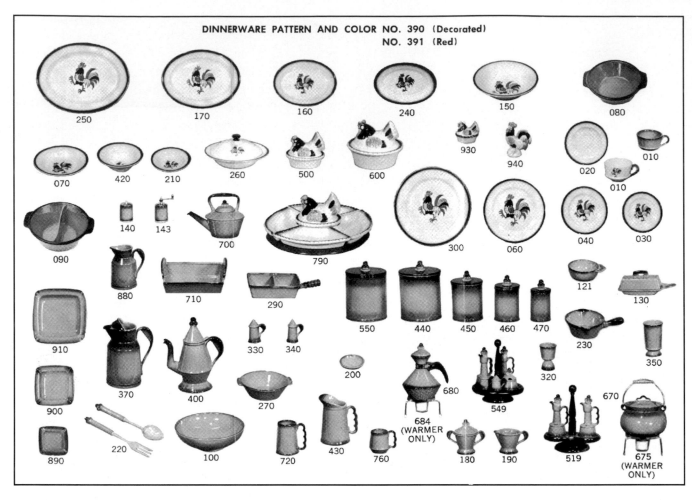

DINNERWARE PATTERN AND COLOR NO. 390 (Decorated)
NO. 391 (Red)

250   170   160   240   150   080
070   420   210   260   500   600   930   940   020   010   010
090   140   143   700   790   300   060   040   030
880   710   290   550   440   450   460   470   121   130
910   330   340   230   350
370   400   270   200   680   549   320   670
900   220   100   720   430   760   684 (WARMER ONLY)   180   190   519   675 (WARMER ONLY)
890

Red Rooster: 1968 brochure.

Red Rooster

Early American with the exciting red coloring that lends style and life to Provincial Ware. The orange or "live-coal" red is a distinct achievement in ceramics. The basic shapes are derived from olden Tole Ware, made from tin… hence the "rivets" on the holloware pieces. The smoky effect on the edges and handles suggest age and enhance the antique feeling. The touches of deep red, straw yellow and leaf green point up the beauty of this distinctive ware. The wide and varied accessories are so beautiful that you'll add to your set and display pieces in hutches, pantry or kitchen.

Red Rooster: rare figural rooster water pitcher.

Red Rooster: pepper shaker and fruit bowl.

Red Rooster: salt box (without wood lid) and basket vegetable.

Red Rooster: flour canister and lid (red) and flour canister and lid (decorated).

Red Rooster: vegetable bowl and lid.

Red Rooster: butter and lid, salad plate, and cup and saucer.

Red Rooster: bread and butter plate and medium pitcher (milk pitcher).

P 390 Red Rooster (Decorated)
P 391 Red Rooster (Red)

(1) Decorated Only **(2) Red Only** **(3) Decorated and Red**

00	010	Cup, 7 oz.	(3)	$11 – 12
02	020	Saucer, 6⅛"	(1)	$3 – 4
03	030	Bread & Butter, 6⅜"	(1)	$8 – 9
04	040	Salad Plate, 7½"	(1)	$10 – 12
06	060	Dinner Plate, 10"	(1)	$13 – 15
07	070	Soup, 8"	(1)	$18 – 20
	080	Vegetable, sm., rnd., 7⅛"	(2)	$35 – 40
	090	Vegetable, div., sm., rnd., 7⅛"	(2)	$40 – 45
10	100	Salad Bowl, 11⅛"	(3)	$75 – 80
12	121	Individual Soup Server, lug, 5"	(3)	$20 – 22
13	500	Hen on Nest	(1)	$90 – 95
14A	140	Salt Shaker/Mill	(3)	$35 – 40
14B	143	Pepper Mill	(3)	$40 – 45
15	150	Vegetable, med., rnd., 10"	(1)	$45 – 50
16	160	Platter, med., oval, 11"	(1)	$35 – 40
17	170	Platter, lg., oval, 13½"	(1)	$45 – 50
18	180	Sugar & Lid, 8 oz.	(3)	$25 – 30
19	190	Creamer, 6 oz.	(3)	$22 – 25
20	200	Coaster, 3¾"	(3)	$18 – 20
21	210	Fruit, 6"	(1)	$12 – 14
22A-B	220	Salad Fork & Spoon Set	(2)	$55 – 60
23	230	Gravy, 1 pt.	(3)	$35 – 40
	240	Platter, sm., oval, 9½"	(1)	$32 – 35
25	250	Platter, ex. lg., oval, 16"	(1)	$75 – 80
26	260	Vegetable & Lid, med., rnd., 1 qt., 10"	(1)	$85 – 95
27	270	Vegetable, basket design, rnd., 8⅛"	(3)	$40 – 45
29	290	Vegetable, div., med., rect., 12"	(3)	$55 – 60
30	300	Buffet Server, rnd., 12¼"	(1)	$65 – 70
32	320	Egg Cup	(3)	$25 – 28
33	330	Salt	(3)	$12 – 14
34	340	Pepper	(3)	$12 – 14
35	350	Tumbler, 11 oz.	(2)	$30 – 32
37	370	Pitcher, lg., 2¼ qt.	(3)	$75 – 80
40	400	Coffee Pot & Lid, 42 oz., 6 cup	(3)	$110 – 120
42	420	Cereal, 7¼"	(1)	$14 – 16
43	430	Pitcher, med., 1 qt.	(3)	$55 – 60
44	440	Flour Canister & Lid	(3)	$75 – 80
45	450	Sugar Canister & Lid	(3)	$65 – 70
46	460	Coffee Canister & Lid	(3)	$55 – 60
47	470	Tea Canister & Lid	(3)	$45 – 50

50	130	Butter & Lid	(3)	$60 – 65
51-51	519	Cruet Set, 2-piece, complete	(3)	$95 – 100
	510	Cruet Oil & Lid, 7 oz.	(3)	$32 – 35
	515	Cruet Vinegar & Lid, 7 oz.	(3)	$32 – 35
	518	Cruet Wood Base for 2-pc. Set		$28 – 30
51-54	549	Cruet Set, 5-piece, complete	(3)	$155 – 170
	510	Cruet Oil & Lid, 7 oz.	(3)	$32 – 35
	515	Cruet Vinegar & Lid, 7 oz.	(3)	$32 – 35
	520	Cruet Mustard & Lid, 4 oz.	(3)	$25 – 28
	530	Cruet Salt	(3)	$18 – 20
	540	Cruet Pepper	(3)	$18 – 20
	548	Cruet Wood Base for 5-Piece Set		$28 – 30
55	550	Cookie Jar & Lid	(3)	$85 – 90
60	600	Casserole & Lid, chicken cover, 1 qt. 10 oz.	(1)	$130 – 140
67	670	Kettle Casserole & Lid, 2 qt. 12 oz.	(3)	$110 – 120
67W	675	Kettle Casserole Warmer, med., metal		$30 – 35
68	680	Coffee Carafe & Lid, 44 oz., 6 cup	(3)	$120 – 130
68W	684	Coffee Carafe Warmer, sm., metal		$30 – 35
70	700	Teapot & Lid, 42 oz., 6 cup	(3)	$110 – 120
71	710	Bread Server, 9½"	(3)	$60 – 65
72	720	Mug, no lid, lg., 1 pt.	(3)	$30 – 32
76	760	Mug, 8 oz.	(3)	$20 – 22
78		Turkey Platter, 22½"	(1)	$190 – 215
79 799 (790)		Lazy Susan Set, 7-piece, complete	(1)	$180 – 190
	791	Lazy Susan End Dish, two	(2)	$30 – 32
	792	Lazy Susan Side Dish, two	(2)	$30 – 32
	795	Lazy Susan Wood Base	(1)	$28 – 30
	500	Hen on Nest	(1)	$90 – 95
88	880	Pitcher, sm., 1½ pt.	(3)	$40 – 45
90	900	Ashtray, med., 6⅜"	(3)	$20 – 22
91	910	Ashtray, lg., 8¼"	(3)	$25 – 28
92		Ashtray, 10"	(3)	$30 – 35
93	930	Hen on Nest Salt	(1)	$25 – 28
94	940	Rooster Pepper	(1)	$25 – 28
96	890	Ashtray, sm., 4½"	(3)	$16 – 18
98		3-Divided Server, med., 13¼"	(1)	$110 – 120

(continued)

Although research uncovered no brochure listings for the following items, most are believed to have been produced in the Red Rooster and Colonial Heritage patterns.

05	Luncheon Plate, 9"	$15 – 18	80	Cigarette Box	$85 – 90
36	Candle Holder	$35 – 40	81	Match Box	$75 – 80
41	Jam & Mustard	$55 – 60	82	Spice Box Planter	$70 – 75
46-31	3-Tier Tray	$85 – 95	83	Dower Chest	$90 – 95
48	Soup Tureen & Lid	$300 – 325	84	Sprinkling Can	$85 – 90
49	Soup Tureen Ladle	$35 – 40	85	Steeple Clock	$85 – 90
56-59	Pipkin Set	$180 – 190	86	Salt Box	$110 – 120
72	Mug with Lid, lg., 1 pt.	$45 – 50	95	Ashtray, 12"	$35 – 40

Colonial Heritage: sugar and lid, large platter, and creamer.

Colonial Heritage: match box.

Colonial Heritage: bread server and divided vegetable.

Colonial Heritage: gravy, salad plate, and bread and butter plate.

Colonial Heritage

Colonial Heritage blends perfectly with casual and informal Modern as well as with Early American, English Farmhouse, Cape Cod, and Swedish. Designed under the art direction of Allen & Shaw, the antique mood of this festive dinnerware is enhanced by the smoky effect on the handles and edges. The basic shapes are derived from Early American folk art, and are similar to pieces made in pewter, tin, and wood. Hence, the simulated "rivets" on the holloware. The "live-coal" red is a distinct achievement in ceramics. The warm, off-white glaze plus the rich leaf green and dark coffee brown accents on the edges and handles provide the antique mood of this festive dinnerware.

P 380 Colonial Heritage

* Items Produced Both Decorated & Red

No.	Item	Price
00	* Cup	$10 – 11
02	Saucer	$3 – 4
03	Bread & Butter	$7 – 8
04	Salad Plate	$10 – 11
06	Dinner Plate	$13 – 14
07	Soup	$18 – 20
10	Salad Bowl	$75 – 80
12	*Individual Soup Server, lug	$20 – 22
13	Hen On Nest	$90 – 95
14A	*Salt Shaker/Mill	$35 – 40
14B	*Pepper Mill	$40 – 45
15	Vegetable, med., rnd.	$45 – 50
16	Platter, med., oval	$35 – 40
17	Platter, lg., oval	$45 – 50
18	*Sugar & Lid	$25 – 30
19	*Creamer	$22 – 25
20	*Coaster	$18 – 20
21	Fruit	$12 – 14
22A-B	*Salad Fork & Spoon Set	$55 – 60
23	*Gravy	$35 – 40
25	Platter, ex. lg., oval	$75 – 80
26	Vegetable & Lid, med., rnd.	$85 – 95
27	*Vegetable, basket design, rnd.	$40 – 45
29	*Vegetable, div., med., rect.	$55 – 60
30	Buffet Server, rnd.	$65 – 70
32	Egg Cup	$25 – 28
33	*Salt	$12 – 14
34	*Pepper	$12 – 14
37	Pitcher, lg.	$75 – 80
40	*Coffee Pot & Lid	$110 – 120
42	Cereal	$14 – 16
43	*Pitcher, med.	$55 – 60
44	Flour Canister & Lid	$75 – 80
45	Sugar Canister & Lid	$65 – 70
46	Coffee Canister & Lid	$55 – 60
47	Tea Canister & Lid	$45 – 50
50	*Butter & Lid	$60 – 65
51-51	*Cruet Set, 2-piece	$95 – 100
51-54	*Cruet Set, 5-piece	$155 – 170
55	Cookie Jar & Lid	$85 – 90
60	Casserole & Lid, chicken cover	$130 – 140
67	Kettle Casserole & Lid	$110 – 120
67W	Kettle Casserole Warmer, metal	$30 – 35
68	Coffee Carafe & Lid	$120 – 130
68W	Coffee Carafe Warmer, metal	$30 – 35
70	*Teapot & Lid	$110 – 120
71	*Bread Server	$60 – 65
72	*Mug, no lid, lg.	$30 – 32
76	*Mug, 8 oz.	$20 – 22
78	Turkey Platter	$190 – 215
79	Lazy Susan Set	$180 – 190
88	Pitcher, sm.	$40 – 45
90	Ashtray, med., 6⅜"	$20 – 22
91	Ashtray, lg., 8¼"	$25 – 28
92	Ashtray, 10"	$30 – 35
93	Hen on Nest Salt	$25 – 28
94	Rooster Pepper	$25 – 28
96	Ashtray, sm., 4½"	$15 – 18

P 120 Provincial Blue, P 140 Homestead Provincial, P 190 California Provincial, P 380 Colonial Heritage, P 390 Red Rooster
Additional Items

1-Tier Tray, metal divider	$35 – 40
2-Tier Tray, metal divider	$50 – 60
3-Tier Tray, metal divider	$65 – 75
Small Flower Pot, 4¾"	$55 – 65
Medium Flower Pot, size unknown	$70 – 80
Large Flower Pot, 6½"	$85 – 95
Figural Rooster Water Pitcher, 14"	$400+
3-Divided Server, sm.	$100 – 115
Snack Plate with Handle & Well, 13½" x 7¼"	$110 – 115
Square Divided Dish with Handle	$95 – 110
4-Piece Wall Set (Planter, Water Tank & 2 Candle Holders)	$450+
Large Mug with Spout	$90 – 100
Figural Hen Egg Cup	$55 – 65

Colonial Heritage: cup and saucer, dinner plate, and coffee pot and lid.

Colonial Heritage: coaster and fruit bowl.

Happy Time: bread server and large mug.

Happy Time: lug soup bowl, chop plate, and rare large mug with spout.

Country Side: dinner plate.

Winter Scene: 22½" turkey platter.

P — Winter Scene			
00	Cup. $12 – 15	06	Dinner Plate . . . . $18 – 20
02	Saucer . . . . $4 – 5	78	Turkey Platter . . . . $200 – 225

Provincial Shape

Part II: P 480 Jamestown (1957)

P 550 Provincial Rose (1958)

P 490 Provincial Fruit (1960)

P 510 Golden Fruit (1961)

P 370 Cape Cod (1961)

P 350 Blueberry Provincial (1962)

P 360 Provincial Flower (1962)

P 380 Rooster Bleu (1966)

P 012 Provincial Whitestone (1977)

Jamestown presented a major redesign and restyling of many Provincial items. These changes by Allen and Shaw affected the composition and look of the Provincial patterns released from the late 50s through the 70s. The all-white Jamestown, a large pattern ornamented with maple and brass appointments, recalled the white ironstone dinnerware of the colonial period. While retaining the basic Provincial shape, plate and bowl sizes were increased slightly. The medium and large platters were rectangular. The Tole Ware rivet styling was added to plates, platters, and most bowls. The larger, taller cup had slanted, straight sides. Among the serving pieces, the butter, sugar, creamer, salt and pepper, coffee pot, teapot, and milk pitcher were redesigned. The sugar received a stick handle and was supported by small feet. The coffee pot lost its sharply angular contours, becoming a straight-sided design with a rounded lid and straight spout. The teapot copied the shape of the kettle casserole and added a brass handle, short spout, and small feet. Heart-shaped finials adorned many of the lids. The figural matchbox salt and pepper and the handled basket sauce boat were delightful designs unique to Jamestown.

Although it offered a smaller selection of major serving items, the lovely Provincial Rose duplicated the shapes and designs of Jamestown except for the matchbox salt and pepper. The addition of smoky charcoal edges, handles, and finials contrasted with its rose, brown, green, and wheat coloring.

Provincial Fruit, Golden Fruit, Blueberry Provincial, and Provincial Flower were a mixture of the original Provincial shapes and Jamestown's alterations. Since they were not compatible with the fruit and flower motifs, all hen and rooster shapes were omitted from these patterns. Plates and bowls retained the larger size and the rivet styling of Jamestown. Platters, however, reverted to oval shapes. Of the major serving pieces, the butter, sugar, creamer, salt and pepper, and teapot adopted the initial Provincial styling while the coffee pot and milk pitcher retained Jamestown's redesign. The items in Cape Cod repeated the shapes of these four patterns except for the substitution of Jamestown's rectangular platters and the original coffee pot design. Of these five patterns, Provincial Fruit became very popular.

Rooster Bleu revived Mel Shaw's rooster design in a colorful variation of brilliant blues and greens with orange and yellow on a tinted, off-white background. Floral designs on the border and underneath the rooster enlivened the original design and enhanced the country French Provincial look of the set. A small pattern of 19 items, Rooster Bleu repeated the larger size plates, bowls, and platter minus the rivet styling. The cup and saucer were adopted from Red Rooster. All other items followed the original Provincial shapes including the coffee pot.

Reminiscent of Jamestown, Provincial Whitestone was a large, all-white 1977 reissue of Provincial items that included many of the major serving items.

Complete the charm of a colonial setting... with these "heirloom" open stock pieces! Oven and detergent proof

Jamestown: 1957 brochure (above and below right).

Jamestown

These classic, functional designs have held their charm for hundreds of years, and blend perfectly with today's finest trends in home decoration — casual and informal Modern, Early American, English Farmhouse, Cape Cod, and Swedish.

The beautiful white glaze matches the original Ironstone ware of the colonists, and many of the basic shapes are reminiscent of old time Toleware — pieces made in tin, pewter, and wood. Hence the "simulated rivets" on the holloware.

Designed under the art direction of Allen & Shaw, this new white ware with its maple and brass appointments will fill a definite need for those discriminating people who want the grace and charm of a truly authentic Provincial pattern.

The American Style in Dinnerware

Provincial Rose: 1961 brochure.

Provincial Rose
Reminiscent of beautiful 18th Century country homes, Provincial Rose epitomizes today's decorating trend — "the new look of elegance." Styled in traditional provincial colors of delicate rose, brown, green, wheat, it blends harmoniously with your dining decor — whether maple, walnut, or mahogany.

P 480 Jamestown, P 550 Provincial Rose
Add 10% for P 550 Provincial Rose

No.	Item	Price
00	Cup	$8 – 9
02	Saucer	$3 – 4
03	Bread & Butter	$6 – 7
04	Salad Plate	$8 – 9
06	Dinner Plate	$11 – 12
07	Soup	$14 – 16
10	Salad Bowl	$60 – 65
12	Individual Soup Server, lug	$16 – 18
14A	Salt Shaker/Mill	$30 – 32
14B	Pepper Mill	$32 – 35
15	Vegetable, med., rnd.	$35 – 40
16	Platter, med., rect., 11"	$30 – 35
17	Platter, lg., rect., 13"	$35 – 40
18	Sugar & Lid	$30 – 32
19	Creamer	$28 – 30
21	Fruit	$10 – 11
22A-B	Salad Fork & Spoon Set	$45 – 50
23	Gravy	$30 – 32
26	Vegetable & Lid, med., rnd.	$65 – 75
27	Vegetable, basket design, rnd.	$32 – 35
29	Vegetable, div., med., rect.	$45 – 50
30	Buffet Server, rnd.	$55 – 60
33	Salt	$14 – 16
34	Pepper	$14 – 16
37	Pitcher, lg.	$60 – 65
40	Coffee Pot & Lid	$80 – 90
42	Cereal	$11 – 12
43	Pitcher, med.	$45 – 50
44	Flour Canister & Lid	$60 – 65
45	Sugar Canister & Lid	$50 – 55
46	Coffee Canister & Lid	$40 – 45
47	Tea Canister & Lid	$30 – 35
50	Butter & Lid	$45 – 50
51-51	Cruet Set, 2-piece (Vinegar & Oil)	$75 – 85
51-54	Cruet Set, 5-piece	$125 – 140
55	Cookie Jar & Lid	$70 – 75
67	Kettle Casserole & Lid	$80 – 90
67W	Kettle Casserole Warmer, metal	$30 – 35
68	Coffee Carafe & Lid	$85 – 95
68W	Coffee Carafe Warmer, metal	$30 – 35
70	Teapot & Lid	$100 – 110
71	Bread Server	$50 – 55
72	Mug, no lid, lg.	$25 – 28
76	Mug, 8 oz.	$16 – 18
88	Pitcher, sm.	$32 – 35

P480 Jamestown Additions

No.	Item	Price
05	Luncheon Plate	$12 – 14
13	Hen on Nest	$75 – 80
32	Egg Cup	$20 – 22
41	Jam & Mustard	$45 – 50
46-31	3-Tier Tray	$70 – 80
48	Soup Tureen & Lid	$250 – 275
49	Soup Tureen Ladle	$30 – 32
56-59	Pipkin Set	$165 – 175
60	Casserole & Lid, chicken cover	$110 – 120
62	Sauce Boat	$45 – 50
78	Turkey Platter	$170 – 195
79	Lazy Susan Set	$160 – 170
81	Match Box	$60 – 65
84	Sprinkling Can	$70 – 75
86	Salt Box	$90 – 100
93	Hen on Nest Salt	$20 – 22
94	Rooster Pepper	$20 – 22

The American Style
in Dinnerware

Provincial Rose: 1961 brochure.

Provincial Fruit

This exciting dinnerware will add luster to any contemporary Provincial home. You'll fall in love with the Early American shapes, designed from authentic antiques. To really appreciate how Provincial Fruit will blend with your home decoration you must see the hand-painted permanent orchard colors of wine-apple red, soft-yellow peach, the subtle leaf greens against the pleasing stippled satin finish and olive rim.

Provincial Fruit: sugar and lid, creamer, salad plate, bread and butter plate, and salt and pepper shakers.

Provincial Fruit: 1968 brochure.

Provincial Fruit: cup and saucer, dinner plate, and salad plate.

Provincial Fruit: vegetable and lid.

Provincial Fruit: three-divided server.

Provincial Fruit: tea canister and lid and coffee canister and lid.

Golden Fruit
Hand decorated in honey browns, cinnamon, and spice — plus neutral shades of gold to blend happily with all Provincial and Early American — as well as Contemporary furnishings! A delight to view — a delight to serve on for guests or family.

Golden Fruit: lug soup bowl, dinner plate, bread and butter plate, and tumbler.

Golden Fruit: basket vegetable, large platter, and medium platter.

Golden Fruit: cup and saucer, dinner plate, and coffee pot and lid.

Cape Cod: 1965 brochure.

Cape Cod
The great beauty originally created by Colonial craftsmen has been rediscovered in this elegantly-styled dinnerware. It brings you the warm, familiar qualities of the past with the simplicity and at the same time sophistication we like in today's home decor. You'll love the soft blue, and cobalt combined in hand-painted flower forms and interesting shapes from California.

Cape Cod: sugar and lid, creamer, soup bowl, and fruit bowl.

Blueberry Provincial:
1962 brochure.

Blueberry Provincial:
1962 brochure.

Blueberry Provincial
Be the envied hostess when you grace your table with this lustrous, hand-painted earthenware from California! Metlox designers created it from Early American shapes with your home in mind. Blues dominate the background, with leaf and olive-green petals, lemon-yellow blossoms.

Provincial Flower
We are truly proud to present this unusual dinnerware pattern, hand painted, with beauty only achievable in quality earthenware. It is beauty you can afford to use every day, as well as for company service. The colors harmonize with your home decor — cinnamon, rust and tangerine, with accents of lemon-yellow and leaf-green. Provincial Flower combines the charm of Provincial with today's contemporary colors.

Provincial Flower:
salt and pepper shakers, dinner plate, and teapot and lid.

P 350 Blueberry Provincial, P 360 Provincial Flower, P 370 Cape Cod, P 490 Provincial Fruit, P 510 Golden Fruit

Deduct 15% for P 370 Cape Cod   ***Cape Cod only**

00	010	Cup, 7 oz.	$9 – 10
02	020	Saucer, 6¼"	$3 – 4
03	030	Bread & Butter, 6½"	$7 – 8
04	040	Salad Plate, 7½"	$9 – 10
06	060	Dinner Plate, 10½"	$12 – 13
07	070	Soup, 8½"	$16 – 18
08	080	Vegetable, sm., rnd., 7⅛"	$32 – 35
10	100	Salad Bowl, 11⅛"	$65 – 70
12	121	Individual Soup Server, lug, 5"	$18 – 20
13	130	Butter & Lid	$50 – 55
14A	140	Salt Shaker/Mill	$32 – 35
14B	143	Pepper Mill	$35 – 40
15	150	Vegetable, med., rnd., 10"	$40 – 45
16	160	Platter, med., oval, 11"	$35 – 40
16	160	*Platter, med., rect., 11"	$30 – 35
17	170	Platter, lg., oval, 13½"	$40 – 45
17	170	*Platter, lg., rect., 13"	$35 – 40
18	180	Sugar & Lid, 8 oz.	$22 – 25
19	190	Creamer, 6 oz.	$20 – 22
21	210	Fruit, 6¼"	$11 – 12
22A-B	220	Salad Fork & Spoon Set	$50 – 55
23	230	Gravy, 1 pt.	$32 – 35
25	250	Platter, ex. lg., oval, 16" (except Cape Cod)	$65 – 70
26	260	Vegetable & Lid, med., rnd., 1 qt., 10"	$75 – 85
27	270	Vegetable, basket design, rnd., 8⅛"	$35 – 40
29	290	Vegetable, div., med., rect., 12"	$50 – 55
30	300	Buffet Server, rnd., 12¼"	$60 – 65
33	330	Salt	$11 – 12
34	340	Pepper	$11 – 12
35	350	Tumbler, 11 oz.	$28 – 30
37	370	Pitcher, lg., 2¼ qt.	$65 – 70
40	400	Coffee Pot & Lid, 49 oz., 7 cup.	$90 – 100
40	400	*Coffee Pot & Lid, 42 oz., 6 cup.	$75 – 85
42	420	Cereal, 7¼"	$12 – 14
43	430	Pitcher, med., 1 qt.	$50 – 55
70	700	Teapot & Lid, 42 oz., 6 cup.	$90 – 100
71	710	Bread Server, 9½"	$55 – 60
72	720	Mug, lg., 1 pt.	$28 – 30
76	760	Mug, 8 oz.	$18 – 20
88	880	Pitcher, sm., 1½ pt.	$35 – 40
98	980	3-Divided Server, med., 13¼"	$100 – 110

P 490 Provincial Fruit, P 510 Golden Fruit Additions

20	200	Coaster, 3¾"	$16 – 18
32	320	Egg Cup	$22 – 25
44	440	Flour Canister & Lid	$65 – 70
45	450	Sugar Canister & Lid	$55 – 60
46	460	Coffee Canister & Lid	$45 – 50
47	470	Tea Canister & Lid	$35 – 40
51-51	519	Cruet Set, 2-piece, complete	$85 – 90
	510	Cruet Oil & Lid, 7 oz.	$28 – 30
	515	Cruet Vinegar & Lid, 7 oz.	$28 – 30
	518	Cruet Wood Base for 2-Pc. Set	$28 – 30
51-54	549	Cruet Set, 5-pc., complete	$140 – 150
	510	Cruet Oil & Lid, 7 oz.	$28 – 30
	515	Cruet Vinegar, & Lid, 7 oz.	$28 – 30
	520	Cruet Mustard & Lid, 4 oz.	$22 – 25
	530	Cruet Salt	$16 – 18
	540	Cruet Pepper	$16 – 18
	548	Cruet Wood Base for 5-Pc. Set	$28 – 30
55	550	Cookie Jar & Lid	$75 – 80
68	680	Coffee Carafe & Lid, 42 oz., 6 cup.	$95 – 105
68W	684	Coffee Carafe Warmer, metal	$30 – 35
90	900	Ashtray, med., 6⅜"	$18 – 20
91	910	Ashtray, lg., 8¼"	$22 – 25
96	890	Ashtray, sm., 4½"	$14 – 16

P 012 Provincial Whitestone

010	Cup, 7 oz.	$8 – 9
020	Saucer, 6¼"	$3 – 4
030	Bread & Butter, 6½"	$6 – 7
040	Salad Plate, 7½"	$8 – 9
060	Dinner Plate, 10½"	$11 – 12
070	Soup, 8½"	$14 – 16
080	Vegetable, sm., rnd., 7⅛"	$30 – 32
121	Individual Soup Server, lug, 5"	$16 – 18
130	Butter & Lid	$45 – 50
150	Vegetable, med., rnd., 10"	$35 – 40
160	Platter, med, oval, 11"	$30 – 35
170	Platter, lg., oval, 13½"	$35 – 40
180	Sugar & Lid, 8 oz.	$20 – 22
190	Creamer, 6 oz.	$18 – 20
210	Fruit, 6¼"	$10 – 11
230	Gravy, 1 pt.	$30 – 32
260	Vegetable & Lid, med., rnd., 1 qt., 10"	$65 – 75
270	Vegetable, basket design, rnd., 8⅛"	$32 – 35

(continued)

290	Vegetable, div., med., rect., 12"	$45 – 50	549	Cruet Set, 5-pc., complete		$125 – 140
300	Buffet Server, rnd., 12¼"	$55 – 60	510	Cruet Oil & Lid, 7 oz.		$25 – 28
320	Egg Cup	$20 – 22	515	Cruet Vinegar & Lid, 7 oz.		$25 – 28
330	Salt	$9 – 10	520	Cruet Mustard & Lid, 4 oz.		$20 – 22
340	Pepper	$9 – 10	530	Cruet Salt		$14 – 16
350	Tumbler, 11 oz.	$22 – 25	540	Cruet Pepper		$14 – 16
370	Pitcher, lg., 2¼ qt.	$60 – 65	548	Cruet Wood Base for 5-Pc. Set		$28 – 30
400	Coffee Pot & Lid, 49 oz., 7 cup	$80 – 90	600	Casserole & Lid, chicken cover,		
420	Cereal, 7¼"	$11 – 12		1 qt. 10 oz.		$110 – 120
430	Pitcher, med., 1 qt.	$45 – 50	670	Kettle Casserole & Lid, 2 qt. 12 oz.		$80 – 90
500	Hen on Nest	$75 – 80	700	Teapot & Lid, 42 oz., 6 cup		$80 – 90
519	Cruet Set, 2-pc., complete	$75 – 85	710	Bread Server, 9 ½"		$50 – 55
	510 Cruet Oil & Lid, 7 oz.	$25 – 28	720	Mug, lg., 1 pt.		$25 – 28
	515 Cruet Vinegar & Lid, 7 oz.	$25 – 28	760	Mug, 8 oz.		$16 – 18
	518 Cruet Wood Base for 2-Pc. Set	$28 – 30	880	Pitcher, sm., 1½ pt.		$32 – 35

Rooster Bleu

An outstanding achievement in dinnerware for your home

The American Style in Dinnerware

Rooster Bleu

A new jaunty version of Poppytrail's famous Rooster pattern. Same basic stride and strut, but in bright decorator blues, greens, brick orange and yellow accents against a tinted cream-white background. Authentic Early American and Continental Provincial accessories — the smart "Country-Flavor" French Provincial hand-painted beauty.

Rooster Bleu: 1968 brochure.

P 380 Rooster Bleu

010	Cup, 7 oz.	$9 – 10	190	Creamer, 6 oz.	$20 – 22
020	Saucer, 6⅛"	$3 – 4	210	Fruit, 6¼"	$11 – 12
030	Bread & Butter, 6½"	$7 – 8	230	Gravy, 1 pt.	$32 – 35
040	Salad Plate, 7½"	$9 – 10	290	Vegetable, div., med., rect., 12"	$50 – 55
060	Dinner Plate, 10½"	$12 – 13	330	Salt	$11 – 12
070	Soup, 8½"	$16 – 18	340	Pepper	$11 – 12
130	Butter & Lid	$50 – 55	400	Coffee Pot & Lid, 42 oz., 6 cup	$90 – 100
150	Vegetable, med., rnd., 10"	$40 – 45	420	Cereal, 7¼"	$12 – 14
170	Platter, lg., oval, 13½"	$40 – 45	700	Teapot & Lid, 42 oz., 6 cup	$90 – 100
180	Sugar & Lid, 8 oz.	$22 – 25			

SCULPTURED DAISY

Provincial Shape

Two sculptured and three embossed patterns were created on the Provincial shape. Sculptured Daisy, introduced in 1964, was designed by Allen and Shaw after the appeal of sculptured designs was established by the great success of Sculptured Grape in 1963. The detailed, realistic carvings featured white daisies with wheat-yellow centers and green leaves tightly spaced on the borders of flatware and bowls; arranged in bouquets on the sides of holloware; clustered on lid finials; and massed together to cover entirely the vegetable and casserole lids. The wide rims of Provincial's flatware provided ample room for the luxuriant sculptured design. Provincial's basket weave exterior, suggestive of a flower basket, was added to the vegetable bowls, casserole, baker, butter, and gravy. The shape and size of most items closely resembled Provincial Fruit. However, several changes were effected to better coordinate the overall look of the pattern. The size of the salad bowl and large platter were increased to accommodate the sculptured design. Several shapes were redesigned including the salad bowl, salt and pepper, and the vegetable and lid. The Provincial stick-handled gravy was renamed for use as a sauce boat. Two items were adopted from other shapes — the gravy with attached plate from Navajo and the butter from the sculptured Traditional patterns. The oval baker was a new item appearing only in this Provincial pattern.

Sculptured Daisy became an immediate bestseller. Daisy Accessories, a compatible artware line featuring the same sculptured styling, was created to capitalize on the popularity of the dinnerware pattern. Oh' Susanna, a smaller pattern consisting of 20 Sculptured Daisy

items, intensified the color scheme by painting the daisies as bright, brown-eyed susans.

Chantilly Blue, a lovely embossed pattern designed and modeled by Bob Chandler, displayed a graceful bird perched among tree limbs with a tree branch border design. Double blue banding added a color accent to the Provincial shape items.

Wicker White showcased an embossed wicker weave pattern on ten all-white Provincial items. Wicker Strawberry added a strawberry vine design, reminiscent of P 590 California Strawberry on the Traditional shape, to the dinner plate and salad plate, and strawberry finials to the coffee pot and sugar lids. Strawberry Accessories (Second Series) was an artware line intended to coordinate with Wicker Strawberry.

The importance of the Provincial shape to Metlox cannot be overemphasized. The Ivy shape had established the company's credibility as an innovator under Evan K. Shaw's leadership. The first three Provincial patterns elevated its reputation to the stature of Franciscan Ceramics. No other Metlox shape produced as many successful dinnerware patterns. With the company financially secure during the early 1950s, Shaw allowed his design department to experiment freely with new dinnerware shapes and artware lines. As paraphrased by Ted Ball, Poppytrail Sales Division manager, Shaw, when asked about the secret of his success at Metlox, reportedly said, "We had the guts to paint a chicken on a dinner plate and continued to do the unusual in a colorful way..."

Sculptured Daisy: 1975 brochure.

Sculptured Daisy
Once in a while a dinnerware pattern comes along that is breathtaking! Here is the friendly daisy in all its beauty. The free, graceful petals are carved and raised on the shoulder of the rim plate. It features white petals with wheat-yellow centers and green leaves — all vividly held together with light umber accent shading.

Sculptured Daisy: butter and lid.

DINNERWARE PATTERN AND COLOR NO. 270

Sculptured Daisy: 1975 brochure.

Sculptured Daisy: tumbler, rim soup bowl, salad plate, and mug.

Sculptured Daisy: salad bowl.

Sculptured Daisy: cup and saucer, large platter, and gravy with fastand.

Sculptured Daisy: cereal bowl and medium vegetable bowl.

Oh' Susanna

The Brown Eyed Susan is sculptured on the shoulder of the rim plate. The raised petals are hand painted in Sun Yellow with Brown Centers and Green Leaves. A Light Umber wash accents the decoration. A glossy Rich White glaze seals in the colors permanently. The delightful accessories feature Floral Knobs.

Oh' Susanna: 1976 brochure.

P 270 Sculptured Daisy, P 271 Oh' Susanna
Deduct 10% for P 271 Oh' Susanna

010	Cup, 6 oz.	$9 – 10
020	Saucer, 6¼".	$3 – 4
030	Bread & Butter, 6¼"	$7 – 8
040	Salad Plate, 7½"	$9 – 10
060	Dinner Plate, 10½"	$12 – 13
070	Soup, 8¼".	$16 – 18
090	Vegetable, div., sm., rnd., 7"	$35 – 40
130	Butter & Lid	$50 – 55
150	Vegetable, med., rnd., 10"	$40 – 45
170	Platter, lg., oval, 14¼".	$40 – 45
180	Sugar & Lid, 8 oz.	$28 – 30
190	Creamer, 6 oz.	$20 – 22
210	Fruit, 6½"	$11 – 12
230	Gravy, Fastand, 1 pt.	$32 – 35
290	Vegetable, div., med.	$45 – 50
330	Salt	$11 – 12
340	Pepper	$11 – 12
400	Coffee Pot & Lid, 8 cup	$90 – 100
420	Cereal, 7¼".	$13 – 14
700	Teapot & Lid, 7 cup	$90 – 100

P 270 Sculptured Daisy Additions

050	Luncheon Plate.	$14 – 16

(A brochure dated December 1, 1980, lists this item as scheduled for production during spring 1981. Its appearance has not been verified from subsequent brochure material.)

080	Vegetable, sm., rnd., 7"	$32 – 35
100	Salad Bowl, 12⅛"	$65 – 70
160	Platter, med., oval, 11"	$35 – 40
220	Salad Fork & Spoon Set	$50 – 55
240	Platter, sm., oval, 9½"	$30 – 35
260	Vegetable & Lid, med., 1 qt.	$70 – 75
300	Buffet Server, rnd., 12¼"	$60 – 65
350	Tumbler, 11 oz.	$28 – 30
370	Pitcher, lg., 2 qt.	$65 – 70
430	Pitcher, med., 1 qt.	$50 – 55
600	Casserole & Lid, 1½ qt.	$85 – 90
620	Sauce Boat, 1 pt.	$35 – 40
630	Oval Baker, 11"	$45 – 50
760	Mug, 8 oz.	$18 – 20
880	Pitcher, sm., 1½ pt.	$35 – 40

P 145 Chantilly Blue

010	Cup.	$9 – 10
020	Saucer	$3 – 4
040	Salad Plate	$9 – 10
060	Dinner Plate	$12 – 13
150	Vegetable, med., rnd.	$35 – 40
170	Platter, lg., oval	$40 – 45
180	Sugar & Lid	$22 – 25
190	Creamer	$20 – 22
400	Coffee Pot & Lid	$90 – 100
420	Cereal	$13 – 14

Wicker Strawberry, Wicker White
Add 20% for strawberry designs (*).

010	Cup.	$7 – 08
020	Saucer	$2 – 3
040	*Salad Plate	$7 – 8
060	*Dinner Plate	$9 – 10
170	Platter.	$25 – 30
180	*Sugar & Lid	$18 – 20
190	Creamer	$16 – 18
270	Vegetable, basket design	$25 – 28
400	*Coffee Pot & Lid	$55 – 60
420	Cereal.	$10 – 11

Chantilly Blue: Metlox brochure.

Wicker Strawberry: Metlox brochure.

P 220 California Peach Blossom (1952)
P 250 California Golden Blossom (c.1953)

California Peach Blossom and California Golden Blossom were the first sculptured patterns manufactured by Metlox. Allen and Shaw pioneered the concept of sculpturing designs in 1952, an experimental Metlox design technique which involved intricate, detailed in-mold carving quite different from embossing. Bob Allen created the item shapes, Mel Shaw contributed the peach blossom and brown branch handle designs, and Frank Irwin modeled the shapes.

Both patterns had the same design and item selection; the only difference was that Peach Blossom featured hand-decorated pink flowers with yellow centers as opposed to Golden Blossom's yellow flowers with green centers. Contrary to the styling of later sculptured patterns where the carvings completely encircled the wide rim of flatware and bowls, the flowered branch covered only about two-thirds of the interior sloping sides of these items. Blossom finials enhanced the delicate, quasi-oriental appearance of the patterns. Except for the circular lug soup and the coaster, the plates and bowls were square designs with gracefully curving sides that gently dipped between modestly upraised, rounded corners. The same styling characterized the rectangular platters. The 9½" dinner plate was actually luncheon size. A special off-center look was achieved by the elongated handle of the gravy, celery dish, and jam and jelly which extended outwards from the main body. The butter lid also fit off-center on its oval bottom.

The moderate success of both patterns did not immediately lead to the creation of other sculptured designs. However, the shape of many Blossom items influenced the subsequent development of the Shoreline and Freeform shapes.

California Peach Blossom: interior of gravy and butter and lid.

California Peach Blossom: 1961 brochure.

California Peach Blossom
For Those Who Like Lovely Things...Each raised petal is done in exquisite, "orchard-freshness" detail, hand painted under glaze. True-to-life peach blossom pink and brown stems are reflected against a background of snowy white. Casual and functional in the modern manner, yet daintily at home with all types of linen and silverware.

California Peach Blossom: small platter, dinner plate, bread and butter plate, tumbler, and cup and saucer.

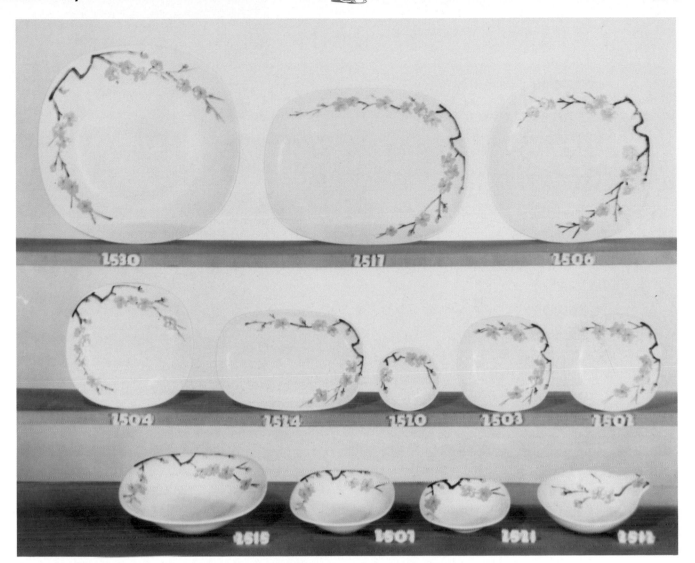

California Golden Blossom: Metlox archive photo.

P 220 California Peach Blossom, P 250 California Golden Blossom

00	Cup	$11 – 12	21	Fruit	$12 – 14
02	Saucer	$3 – 4	23	Gravy	$40 – 45
03	Bread & Butter	$8 – 9	24	Small Platter	$35 – 40
04	Salad Plate	$11 – 12	26	Covered Vegetable	$80 – 90
06	Dinner Plate	$14 – 15	28	Jam & Jelly	$45 – 50
07	Soup	$16 – 18	29	Divided Vegetable	$50 – 55
10	Salad Bowl	$85 – 95	30	Chop Plate	$65 – 75
12	Lug Soup	$22 – 25	33	Salt	$14 – 15
13	Butter & Lid	$60 – 65	34	Pepper	$14 – 15
15	Vegetable	$40 – 45	35	Tumbler	$25 – 28
17	Platter, 13"	$45 – 50	37	Water Pitcher	$75 – 85
18	Sugar & Lid	$28 – 30	39	Celery Dish	$40 – 45
19	Creamer	$25 – 28	40	Coffee Pot & Lid	$90 – 100
20	Coaster	$18 – 20	70	Teapot & Lid	$90 – 100

Shoreline Shape

P 230 Shoreline (1953)
    Deep Sea Green
    Driftwood Brown
    Horizon Blue
    Seafoam White
    Surf Chartreuse
    Wet Sand Beige

P 260 Indian Summer (1953)
P 270 Central Park (1953)

Shortly after the release of California Peach Blossom, Allen and Shaw decided to design a new, more modern shape utilizing the form and styling of Blossom flatware, bowls, and selected serving pieces. Their desire to give the shape, later named Shoreline, a simple, contemporary look precluded the use of other Blossom items, thereby necessitating the creation of a different cup, sugar, creamer, coaster, gravy, divided vegetable, salt, pepper, tumbler, and pitcher. The 10½" dinner plate replaced Blossom's 9½" dinner plate which became the luncheon plate. A special design feature was the elevated loop handle of the sugar, creamer, and gravy. Curiously, several standard Metlox dinnerware items — the butter, covered vegetable, coffee pot, and teapot — were never included in the Shoreline shape. The probable reason was that Evan K. Shaw wanted to be certain of the saleability of Shoreline's contemporary designs before expanding the shape.

Metlox released only three patterns, all employing new design concepts, on the shape. Shoreline, Metlox's first solid color pattern under Shaw's leadership, emphasized each item's distinct shape by the absence of patterns or sculpturing. This treatment, a favorite of Shaw's, was repeated with several later patterns. Shoreline, inspired by various shades of the California coastline, was produced in six colors all popular in the early 1950s. Contrary to later company practice, colors were not assigned separate pattern numbers.

Indian Summer and Central Park, both featuring individual olive green, reddish-brown, and yellow leaf shapes on light beige and white backgrounds respectively, were the company's first decal patterns. Poor sales coupled with the expensiveness of decal decoration resulted in a brief production run for both patterns.

Shoreline: sugar and lid, small platter, and creamer.

Shoreline: salt and pepper shakers, dinner plate, and cup and saucer.

Shoreline

Distinctive Shapes in Coast-of-California Colors Created after long study of the decorating desires of home makers who want something different. Designed under the art direction of Allen & Shaw, the shapes are ultra modern. The popular colors are based upon surveys made by authoritative home magazines like House Beautiful and House & Garden.

Six Colors:

Deep Sea Green   *Surf Chartreuse*
Seafoam White   *Horizon Blue*
Driftwood Brown   *Wet Sand Beige*

Shoreline: 1953 brochure.

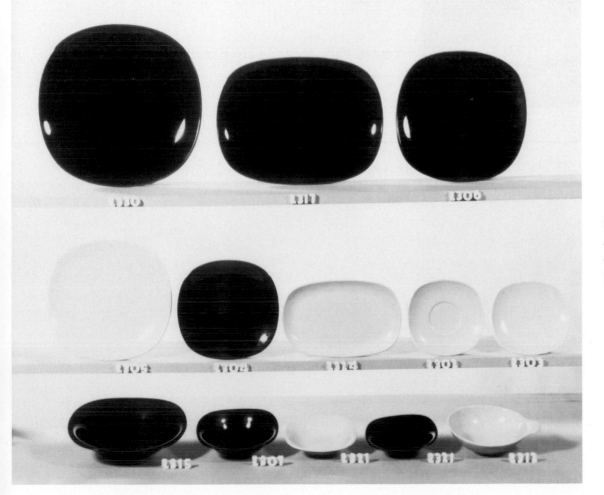

Shoreline: Metlox archive photo.

Central Park

An outstanding achievement in the decorator's and ceramist's art! Nature's own subtly colored leaves, permanently imbedded in smooth glaze, assures a lifetime of use and loveliness.

The shapes are ultra-modern and functional. The warmth and simplicity of Central Park makes this pattern blend well, too, with new textured table mats, cloths and draperies, and with either Provincial or casual home decoration.

Central Park: Metlox archive photo.

P 230 Shoreline, P 260 Indian Summer, P 270 Central Park

00	Cup	$8 – 9	20	Coaster	$14 – 16
02	Saucer	$2 – 3	21	Fruit	$10 – 12
03	Bread & Butter	$6 – 7	23	Gravy	$25 – 28
04	Salad Plate	$8 – 9	24	Small Platter	$28 – 30
05	Luncheon Plate	$12 – 14	28	Jam & Jelly	$35 – 40
06	Dinner Plate	$10 – 11	29	Divided Vegetable	$35 – 40
07	Rim Soup	$14 – 15	30	Chop Plate	$40 – 45
10	Salad Bowl	$50 – 55	33	Salt	$9 – 10
12	Lug Soup	$18 – 20	34	Pepper	$9 – 10
15	Vegetable Dish	$30 – 32	35	Tumbler	$20 – 22
17	Large Platter	$32 – 35	37	Pitcher	$45 – 50
18	Sugar & Lid	$22 – 25	39	Celery Dish	$32 – 35
19	Creamer	$16 – 18			

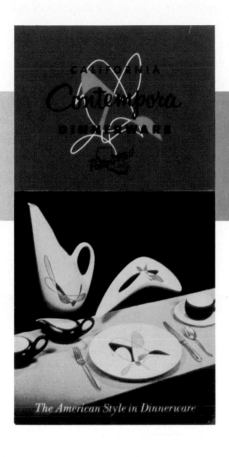

Freeform Shape

P 310 California Freeform (1954)
P 320 California Mobile (1954)
P 330 California Aztec (1955)
P 340 California Contempora (1955)

Frank Irwin was the primary instigator, designer, and modeler of the impressive, ultra-modern Freeform shape. Irwin, who had a special flair for abstract art, was an acknowledged devotee of Henry Moore, the English fine artist noted for his large, abstract sculptures in stone, fiber glass, bronze, and clay, and Alexander Calder, a renowned sculptor of wire and flat steel who popularized the mobile as an art form. Ironically, the Freeform shape began as a dinnerware set Irwin intended to fashion for himself when, due to an extended illness, Evan K. Shaw was absent from the plant for several months. As Irwin worked on the designs, Allen and Shaw lent their support as did sales representatives who believed the shape could compete successfully with other modernistic patterns such as Russel Wright's American Modern by Steubenville Pottery. A surreptitious pilot production of the set was produced without Shaw's approval shortly before his return. Although Shaw, an avowed admirer of traditional dinnerware designs, was unappreciative of the avant-garde shapes, to his credit he nevertheless decided to produce them. Irwin designed the delightful mobile pattern, imitative of Calder's amorphous wire inventions, which decorated California Freeform, California Mobile, and California Contempora. Bob Allen conceived the California Aztec pattern, a mystical, primitive Indian design. Shaw was perplexed yet pleased by the success of the four patterns which added yet another dimension to Metlox's diverse dinnerware shapes.

Although often regarded as identical patterns consisting of the same item shapes, the Freeform patterns were actually released in two versions: California Freeform and California Mobile in 1954, and California Aztec and California Contempora in 1955. The major differences were the redesigning of many common items in the 1955 patterns and the use of contrasting textured glazes — gloss glaze for Freeform and Mobile and satin glaze for Aztec and Contempora.

Freeform and Mobile continued the square and rectangular flatware designs used in the Blossom and Shoreline shapes. The soup and lug soup of these shapes were also retained. The vegetable bowl and fruit, however, introduced a round styling in which one side flared dramatically upward and outward opposite a less pronounced raised side. The cup, sugar, creamer, coaster, gravy, salt, pepper, jam and jelly, divided vegetable, and celery dish were other borrowed Shoreline shapes. Irwin's primary contributions were the major serving pieces — the covered vegetable, water pitcher, coffee pot, jaw bone, twin vegetable, handle vegetable, and beverage server and juice cup/lid.

Aztec and Contempora presented an extensive redesign including coupe-shaped plates and oval platters. The soup bowl adopted the flared design, and a new gravy imitated the off-center stance of the earlier Blossom shape gravy. A butter dish and an II" oval platter were additions to both patterns while Aztec added a cocoa mug and Contempora a milk pitcher which also appeared in Mobile. Contempora introduced two-toned holloware, a new design concept, on a limited basis with a black and white cup, sugar, creamer, salt, pepper, and the tall coffee pot.

The cigarette box, small and large ashtrays, and three flower pots were produced only in Freeform, Mobile, and Contempora. Various tier servers, each with a metal divider, were offered but never listed in company leaflets.

Never conceived as a homogeneous set, the look of the Freeform shape certainly reflects its name. The contours of many of the serving pieces are suggestive of the erratic, meandering scribbling of the mobile design. A diverse mixture of abstract, asymmetrical, flared, off-center, slanted, loop, cone, hourglass, boomerang, and "W" shapes, as well as circles, squares, and ovals give the impression of unrestrained creative freedom unleashed on a dining room table. Towering above this wonderful multiplicity stand the unique tall coffee pot and beverage server. It is not surprising that the traditionalist Evan K. Shaw was unmoved by Freeform's indulgent excesses. Today's collectors, however, consider the Freeform shape to be one of the finest achievements in 1950s avant-garde dinnerware design.

California Freeform: Metlox archive photo.

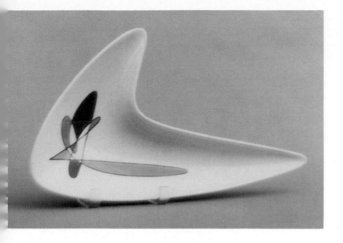

California Freeform: jaw bone.

California Freeform
Trend Setting . . . created for moderns who want something different. Cocoa, chartreuse and sharp yellow against a background of palest grey, "textured" with tiny dots of color; decoration of these novel designs is painted by hand . . .

California Freeform: 13" platter and small platter.

California Freeform: covered vegetable and handle vegetable.

California Mobile
Talk of the Town
Modern abstract design — in distinctive shades of purple, yellow, turquoise, and pink — on a pale grey, flecked background.

California Mobile: dinner plate and gravy.

California Mobile: jam and jelly, 13" platter, and lug soup.

California Mobile: Metlox archive photo.

California Mobile: beverage server and milk pitcher.

California Mobile: tumbler, 4" flower pot, and gravy.

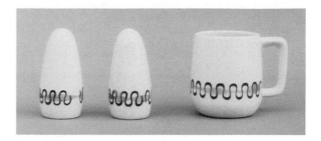

California Aztec: salt and pepper shakers and cocoa mug.

California Aztec: creamer and sugar and lid.

California Aztec: water pitcher.

California Aztec: coffee pot and lid.

California Aztec: Metlox archive photo.

California Aztec: cup and saucer, tumbler, coaster, juice cup, and black cup and saucer.

California Aztec
Textured! Bold! Primitive!
The subdued effect of grey and black on the soft grey-flecked satin glaze should prove a welcome relief to the discriminating homemaker. The neutral shades and primitive pattern of Aztec blend decoratively with your colored table mats and napkins.

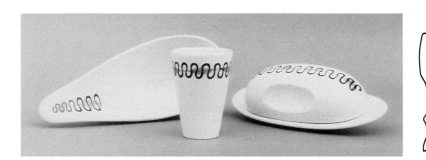

California Aztec: gravy, juice cup, and butter and lid.

California Aztec: twin vegetable.

California Aztec: beverage server and juice cup/lid and tumblers.

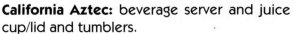

California Contempora: gravy, 13" platter, and tumbler.

California Contempora: chop plate and beverage server.

California Contempora: two-tier server with metal divider.

California Contempora
Modern Free-Form Design
Done in pink, black and grey, with black and white,
two toned holloware. In tune with the new trend
toward textured finishes, with satin-
flecked glaze. Sets the mood for gay
entertaining and casual family meals.

California Contempora: 1955 brochure.

P 310 California Freeform, P 320 California Mobile, P 330 California Aztec, P 340 California Contempora
Value P 330 California Aztec at the lower end of the scale.

00	Cup	$16 – 18		**P 310 California Freeform Additions**	
02	Saucer	$4 – 5	69	Cigarette Box	$115 – 125
03	Bread and Butter	$11 – 12	87	Small Ashtray	$40 – 45
04	Salad Plate	$15 – 18	89	Large Ashtray	$50 – 55
05	Luncheon Plate	$32 – 35	97	Flower Pot, 3".	$55 – 60
06	Dinner Plate	$20 – 25	98	Flower Pot, 4".	$65 – 70
07	Soup	$22 – 25	99	Flower Pot, 6".	$75 – 80
10	Salad Bowl	$300+			
12	Lug Soup	$30 – 35		**P 320 California Mobile Additions**	
15	Vegetable Dish	$50 – 55	43	Milk Pitcher.	$180 – 200
17	Platter, 13"	$65 – 70	69	Cigarette Box	$115 – 125
18	Sugar & Lid	$50 – 55	87	Small Ashtray	$40 – 45
19	Creamer	$22 – 25	89	Large Ashtray	$50 – 55
20	Coaster	$28 – 30	97	Flower Pot, 3".	$55 – 60
21	Fruit	$15 – 18	98	Flower Pot, 4".	$65 – 70
23	Gravy	$40 – 45	99	Flower Pot, 6".	$75 – 80
24	Small Platter	$45 – 50			
26	Covered Vegetable	$300+		**P 330 California Aztec Additions**	
28	Jam & Jelly	$55 – 60	13	Butter & Lid	$95 – 100
29	Divided Vegetable	$90 – 95	16	Oval Platter, 11"	$55 – 60
30	Chop Plate	$80 – 85	76	Cocoa Mug	$35 – 40
33	Salt	$20 – 25			
34	Pepper	$20 – 25		**P 340 California Contempora Additions**	
35	Tumbler	$45 – 50	13	Butter & Lid	$95 – 100
37	Water Pitcher	$210 – 230	16	Oval Platter, 11"	$55 – 60
39	Celery Dish	$50 – 55	43	Milk Pitcher.	$180 – 200
40	Coffee Pot & Lid	$225 – 250	69	Cigarette Box	$115 – 125
64	Jaw Bone	$115 – 125	87	Small Ashtray	$40 – 45
65	Twin Vegetable	$180 – 200	89	Large Ashtray	$50 – 55
66	Handle Vegetable	$180 – 200	97	Flower Pot, 3".	$55 – 60
80-80½	Beverage Server & Juice Cup/Lid	$225 – 250	98	Flower Pot, 4".	$65 – 70
80½	Juice Cup	$40 – 45	99	Flower Pot, 6".	$75 – 80
—	Two-Tier Server (Salad Plate and Bread & Butter)	$60 – 65			
—	Two-Tier Server (Dinner Plate and Bread & Butter)	$80 – 85			

CALIFORNIA
Del Rey
DINNERWARE
Poppytrail

The American Style in Dinnerware

Confetti Shape

P 420 California Del Rey (1955)
P 430 California Confetti (1955)
P 370 Mardi Gras (1955)
Red
Black
White
P 350 Street Scene (1956)

The Confetti shape combined selected items from the Freeform shape's Aztec-Contempora group with new, compatible designs by Allen and Shaw. Freeform's coupe-shaped plates, oval platters, and flared bowls were used along with the gravy, jam and jelly, divided vegetable, tumbler, celery dish, and flower pots. None of the extravagant Freeform major serving pieces were included. The new items — the cup, butter, sugar, creamer, covered vegetable, salt, pepper, water pitcher, coffee pot, milk pitcher, and teapot — were less abstract designs with smoother contours that blended effectively with the Freeform items. The addition of white bow finials and half-heart handles added a decorative touch. When compared to the audacity of the Freeform patterns, Confetti's styling appeared graceful and conservative, yet still quite contemporary.

California Del Rey and California Confetti featured two-toned holloware in blue and white and pink and white respectively. This design concept, introduced on a limited basis by Contempora, was repeated often in later patterns. Like Aztec, Del Rey sported a primitive pattern while Confetti sprinkled very tiny pink, turquoise, and black flakes on a

white background. Continuing the solid color decoration of the Shoreline patterns, Mardi Gras presented Confetti shape items in red, white, or black. Archive photos of Mardi Gras picture the Freeform jaw bone, which would lead one to surmise that other Freeform major serving items, omitted in the other Confetti shape patterns, may have been included in this pattern. Street Scene was the invention of Mel Shaw who created the detailed, delightful sketches of Parisian street life and neighborhoods after a visit to Europe. Two-toned turquoise and white holloware was used for this pattern. Brochure listings for Mardi Gras and Street Scene could not be obtained but were probably very similar to Del Rey and Confetti.

The development of the Blossom, Shoreline, Freeform, and Confetti shapes demonstrates the evolutionary-like design process that was a characteristic of the Metlox design department during the 1950s. Each subsequent, new shape was formed by continuing some items from the last shape while redesigning others and/or adding new designs. It is a remarkable achievement that such different, innovative, contrasting shapes were created in this manner.

Here is a primitive pattern boldly brush-stroked with color and combined with two-tone turquoise holloware for a bright, but not "too busy" effect. The graceful design shows to advantage on every occasion.

Oven tested and dishwasher safe. Designed under the direction of Allen & Shaw. Buy the "bargain" starter set and add extra pieces from time to time.

METLOX MFG. CO.
Manhattan Beach, California

California Del Rey
Here is a primitive pattern boldly brush-stroked with color and combined with two-tone turquoise holloware for a bright, but not "too busy" effect. The graceful design shows to advantage on every occasion.

California Del Rey: 1955 brochure.

California Del Rey: milk pitcher, bread and butter plate, and tumbler.

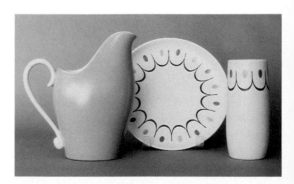

California Del Rey: butter and lid, dinner plate, and teapot and lid.

California Del Rey: sugar and lid, creamer, dinner plate, and coffee pot and lid.

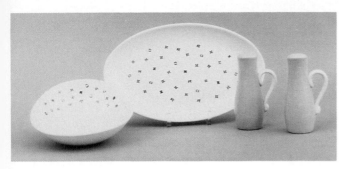

California Confettl: fruit bowl, small platter, salt and pepper shakers.

California Confetti
Developed to fill the demand for an overall chintz pattern. In the modern trend. Two-tone pink and white holloware, this "traditional-modern" pattern is handsome and supremely practical.

California Confetti: cup and saucer, dinner plate, and creamer.

California Confetti: Metlox archive photo.

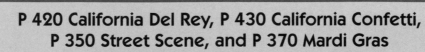
P 420 California Del Rey, P 430 California Confetti, P 350 Street Scene, and P 370 Mardi Gras
Deduct 20% for P 350 Street Scene and 30% for P 370 Mardi Gras

00	Cup	$12 – 13	28	Jam & Jelly	$45 – 50
02	Saucer	$4 – 5	29	Divided Vegetable	$60 – 65
03	Bread & Butter	$9 – 10	30	Chop Plate	$65 – 70
04	Salad Plate	$12 – 14	33	Salt	$16 – 18
05	Luncheon Plate	$22 – 25	34	Pepper	$16 – 18
06	Dinner Plate	$16 – 18	35	Tumbler	$30 – 32
07	Soup	$16 – 18	37	Water Pitcher	$85 – 95
12	Lug Soup	$22 – 25	39	Celery Dish	$40 – 45
13	Butter & Lid	$60 – 65	40	Coffee Pot & Lid	$115 – 125
15	Vegetable Dish	$45 – 50	43	Milk Pitcher	$75 – 85
17	Platter, 13"	$45 – 50	70	Teapot & Lid	$115 – 125
18	Sugar & Lid	$30 – 32	97	Flower Pot, 3"	$40 – 45
19	Creamer	$28 – 30	98	Flower Pot, 4"	$50 – 55
20	Coaster	$22 – 25	99	Flower Pot, 6"	$60 – 65
21	Fruit	$12 – 14			
23	Gravy	$35 – 40		**P 420 California Del Rey Additions**	
24	Small Platter	$35 – 40	10	Salad Bowl	$85 – 95
26	Covered Vegetable	$90 – 100	16	Oval Platter, 11"	$40 – 45

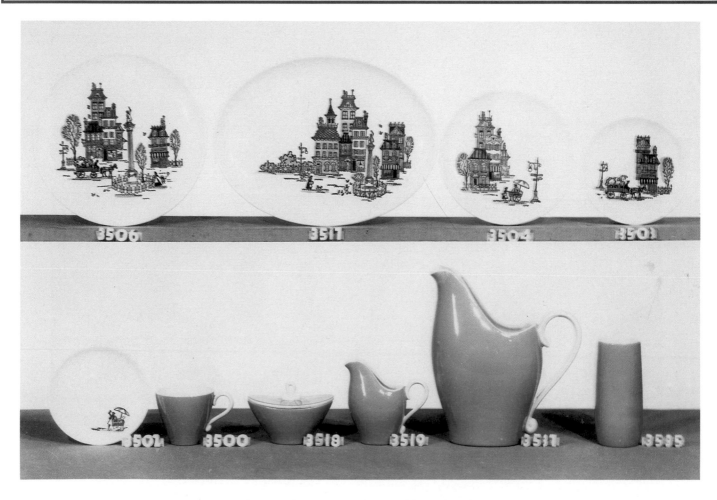

Street Scene: Metlox archive photo.

Street Scene: chop plate.

Mardi Gras: Metlox archive photo.

Navajo/Tempo Shape

P 470 Navajo (1956)

P 520 Pepper Tree (1957)

P 450 California Geranium (1958)

P 540 California Palm (1958)

P 460 Luau (1959)

P 440 California Tempo Series

    P 441 Walnut with Sky Blue (1960)

    P 442 Walnut with Yellow Gold (1960)

    P 443 Walnut with Beige (1960)

    P 444 Walnut with Terra Cotta (1960)

    P 445 Walnut with Olive Green (1960)

    P 446 Walnut with White (1960)

P 530 Painted Desert (1960)

P 410 Palm Springs (1962)

P 430 Golden Scroll (1962)

P 130 Mayan Necklace (1964)

P 150 Fleur-de-lis (1964)

The Navajo shape, inspired by Native American art work of the American Southwest and designed by Allen and Shaw, continued the contemporary look of the Freeform patterns while tempering their unrestrained design. Asymmetrical, off-center, and freeform designs were abandoned in favor of more symmetrical and geometrical shapes. The most notable stylistic features of Navajo were the following: wide, raised rims on plates, platters, and most bowls; an emphasis on rectangular shapes; steep, almost vertical sides on deep bowls; straight edges or uniform curves on most items; and perpendicular handles.

Navajo, with 52 items, was one of the largest shapes produced. Several new pieces were designed for this shape — the espresso mug and saucer, the chip and dip, and the divided servers. The tall coffee pot and the beverage server and juice cup/lid were carryovers from the Freeform patterns. The smaller coffee server was included to offer a more typical coffee pot design. The vinegar and oil cruets were miniature replicas of the tall coffee pot. The no. 28 jam and jelly, a

rimmed, divided bowl on a pedestal, was replaced by the no. 28 small divided vegetable, a rectangular design which, though less impressive, harmonized better with the overall design concept.

The first pattern, Navajo, enhanced the Southwestern look with a primitive design reminiscent of Aztec. Pepper Tree followed with a simple, abstract leaf design. Both of these successful patterns utilized decorative features that were used on later patterns of this shape — solid color and/or two-toned accessory items, and the use of satin glazes with textures and/or color tints.

A redesigning of some items began as early as 1958. The popular, award-winning California Geranium, which presented the flower as an artist's abstract sketch, radically narrowed the rims of plates, platters, and bowls. The most significant changes, however, were introduced in California Tempo, another large group considered by designers Allen and Shaw to be a separate though closely related shape. The Tempo shape repeated 29 Navajo serving items — the butter, salt mill, pepper mill, sugar, creamer, salad fork and spoon set, gravy, ladle, covered vegetable, small divided vegetable, salt, pepper, tumbler, water pitcher, coffee pot, milk pitcher, two-quart covered casserole, casserole warmer, sauce boat, oval baker, teapot, espresso mug, espresso saucer, chip and dip, cocoa mug, coffee server, one-pint pitcher, small three-divided server and medium three-divided server. Ten items — the soup, lug soup, individual casserole and lid, coaster, pedestal jam and jelly, vinegar cruet, oil cruet, twin vegetable, beverage server, and juice cup — were deleted while nine items — the small vegetable, barbecue plate, four-piece canister set, ceramic warmer, handled open vegetable, and compote — were added. Coupe-shaped flatware, oval platters, and concave bowls, all with very narrow edges, replaced Navajo's wide rims and steep-sided styling. The cup and divided vegetable were redesigned. The overall result of these changes and alterations was a smoother, simpler look. California Tempo showcased two-tone decoration by juxtaposing walnut with six separate color choices. The four-piece canister set, included only in California Tempo, was also used as a shape design for several canister sets and cookie jars by the Artware Division.

The remaining seven smaller patterns featured abstract or primitive designs similar to Aztec, Navajo, and Pepper Tree. The item selection for each of these patterns was a different ingenious combination, sometimes including individual items from both the Navajo and Tempo shapes as well as California Geranium's narrow rim styling. Evan K. Shaw's practice of varying the set composition of patterns on a given shape was exemplified by the diversified makeup of these seven patterns.

Metlox's development of contemporary shapes, the primary design emphasis of the company from the mid to late 1950s, ceased temporarily after the Navajo and Tempo shapes. Shaw had allowed and supported modernistic and experimental patterns and shapes that were not particularly suited to his personal tastes. The 1960s would belong to his ideas and preferences.

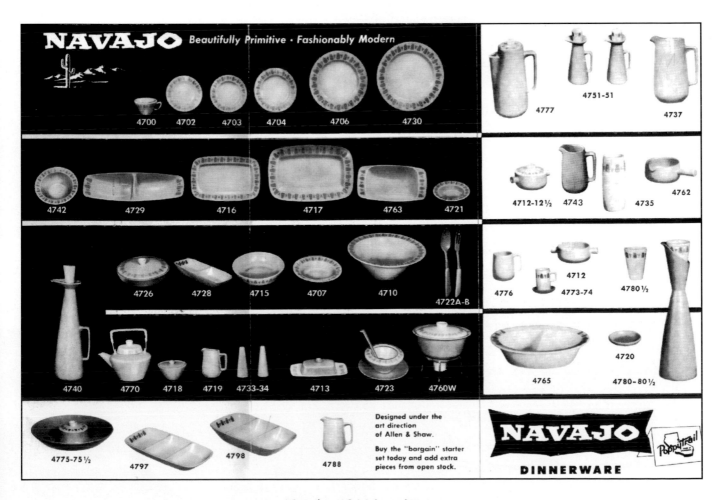

Navajo: 1961 brochure.

Navajo: cup and saucer, dinner plate, salad plate, pepper shaker, and salt shaker.

Navajo
Desert Enchantment is yours...
Primitive art shapes molded into ultra-modern dinnerware, whose colors reflect the sun baked sands and turquoise skies of the Southwest. Made by talented California craftsmen. Pleasing designs permanently painted under satin glaze.

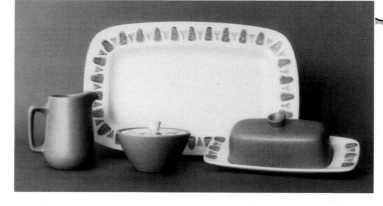

Navajo: large platter, creamer, sugar and lid, and butter and lid.

Pepper Tree: cup and saucer, salad plate, and juice cup.

Pepper Tree
Let the soft warm suggestion of a California day enhance your table setting with handcrafted Pepper Tree that may be used for any occasion and whose colors harmonize with just about everything. The leaf pattern is done in exciting new colors of bronze-green and sun-gold, and the shapes are inspired by the primitive art of the Southwest. The textured body and satin-finish green glaze are new developments from Poppytrail.

Pepper Tree: butter and lid, dinner plate, and gravy with fastand.

Pepper Tree: divided vegetable.

Pepper Tree: vegetable bowl, cereal bowl, and creamer.

P 470 Navajo, P 520 Pepper Tree
Deduct 15% for P 520 Pepper Tree

00	Cup	$11 – 12	35	Tumbler, 10 oz.	$30 – 32
02	Saucer	$3 – 4	37	Water Pitcher, 2 qt.	$65 – 70
03	Bread & Butter, 6½"	$8 – 9	40	Coffee Pot & Lid, 10 cup	$160 – 175
04	Salad Plate, 7½"	$11 – 12	42	Cereal, 7¼"	$14 – 16
06	Dinner Plate, 10½"	$14 – 15	43	Milk Pitcher, 1 qt.	$50 – 55
07	Soup, 8"	$18 – 20	51-V	Vinegar Cruet & Stopper	$25 – 28
10	Salad Bowl, 12"	$80 – 90	51-O	Oil Cruet & Stopper	$25 – 28
12	Lug Soup	$20 – 22	60	Covered Casserole, 2 qt.	$85 – 95
12-12½	Individual Casserole & Lid	$25 – 28	60W	Covered Casserole Warmer	$30 – 35
13	Butter & Lid	$60 – 65	62	Sauce Boat	$32 – 35
15	Vegetable, 9½"	$35 – 40	63	Oval Baker	$40 – 45
16	Rectangular Platter, med., 11"	$35 – 40	65	Twin Vegetable	$45 – 50
17	Rectangular Platter, lg., 13"	$40 – 45	70	Teapot & Lid, 7 cup	$85 – 95
18	Sugar & Lid	$25 – 28	76	Cocoa Mug, 8 oz.	$18 – 20
19	Creamer	$22 – 25	77	Coffee Server & Lid, 8 cup	$85 – 95
20	Coaster	$20 – 22	80-80½	Beverage Server & Juice Cup/Lid.	$160 – 175
21	Fruit, 6"	$12 – 14	80½	Juice Cup	$28 – 30
22A-B	Salad Fork & Spoon Set	$60 – 65	88	Pitcher, 1 pt.	$35 – 40
23	Gravy, Fastand	$35 – 40			
—	Gravy Ladle	$20 – 22		**P 470 Navajo Additions**	
26	Covered Vegetable	$70 – 75	14A	Salt Mill	$32 – 35
28	Jam & Jelly	$65 – 70	14B	Pepper Mill	$35 – 40
28	Small Divided Vegetable	$40 – 45	73	Espresso Mug	$18 – 20
29	Divided Vegetable	$55 – 60	74	Espresso Saucer	$6 – 8
30	Chop Plate, 13"	$60 – 65	75	Chip N' Dip & Lid	$50 – 55
33	Salt	$16 – 18	97	3-Divided Server, sm.	$45 – 50
34	Pepper	$16 – 18	98	3-Divided Server & Lid, med.	$55 – 60

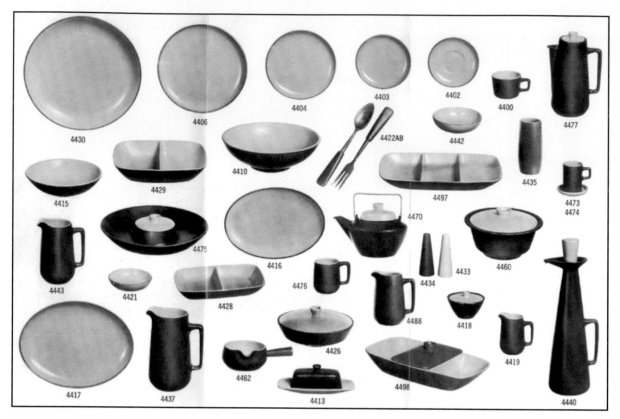

4430
4406
4404
4403
4402
4400
4477
4422AB
4442
4415
4429
4410
4435
4497
4473
4474
4443
4475
4416
4470
4460
4433
4434
4421
4476
4488
4418
4428
4426
4419
4417
4437
4462
4413
4498
4440

**California
Tempo:**
1961
brochure.

California Tempo
The table fashion of our times . . .
Hand-crafted and smartly styled for today's casual
indoor and outdoor living. A rich, walnut back-
ground accents the color of your choice. The
blending two-tones enhance your home's decor.
Contemporary shapes designed to keep you up to
the minute in fashion table settings.

**California
Tempo:** 1961
brochure.

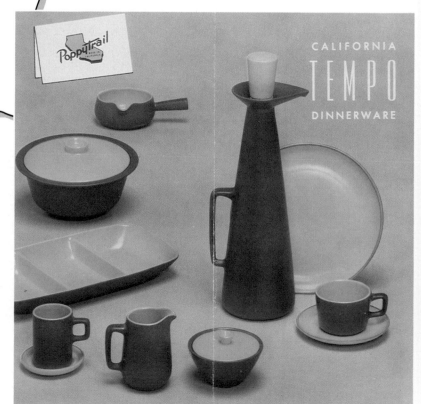

California Tempo: additional pieces and color photo from 1968 brochure.

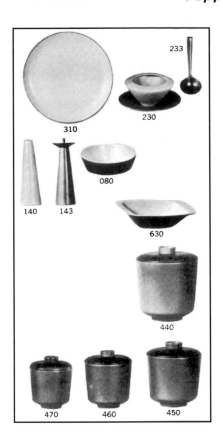

P 440 California Tempo

00	Cup	$8 – 9	34	Pepper	$12 – 13
02	Saucer	$2 – 3	35	Tumbler, 10 oz.	$22 – 25
03	Bread & Butter, 6¼"	$6 – 7	37	Water Pitcher, 2 qt.	$50 – 55
04	Salad Plate, 8"	$8 – 9	40	Coffee Pot & Lid, 10 cup	$110 – 120
06	Dinner Plate, 10½"	$10 – 11	42	Cereal, 6"	$11 – 12
08	Small Vegetable, 7½"	$22 – 25	43	Milk Pitcher, 1 qt.	$38 – 40
10	Salad Bowl, 11"	$50 – 55	44	Flour Canister & Lid	$30 – 35
13	Butter & Lid	$45 – 50	45	Sugar Canister & Lid	$25 – 30
14A	Salt Mill	$25 – 28	46	Coffee Canister & Lid	$22 – 25
14B	Pepper Mill	$28 – 30	47	Tea Canister & Lid	$20 – 22
15	Vegetable, 9"	$28 – 30	59	Warmer (ceramic)	$28 – 30
16	Oval Platter, med., 11"	$28 – 30	60	Covered Casserole, 2 qt.	$60 – 65
17	Oval Platter, lg., 13"	$30 – 35	60W	Covered Casserole Warmer	$30 – 35
18	Sugar & Lid	$20 – 22	62	Sauce Boat, 1 pt.	$25 – 28
19	Creamer	$18 – 20	63	Oval Baker, 24 oz.	$30 – 32
21	Fruit, 6"	$9 – 10	67	Handled Open Vegetable	$40 – 45
22A-B	Salad Fork & Spoon Set	$45 – 50	70	Teapot & Lid, 7 cup	$65 – 75
23	Gravy, Fastand, 18 oz.	$28 – 30	73	Espresso Mug	$15 – 16
—	Gravy Ladle	$15 – 18	74	Espresso Saucer	$5 – 6
26	Covered Vegetable, 1 qt.	$50 – 55	75	Chip N' Dip & Lid	$40 – 45
28	Small Divided Vegetable, 10" (aka Jam & Jelly)	$30 – 32	76	Cocoa Mug, 8 oz.	$15 – 16
29	Divided Vegetable, 11"	$32 – 35	77	Coffee Server & Lid, 7 cup	$65 – 75
30	Chop Plate, 13"	$40 – 45	84	Compote	$40 – 45
31	Barbecue Plate, 12"	$35 – 40	88	Pitcher, 1 pt.	$28 – 30
33	Salt	$12 – 13	97	3-Divided Server, sm., 14"	$38 – 40
			98	3-Divided Server & Lid, med., 13½"	$45 – 50

California Palm
Modern shapes, hand decorated in soft aqua, gold and avocado-green palm leaves — against a background of warm, off-white satin glaze.

California Palm: 1958 brochure.

Palm Springs: 1962 brochure.

Palm Springs
Poppytrail designers captured the new trend in home decoration with this ochre and orange on white dinnerware. Solid tone "ochre," "yellow gold" accessories keep your table in style for years and years . . . Serving your guests and family on Palm Springs dinnerware is a feast — for the eyes!

Palm Springs: 1962 brochure.

Golden Scroll

The discriminating home maker understands the subtle effect of gold and cinnamon decorated dinnerware, done in the modern manner by America's leading earthenware designers... This pattern will win compliments for the hostess — and enthusiasm from her family. Bold, primitive shapes, soft-cinnamon flecked satin glaze.

Golden Scroll: cup and saucer, dinner plate, salad plate, and bread and butter plate.

Fleur-de-lis

Perfect for entertaining or every day use. Fashionable lacy look, so soft, feminine and smart. Avocado green and blue set off against a blue-tinted, white background.

Mayan Necklace

Ancient civilization and culture design theme in soft beige, against a tinted, off-white finish glaze, that conveys a stone-texture effect.

California Geranium

Hand painted artist's floral sketch, worthy of a canvas! The superb red, hand-decorated blossoms, soft warm green leaves create a fresh-as-a-spring-garden effect. New, smartly-styled contemporary shapes make it as much at home in your modern dining room as your casual patio serving.

California Geranium:
large platter.

P 130 Mayan Necklace, P 150 Fleur-de-lis, P 410 Palm Springs, P 430 Golden Scroll, P 450 California Geranium, P 460 Luau, P 530 Painted Desert, P 540 California Palm

Add 20% for P 450 California Geranium

00	Cup	$7 –	8
02	Saucer	$2 –	3
03	Bread & Butter	$5 –	6
04	Salad Plate	$7 –	8
06	Dinner Plate	$9 –	10
07	Soup	$12 –	13
13	Butter & Lid	$40 –	45
15	Vegetable	$25 –	28
17	Platter, lg.	$28 –	30
18	Sugar & Lid	$18 –	20
19	Creamer	$16 –	18
21	Fruit	$8 –	9
29	Divided Vegetable	$30 –	32
33	Salt	$10 –	11
34	Pepper	$10 –	11
42	Cereal	$10 –	11
70	Teapot & Lid	$55 –	60
77	Coffee Server & Lid	$55 –	60

P 130 Mayan Necklace Additions

23	Gravy, Fastand	$25 –	28
—	Gravy Ladle	$14 –	15

P 150 Fleur-de-lis Addition

23	Gravy, Fastand	$25 –	28

P 410 Palm Springs Additions

14A	Salt Mill	$22 –	25
14B	Pepper Mill	$25 –	28
20	Coaster	$14 –	15
23	Gravy, Fastand	$25 –	28
—	Gravy Ladle	$14 –	15
26	Covered Vegetable	$45 –	50
28	Small Divided Vegetable	$28 –	30
30	Chop Plate	$35 –	40
35	Tumbler	$20 –	22
37	Water Pitcher	$45 –	50
40	Coffee Pot & Lid	$100 –	110

43	Milk Pitcher	$35 –	38
60	Covered Casserole	$55 –	60
60W	Covered Casserole Warmer	$30 –	35
62	Sauce Boat	$22 –	25
63	Oval Baker	$28 –	30
76	Cocoa Mug	$14 –	15
88	Pitcher, 1 pt.	$25 –	28
97	3-Divided Server, sm.	$35 –	38
98	3-Divided Server & Lid, med.	$40 –	45

P 430 Golden Scroll Additions

10	Salad Bowl	$45 –	50
16	Platter, med.	$25 –	28
20	Coaster	$14 –	15
22A-B	Salad Fork & Spoon Set	$40 –	45
26	Covered Vegetable	$45 –	50
30	Chop Plate	$35 –	40
35	Tumbler	$20 –	22
37	Water Pitcher	$45 –	50
40	Coffee Pot & Lid	$100 –	110
43	Milk Pitcher	$35 –	38
62	Sauce Boat	$22 –	25
76	Cocoa Mug	$14 –	15
88	Pitcher, 1 pt.	$25 –	28

P 450 California Geranium Additions

10	Salad Bowl	$60 –	65
12	Lug Soup	$18 –	20
16	Platter, med.	$30 –	35
22A-B	Salad Fork & Spoon Set	$50 –	55
23	Gravy, Fastand	$30 –	35
—	Gravy Ladle	$18 –	20
26	Covered Vegetable	$55 –	60
30	Chop Plate	$45 –	50
60	Covered Casserole	$65 –	70
60W	Covered Casserole Warmer	$30 –	35
62	Sauce Boat	$28 –	30

(continued)

P 460 Luau Additions

16	Platter, med.	$25 – 28
23	Gravy, Fastand	$25 – 28
26	Covered Vegetable	$45 – 50
30	Chop Plate	$35 – 40
40	Coffee Pot & Lid	$100 – 110
60	Covered Casserole	$55 – 60
60W	Covered Casserole Warmer	$30 – 35
76	Cocoa Mug	$14 – 15

P 530 Painted Desert Additions

23	Gravy, Fastand	$25 – 28
30	Chop Plate	$35 – 40
73	Espresso Mug	$14 – 15
74	Espresso Saucer	$4 – 5
75	Chip N' Dip & Lid	$38 – 40
76	Cocoa Mug	$14 – 15
98	3-Divided Server & Lid, med.	$40 – 45

P 540 California Palm Additions

10	Salad Bowl	$45 – 50
12	Lug Soup	$15 – 16
12-12½	Individual Casserole & Lid	$20 – 22
16	Platter, med.	$25 – 28
22A-B	Salad Fork & Spoon Set	$40 – 45
23	Gravy, Fastand	$25 – 28
26	Covered Vegetable	$45 – 50
28	Jam & Jelly	$28 – 30
30	Chop Plate	$35 – 40
36	Candle Holder	$22 – 25
40	Coffee Pot & Lid	$100 – 110
51-V	Vinegar Cruet & Stopper	$18 – 20
51-O	Oil Cruet & Stopper	$18 – 20
60	Covered Casserole	$55 – 60
60W	Covered Casserole Warmer	$30 – 35
62	Sauce Boat	$22 – 25
63	Oval Baker	$28 – 30
76	Cocoa Mug	$14 – 15

Traditional Shape

Part I:
- P 560 Woodland Gold (1959)
- P 570 California Rose (1959)
- P 580 Tropicana (1960)
- P 590 California Strawberry (1961)
- P 580 Mission Verde (1966)
- P 585 Mission Gold (1966)
- P 561 Gold Dahlia (1968)
- P 562 Blue Dahlia (1969)

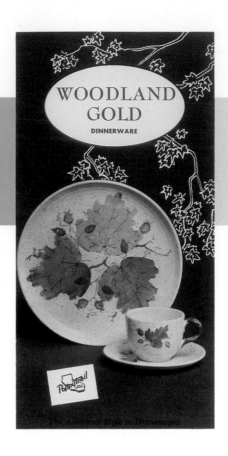

Throughout the 1950s Metlox securely established its reputation with dinnerware patterns produced on unusual, distinctive shapes, i.e. the Early American Provincial, the avant-garde Freeform, and the modernistic Navajo and Tempo. Allen and Shaw's Traditional, styled on simpler, more familiar — Metlox used the description "universal" — shapes was counterpoint to these earlier shapes with its overall emphasis on common rather than unique designs and contours. Metlox's intent, however, was a further diversification of its already varied output, not a conservative, reactionary abandonment of the experimentation of the past. Evan K Shaw, who actually preferred authentic, traditional dinnerware designs, was delighted with the new shape. Traditional quickly became the Poppytrail Division's dominant shape of the 1960s. The initial designs were followed by two sculptured versions of the shape. The successes of many of its patterns rivaled those of Provincial shape patterns during the 1950s.

The original Traditional shape (also commonly referred to as the Woodland Gold shape by company employees) utilized only coupe shape styling. Wide rims were noticeably absent on all flatware and bowls. A studio potter's effect was achieved by the addition of a pronounced raised ring pattern on the interior edge of flatware and bowls, and on the exteriors of serving pieces. Hol-

loware items were predominantly bulbous shapes. Vine handles and finials added a decorator's touch. Woodland Gold and California Strawberry, the two most popular patterns, were large sets with various open stock items, including a four-piece canister set with ceramic lids. The other patterns offered smaller selections. The most attractive of these were California Rose, picturing a stem cutting with an open rose, buds, and leaves, and Tropicana, depicting a colorful assortment of fruit. According to the Metlox files, Mission Gold was never released as an active pattern.

Special attention was focused on the development of California Strawberry. A strawberry vine design decorated the flatware and bowls with solid color avocado green holloware. Strawberry fruit, flower, and leaf clusters served as lid finials. The strawberry vine design was accented with a rich, vivid red, one of hand-decorated earthenware's most challenging colors to accurately reproduce. This on-glaze, selenium-enriched color, created by the glaze department's wizard John Johnson, was a variant shade of P 390 Red Rooster's "live-coal" red. The new red was showcased in Strawberry Accessories, a complementary Artware Division line featuring realistic strawberry and leaf shaped items that coordinated with California Strawberry.

DINNERWARE PATTERN AND COLOR NO. 560

030
040
060
170
160
300
070
260
600
700
760
100
190
330
230
400
830
010   020
220
180
080
121
630
620
210
WOODLAND GOLD
DINNERWARE
290
420   340
150
660
370
430
880   090
130   350

440   450   460   470

Woodland Gold: 1972 brochure. Pattern designed by George Newsome.

Woodland Gold

The universal shapes retain hand crafted touch of the potter's wheel and will complement all styles of home decor. Each item hand decorated with delicate colors of cocoa, gold and burnt sienna which are permanently retained under a soft, satin fleck glaze.

Woodland Gold: individual soup server, buffet server, and cheese server and lid.

Woodland Gold: salad bowl and salad fork and spoon set.

Woodland Gold: large 2¼ quart pitcher and small 1½ pint pitcher.

Woodland Gold: pepper shaker, salt shaker, medium platter, and butter and lid.

Woodland Gold: cup and saucer, dinner plate, and medium 1¼ quart vegetable and lid.

Woodland Gold: sugar and lid, teapot and lid, and creamer.

California Strawberry: coffee pot and lid, mug, and teapot and lid.

California Strawberry: cup and saucer, dinner plate, salt shaker, and bread and butter plate.

California Strawberry: medium divided vegetable and salad bowl.

California Strawberry

One of the most difficult colors to achieve in hand decorating fine earthenware is the "just right" luscious red, used as an accent in this delightful pattern. Balancing the hand-painted strawberries are the subtle avocado-green leaves, with solid tone avocado green color in the uniquely-shaped holloware. Colors are detergent proof under honey-toned glaze.

Note, too, the unique Strawberry knobs that make for exciting conversation pieces.

California Strawberry: fruit bowl, large platter, and medium 1¼ quart pitcher.

California Strawberry: creamer, sugar and lid, salad plate, and butter and lid.

103

P 560 Woodland Gold, P 590 California Strawberry

010	Cup, 7 oz.	$9 – 10
020	Saucer, 6"	$3 – 4
030	Bread & Butter, 6⅜"	$7 – 8
040	Salad Plate, 8"	$9 – 10
060	Dinner Plate, 10¼"	$12 – 13
070	Soup, 6¾"	$14 – 15
080	Vegetable, sm., rnd., 8⅛"	$30 – 35
090	Vegetable, div., sm., rnd., 8½" (aka Jam & Jelly)	$35 – 40
100	Salad Bowl, 11"	$55 – 60
121	Individual Soup Server, lug, 6¾"	$16 – 18
130	Butter & Lid, oval	$50 – 55
150	Vegetable, med., rnd., 9"	$35 – 40
160	Platter, med., oval, 11"	$30 – 35
170	Platter, lg., oval, 13"	$35 – 40
180	Sugar & Lid, 12 oz.	$22 – 25
190	Creamer, 10 oz.	$20 – 22
210	Fruit, 5⅜"	$11 – 12
220	Salad Fork & Spoon Set	$50 – 55
230	Gravy, Fastand, 1¼ pt.	$32 – 35
260	Vegetable & Lid, med., 1¼ qt.	$65 – 70
290	Vegetable, div., med., rnd., 9"	$40 – 45
300	Buffet Server, rnd., 13¼"	$50 – 55
330	Salt	$10 – 12
340	Pepper	$10 – 12
350	Tumbler, 12 oz.	$22 – 25
370	Pitcher, lg., 2¼ qt.	$55 – 60
400	Coffee Pot & Lid, 8 cup	$80 – 90
420	Cereal, 5⅝"	$13 – 14
430	Pitcher, med., 1¼ qt.	$40 – 45
440	Flour Canister & Lid	$65 – 70
450	Sugar Canister & Lid	$55 – 60
460	Coffee Canister & Lid	$45 – 50
470	Tea Canister & Lid	$35 – 40
620	Sauce Boat, 1¼ pt.	$35 – 40
630	Oval Baker, 11"	$40 – 45
660	Vegetable & Lid, lg., 2 qt.	$80 – 85
700	Teapot & Lid, 6 cup	$90 – 100
760	Mug, 8 oz.	$18 – 20
880	Pitcher, sm., 1½ pt.	$30 – 35

P 560 Woodland Gold Additions

600	Casserole & Lid, 1½ qt.	$75 – 80
830	Cheese Server & Lid (aka Butter & Lid, rnd.)	$60 – 65

P 590 California Strawberry Addition

240	Platter, sm., oval, 9½"	$28 – 30

Mission Verde

...pleasing warmth of intricate design plus outstanding contemporary coloring. Elegant shapes show the hand-turned potters' art. Avocado greens in lacy design seem to melt into the soft, grey-white background, with an overall rich stoneware glaze effect. Distinctive vine handles. So compatible it coordinates with any table background of wood or linen — for the most delightful Provincial dining atmosphere.

Mission Verde:
1966 brochure.

Gold Dahlia

Gold Dahlia:
1974 brochure.

Gold Dahlia

Gold dahlia petals, honoring the artistry of Anders Dahl*, embellish soft orange centers in a blend reminiscent of a brilliant California sun. And each smiles through leaves of spring green "under glaze" on a background of golden honey.

*Swedish botanist from whom the word "dahlia," in 1789, received its name.

Blue Dahlia

Sun speckled centers sparkle from alluring azure petals. Leaves of spring green glisten from a moss background. Together "under glaze" they form a garden of blue dahlias hand crafted in the manner of the studio potter.

Blue Dahlia

Blue Dahlia:
1974 brochure.

P 561 Gold Dahlia, P 562 Blue Dahlia, P 570 California Rose, P 580 Tropicana, P 580 Mission Verde

No.	Item	Price	No.	Item	Price
010	Cup, 7 oz.	$6 – 7	700	Teapot & Lid, 6 cup	$45 – 50
020	Saucer, 6"	$2 – 3			
030	Bread & Butter, 6⅜"	$4 – 5	**P 561 Gold Dahlia and P 562 Blue Dahlia Additions**		
040	Salad Plate, 8"	$6 – 7	080	Vegetable, sm., rnd., 8⅛"	$18 – 20
060	Dinner Plate, 10¼"	$8 – 9	090	Vegetable, div., sm., rnd., 8½"	$20 – 22
070	Soup, 6¾"	$11 – 12	121	Individual Soup Server, lug, 6¾"	$12 – 14
130	Butter & Lid, oval	$28 – 30	160	Platter, med., oval, 11"	$20 – 22
150	Vegetable, med., rnd., 9"	$20 – 22	240	Platter, sm., oval, 9½"	$18 – 20
170	Platter, lg., oval, 13"	$22 – 25	630	Oval Baker, 11"	$22 – 25
180	Sugar & Lid, 12 oz.	$16 – 18	760	Mug, 8 oz.	$14 – 15
190	Creamer, 10 oz.	$14 – 16			
210	Fruit, 5⅜"	$7 – 8	**P 570 California Rose Additions**		
230	Gravy, Fastand, 1¼ pt.	$18 – 20	121	Individual Soup Server, lug, 6¾"	$19 – 14
290	Vegetable, div., med., rnd., 9"	$22 – 25	160	Platter, med., oval, 11"	$20 – 22
330	Salt	$8 – 9	260	Vegetable & Lid, med., 1¼ qt.	$35 – 40
340	Pepper	$8 – 9	300	Buffet Server, rnd., 13¼"	$25 – 28
400	Coffee Pot & Lid, 8 cup	$45 – 50	630	Oval Baker, 11"	$22 – 25
420	Cereal, 5⅝"	$9 – 10	760	Mug, 8 oz.	$14 – 15

Traditional Shape

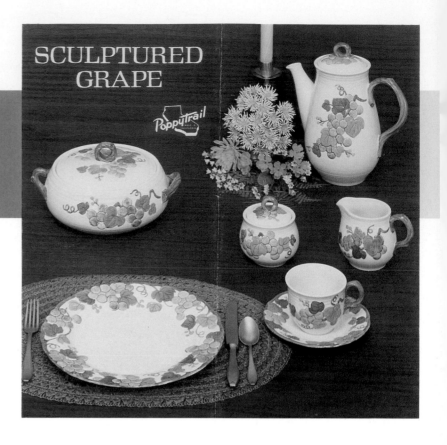

SCULPTURED GRAPE

Poppytrail

Part II: P 240 Sculptured Grape (1963)

P 250 Antique Grape (1964)

P 260 Vintage Pink (1965)

P 241 Grape Arbor (1975)

P 310 Sculptured Zinnia (1964)

P 311 Floralace (1975)

P 056 Lavender Blue (1980)

P 146 Memories (early 1980s)

Metlox's first sculptured designs, California Peach Blossom (1952) and Golden Blossom, were moderately successful patterns. For a long time Allen and Shaw contemplated creating other sculptured patterns. During the 1950s, however, the company's preoccupation with Freeform, Navajo, Tempo, and Confetti, shapes not appropriate for carved designs, delayed the opportunity. The creation of Traditional shape, with its simpler styling and contours, offered the ideal shapes. With Evan K. Shaw's wholehearted approval, a grape design by Allen and Shaw was chosen as the theme. Entrusted to the extraordinary modeling abilities of Frank Irwin and Bob Chandler, the development process was slowed only by Evan K. Shaw's constant revisions. Convinced that the pattern would become very popular, Shaw insisted that every detail be perfect. For over a year, numerous models of the dinner plate, the item always designed first to set the tone and style of the complete pattern, were rejected until one meeting Shaw's standards was created. As usual, Shaw's perfectionist attitude reaped huge profits for the company as Sculptured Grape, finally released in 1963, was an instantaneous success.

Significant alterations and an increase in bowl and flatware sizes were necessary to accomodate the grape carvings while allowing ample smooth surfaces for food. Therefore, a wide rim was added to all of the coupe shape plates and platters and a gentler, more gradual incline to the edges of bowls. Most serving pieces retained their original design and dimensions. The vine handles and finials — very fitting for a grape design — remained along with a lightly impressed suggestion of the studio potter rings design. Delicately scalloped edges added a decorator's flair. The luncheon plate, jam and jelly, and footed compote were additions. Of the three other decorated versions of the Sculptured Grape design, Antique Grape sold very well. In 1988, the design was revived for Sonoma and Mission, two very different patterns (see Late Dinnerware Patterns).

The immediate popularity of Sculptured Grape led to the rapid development and release of Sculptured Zinnia, composed of many of the same items. The only difference was the substitution of a carved zinnia design. Sculptured Zinnia was also produced in three color variations. Especially beautiful and noteworthy were Helen McIntosh's Lavender Blue and Memories which painted the zinnia design in soft lavender, pink, and green, and finished it with a blue tint glaze and a clear glaze respectively.

DINNERWARE PATTERN AND COLOR NO. 240

Sculptured Grape: 1975 brochure.

Sculptured Grape

Those who appreciate the finer things in their daily lives really will enjoy this last word in table service. Sculptured Grape is the culmination of our designers' long dream to represent Nature's beauty in functional dinnerware. About this unique design . . . This pattern was contemplated and in development by us for over ten years. Our designers, whose combined experience represents well over one hundred fifty years, painstakingly had to make change after change in each piece, until the smallest detail of dimension, carving, depth, shape and color were in proper balance and harmony. Only in this deliberate, dedicated way could they have brought forth this unusual pattern, destined to be a "classic" far into the future.

One great advantage our designers had was that the material they work with is Earthenware. Sculptured Grape could not have been done as effectively in china, ironstone or plastic. Only superior Earthenware could reproduce the full, rich combinations of the green, blue, and brown tones that blend so well with the colors used in your individual home deocration.

Our designers knew that our talented California hand crafters and hand decorators, some of whom have been with Poppytrail for over twenty-five years, would produce Sculptured Grape perfectly and in accordance with the original design, quality concept. The decorator who hand painted your set proudly marked her "signature mark" on the back of each plate.

Sculptured Grape in your home will stand the test of time because it is durable and because of its basic heirloom quality of design. It is an open stock pattern that enables you to add new, dramatic accessory pieces — to enhance further the dining pleasure of your friends and family.

Sculptured Grape: sugar canister and lid.

Sculptured Grape: cup and saucer, dinner plate, and coffee pot and lid.

Sculptured Grape: bread and butter plate and butter and lid.

Sculptured Grape: salad plate and medium 1¼ quart pitcher.

Sculptured Grape: medium one quart vegetable and lid and gravy with fastand.

Sculptured Grape: tumbler.

Antique Grape: medium platter and coffee canister and lid.

Antique Grape

The discriminating homemaker will proudly entertain with this sculptured pattern, and delight her family with its smart beauty. The carved grapes and leaves — raised on the soft-beige, antique finish, against a warm-white background — gives the feeling of elegance and the richness you look for in serving with beautiful dinnerware.

Antique Grape: cup and saucer, dinner plate, pepper shaker, and medium one quart vegetable and lid.

P 240 Sculptured Grape, P 250 Antique Grape

No.	Item	Price		No.	Item	Price
010	Cup, 7 oz.	$11 – 12		280	Jam & Jelly, 8⅛"	$50 – 55
020	Saucer, 6⅛"	$3 – 4		290	Vegetable, div., med., rnd., 9½"	$45 – 50
030	Bread & Butter, 6⅜"	$8 – 9		300	Buffet Server, rnd., 12⅛"	$65 – 75
040	Salad Plate, 7½"	$10 – 12		330	Salt	$12 – 13
050	Luncheon Plate, 9"	$15 – 18		340	Pepper	$12 – 13
060	Dinner Plate, 10½"	$14 – 15		350	Tumbler, 12 oz.	$25 – 28
070	Soup, 8⅛"	$18 – 20		370	Pitcher, lg., 2¼" qt.	$60 – 65
080	Vegetable, sm., rnd., 8½"	$35 – 40		400	Coffee Pot & Lid, 8 cup	$90 – 100
090	Vegetable, div., sm., rnd., 8½"	$40 – 45		420	Cereal, 7⅜"	$14 – 16
100	Salad Bowl, 12⅛"	$70 – 75		430	Pitcher, med., 1¼ qt.	$45 – 50
130	Butter & Lid	$55 – 60		440	Flour Canister & Lid	$70 – 75
150	Vegetable, med., rnd., 9½"	$40 – 45		450	Sugar Canister & Lid	$60 – 65
160	Platter, med., oval, 12½"	$40 – 45		460	Coffee Canister & Lid	$50 – 55
170	Platter, lg., oval, 14¼"	$45 – 50		470	Tea Canister & Lid	$40 – 45
180	Sugar & Lid, 10 oz.	$25 – 28		620	Sauce Boat, 1 pt.	$40 – 45
190	Creamer, 10 oz.	$22 – 25		630	Oval Baker, 10¼"	$45 – 50
210	Fruit, 6"	$12 – 14		660	Vegetable & Lid, lg., 2 qt.	$90 – 95
220	Salad Fork & Spoon Set	$55 – 60		700	Teapot & Lid, 6 cup	$100 – 110
230	Gravy, Fastand, 1 pt.	$35 – 40		760	Mug, 8 oz.	$20 – 22
240	Platter, sm., oval, 9⅝"	$35 – 40		840	Footed Compote, 8½"	$65 – 70
260	Vegetable & Lid, med., 1 qt.	$75 – 80		880	Pitcher, sm., 1½ pt.	$35 – 40

Vintage Pink: cereal bowl, large platter, and dinner plate.

Vintage Pink

Sculptured "Pink Champagne" colored grapes accented with deeper cranberry tones and balanced with live chartreuse green leaves and natural vines — Go as Formal as you like, yet retain the warm beauty that says use me every day.

Vintage Pink: medium vegetable bowl.

Grape Arbor

"Grape Arbor" is a Poppytrail Sculptured Pattern inspired by the beautiful subtle colors of white wine grapes... Malaga, Sauterne, Balsac, Chablis. The leaves are parrot green and olive, and the vines cling to Arbor's tinted white background. "Grape Arbor" means a beautiful table for every day and company too...

Grape Arbor: mug, large platter, and gravy with fastand.

Grape Arbor: cup and saucer, dinner plate, salad plate, and creamer.

P 241 Grape Arbor, P 260 Vintage Pink

010	Cup, 7 oz.	$9 – 10		240	Platter, sm., oval, 9⅝"	$30 – 35
020	Saucer, 6⅛"	$3 – 4		260	Vegetable & Lid, med., 1 qt.	$65 – 70
030	Bread & Butter, 6⅜"	$7 – 8		290	Vegetable, div., med., rnd., 9½"	$40 – 45
040	Salad Plate, 7½"	$9 – 10		300	Buffet Server, rnd., 12⅛"	$55 – 65
060	Dinner Plate, 10½"	$12 – 13		330	Salt	$10 – 12
070	Soup, 8⅛"	$16 – 18		340	Pepper	$10 – 12
090	Vegetable, div., sm., rnd., 8½"	$35 – 40		400	Coffee Pot & Lid, 8 cup	$80 – 90
100	Salad Bowl, 12⅛"	$60 – 65		420	Cereal, 7⅜"	$13 – 14
130	Butter & Lid	$50 – 55		660	Vegetable & Lid, lg., 2 qt.	$80 – 85
150	Vegetable, med., rnd., 9½"	$35 – 40		700	Teapot & Lid, 6 cup	$90 – 100
170	Platter, lg., oval, 14¼"	$40 – 45		760	Mug, 8 oz.	$18 – 20
180	Sugar & Lid, 10 oz.	$22 – 25				
190	Creamer, 10 oz.	$20 – 22			**P 241 Grape Arbor Additions**	
210	Fruit, 6"	$11 – 12		080	Vegetable, sm., rnd., 8½"	$30 – 35
220	Salad Fork & Spoon Set	$50 – 55		160	Platter, med., oval, 12½"	$35 – 40
230	Gravy, Fastand, 1 pt.	$32 – 35		630	Oval Baker, 10¼"	$40 – 45

Sculptured Zinnia

Sculptured Zinnia, so bold and different, and understandably right in fashion, because flowers have always been used for beautiful table settings.

The Zinnias are carved with minute attention to detail, and hand painted in the luxurious combination of yellow-gold, orange, greens, and browns, against a cream-white background.

Sculptured Zinnia:
1975 brochure.

Sculptured Zinnia:
sugar and lid, teapot and lid, and creamer.

Sculptured Zinnia: cup and saucer, dinner plate, and coffee pot and lid.

Sculptured Zinnia: butter and lid.

P 310 Sculptured Zinnia

010	Cup, 7 oz.	$9 – 10	190	Creamer, 10 oz.	$20 – 22
020	Saucer, 6⅛"	$3 – 4	210	Fruit, 6"	$11 – 12
030	Bread & Butter, 6⅜"	$7 – 8	220	Salad Fork & Spoon Set	$50 – 55
040	Salad Plate, 7½"	$9 – 10	230	Gravy, Fastand, 1 pt.	$32 – 35
060	Dinner Plate, 10½"	$12 – 13	260	Vegetable & Lid, med., 1 qt.	$65 – 70
070	Soup, 8⅛"	$16 – 18	290	Vegetable, div., med., rnd., 9½"	$40 – 45
080	Vegetable, sm., rnd., 8½"	$30 – 35	330	Salt	$10 – 12
090	Vegetable, div., sm., rnd., 8½"	$35 – 40	340	Pepper	$10 – 12
100	Salad Bowl, 12⅛"	$60 – 65	400	Coffee Pot & Lid, 8 cup	$80 – 90
130	Butter & Lid	$50 – 55	420	Cereal, 7⅜"	$13 – 14
150	Vegetable, med., rnd., 9½"	$35 – 40	660	Vegetable & Lid, lg., 2 qt.	$80 – 85
160	Platter, med., oval, 12½"	$35 – 40	700	Teapot & Lid, 6 cup	$90 – 100
170	Platter, lg., oval, 14¼"	$40 – 45	760	Mug, 8 oz.	$18 – 20
180	Sugar & Lid, 10 oz.	$22 – 25			

Floralace

The Zinnia is sculptured with infinite attention to the detail of every petal. The raised carving of the snow white flowers is accented by the jeweled glazelets that color the petals. This citron color is also the glossy beauty of the total background. Vine handles and knobs — so feminine — so lacey.

Floralace: 1976 brochure.

Lavender Blue:
Metlox brochure.

Sculptured Zinnia

Lavender Blue

P 311 Floralace, P 056 Lavender Blue

Deduct 10% for P 311 Floralace.

010	Cup, 7 oz.	$9 – 10
020	Saucer, 6⅛"	$3 – 4
030	Bread & Butter, 6⅜"	$7 – 8
040	Salad Plate, 7½"	$9 – 10
060	Dinner Plate, 10½"	$12 – 13
070	Soup, 8⅛"	$16 – 18
130	Butter & Lid	$50 – 55
150	Vegetable, med., rnd., 9½"	$35 – 40
170	Platter, lg., oval, 14¼"	$40 – 45
180	Sugar & Lid, 10 oz.	$22 – 25
190	Creamer, 10 oz.	$20 – 22
210	Fruit, 6"	$11 – 12
230	Gravy, Fastand, 1 pt.	$32 – 35
290	Vegetable, div., med., rnd., 9½"	$40 – 45
330	Salt	$10 – 12
340	Pepper	$10 – 12
400	Coffee Pot & Lid, 8 cup	$80 – 90
420	Cereal, 7⅜"	$13 – 14
700	Teapot & Lid, 6 cup	$90 – 100

P 056 Lavender Blue Addition

760	Mug, 8 oz.	$18 – 20

(A brochure dated December 1, 1980, lists this item as scheduled for production during spring 1981. Its appearance cannot be verified from subsequent brochure material.)

Memories

Memories: Metlox brochure.

P 146 Memories

010	Cup, 7 oz.	$9 – 10
020	Saucer, 6⅛"	$3 – 4
030	Bread & Butter, 6⅜"	$7 – 8
040	Salad Plate, 7½"	$9 – 10
060	Dinner Plate, 10½"	$12 – 13
070	Soup, 8⅛"	$16 – 18
150	Vegetable, med., rnd., 9½"	$35 – 40
170	Platter, lg., oval, 14¼"	$40 – 45
180	Sugar & Lid, 10 oz.	$22 – 25
190	Creamer, 10 oz.	$20 – 22
210	Fruit, 6"	$11 – 12
400	Coffee Pot & Lid, 8 cup	$80 – 90
420	Cereal, 7⅜"	$13 – 14
760	Mug, 8 oz.	$18 – 20

American Tradition Shape

After the initial success of the first Traditional shape patterns, Evan K. Shaw and the design department discussed the possibility of creating another shape based on familiar, authentic dinnerware shapes. Shaw hoped a second shape, similar to the Traditional shape yet conceptually different, would be equally profitable. The result was American Tradition, inspired and influenced by the thick, rugged designs of Early American white ironstone. American Tradition was designed by Allen and Shaw after extensive research and a thorough study of museum examples. Although the heavy, masculine appearance and basic contours of the originals were retained, Allen and Shaw refined the shapes to impart a Spanish flavor enhanced by elegant decorative stylings: gracefully upturned wide rims; delicately scalloped edges on the overall design; alternating widely spaced ridges on the rims of flatware, bowls, and serving piece exteriors; and detailed leaf carvings on handles, spouts, and lids. A delightful new item was the salad/dessert plate which was included in some of the patterns as a substitute for or addition to the slightly smaller salad plate.

The La Mancha (Spanish for "the stain") patterns were solid gold, green, or white sets highlighted with double charcoal borders. This border distinguished La Mancha White from Tradition White, an all-white pattern. The La Mancha patterns featured a brown Spanish medallion on the salad/dessert plate only. Three sculptured patterns — Sculptured Berry, Autumn Berry, and the all-white Winter Berry — appeared on the shape. P 054 American Heritage was released as a dinnerware pattern as well as a larger gourmet set. The dinnerware pattern is included here while the gourmet set is listed with its three counterpart sets in the Vernonware Division section. Marigold was a decal decorated pattern. Although its patterns never attained the popularity of those on other traditional shapes, American Tradition epitomized Metlox's "shape of beauty," as it was aptly described in company literature.

Colonial Garden: bread and butter plate.

114

Colonial Garden: 1973 brochure.

Colonial Garden
Beauty in the "American Tradition"
This authentic shape and pattern is an outstanding achievement in traditional dinnerware. Over four and one-half years went into the planning and design of its shape called "American Tradition." Over a year was spent in modeling and carving. Colonial Garden's blue on blue, hand-decorated pattern is rich and colorful. A fitting complement to its elegant shape.

Golden Garden
Beauty in the "American Tradition"
Golden Garden's yellow, rust, orange and green, hand-decorated pattern is rich and colorful.

Golden Garden: 1973 brochure.

Golden Garden:
coffee pot and lid.

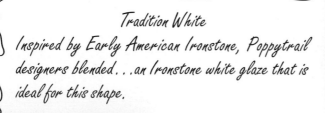

Tradition White
Inspired by Early American Ironstone, Poppytrail designers blended...an Ironstone white glaze that is ideal for this shape.

Tradition White: 1973 brochure.

Tradition White:
butter and lid.

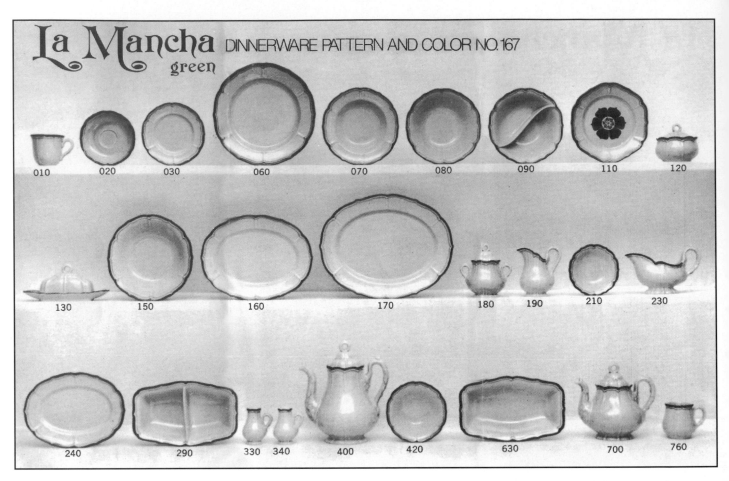

La Mancha green

DINNERWARE PATTERN AND COLOR NO. 167

010 020 030 060 070 080 090 110 120

130 150 160 170 180 190 210 230

240 290 330 340 400 420 630 700 760

La Mancha Green: 1975 brochure.

La Mancha Green
Poppytrail matched the color of the richest green sea moss and applied it to a gracefully carved traditional shape. Then hand painted double borders of deep charcoal brown. And added a brown medallion to the salad/dessert plate that lends a "Don Quixote" touch to this elegantly carved dinnerware.

La Mancha Green:
1975 brochure.

La Mancha green

La Mancha Gold: cup and saucer, dinner plate, and salad/dessert plate.

La Mancha Gold: cereal bowl, medium platter, and soup bowl.

La Mancha Gold: sugar and lid, teapot and lid, and gravy.

La Mancha Gold: divided vegetable and oval baker.

La Mancha Gold
Double charcoal borders highlight the jeweled gold glaze on glaze. The medallion decorated salad plate adds fashion excitement to the deep, graceful carving of the pattern. La Mancha Gold is a California golden sunset designed to become the happy conversation piece of your many dining occasions.

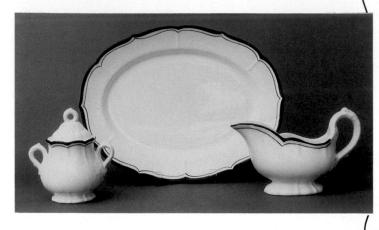

La Mancha White

Lovely La Mancha White…the contemporary look on the elegantly carved traditional shape. Double charcoal borders band the gleaming white pattern. The decorated salad/dessert plate adds the designer touch to this "Don Quixote" inspired dinnerware. Milady can accessorize for formal or informal occasions to please the most discriminating guest. And she will be pleased to know that La Mancha White — like all fine Poppytrail dinnerware — is durable and dishwasher, detergent and oven safe.

La Mancha White: sugar and lid, large platter, and gravy.

La Mancha White: salt and pepper shakers, dinner plate, and salad/dessert plate.

P 161 Colonial Garden, P 163 Golden Garden, P 164 Tradition White, P 165 La Mancha Gold, P 167 La Mancha Green, P 168 La Mancha White

010	Cup, 7 oz.	$9 – 10
020	Saucer, 5¾"	$3 – 4
030	Bread & Butter, 6½"	$7 – 8
060	Dinner Plate, 10¾"	$12 – 13
070	Soup, 8⅛"	$16 – 18
110	Salad/Dessert Plate, 8¼"	$11 – 12
130	Butter & Lid	$50 – 55
150	Vegetable, med., rnd., 8⅞"	$30 – 35
170	Platter, lg., oval, 14¼"	$35 – 40
180	Sugar & Lid, 12 oz.	$22 – 25
190	Creamer, 9 oz.	$20 – 22
210	Fruit, 5½"	$11 – 12
230	Gravy, 12 oz.	$25 – 28
290	Vegetable, div., med., 10¾"	$40 – 45
330	Salt	$10 – 12
340	Pepper	$10 – 12
400	Coffee Pot & Lid, 8 cup	$80 – 90
420	Cereal, 6⅝"	$13 – 14
700	Teapot & Lid, 6 cup	$85 – 95

P 161 Colonial Garden, P 163 Golden Garden, 164 Tradition White Addition

040	Salad Plate, 7⅝"	$9 – 10

P 165 La Mancha Gold, P 167 La Mancha Green, P 168 La Mancha White Additions

080	Vegetable, sm., rnd., 8"	$28 – 30
090	Vegetable, div., sm., rnd., 8"	$30 – 35
120	Individual Soup Server & Lid, 12 oz.	$25 – 30
121	Individual Soup Server, No Lid, 12 oz.	$16 – 18
160	Platter, med., oval, 11¾"	$32 – 35
240	Platter, sm., oval, 10"	$30 – 32
630	Oval Baker, 10¾"	$35 – 40
760	Mug, 10 oz.	$18 – 20

Sculptured Berry Is...
Delicate and graceful carving on a Traditional
Shape... The Berries, Leaves, and Blossoms are
hand painted with nature's colors; Soft Raspberry
fruit, Pink blossoms, Multi-color Green Leaves
and Yellow stamen. The scalloped border of the
rim plate is edged in Leaf Green. This dramatic
Sparkling beauty is enhanced by a Bone White
glossy background.

Sculptured Berry:
1976 brochure.

Sculptured Berry:
cup and saucer and
large platter.

Autumn Berry:
small vegetable bowl,
large platter,
and sugar and lid.

Autumn Berry:
1979 Metlox
brochure.

American Heritage:
Metlox brochure.

American Heritage

Quail Ridge: coffee pot and lid.

Quail Ridge: 1979 brochure.

Quail Ridge:
Metlox brochure.

Sorrento:
Metlox brochure.

P 027 Autumn Berry, P 052 Quail Ridge, P 053 Sorrento, P 054 American Heritage, P 181 Sculptured Berry, P — Winter Berry

010	Cup, 7 oz.	$9 – 10
020	Saucer, 5¾"	$3 – 4
030	Bread & Butter, 6½"	$7 – 8
040	Salad Plate, 7⅝"	$9 – 10
060	Dinner Plate, 10¾"	$12 – 13
070	Soup, 8⅛"	$16 – 18
130	Butter & Lid	$50 – 55
150	Vegetable, med., rnd., 8⅞"	$30 – 35
170	Platter, lg., oval, 14¼"	$35 – 40
180	Sugar & Lid, 12 oz.	$22 – 25
190	Creamer, 9 oz.	$20 – 22
210	Fruit, 5½"	$11 – 12
230	Gravy, 12 oz.	$25 – 28
290	Vegetable, div., med., 10¾"	$40 – 45
330	Salt	$10 – 12
340	Pepper	$10 – 12
400	Coffee Pot & Lid, 8 cup	$80 – 90
420	Cereal, 6⅝"	$13 – 14
700	Teapot & Lid, 6 cup	$85 – 95

P 027 Autumn Berry Additions

080	Vegetable, sm., rnd., 8"	$28 – 30
160	Platter, med., oval, 11¾"	$32 – 35
760	Mug, 8 oz.	$18 – 20

P 052 Quail Ridge Additions

080	Vegetable, sm., rnd., 8"	$28 – 30
110	Salad/Dessert Plate, 8¼"	$11 – 12
160	Platter, med., oval, 11¾"	$32 – 35
620	Casserole & Lid, 2 qt.	$75 – 80
760	Mug, 8 oz.	$18 – 20

P 053 Sorrento, P 054 American Heritage Addition

760	Mug, 8 oz.	$18 – 20

(A brochure dated December 1, 1980, lists this item as scheduled for production in P 053 Sorrento during spring 1981. Its appearance has not been verified from subsequent brochure material.)

P 181 Sculptured Berry, P —- Winter Berry Additions

080	Vegetable, sm., rnd., 8"	$28 – 30
160	Platter, med., oval, 11¾"	$32 – 35
620	Casserole & Lid, 2 qt.	$75 – 80
760	Mug, 8 oz.	$18 – 20

(A brochure dated December 1, 1980, lists these items as scheduled for production during spring 1981. Their appearance has not been verified from subsequent brochure material.)

Marigold: Metlox brochure*.

*Poor quality, only photo available.

P 079 Marigold

010	Cup, 7 oz.	$8 – 9
020	Saucer, 5¾"	$2 – 3
040	Salad Plate, 7⅝"	7 – 8
060	Dinner Plate, 10¾"	$10 – 11
150	Vegetable, med., rnd., 8⅞"	$28 – 30
170	Platter, lg., oval, 14¼"	$30 – 35
180	Sugar & Lid, 12 oz.	$20 – 22
190	Creamer, 9 oz.	$18 – 20
400	Coffee Pot & Lid, 8 cup	$65 – 75
420	Cereal, 6⅝"	$11 – 12

Studio Potter Shape

Part I: P 570 Indigo (1969)

P 571 Bandero (1969)

P 572 Carmel (1969)

P 573 San Clemente La Casa Brown (1970)

P 574 San Clemente Spanish Yellow (1970)

P 575 Marina (1970)

P 576 San Clemente Laguna Blue (1970)

P 577 Flamenco Red (1971)

P 578 Medallion Red (1971)

P 586 California Orchard (1973)

P 003 Moulin Rouge (aka Tiffany Blue) (1976)

P 004 Sandflower (1976)

During the late 1960s, Evan K Shaw determined that the Poppytrail Division needed a new contemporary shape that would be competitive with similar lines from other companies. Sales of the modernistic Navajo and Tempo patterns had diminished greatly and many of their patterns were already discontinued. Shaw decided on simple shapes that resembled hand-thrown stoneware. For this purpose, Metlox hired John Karrash, a Los Angeles ceramicist who specialized in stoneware studio pottery. Karrash worked at Metlox for about six months creating various hand-thrown dinnerware items and glazes for them. The Studio Potter shape evolved from his models and was augmented with complementary designs from Metlox's design department. A total of 34 patterns with assigned company numbers plus 26 Colorstax and ten Colorbands patterns were produced on this shape. Studio Potter was Metlox's primary shape of the 70s and 80s.

The first group featured wide, upraised rims on the flatware. The hand-thrown effect was achieved by concentric impressions or grooves lightly molded into each piece as though shaped by a pot-ter's fingertips at the studio wheel. A unique item in this group was the beverage server urn, lid, and warmer, a truly impressive piece included only in patterns P 570, P 571, P 572, P 573, P 574, and P 576.

The first nine patterns were introduced from 1969 to 1971. At the same time Metlox released a series of five oven-to-table gourmet-ware lines in the Artware Division that were merchandised separately and not included in these patterns. These lines were P 140 Gourmet, P 141 Flamenco Red Serving Accessories, P 142 Casual Cookery White, P 143 La Casa Brown Gourmet, and P 144 Casual Cookery Yellow (aka Gourmet Spanish Yellow). P 141, P 143, and P 144 were named after the dinnerware patterns P 577, P 573, and P 574 respectively. Metlox defined "gourmetware" as items designed for the cooking and serving of food. These lines included casseroles, a soup tureen, lasagna servers, and other items that were useful additions to the dinnerware patterns. Their design and styling, especially the circular potter's grooves on the exteriors of all items, blended harmoniously with the patterns.

010   020   030   040   060   420   210

080   150   240   160   170

090   290

190   180   120   230   130   330   340

800/803

600   700   070   400   630   760

bandero

Bandero: 1975 brochure.

Bandero
Smoke grey rings spiral outward to announce a banded border of ultramarine blue and chestnut brown while free flowing flowers dance merrily on the hand crafted holloware. A fun loving pattern created in the hand turned manner of the studio potter. Bonny Bandero... the happy difference in fine dinnerware.

Bandero: 1975 brochure.

Indigo
Ultramarine blue blossoms burst forth from a mercury grey background to announce the pattern. Free flowing flowers. Unruly. Undefined. Beautifully banded. The hand-turned look, superbly crafted in the manner of the studio potter. Indigo. Equally at home in any decor. Designed for now and every dining occasion.

Carmel

On a background of golden honey, Poppytrail added free flowing flowers in hand painted brush strokes of cinnamon and burnt umber. Under glaze they set a casual mood so indicative of today's trend in indoor or outdoor entertaining. The creation of Carmel was expressly for those who wish to share its hand painted beauty.

Carmel: Metlox brochure.

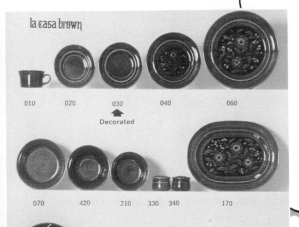

**San Clemente
La Casa Brown:**
1974 brochure.

San Clemente La Casa Brown

Sun splashed wild flowers flowing freely o'er the banks of the Rio Grande are subject matter sufficient to inspire a dozen patterns. Yet, La Casa Brown states its case in a moving manner that reflects the individuality of the pattern. Medium to dark tones of earthy brown house sun speckled wild flowers hand painted in the manner of the studio potter.

**San Clemente
La Casa Brown:**
1974 brochure.

**San Clemente
La Casa Brown:**
Metlox brochure.

San Clemente Laguna Blue
Rich tones of Laguna Blue serve as the perfect foil for iridescent off-white and blue wild flowers that flow freely around the pattern, sealed in a glaze of polished beauty. Here, the California mood for dining and entertaining is translated on fine dinnerware in the new San Clemente studio series by Poppytrail.

San Clemente Laguna Blue:
1974 brochure.

San Clemente Laguna Blue:
Metlox brochure.

San Clemente Spanish Yellow
Spanish Yellow, one of the new San Clemente studio series by Poppytrail, captures the nostalgia of a Spanish sunset shining brilliantly on a field of wild flowers. The earthy tones of this wonderfully hospitable pattern serve as a stimulus for imaginative table settings, particularly appropriate for the California mood in casual dining and entertaining.

San Clemente Spanish Yellow:
Metlox brochure.

Marina

Marina:
Metlox brochure.

Flamenco Red

"Flamenco Red" — For the exciting, unusual table — A live, rich red shaded with a charcoal brown edge accent. A hand turned studio potters shape with potters tool texture to enhance shape and color... Flamenco Red provides drama, and daring with smart styling...

FLAMENGO RED BY POPPYTRAIL

Flamenco Red:
Metlox brochure.

Medallion Red

Here is fine dinnerware to go with the provocative you for your most festive dining occasions — an Aztec inspired sunburst in hues of golden yellow, bittersweet and charcoal brown explodes across the hand crafted studio shaped pattern against a background of fiery red.

Medallion Red:
Metlox brochure.

California Orchard:
Metlox brochure.
California Orchard is noted for its apple and grape cluster finials.

Moulin Rouge
Exciting . . . hand-painted red, yellow, green and blue floral in the Tiffany glass mode. Elegant, yet so casual, a design for all times, fun, French and saucy.

Moulin Rouge:
1977 brochure.

Sandflower
Hand painted golden yellow blossoms with terra cotta stamen and free flowing spear leaves on a deep sand color background. Accent sand color on accessories.

Sandflower:
1977 brochure.

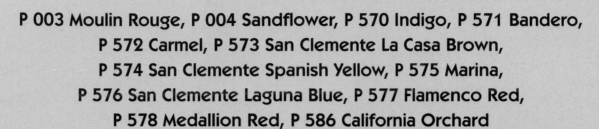

P 003 Moulin Rouge, P 004 Sandflower, P 570 Indigo, P 571 Bandero, P 572 Carmel, P 573 San Clemente La Casa Brown, P 574 San Clemente Spanish Yellow, P 575 Marina, P 576 San Clemente Laguna Blue, P 577 Flamenco Red, P 578 Medallion Red, P 586 California Orchard

010	Cup, 7 oz.	$7 – 8
020	Saucer, 6"	$2 – 3
030	Bread & Butter, 6½"	$5 – 6
040	Salad Plate, 7¾"	$7 – 8
060	Dinner Plate, 10½"	$9 – 10
070	Soup, 7¼"	$12 – 13
130	Butter & Lid	$30 – 35
150	Vegetable, med., rnd., 9"	$22 – 25
170	Platter, lg., oval, 13⅛"	$25 – 30
180	Sugar & Lid, 11 oz.	$18 – 20
190	Creamer, 11 oz.	$16 – 18
210	Fruit, 5½"	$8 – 9
230	Gravy, 1 pt.	$22 – 25
330	Salt	$8 – 9
340	Pepper	$8 – 9
400	Coffee Pot & Lid, 6 cup	$50 – 55
420	Cereal, 6½"	$10 – 11
700	Teapot & Lid, 4½ cup	$50 – 55

P 571 Bandero & P 572 Carmel Additions

080	Vegetable, sm., rnd., 8¼"	$20 – 22
090	Vegetable, div., sm., rnd., 8¼"	$22 – 25
120	Individual Soup Server & Lid, 12 oz.	$20 – 22
121	Individual Soup Server, no lid, 12 oz.	$12 – 14
160	Platter, med., oval, 10⅞"	$22 – 25
240	Platter, sm., oval, 9⅝"	$20 – 22
290	Vegetable, div., med., rnd., 9"	$25 – 30
480	Soup Tureen & Lid (Bandero only)	$55 – 60
600	Casserole & Lid, 2 qt.	$40 – 45
630	Oval Baker, 10¾"	$25 – 30
760	Mug, 10 oz.	$14 – 15
809	Beverage Server Urn, Lid & Warmer, 18 cup	$85 – 95

P 570 Indigo, P 573 San Clemente La Casa Brown, P 574 San Clemente Spanish Yellow, P 576 San Clemente Laguna Blue Additions

290	Vegetable, div., med., rnd., 9"	$25 – 30
600	Casserole & Lid, 2 qt.	$40 – 45
760	Mug, 10 oz.	$14 – 15
809	Beverage Server Urn, Lid & Warmer, 18 cup	$85 – 95

P 575 Marina Additions

290	Vegetable, div., med., rnd., 9"	$25 – 30
600	Casserole & Lid, 2 qt.	$40 – 45
760	Mug, 10 oz.	$14 – 15

P 577 Flamenco Red, P 578 Medallion Red Addition

290	Vegetable, div., med., rnd., 9"	$25 – 30

P 586 California Orchard Additions

290	Vegetable, div., med., rnd., 9"	$25 – 30
600	Casserole & Lid, 2 qt.	$40 – 45

P 004 Sandflower Additions

080	Vegetable, sm., rnd., 8¼"	$20 – 22
160	Platter, med., oval, 10⅞"	$22 – 25
290	Vegetable, div., med., rnd., 9"	$25 – 30

P 003 Moulin Rouge Additions

080	Vegetable, sm., rnd., 8¼"	$20 – 22
160	Platter, med., oval, 10⅞"	$22 – 25
290	Vegetable, div., med., rnd., 9"	$25 – 30
760	Mug, 8 oz.	$14 – 15

(A brochure dated December 1, 1980, lists this item as scheduled for production in spring 1981. Its appearance has not been verified from subsequent brochure material.)

Studio Potter Shape

Part II: Impression Series
              P 320 White (1971)
              P 321 Yellow (1971)
              P 322 Orange (1971)
              P 323 Green (1971)
           P 581 Wild Poppy (1972)
           P 583 Matilija (1974)

This group introduced a major redesign of the original Studio Potter shape. Flatware became slightly larger coupe shapes with narrower rims. A large round platter, actually a chop plate, replaced the earlier oval design. With a smoother surface, the potter's groove texture was less visible and tactile. The most noticeable change was the addition of the tall, slim coffee pot. The cup was also redesigned as a taller, narrower mug shape to match the new coffee pot.

Strikingly different patterns were also created. The Impression Series featured geometric designs carved intaglio-style on the exteriors of many serving pieces. White and pastels superseded the bright colors of the earlier patterns. Wild Poppy was the first Metlox pattern to use decals instead of hand painting since Indian Summer and Central Park in 1953. Elaine Masnick designed the flamboyant, colorful decals. Wild Poppy was so immediately successful that a second decal version, Matilija (White Poppy), was released two years later.

Impression:
1971 brochure.

Impression

The 'king' size coupe dinner plate with narrow rim begins the 'impression.' The cup, slim with carved geometrics, sets the theme for the beautiful accessories highlighted by the tall, graceful coffee server. Impression's bright pastel solid colors are all accented with light maple sugar color borders that match the accessories. Set a romantic table for two — go 'bold' as you like for Impression accents the wildest fabric colors and materials, yet its pastels will brighten up beige or neutral mats or natural wood finishes.

Available in Spectrum bright —

P 320 Impression White	P 321 Impression Yellow
P 322 Impression Orange	P 323 Impression Green

Impression: 1971 brochure.

Wild Poppy: 1975 brochure.

Wild Poppy: cup and saucer, salad plate, and creamer.

Wild Poppy: gravy, dinner plate, and bread and butter plate.

Wild Poppy
The glorious burst of color of poppies in full bloom...
Seven shades of Oranges, Yellows and Greens blended onto a Tint Green Background. A large functional 10³/₄ inch coupe dinner plate, a wonderful cup matches the tall, gracefully slim Coffee Pot smothered with Wild Poppies. Beautiful lines and style.

Wild Poppy:
Metlox brochure.

Matilija
(White Poppy)

Matilija: Metlox brochure.

Matilija (White Poppy)
In the Matilija Canyon in California grows huge White Poppies... named by the Native Indians — 'Matilija.' One of Poppytrail's most beautiful Patterns and so Versatile... Coordinates with Greens, Browns, Yellows, Oranges, Blues. An Emerald Green Center with Citron Accent Spray... with multi-Green Stems on a Soft White, Glossy Background.

Matilija:
large round platter.

P 320 – 23 Impression Series, P 581 Wild Poppy, P 583 Matilija (White Poppy)

No.	Item	Price	No.	Item	Price
010	Cup, 7 oz.	$9 – 10	230	Gravy, 1 pt.	$28 – 30
020	Saucer, 6¼".	$3 – 4	290	Vegetable, div., med., rnd., 9"	$35 – 40
030	Bread & Butter, 6⅞"	$7 – 8	330	Salt	$10 – 12
040	Salad Plate, 8".	$9 – 10	340	Pepper	$10 – 12
060	Dinner Plate, 10¾"	$12 – 13	400	Coffee Pot & Lid, tall, 10 cup	$80 – 90
070	Soup, 7¼".	$15 – 16	420	Cereal, 6½"	$13 – 14
130	Butter & Lid	$45 – 50	700	Teapot & Lid, 4½ cup	$70 – 80
150	Vegetable, med., rnd., 9"	$30 – 35			
170	Platter, lg., rnd., 13¼".	$35 – 40		**P 320 – 23 Impression Series Additions:**	
180	Sugar & Lid, 11 oz.	$22 – 25	600	Casserole & Lid, 2 qt.	$55 – 60
190	Creamer, 11 oz.	$20 – 22	760	Mug, 10 oz.	$16 – 18
210	Fruit, 5½"	$11 – 12			

Studio Potter Shape

Part III: P 002 Geranium (1976)
P 005 Pomegranate (1976)
P 006 Tiffany (aka Tiffany Green) (1976)
P 007 Tiffany Yellow (1976)

These hand-painted patterns resulted from a combination of various items from the two previous Studio Potter groups. The oval platters and shorter six-cup coffee pot of the first group, and the coupe shape flatware and tall cup of the second were included. All other items, common shapes to both groups, were unchanged. Geranium, however, utilized the tall coffee pot in lieu of the shorter one.

Geranium
Hand painted California Geranium with red and orange petals and natural multigreen leaves. The accessories all decorated and accented with red and orange blossoms beautifully casual.

Geranium:
1977 brochure.

135

Pomegranate
The luscious exotic pomegranate, bursting ripe. Hand painted on a large coupe plate. Brownish orange, yellows, greens, and earth tones with speckled background. Very smart, casual elegance.

Pomegranate:
1977 brochure.

Tiffany: 1977 brochure.

Tiffany
A rich, hand-painted grouping of fruits and foliage in the distinctive, brilliant Tiffany glass style. Vibrant colors... blue, yellow and mauve, accented with glazier's green hollow ware set a charming table... Green banded... with green accessories...

Tiffany Yellow
Hand painted fruits and leaves in glazier's greens, blues, mauve, yellows. Light and alive in Poppytrail's design version of famous Tiffany style... Yellow banded... with yellow accessories...

P 002 Geranium, P 005 Pomegranate, P 006 Tiffany, P 007 Tiffany Yellow

No.	Item	Price		No.	Item	Price
010	Cup, 7 oz.	$7 – 8		190	Creamer, 11 oz.	$16 – 18
020	Saucer, 6¼"	$2 – 3		210	Fruit, 5½"	$8 – 9
030	Bread & Butter, 6⅞"	$5 – 6		230	Gravy, 1 pt.	$22 – 25
040	Salad Plate, 8"	$7 – 8		290	Vegetable, div., med., rnd., 9"	$25 – 30
060	Dinner Plate, 10¾"	$9 – 10		330	Salt	$8 – 9
070	Soup, 7¼"	$12 – 13		340	Pepper	$8 – 9
080	Vegetable, sm., rnd., 8¼"	$20 – 22		400	Coffee Pot & Lid, 6 cup (except P 002 Geranium)	$50 – 55
130	Butter & Lid	$30 – 35		420	Cereal, 6½"	$10 – 11
150	Vegetable, med., rnd., 9"	$22 – 25		700	Teapot & Lid, 4½ cup	$50 – 55
160	Platter, med., oval, 10⅞"	$22 – 25		770	Coffee Server & Lid, tall, 10 cup, (P 002 Geranium only)	$65 – 70
170	Platter, lg., oval, 13¼"	$25 – 30				
180	Sugar & Lid, 11 oz.	$18 – 20				

Studio Potter Shape

Part IV: P 591 California Whitestone (1975)
Fashion Plates
P 592 Red (1976)
P 593 Yellow (1976)
P 594 Green (1976)
P 595 Blue (1976)
P 001 California Brownstone (1976)

California Whitestone represented Metlox's ultimate gourmet dinnerware pattern, a solid white amalgamation combining the original Studio Potter set with most of the Artware Division's Gourmetware lines and Vegetable Line items. The resulting enormous pattern included the tall and short coffee pots, the beverage server, a mixing bowl set, three casseroles, two lasagna servers, three tureens, and six vegetable canisters, as well as numerous dinnerware items and food serving accessories. The Fashion Plates, open stock dinner plates with a white rim surrounding a red, yellow, green, or blue center, were specifically offered to add splashes of color to California Whitestone.

California Brownstone (aka Coco/Blanc) was a condensed chocolate and white version of Whitestone minus the Vegetable Line items. Individual pieces were either solid brown, solid white, or a combination of the two.

California Whitestone:
1977 brochure.

California Whitestone
A. Cabbage tureen set. B. Coffee server.
C. Oval baker. D. Small platter. E. Large platter.
F. Lasagna server. G. Beverage urn. H. Casserole dish with lid.
Be sure to ask your dealer to show you all of the versatile and appealing pieces in the California Whitestone line.

California Whitestone: Metlox brochure.

California Whitestone
Beautiful, versatile white, dramatic on bold colors... smart on patterned cloths, elegant or casual, as you please. Handsome, gourmet accessories create a stunning buffet. Ideal for oven-to-table service. Safe in freezer, dishwasher, oven, microwave.

P 591 California Whitestone

010	Cup, 7 oz.	$7 – 8
020	Saucer, 6"	$2 – 3
030	Bread & Butter, 6½"	$5 – 6
040	Salad Plate, 7¾".	$7 – 8
060	Dinner Plate, 10½"	$9 – 10
070	Soup, 7¼"	$12 – 13
100	Salad Bowl, 12⅛".	$35 – 40
101	Mixing Bowl, sm.	$20 – 25
102	Mixing Bowl, med.	$25 – 30
103	Mixing Bowl, lg.	$30 – 35
120	Individual Soup Server & Lid, 12 oz.	$20 – 22
121	Individual Soup Server, No Lid, 12 oz.	$12 – 14
130	Butter & Lid	$30 – 35
150	Vegetable, med., rnd., 9"	$22 – 25
160	Platter, med., oval, 10⅞"	$22 – 25
170	Platter, lg., oval, 13⅛"	$25 – 30
180	Sugar & Lid, 11 oz.	$18 – 20
190	Creamer, 11 oz.	$16 – 18
210	Fruit, 5½"	$8 – 9
230	Gravy, 1 pt.	$22 – 25
240	Platter, sm., oval, 9⅝"	$20 – 22
300	Buffet Server, rnd., 13¼"	$30 – 35
330	Salt, sm.	$8 – 9
331	Salt, lg.	$14 – 15
340	Pepper, sm.	$8 – 9
341	Pepper, lg.	$14 – 15
380	Individual Baker, 8⅜"	$18 – 20
385	Au Gratin, 9⅜"	$20 – 22
387	Quiche Server, 10½"	$30 – 32
400	Coffee Pot & Lid, 6 cup	$50 – 55
420	Cereal, 6½"	$10 – 11
450	Canister & Lid, 2 qt.	$40 – 45

480	Soup Tureen & Lid W/H, 5 qt.	$55 – 60
490	Soup Tureen Ladle, 11"	$18 – 20
620	Casserole & Lid W/H, 2 qt.	$40 – 45
630	Oval Baker, 10¾"	$25 – 30
640	Casserole & Lid W/H, 4 qt.	$50 – 55
660	Casserole & Lid W/H, 6 qt.	$60 – 65
700	Teapot & Lid, 4½ cup	$50 – 55
760	Mug, 10 oz.	$14 – 15
770	Coffee Server & Lid, tall, 10 cup	$65 – 70
780	Lasagna Server W/H, lg., 15¾ x 10½ x 2⅝".	$40 – 45
781	Lasagna Server W/H, med., 13 x 8 x 2⅝"	$35 – 40
809	Beverage Server Urn, Lid & Warmer, 18 cup	$85 – 95

Vegetable Line & Serving Accessory Additions

050	Artichoke Plate, 9⅞"	$30 – 35
080	Cabbage Bowl, 8"	$14 – 16
300	Leaf Buffet Plate, 11"	$28 – 30
386	Asparagus Plate, 8½ x 4"	$25 – 28
440	Corn Canister & Lid, 2½ qt.	$70 – 80
450	Squash Canister & Lid, 2½ qt.	$120 – 140
450	Broccoli Canister & Lid, 1½ qt.	$95 – 110
460	Eggplant Canister & Lid, 1¼ qt.	$100 – 120
470	Pepper Canister & Lid, 1½ pt.	$80 – 100
470	Artichoke Sauce Server & Lid, 1½ pt.	$45 – 50
480	Tomato Tureen & Lid, 3 qt.	$75 – 85
480	Cabbage Tureen & Lid, 3 qt.	$95 – 105
490	Cabbage Tureen Ladle, 11"	$18 – 20
500	Individual Corn Server, 11"	$15 – 16
740	Shell Chip & Dip, 12½"	$30 – 35

California Brownstone

Chocolate and white. An interplay of brown and white with all the style smartness that allows clever tabletop settings. Talk about cook and serve, California Brownstone has six quart casseroles, oven bakers, salad bowls, au gratins — over 30 open stock accessories. Safe in oven — freezer — microwave ovens.

California Brownstone: 1979 brochure.

Fashion Plates

Dinnerplates of sparkling bright red, yellow, green or blue centers with white rims. They mix or match with over 30 Whitestone accessories. Start with basic white and mix with the color or colors you like for fashion plate table top.

Fashion Plates

060	Dinner Plate, 10½"	$10 – 11

P 001 California Brownstone (aka Coco/Blanc)

(1) Brown   (2) White   (3) Brown/White   (4) Brown Bottom/White Lid

010	Cup, 7 oz..	(2)	$7 – 8	
020	Saucer, 6"	(1)	$2 – 3	
040	Salad Plate, 7¾"	(3)	$7 – 8	
060	Dinner Plate, 10½"	(3)	$9 – 10	
070	Soup, 7¼"	(1)	$12 – 13	
100	Salad Bowl, 12⅛"	(1)	$35 – 40	
130	Butter & Lid	(4)	$30 – 35	
150	Vegetable, med., rnd., 9"	(1)	$22 – 25	
160	Platter, med., oval, 10⅞".. . . .	(3)	$22 – 25	
170	Platter, lg., oval, 13⅛"	(3)	$25 – 30	
180	Sugar & Lid, 11 oz..	(4)	$18 – 20	
190	Creamer, 11 oz.	(2)	$16 – 18	
210	Fruit, 5½"	(1)	$8 – 9	
230	Gravy, 1 pt..	(1)	$22 – 25	
240	Platter, sm., oval, 9⅝"	(3)	$20 – 22	
330	Salt.	(2)	$8 – 9	
340	Pepper	(1)	$8 – 9	
385	Au Gratin, 9⅜"	(1)	$20 – 22	
400	Coffee Pot & Lid, 6 cup	(4)	$50 – 55	
420	Cereal, 6½"	(1)	$10 – 11	
480	Soup Tureen & Lid W/H, 5 qt.. . .	(4)	$55 – 60	
490	Soup Tureen Ladle, 11"	(2)	$18 – 20	
620	Casserole & Lid W/H, 2 qt. . . .	(4)	$40 – 45	
640	Casserole & Lid W/H, 4 qt. . . .	(4)	$50 – 55	
660	Casserole & Lid W/H, 6 qt. . . .	(4)	$60 – 65	
700	Teapot & Lid, 4½ cup	(4)	$50 – 55	
760	Mug, 10 oz.	(1)	$14 – 15	
770	Coffee Server & Lid, tall, 10 cup	(4)	$65 – 70	
780	Lasagna Server W/H, lg., 15¾ x 10½ x 2⅝"	(1)	$40 – 45	
781	Lasagna Server W/H, med., 13 x 8 x 2⅝"	(1)	$35 – 40	

Studio Potter Shape

Part V: P 008 Primary Red (1977)
P 010 Primary Blue (1977)
P 022 Primary Blue Daisies (1978)
P 024 Primary Red Daisies (1978)
P 025 Primary Yellow (1978)
P 026 Primary Yellow Daisies (1978)

Primary Yellow, Red & Blue

The Primary patterns were gourmet dinnerware sets similar in composition to California Brownstone, i.e. lacking the Vegetable Line items but including most of the pieces from the Gourmetware lines. The slightly larger coupe shape flatware with narrow rim and faint grooves replaced the wide rim and pronounced groove styling of Whitestone and Brownstone. A red, blue, or yellow color band decorated the rim of each item. Many of the accessories had an additional color band. Each Daisies pattern featured an abstract floral design on the plates, cups, and platters.

Primary Red:
cup and saucer,
dinner plate, and
salad plate.

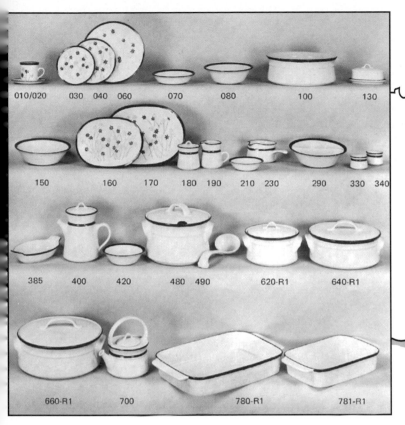

Primary Red, Primary Blue, Primary Yellow A narrow color border... accented by a brown rim edging. Smartly simple for today's informal entertaining. Big, deep cups keep liquids warm... gourmet-type baking-serving casseroles and lasagna dishes, au gratin bakers and a handsome, covered tureen with matching ladle, all are ideal for oven-to-table service... Safe in freezer, dishwasher, Microwave oven.

Primary Red Daisies: 1979 brochure. Same design as Primary Red, Blue, and Yellow with the addition of an abstract daisy pattern on the plates, cup, and platters.

P 008 Primary Red, P 010 Primary Blue, P 022 Primary Blue Daisies, P 024 Primary Red Daisies, P 025 Primary Yellow, P 026 Primary Yellow Daisies

No.	Item	Price		No.	Item	Price
010	Cup, 7 oz.	$7 – 8		290	Vegetable, div., med., rnd., 9"	$25 – 30
020	Saucer, 6¼"	$2 – 3		330	Salt	$8 – 9
030	Bread & Butter, 6⅞"	$5 – 6		340	Pepper	$8 – 9
040	Salad Plate, 8"	$7 – 8		385	Au Gratin, 9⅜"	$20 – 22
060	Dinner Plate, 10¾"	$9 – 10		400	Coffee Pot & Lid, 6 cup	$50 – 55
070	Soup, 7¼"	$12 – 13		420	Cereal, 6½"	$10 – 11
080	Vegetable, sm., rnd., 8¼"	$20 – 22		480	Soup Tureen & Lid W/H, 5 qt.	$55 – 60
100	Salad Bowl, 12⅛"	$35 – 40		490	Soup Tureen Ladle, 11"	$18 – 20
130	Butter & Lid	$30 – 35		620	Casserole & Lid W/H, 2 qt.	$40 – 45
150	Vegetable, med., rnd., 9"	$22 – 25		640	Casserole & Lid W/H, 4 qt.	$50 – 55
160	Platter, med., oval, 10⅞"	$22 – 25		660	Casserole & Lid W/H, 6 qt.	$60 – 65
170	Platter, lg., oval, 13¼"	$25 – 30		700	Teapot & Lid, 4½ cup	$50 – 55
180	Sugar & Lid, 11 oz.	$18 – 20		780	Lasagna Server W/H, lg., 15¾ x 10½ x 2⅝"	$40 – 45
190	Creamer, 11 oz.	$16 – 18				
210	Fruit, 5½"	$8 – 9		781	Lasagna Server W/H, med., 13 x 8 x 2⅝"	$35 – 40
230	Gravy, 1 pt.	$22 – 25				

Studio Potter Shape

Part VI: Colorstax

P 028 Sand (1978)
P 029 Chocolate (1978)
P 030 Terra Cotta (1978)
P 031 Forest Green (1978)
P 032 Fern Green (1978)
P 033 Midnight Blue (1978)
P 034 Sky Blue (1978)
P 035 Yellow (1978)
P 036 White (1978)
P 061 Cranberry
P 063 Aqua
P 064 Plum (1980)
P 065 Apricot (1980)
P 066 Black (1980)
P 073 Rose (early 1980s)
P 074 Jade (early 1980s)

Colorstax and Colorbands

P 075 Lilac (early 1980s)
P 076 Canary (early 1980s)
P 080 Brick (1984)
P 081 Camel (1984)
P 082 Evergreen (1984)
P 083 Pewter (1984)
P 084 Pumpkin (1984)
P 085 Silver (1984)
P 086 Wheat (1984)
P 088 French Blue

Colorbands
P 044 Sand (1979)
P 045 Chocolate (1979)
P 046 Terra Cotta (1979)
P 047 Forest Green (1979)
P 048 Fern Green (1979)
P 049 Midnight Blue (1979)
P 050 Sky Blue (1979)
P 051 Yellow (1979)
— Cranberry
— Aqua

Metlox's initial dinnerware patterns, produced during the Prouty years from 1932 through the early 1940s, were popular solid color sets with satin-matte or high-gloss glazes that paralleled similar lines of Gladding-McBean, Bauer, Catalina Island, and other California potteries. After World War II solid patterns lost their appeal to consumers. Evan K. Shaw always felt a special affinity for solid color dinnerware because it highlighted shapes without the distraction of designs. He usually was dissuaded from producing these patterns by his design department and sales staff who felt solid colors were dated and unappealing. During the 1950s and 60s Metlox's few solid color patterns were either moderate successes or failures. Therefore, Metlox typically relegated solid colors to accent pieces in patterns with designs or two-tone patterns. Consumer taste began to change during the 1970s. With the growing popularity of Homer Laughlin's Fiesta and Bauer's Ring series among collectors, Shaw was convinced circumstances were ideal for introducing a new series featuring solid colors. The result was Colorstax.

Studio Potter provided the perfect shape for Colorstax. The contours of the wide, elevated rim surrounding a lower center — and especially the circular groove pattern — were enhanced by solid colors and a high-gloss glaze without the addition of a design. The original Studio Potter items were used as they were except for a redesigned, larger soup bowl. Additions followed the same styling. Since Colorstax did not require detailed, time-consuming hand painting, production costs were substantially lowered and the series could be retailed relatively inexpensively.

The development of Colorstax was an intricate evolutionary process. The original 1978 patterns, consisting of only 20 items, were interesting both for what was included (unusual items such as a three-piece mixing bowl set, large salt and pepper, a canister and lid, individual baker, au gratin, and corn server), as well as what was left out (standard Metlox items such as a cup, bread and butter plate, butter dish, medium platter, fruit bowl, gravy, coffee pot, and teapot). The nine-ounce mug instead of a cup was intended for the saucer. With the exception of the coffee pot and teapot, by 1980 the above standard items plus a candlestick were added. In fact, the coffee pot and the teapot were listed only once in a 1984 brochure. Early 1980s leaflets advertised the following Artware Division Gourmetware line items available in white only as part of Colorstax: 2-quart, 4-quart, and 6-quart covered casseroles, large and medium lasagna servers, and a 5-quart covered tureen and ladle. Curiously, during the early 1980s as the number of available colors increased, the number of items slightly decreased. In one leaflet only 17 items constituted the pattern. The mixing bowl set, large salt and pepper, canister, candlestick, baker, and corn server were discontinued during this period. After 1985 the number of Colorstax items was gradually increased. Thirty-two items were offered in 1987 including a demitasse cup and saucer, a large cup and saucer, the Carousel mug in addition to the Colorstax mug, a barbecue plate, a soup bowl, a salad bowl, two buffet plates, a soup tureen and ladle, and the candlestick. By 1988 forty-five items were listed. Important additions were the large and extra large platters, three flower pots with saucers, two casseroles, an oval baker, three banana leaves (adapted from Lotus), and the reappearance of the mixing bowl set.

The first nine colors were released in 1978. As the popularity of Colorstax grew, John Johnson's glaze department developed unusual variant shades of primary colors for the series. A "true" red, green, and blue — commonplace dinnerware colors — were avoided in favor of hues such as cranberry, brick, evergreen, aqua, rose, and apricot. Each color was assigned its own pattern number. Colors were discontinued if sales were poor. Most of the Colorstax colors also decorated the Lotus dinnerware series.

Colorbands were open stock white dinner and salad plates with two separate bands of color on the edge and the incline of the wide rim. When combined with Colorstax, they provided a dramatic contrast in white. Produced only in the first ten colors (logically skipping white), they were discontinued by 1984.

Since Colorstax items and colors were added and dropped at various times throughout its 12-year history, it is possible that the complete set in one single color may have been produced in only a few of the color choices. New additions were frequently introduced in only some of the currently available colors. Of the original colors, sky blue, yellow, midnight blue, sand, and white were continually produced from 1978 to 1989. Other long-run colors were aqua, rose, apricot, canary, jade, lilac, black, and cranberry. P 080 through P 086 were "active" colors for a short time only. Forest green was discontinued almost immediately; french blue was a late color addition. Therefore, although Colorstax was not conceived or merchandised as a series of "mix and match" solid colors, collectors wishing to acquire the entire set should consider this an option. Seemingly countless unusual color combinations of contrasting or blending shades offer a variety of beautiful possibilities.

Colorstax was Metlox's bestselling product throughout the 1980s. Its popularity reflected the buying public's renewed interest in solid color dinnerware and justified Evan K. Shaw's decision to produce it. Together with Lotus and many successful cookie jars, Colorstax sustained the company economically until its close in 1989.

Colorstax:
Metlox brochure.

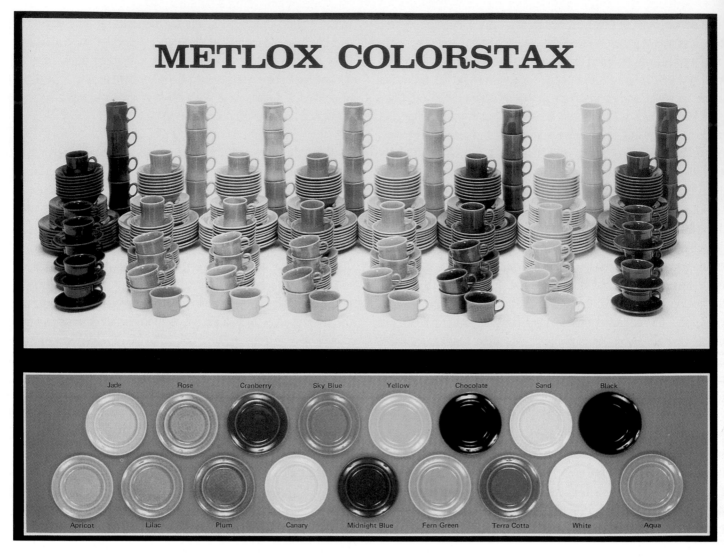

Colorstax: Metlox brochure.

Colorstax: large cups and saucers.

Colorstax: large cup,
fruit bowl, and Colorstax mug.

Colorstax: sugar and lid, dinner plate, and creamer.

Colorstax: large cup, large platter, and Colorstax mug.

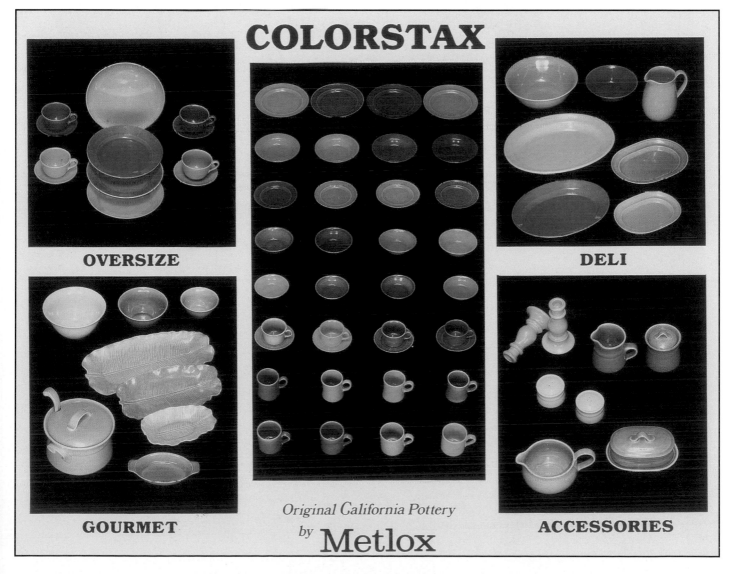

Colorstax: Metlox brochure.

Metlox Colorstax - The In Look

Solid colors are
clicking like never before.
Metlox offers nine colors on timeless
shapes turned in the manner of the studio potter. Colors
are sand, chocolate, terra cotta, yellow, fern green, forest green, sky blue,
white and midnight blue. Priced to retail in volume. Safe in dishwasher, oven and
microwave. (Not shown: Creamer, Sugar and Lid, Lg. Platter, Med. Vegetable in all colors.
2qt., 4qt., 6qt. covered casseroles, large and medium lasagnas, individual au gratins, 5qt. tureen, lid and ladle. Available in white only.)

Metlox Colorbands - New

METLOX POTTERIES   P.O. Box 8, Manhattan Beach, California 90266

Colorstax and Colorbands: Metlox brochure.

Colorstax

010	Cup, 7 oz.		$8 – 9	102	Mixing Bowl, med., 44 oz.	$30 – 35
011	Cup, lg., 16 oz.		$18 – 20	103	Mixing Bowl, lg., 84 oz.	$35 – 40
016	Cup, demitasse, 5 oz.		$16 – 18	130	Butter & Lid	$35 – 40
017	Saucer, demitasse		$3 – 4	150	Vegetable, med., rnd., 9"	$25 – 30
020	Saucer, 6"		$2 – 3	160	Platter, med., oval, 10⅞".	$25 – 30
021	Saucer, lg., 7"		$4 – 5	170	Platter, lg., oval, 13⅛"	$30 – 35
030	Bread & Butter, 6½"		$6 – 7	180	Sugar & Lid, 11 oz.	$20 – 22
040	Salad Plate, 7¾"		$8 – 9	190	Creamer, 11 oz.	$18 – 20
060	Dinner Plate, 10½"		$11 – 12	210	Fruit, 5½"	$9 – 10
061	BBQ Plate, 3-part, 11"		$20 – 22	230	Gravy, 1 pt.	$25 – 28
070	Soup, 8½"		$14 – 16	250	Platter, serving, lg., 16"	$40 – 45
100	Salad Bowl, 13"		$40 – 45	300	Buffet Plate, rim, 12"	$35 – 40
101	Mixing Bowl, sm., 16 oz.		$25 – 30	301	Buffet Plate, coupe, 13"	$35 – 40

(continued)

330	Salt, sm.	$9 – 10	620	Casserole & Lid, 2 qt.	$45 – 50
331	Salt, lg.	$16 – 18	700	Teapot & Lid, 4½ cup	$55 – 60
340	Pepper, sm.	$9 – 10	760	Mug, 9 oz. (Colorstax)	$16 – 18
341	Pepper, lg.	$16 – 18	761	Mug, 9 oz. (Carousel)	$14 – 15
360	Candlestick	$22 – 25	782	Oval Baker, 13"	$35 – 40
370	Water Pitcher, 2 qt.	$45 – 50	785	Platter, serving, ex. lg., 19"	$50 – 55
380	Individual Baker, rnd., 8⅜"	$20 – 22	815	Banana Leaf, 11"	$35 – 40
385	Au Gratin, oval, 9⅜"	$22 – 25	816	Banana Leaf, 15"	$45 – 50
400	Coffee Pot & Lid, 6 cup	$55 – 60	817	Banana Leaf, 20"	$55 – 60
420	Cereal, 6½"	$11 – 12			
450	Canister & Lid, 2 qt.	$45 – 50			
480	Soup Tureen & Lid, 5 qt.	$60 – 65			

These gourmet items were sold as accessories to Colorstax in the early 1980s. They were available in white only.

490	Soup Tureen Ladle	$20 – 22	480	Soup Tureen & Lid, 5 qt.	$55 – 60
500	Individual Corn Server	$16 – 18	490	Soup Tureen Ladle	$18 – 20
560	6" Flower Pot	$18 – 20	620	Casserole & Lid, 2 qt.	$40 – 45
561	Saucer for 6" and 7" Flower Pots	$7 – 8	640	Casserole & Lid, 4 qt.	$50 – 55
570	7" Flower Pot	$20 – 22	660	Casserole & Lid, 6 qt.	$60 – 65
580	8" Flower Pot	$22 – 25	780	Lasagna Server, lg.	$40 – 45
581	Saucer for 8" Flower Pot	$9 – 10	781	Lasagna Server, med.	$35 – 40
610	Casserole & Lid, 1 qt.	$35 – 40			

Colorbands

040	Salad Plate, 7¾"	$8 – 9	060	Dinner Plate, 10½"	$11 – 12

Studio Potter Shape

These four small sets on the redesigned Studio Potter shape were composed of place setting and completer set items plus a coffee pot. Each realistic botanical hand painting covered the entire surface of the dinner plate. The following color descriptions appeared in the Metlox files: Silver Dollar (brown), Dill (blue), Eucalyptus (green), and Bottle Brush (rust).

Part VII: Botanical Collection
   P 053 Silver Dollar (1979)
   P 054 Dill (1979)
   P 055 Eucalyptus (1979)
   P 056 Bottle Brush (1979)

Botanical Collection
P 053 Silver Dollar, P 054 Dill, P 055 Eucalyptus, P 056 Bottle Brush

010	Cup, 7 oz.	$6 – 7	170	Platter, lg., oval, 13¼"	$22 – 25
020	Saucer, 6¼"	$2 – 3	180	Sugar & Lid, 11 oz.	$16 – 18
040	Salad Plate, 8"	$6 – 7	190	Creamer, 11 oz.	$14 – 16
060	Dinner Plate, 10¾"	$8 – 9	400	Coffee Pot & Lid, 6 cup	$45 – 50
150	Vegetable, med., rnd., 9"	$20 – 22	420	Cereal, 6½"	$9 – 10

Natural Shape

California Naturals Group
   P 013 Strawflower (1977)
   P 014 Calico (1977)
   P 015 Macramé (1977)
   P 016 Wildflower (1977)
   P 017 William (1977)
P 018 Iris (1978)
P 020 Rhythm (1978)
P 021 Blues (1978)
P 023 Marguerite (1978)

The Natural shape, used for a limited time in 1977 – 78, appeared in nine patterns. The release of these patterns coincided with the six Primary patterns, another group of gourmet dinnerware sets, on the redesigned Studio Potter shape. Although sometimes incorrectly considered as just a variation of the Primary patterns, the Natural shape was quite distinctive and separate. Flatware were coupe shapes with a barely noticeable rim. The basic contours of serving pieces were more rounded and tapered rather than vertical and cylindrical. Also, the Natural patterns offered a different assortment of gourmetware items.

The Natural patterns were released in two groups. California Naturals Group (1977) consisted of five gourmet dinnerware patterns. Strawflower, Calico, Macramé, and Wildflower decorated only the flatware with a pattern design. All other items were brown/white combinations or brown solids. William was two-tone brown and white without a design. Of the four additional patterns introduced in 1978, Rhythm, Blues, and Marguerite were gourmet patterns while the very lovely Iris consisted of dinnerware pieces only. Rhythm featured two brown abstract flower stem and bud designs with brown bands on a white background. Blues used the same pattern as a white design on a blue background. Marguerite was graced with a dainty floral design.

Strawflower:
1977 brochure.

Strawflower: 1977 brochure.

Strawflower
Delicate, hand-painted flowers and slender stems, gracefully arranged in a charming pattern of red, orange and green, coordinated with serving accessories in warm browns, with creamy white interiors to make food and drink extra appetizing. Versatile casseroles, oval bakers, two sizes of platters for gourmet cooking and serving. Ideal for oven-to-table service. Safe in freezer, dishwasher, oven, microwave.

Calico
Fresh as a country garden! Quaint, colorful flowerets in tints of orange and rust, with brown stems and leaves coordinated with serving accessories in warm browns, with creamy white interiors . . .

Calico: 1977 brochure.

Macramé

A classic macramé design in tones of orange, rust and brown, coordinated with serving accessories in warm browns, with creamy white interiors . . .

Macramé: 1977 brochure.

Wildflower

A sunny circlet of hand-painted wildflowers decorates the traditional, coupe shape plates coordinated with serving accessories in warm browns, with creamy white interiors . . .

Wildflower: 1977 brochure.

Iris: cup and saucer, dinner plate, and salad plate.

California Naturals Group
P 013 Strawflower, P 014 Calico, P 015 Macramé, P 016 Wildflower, P 017 William

(1) White, Banded Brown   (2) Brown Glaze   (3) Decorated Pattern
(4) Two-Tone: Brown Out/White In   (5) Brown Lid w/White Accented Knob

010	Cup, 7 oz.	(4)	$6 – 7
020	Saucer, 6".	(1)	$2 – 3
030	Bread & Butter, 6⅜"	(3)	$4 – 5
040	Salad Plate, 8"	(3)	$6 – 7
060	Dinner Plate, 10⅛"	(3)	$8 – 9
070	Soup, 6¾"	(4)	$10 – 11
120	Individual Soup Server/Baker & Lid, 10 oz.	(4/5)	$18 – 20
121	Individual Soup Server/Baker, No Lid, 10 oz.	(4)	$10 – 12
130	Butter & Lid.	(1/5)	$28 – 30
150	Vegetable, med., rnd., 1 qt.	(4)	$20 – 22
160	Platter, med., oval, 11"	(3)	$20 – 22
170	Platter, lg., oval, 13"	(3)	$22 – 25
180	Sugar & Lid	(2/5)	$16 – 18
190	Creamer	(4)	$14 – 16
210	Fruit, 5¼"	(4)	$7 – 8
230	Gravy, 1 pt.	(4)	$20 – 22
330	Salt	(2)	$8 – 9
340	Pepper	(2)	$8 – 9
385	Au Gratin, 10½"	(4)	$20 – 22
400	Coffee Pot & Lid, 8 cup	(2/5)	$45 – 50
420	Cereal, 6¾"	(4)	$9 – 10
600	Casserole & Lid, 1 qt.	(4/5)	$30 – 35
610	Casserole & Lid, 2 qt.	(4/5)	$35 – 40
630	Oval Baker, 1 qt.	(4)	$25 – 30
631	Oval Baker, 2 qt.	(4)	$30 – 35
640	Casserole & Lid, 3½ qt.	(4/5)	$40 – 45
700	Teapot & Lid, 4½ cup	(2/5)	$45 – 50

P 018 Iris, P 020 Rhythm, P 021 Blues, P 023 Marguerite
Add 20% for P 018 Iris

010	Cup, 7 oz.	$6 – 7
020	Saucer, 6".	$2 – 3
030	Bread & Butter, 6⅜"	$4 – 5
040	Salad Plate, 8"	$6 – 7
060	Dinner Plate, 10⅛"	$8 – 9
070	Soup, 6¾"	$10 – 11
130	Butter & Lid	$28 – 30
150	Vegetable, med., rnd, 1 qt.	$20 – 22
160	Platter, med., oval, 11"	$20 – 22
170	Platter, lg., oval, 13"	$22 – 25
180	Sugar & Lid	$16 – 18
190	Creamer	$14 – 16
210	Fruit, 5¼"	$7 – 8
230	Gravy, 1 pt.	$20 – 22
330	Salt	$8 – 9
340	Pepper	$8 – 9
400	Coffee Pot & Lid, 8 cup	$45 – 50
420	Cereal, 6¾"	$9 – 10
700	Teapot & Lid, 4½ cup	$45 – 50

P 020 Rhythm, P 021 Blues Additions

600	Casserole & Lid, 1 qt.	$30 – 35
610	Casserole & Lid, 2 qt.	$35 – 40
630	Oval Baker, 1 qt.	$25 – 30
631	Oval Baker, 2 qt.	$30 – 35
640	Casserole & Lid, 3½ qt.	$40 – 45

P 023 Marguerite Additions

120	Individual Soup Server/Baker & Lid, 10 oz.	$18 – 20
121	Individual Soup Server/Baker, No Lid, 10 oz.	$10 – 12
385	Au Gratin, 10½"	$20 – 22
600	Casserole & Lid, 1 qt.	$30 – 35
610	Casserole & Lid, 2 qt.	$35 – 40
630	Oval Baker, 1 qt.	$25 – 30
631	Oval Baker, 2 qt.	$30 – 35
640	Casserole & Lid, 3½ qt.	$40 – 45

Lotus Shape

Lotus (First Series)
- P 146 White (1974)
- P 147 Yellow (1974)
- P 148 Lime (1974)
- P 149 Pink (1974)

Lotus (Second Series)
- P 150 White (1979)
- P 151 Sand (1979)
- P 152 Chocolate (1979)
- P 153 Yellow (1979)
- P 154 Apricot (1979)
- P 155 Black (1979)
- P 156 Grey (1979)
- P 157 Plum (1979)

- P 158 Blue (1979)
- P 159 Green (1979)
- P 162 Cranberry (1979)
- P 166 Aqua (early 1980s)
- P 175 Rose (early 1980s)
- P 178 Jade (early 1980s)
- P 179 Lilac (early 1980s)
- P 182 Canary (early 1980s)
- P 183 Brick (1984)
- P 184 Camel (1984)
- P 189 Chocolate (1984)
- P 191 Evergreen (1984)
- P 192 Midnight Blue (1984)
- P 193 Pewter (1984)
- P 194 Pumpkin (1984)

- P 195 Silver (1984)
- P 196 Wheat (1984)

Decorated Lotus
- P 185 Concord (early 1980s)
- P 186 Wisteria (early 1980s)
- P 187 Fuchsia (early 1980s)
- P 188 Honeysuckle (early 1980s)

The evolution of Lotus was a singular process unparalleled by the development of any other Metlox dinnerware pattern. It demonstrated Evan K. Shaw's tenacious support of a pattern he greatly admired. Although exact names, dates, and places have been forgotten, various company employees verified the following account of Shaw's discovery of Lotus. In the early 1970s Shaw attended a dinner party where the guests were served on a dinnerware pattern based on lotus leaf shapes. Shaw was engrossed by the shapes, which reminded him of the Artware Division's earlier, popular Leaves of Enchantment line. When Shaw learned the pattern was produced by a local backyard potter, he contacted the ceramicist who agreed to sell Metlox the right to produce 15 items as well as their molds, blocks, and cases. Shaw also gave the potter a 30-day consulting contract. Bob Chandler was assigned the task of converting the designs from a hand-cast to an automated, mass-produced line which necessitated the redesigning of all of the items.

The First Series of Lotus was introduced in 1974 in four colors — white, yellow, lime, and pink — and consisted of 16 items with special item numbers. The four banana leaves, then available only in white, were adaptations from Allen and Shaw's Leaves of Enchantment line. Evan K. Shaw, who always felt a deep appreciation for solid color dinnerware, was disappointed but undeterred when the unusual, beautiful patterns were not commercially successful. The patterns, temporarily withdrawn after a year, were released again in 1977. When sales once more were poor, Shaw's enthusiasm for Lotus still remained unchanged. He was convinced the designs were noteworthy; only the timing was premature.

After the initial success of the solid tone Colorstax dinnerware series in 1978, Shaw believed solid colors were finally becoming popular again and Metlox needed Lotus as an elegant, more formal series to complement Colorstax. The Second Series, released in 1979, included only three new items; however, the color selection was increased from four shades to 11. Each color was given a new pattern number and the regular item numbering system was adopted. Throughout the early 1980s, as sales improved dramatically, the number of items and colors was expanded.

The unique sculptured styling of Lotus closely resembled a tropical waterlily leaf, featuring pronounced, asymmetrical veins and irregular, crimped edges. One perplexing problem was how to indicate an easy method of stacking the unusually shaped flatware and bowls. The solution was to include one straight vein in the same place on each item which acted as a stacking guide. The exteriors of serving pieces displayed carved leaf designs. The four banana leaves, shell chip and dip, and individual shell server, although based on different motifs, blended harmoniously with the Lotus items. The four Decorated Lotus patterns, with hand-painted designs on a white background, offered a contrast to the solid colors.

Item selection increased from 19 in 1979 to 30 in 1980. Bob Chandler designed and modeled all new additions. Shortly after 1980, the chop plate, 24" banana leaf, and both tier trays were deleted. However, several new pieces, including the Decorated Lotus dinner plate and salad plate, were added until the series reached a peak selection of 36 items in 1984. The series was condensed drastically

to 23 pieces in 1985, and thereafter remained relatively constant with no new additions. Several serving pieces were discontinued at this time, including the footed dessert, relish server/gravy stand, coffee pot, soup tureen and ladle, casserole and lid, individual shell server, and teapot.

Metlox expanded the active color selection from the initial ten colors in 1979 to a maximum of 23 in 1984. Most of the shades duplicated those of Colorstax, offering a variety of special, non-primary colors created by John Johnson. After 1984 the number of active colors gradually dwindled. From 1979 to 1989 only white, sand, apricot, and cranberry were manufactured continually. Yellow, black, plum, blue, green, aqua, rose, jade, lilac, canary, and midnight blue also were produced for a long period. P 152 Chocolate was dropped in 1980, then reappeared for one year in 1984 as P 189. Grey was produced only in 1979. The other colors had short production runs. Decorated Lotus appeared from the early 1980s until 1985.

Most or all of the entire set was produced in many Lotus colors. The peak years for color choice and item selection coincided in 1984. In most years all currently available items were produced in every active color. Still, the "mix and match" possibilities of Lotus, offering a myriad of blending and contrasting solid tones, should be considered by collectors.

Lotus: cups and saucers,
dinner plate,
and salad plate.

Lotus: cereal bowl, salad plates, and mug.

Lotus: two quart
casserole and lid.

Lotus: salad bowl.

Lotus: butter and lid.

Lotus (First Series): Metlox brochure.

Lotus: large platter.

> *Lotus*
> *Delicately sculptured leaf and flower motifs create a dinnerware of graceful elegance. Super size serving pieces set a sumptuous table in the color of your choice . . .*

Lotus (First Series)

The special item numbers for this line are used below. Some brochure measurements are slightly different from those of the Second Series. The four banana leaf pieces were made only in white.

010	Cup, 7 oz.	$9 – 10
015	Saucer, 6¼"	$4 – 5
020	Bread & Butter, 6"	$7 – 8
025	Salad Plate, 8½"	$9 – 10
030	Dinner Plate, 11"	$12 – 13
035	Buffet Plate, lg., 12½"	$40 – 45
040	Platter, 15"	$50 – 55
045	Chop Plate, 17"	$65 – 70
055	Bowl, 8"	$30 – 35
060	Vegetable Bowl	$40 – 45
075	Salad Bowl, 13½"	$75 – 80
080	Crescent Salad, 8"	$30 – 32
146145	Banana Leaf, 11"	$35 – 40
146150	Banana Leaf, 15"	$45 – 50
146155	Banana Leaf, 20"	$55 – 60
146160	Banana Leaf, 24"	$70 – 75

Lotus (Second Series): Metlox brochure.

Lotus: Metlox brochure.

Lotus (Second Series)

It is not absolutely certain that every piece was produced in each color.

010	Cup, 7 oz.	$9 – 10
016	Demitasse Cup	$20 – 22
020	Saucer, 6"	$4 – 5
[017] 026	Demitasse Saucer	$6 – 8
030	Bread & Butter, 6¼"	$7 – 8
040	Salad Plate, 8"	$9 – 10
060	Dinner Plate, 10½".	$12 – 13
080	Vegetable, sm., 8"	$30 – 35
100	Salad Bowl, 13½".	$75 – 80
110	Crescent Salad, 8"	$30 – 32
130	Butter & Lid	$60 – 65
150	Vegetable, med., 10"	$40 – 45
170	Platter, lg., 14½"	$50 – 55
180	Sugar & Lid, 11 oz.	$28 – 30
190	Creamer, 11 oz.	$25 – 28
210	Fruit, 5½".	$11 – 12
230	Gravy.	$30 – 35
250	Chop Plate, ex. lg., 17"	$65 – 70
300	Buffet Plate, lg., 12½"	$40 – 45
321	Dessert, footed, 4 oz.	$30 – 32
330	Salt	$12 – 14
340	Pepper	$12 – 14
390	Relish Server/Gravy Stand	$32 – 35
400	Coffee Pot & Lid, 6 cup	$110 – 120
420	Cereal, 6¾"	$14 – 15
480	Soup Tureen & Lid	$150 – 160
490	Soup Tureen Ladle	$25 – 28
620	Casserole & Lid, 2 qt.	$95 – 100
700	Teapot & Lid, 4½ cup	$110 – 120
740	Shell Chip & Dip	$50 – 55
741	Shell Server, individual	$30 – 35
760	Mug, 7 oz.	$20 – 22
811	One-Tier Tray	$40 – 45
812	Two-Tier Tray	$50 – 55
[151] 815	Banana Leaf, 11"	$35 – 40
[152] 816	Banana Leaf, 15"	$45 – 50
[153] 817	Banana Leaf, 20"	$55 – 60
[154] 818	Banana Leaf, 24"	$70 – 75

NEW COLORS FOR 1984!!

Evergreen • Midnight Blue • Brick • Chocolate • Wheat • Camel • Pewter • Pumpkin • Silver

Rose • Jade • Lilac • Apricot • Canary • Plum • Blue • Sand • Cranberry • White • Aqua • Black • Fern Green • Yellow

Wisteria • Concord • Fuchsia • Honeysuckle

Lotus: Metlox brochure.

Decorated Lotus

040	Salad Plate, 8"..............	$11 – 12
060	Dinner Plate, 10½"..........	$14 – 15

Late Dinnerware

The death of Evan K. Shaw in 1980 signaled the real beginning of Metlox's economic downturn which intensified as the 1980s progressed. Only the steady sales of Colorstax, Lotus, and popular cookie jars kept the company viable on a precarious, seemingly month-to-month basis. Yet, even under increasingly depressing circumstances, Metlox continued to introduce innovative dinnerware patterns indicative of the creativity, dedication, and pride of the design staff and employees. Melinda Avery was very instrumental in this process as she assumed the guiding role of her late father. No new shapes were created during this period; rather, patterns were developed from existing shapes.

Due to the enormous success of Colorstax and Lotus in the early 1980s and the continuing appeal and popularity of solid color dinnerware, Metlox released three new solid color lines in 1985. Each series, consisting of place setting and completer set items, was based on an earlier shape and was hand decorated with Colorstax colors. The three were intended as solid color design alternatives to the studio potter styling of Colorstax and the leaf and flower motif of Lotus.

1942 was designed after the solid color Yorkshire pattern of the Prouty years. The name 1942 alluded to this period since Yorkshire,

first released in 1937, was produced through the early 1940s. 1942 similarly featured an embossed swirl design on rims and exteriors. The cup, sugar, and creamer were altered to reflect a simpler style.

Traditions was based on the elegant American Tradition shape. Except for modifications of the ornateness of the cup, sugar, and creamer, the original designs were retained.

The Traditional shape provided the inspiration for Galaxy. The pattern name was suggested by the raised rings design, reminiscent of galactic rings, that was a feature of the potter's wheel styling of the Traditional shape items. The sugar and creamer were adapted from the 1942 shapes without the swirl design. Galaxy was also produced with smooth surfaces minus the rings. Two distinct series of Galaxy were released. The First Series (1985) was a limited set of nine items with Colorstax colors. In 1988 the Second Series, which added five items, was introduced in four new colors. This series was incorporated as the dinnerware items of California Harvest and offered as solid color dinnerware additions to Pescado. Galaxy items backstamped "The Ivy" were produced for a local Los Angeles restaurant and did not constitute a separate pattern.

By 1987 many of the dwindling number of retailers handling Metlox dinnerware did not wish to carry solid color patterns other than Colorstax and Lotus. Therefore, the company discontinued 1942, Traditions, and Galaxy (First Series) rather than accumulate potentially unsaleable inventories.

California Spatterware (1987) was a short-lived series which utilized 14 Studio Potter shape items featuring color flecks on a

white background. Four patterns, each using a different Colorstax shade, were produced.

It's about time!! Solid-color fashion California pottery.

1942, Traditions, and Galaxy: Metlox brochure.

Late Dinnerware

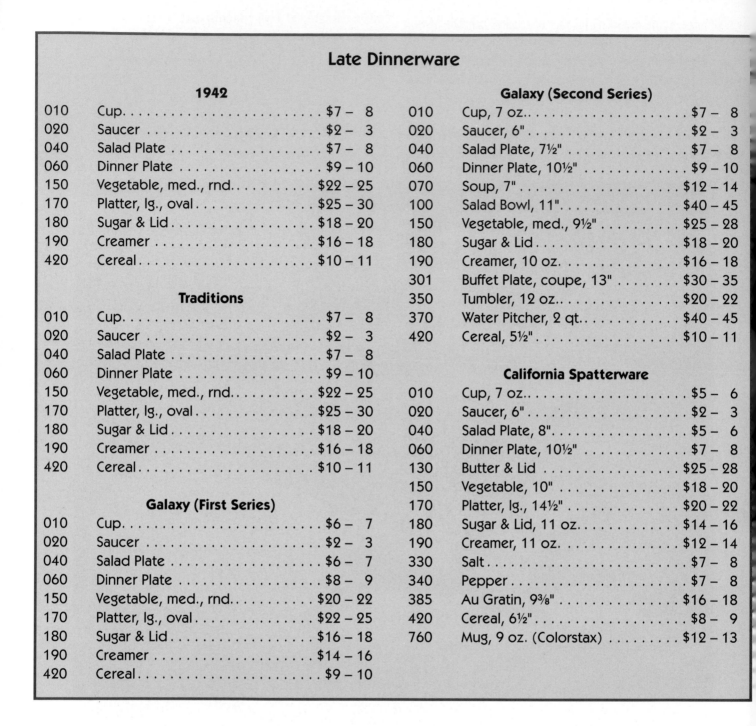

1942

010	Cup	$7 – 8
020	Saucer	$2 – 3
040	Salad Plate	$7 – 8
060	Dinner Plate	$9 – 10
150	Vegetable, med., rnd.	$22 – 25
170	Platter, lg., oval	$25 – 30
180	Sugar & Lid	$18 – 20
190	Creamer	$16 – 18
420	Cereal	$10 – 11

Traditions

010	Cup	$7 – 8
020	Saucer	$2 – 3
040	Salad Plate	$7 – 8
060	Dinner Plate	$9 – 10
150	Vegetable, med., rnd.	$22 – 25
170	Platter, lg., oval	$25 – 30
180	Sugar & Lid	$18 – 20
190	Creamer	$16 – 18
420	Cereal	$10 – 11

Galaxy (First Series)

010	Cup	$6 – 7
020	Saucer	$2 – 3
040	Salad Plate	$6 – 7
060	Dinner Plate	$8 – 9
150	Vegetable, med., rnd.	$20 – 22
170	Platter, lg., oval	$22 – 25
180	Sugar & Lid	$16 – 18
190	Creamer	$14 – 16
420	Cereal	$9 – 10

Galaxy (Second Series)

010	Cup, 7 oz.	$7 – 8
020	Saucer, 6"	$2 – 3
040	Salad Plate, 7½"	$7 – 8
060	Dinner Plate, 10½"	$9 – 10
070	Soup, 7"	$12 – 14
100	Salad Bowl, 11"	$40 – 45
150	Vegetable, med., 9½"	$25 – 28
180	Sugar & Lid	$18 – 20
190	Creamer, 10 oz.	$16 – 18
301	Buffet Plate, coupe, 13"	$30 – 35
350	Tumbler, 12 oz.	$20 – 22
370	Water Pitcher, 2 qt.	$40 – 45
420	Cereal, 5½"	$10 – 11

California Spatterware

010	Cup, 7 oz.	$5 – 6
020	Saucer, 6"	$2 – 3
040	Salad Plate, 8"	$5 – 6
060	Dinner Plate, 10½"	$7 – 8
130	Butter & Lid	$25 – 28
150	Vegetable, 10"	$18 – 20
170	Platter, lg., 14½"	$20 – 22
180	Sugar & Lid, 11 oz.	$14 – 16
190	Creamer, 11 oz.	$12 – 14
330	Salt	$7 – 8
340	Pepper	$7 – 8
385	Au Gratin, 9⅜"	$16 – 18
420	Cereal, 6½"	$8 – 9
760	Mug, 9 oz. (Colorstax)	$12 – 13

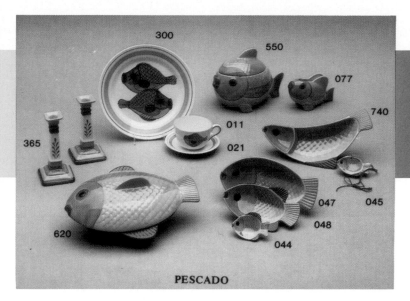

PESCADO

Part II: P 241 Sonoma (1988)
P 242 Mission (1988)
P 095 Holstein Herd (1988)

California Harvest Group
Galaxy Dinnerware (Second Series)
P 095 Delphinium Blue (1988)
P 096 Garden Green (1988)
P 097 Orange (1988)
P 098 Yellow (1988)
758 Decorated Giftware (1988)
756 White Giftware (1988)

Pescado
Solid Colors (Fish Shapes)
P 034 Sky Blue (1988)
P 035 Yellow (1988)
P 036 White (1988)
P 063 Aqua (1988)
P 073 Rose (1988)
199 Hand Decorated (1988)

During the first half of the 1980s, a majority of Metlox's new dinnerware patterns were composed of place setting and completer set items with or without a coffee pot. Disappointing sales of these new releases convinced Melinda Avery that this type of limited set composition, originally adopted as a cost-cutting measure, was not profitable. She decided to experiment with larger, more diverse sets typifying a novel theme or idea and including a number of unusual, nonstandard items.

Sonoma, named after the renowned grape-growing region of California, and Mission resurrected the Sculptured Grape pattern. Both were exceptional in that they were the only Metlox dinnerware patterns produced with a red instead of a white clay body. Sonoma was finished with a clear white glaze, creating a reddish-pink coloring that highlighted the grape design. Mission, a beautiful variation of this idea, featured underglaze blue hand-painted grapes with the white glaze. An unusual selection of serving pieces was included in the patterns.

Holstein Herd emulated the two-tone contrast of the famous cow breed with large black abstract splotches on a white background. Colorstax provided a varied assortment of items for this delightful decoration.

Suggestive of its name, California Harvest combined an opulent selection of decorated giftware items from the Artware Division's vegetable and cabbage lines with the rich colors of the Second Series of Galaxy dinnerware. The seven canisters were realistic shapes hand-painted in vivid, natural hues. The four salad plates of the Vegetable Group (White) displayed decorated embossed vegetables on a white background. Four Cabbage Green and five additional items completed the set, including the turkey tureen and ladle in a decorated and a white version.

The impressive Pescado (Spanish for "fish") was inspired by the fish shapes of the Artware Division's Sea Server line. Several borrowed items — including the fish canister and lid and fish casserole and lid

161

— were augmented with other fish designs to create this fanciful pattern. The original set, consisting of ten items, was released in 1988 in two versions. The hand-decorated set featured brilliantly multicolored fish shapes with matching fish and seaweed designs on the flatware, cup, and candlestick. The solid colors offered the same items in five Colorstax colors. The Second Series of Galaxy dinnerware was combined with Pescado to offer a selection of standard dinnerware items. By 1989 Pescado was limited to the hand-decorated version only. The fish on a cord and 8" fish serving dish were new items. The fish salt and pepper, large fish platter, and teapot and lid were produced shortly before the company closed.

The five 1988 patterns, the last ones introduced by Metlox, were unique sets that signified a new direction for the company under Melinda Avery's leadership. Although well received and critically acclaimed, they were produced in limited quantities for a short period of time. By now the company was in such dire financial straits that large-scale production and extensive nationwide distribution were infeasible. Today a small but growing number of collectors feel that these patterns are some of the most original creations of Metlox's last decade.

Pescado, California Harvest, Sonoma, and Holstein Herd: Metlox brochure.

P 241 Sonoma, P 242 Mission

010	Cup, 7 oz.	$11 – 12	460	Coffee Canister & Lid	$50 – 55
020	Saucer, 6"	$3 – 4	620	Casserole & Lid, 2 qt.	$90 – 95
040	Salad Plate, 8"	$10 – 12	840	Compote, footed, 8½"	$65 – 70
060	Dinner Plate, 10½"	$14 – 15			
070	Soup, 8"	$18 – 20		**P 241 Sonoma Additions**	
100	Salad Bowl, 12"	$70 – 75	130	Butter Dish & Lid	$55 – 60
180	Sugar & Lid	$25 – 28	430	Water Pitcher, 1 qt.	$45 – 50
190	Creamer, 10 oz.	$22 – 25	470	Artichoke Sauce Server & Lid	$55 – 60
300	Buffet Plate, 12"	$65 – 75	760	Mug, 8 oz.	$20 – 22
370	Water Pitcher, 2 qt.	$60 – 65			
440	Flour Canister & Lid.	$70 – 75		**P 242 Mission Addition**	
450	Sugar Canister & Lid	$60 – 65	170	Platter, lg., 14½"	$45 – 50

P 095 Holstein Herd

010	Cup, 7 oz.	$9 – 10	250	Platter, oval, 16"	$50 – 55
011	Cup, lg., 16 oz.	$20 – 22	300	Buffet Plate, rim, 12"	$40 – 45
020	Saucer, 6"	$4 – 5	330	Salt, short	$10 – 12
021	Saucer, lg., 7"	$7 – 8	331	Salt, tall.	$18 – 20
040	Salad Plate, 7½"	$10 – 11	340	Pepper, short	$10 – 12
060	Dinner Plate, 10½"	$13 – 14	341	Pepper, tall	$18 – 20
070	Soup, 8½"	$16 – 18	360	Candlestick, rnd., 5½"	$28 – 30
100	Salad Bowl, 13"	$50 – 55	365	Candlestick, sq., 8"	$32 – 35
101	Mixing Bowl, sm., 16 oz.	$35 – 40	370	Pitcher, 2 qt.	$55 – 60
102	Mixing Bowl, med., 44 oz.	$40 – 45	480	Soup Tureen & Lid, 5 qt.	$75 – 80
103	Mixing Bowl, lg., 84 oz.	$45 – 50	490	Ladle	$22 – 25
130	Butter Dish & Lid.	$45 – 50	760	Mug, 9 oz.	$18 – 20
180	Sugar & Lid, 11 oz.	$25 – 28	761	Mug, Carousel, 9 oz.	$16 – 18
190	Creamer, 11 oz.	$22 – 25	785	Platter, oval, 19"	$60 – 65

California Harvest Group

Galaxy Dinnerware
**095 Delphinium Blue, 096 Garden Green,
097 Orange, 098 Yellow**

010	Cup, 7 oz.	$7 – 8
020	Saucer, 6"	$2 – 3
040	Salad Plate, 7½"	$7 – 8
060	Dinner Plate, 10½"	$9 – 10
070	Soup, 7"	$12 – 14
100	Salad Bowl, 11".	$40 – 45
150	Vegetable, med., 9½"	$25 – 28
180	Sugar & Lid	$18 – 20
190	Creamer, 10 oz.	$16 – 18
301	Buffet Plate, coupe, 13"	$30 – 35
350	Tumbler, 12 oz.	$20 – 22
370	Water Pitcher, 2 qt.	$40 – 45
420	Cereal, 5½"	$10 – 11

758 Decorated Giftware
Salad Plates, embossed

041	Asparagus, 8½"	$18 – 20
042	Corn, 8½"	$18 – 20
043	Carrots, 8½"	$18 – 20
044	Beets, 8½".	$18 – 20

Canisters

430	Squash, 2½ qt.	$150 – 175
435	Tomato, 2 qt.	$100 – 110
440	Corn, 2½ qt.	$90 – 100
450	Broccoli, 1½ qt.	$120 – 135
460	Eggplant, 1½ qt.	$125 – 150
470	Red Pepper, ¾ qt.	$100 – 125
585	Pumpkin, 2½ qt.	$125 – 150

Cabbage Green

070	Soup, 8"	$16 – 18
100	Salad Bowl, 14".	$55 – 60
300	Platter, 14"	$40 – 45
740	Chip & Dip, 12½"	$50 – 55

Additional Pieces

330	Salt, Green Bell Pepper	$18 – 20
340	Pepper, Red Bell Pepper	$18 – 20
500	Corn Server, 11"	$18 – 20
480	Turkey Tureen (758 Decorated)	$175 – 200
490	Turkey Tureen Ladle (758 Decorated)	$28 – 30
480	Turkey Tureen (756 White)	$125 – 140
490	Turkey Tureen Ladle (756 White)	$22 – 25

Pescado

Hand Decorated

011	Cup, lg., 16 oz.	$30 – 35
021	Saucer, lg., 7"	$9 – 10
044	Sauce Dish, Fish, 4"	$25 – 30
045	Fish on a Cord, 4"	$35 – 40
047	Serving Dish, Fish, 11"	$65 – 75
048	Serving Dish, Fish, 8"	$50 – 60
077	Vase, Fish, 8"	$55 – 65
300	Buffet Plate, rim, 12"	$75 – 85
365	Candlestick, sq., 8"	$40 – 45
550	Cookie Jar & Lid, Fish	$300 – 325
620	Casserole & Lid, Fish, 2 qt.	$125 – 150
740	Chip & Dip, Fish, 13½".	$75 – 85

Late, Rare Hand Decorated Additions

250	Fish Platter, ex. lg.	$150 – 175

330	Fish Salt	$35 – 40
340	Fish Pepper.	$35 – 40
700	Teapot & Lid.	$250 – 275

Solid Colors

011	Cup, lg., 16 oz.	$18 – 20
021	Saucer, lg, 7".	$4 – 5
044	Sauce Dish, Fish, 4"	$18 – 20
047	Serving Dish, Fish, 11"	$45 – 50
077	Vase, Fish, 8"	$40 – 45
300	Buffet Plate, rim, 12"	$35 – 40
365	Candlestick, sq., 8"	$25 – 28
550	Cookie Jar & Lid, Fish	$125 – 150
620	Casserole & Lid, Fish, 2 qt.	$80 – 95
740	Chip & Dip, Fish, 13½".	$50 – 55

Vernonware Division

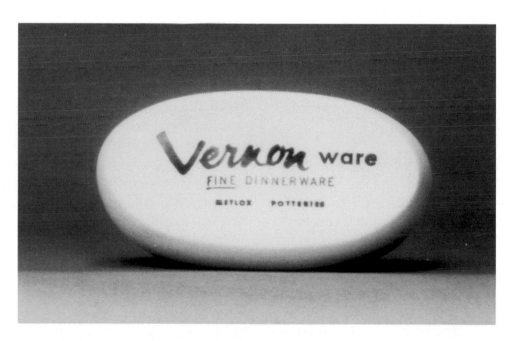

Vernonware dealer sign, 5¾" x 3".

Anytime Shape

V 810 Tickled Pink (1958)

V 820 Heavenly Days (1958)

V 830 Anytime (1958)

V 840 Tisket-A-Tasket

V 850 Sherwood (1958)

V 860 Fancy Free

V 870 Rose-A-Day (1958)

V 880 Year 'Round (1958)

Metlox Potteries established its Vernonware Division in 1958, the year Vernon Kilns ceased production. Evan K. Shaw obtained from Vernon the rights to the well-established names "Vernon," "Vernonware," and "Vernon Ware" for the name of the new division and its patterns. He also purchased the molds, blocks, cases, and equipment necessary to continue production of a number of Vernon Kilns dinnerware patterns. These patterns were the first ones released in the Vernonware Division.

The exact number of continued Vernon patterns is uncertain. Tickled Pink, Heavenly Days, Anytime, Sherwood, and Rose-A-Day, all on Vernon's Anytime shape, were definitely manufactured by Metlox from 1958 through the mid-1960s. These patterns are well-documented in Metlox leaflets. Organdie, a very popular Vernon plaid design on the Montecito shape, was also continued for about a year. However, a listing of the items produced and pattern number could not be found. Organdie was adapted by Metlox on a new shape with different coloring as V 710 Butterscotch in 1960. Metlox company employees have reported that the Vernon patterns Brown Eyed Susan, Homespun, Barkwood, Heyday, Dis 'N Dot, and Young in Heart may have been produced for a short period of time, certainly not more than a year. Metlox company files also mentioned by name only Vernon's Bel Air, Hawaiian Coral, and California Heritage. However, there are no company records, leaflets, pattern numbers, or proof of production for any of these patterns.

The Metlox Anytime shape patterns, the only ones assigned 800 series numbers in the Vernonware Division, are the following: V 810

Tickled Pink, V 820 Heavenly Days, V 830 Anytime, V 840 Tisket-A-Tasket, V 850 Sherwood, V 860 Fancy Free, V 870 Rose-A-Day, and V 880 Year 'Round.

The designs of Tickled Pink, Heavenly Days, Anytime, Sherwood, and Rose-A-Day were unchanged by Metlox. Tisket-A-Tasket was a new Metlox floral design on the Anytime shape. Although there were no available company records, leaflets, or descriptions for Fancy Free, its inclusion in the 800 series would seem to indicate that it was a new pattern on the Anytime shape. Year 'Round, originally produced on Vernon's Year 'Round shape as a yellow, mocha, and gray circular geometric design on a cream textured background, was redesigned as a jewel motif in gray and turquoise with a textured ivory background on the Anytime shape.

At first Metlox manufactured only the identical 35 items of the original Vernon sets. Four new pieces — a 12" salad bowl, wood fork and spoon set with ceramic handles, 9" covered vegetable, and 10¼" oval baker — are listed in a March 15, 1962, leaflet for Tickled Pink and Heavenly Days only. It could not be determined whether or not these items were produced in the other patterns.

Metlox's Anytime shape patterns as well as Organdie are clearly distinguished from Vernon's. Although the backstamps are the same, Metlox always added the words "BY METLOX" under the original Vernon backstamp. In addition, Metlox's items tended to be a little larger and thicker than Vernon's because Metlox's clay body, composed of a slightly different mixture of ingredients, shrank less when fired.

Tickled Pink: tumbler, cup and saucer, chop plate, small one pint pitcher, and medium one quart pitcher.

Heavenly Days
A bright touch of cloudless sky for your table. A contemporary design featuring cool aqua...highlighted with tones of pink and mocha-charcoal on a creamy textured background. All aqua cups and serving pieces add a smart note of color accent.

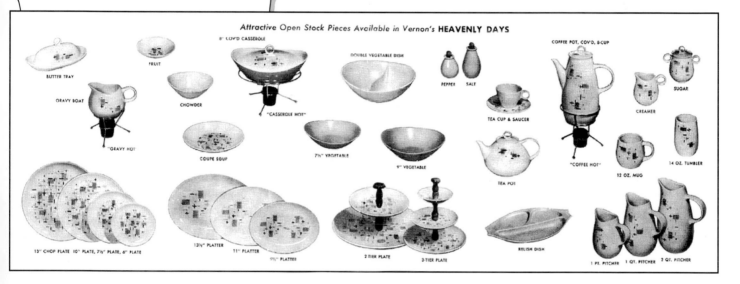

Attractive Open Stock Pieces Available in Vernon's **HEAVENLY DAYS**

BUTTER TRAY — FRUIT — 8" COV'D CASSEROLE — DOUBLE VEGETABLE DISH — PEPPER — SALT — COFFEE POT, COV'D, 8-CUP — SUGAR

GRAVY BOAT — CHOWDER — "CASSEROLE HOT" — TEA CUP & SAUCER — "COFFEE HOT" — CREAMER

"GRAVY HOT" — COUPE SOUP — 7½" VEGETABLE — 9" VEGETABLE — TEA POT — 12 OZ. MUG — 14 OZ. TUMBLER

13" CHOP PLATE, 10" PLATE, 7½" PLATE, 6" PLATE — 13½" PLATTER — 11" PLATTER — 9½" PLATTER — 2-TIER PLATE — 3-TIER PLATE — RELISH DISH — 1 PT. PITCHER, 1 QT. PITCHER, 2 QT. PITCHER

Heavenly Days: 1958 brochure.

Anytime
A subtle abstract pattern in decorator tones of canary yellow, mocha and grey on a creamy textured background combined with mint green serving pieces. A dinnerware new as tomorrow...so right anywhere, anytime.

Anytime:
1958 brochure.

Tisket-A-Tasket: Metlox archive photo.

Tisket-A-Tasket
. . .cheerful as a sunny summer morning! A circlet of golden yellow brown-eyed daisies and gay green leaves on a soft ivory background creates a dinner- ware pattern to brighten every meal.

Sherwood
Warm touches of gold, bronze and brown in a smart leaf design on a beige textured background make Sherwood just right with the fashionable modern woods of your dining room.

Sherwood:
1958 brochure.

Rose-A-Day
Roses for romance and young rosy dreams. Set a table pretty as a picture for just two or for a gay crowd. A refreshing modern version of a traditional floral pattern Rose-A-Day features a wreath of delicate pink roses accented with dark green leaves on a creamy background.

Rose-A-Day: 1958 brochure.

Year 'Round
A distinctive contemporary treatment of jewel-like motifs in subtle silver gray and turquoise tones on a textured ivory background. Richly decorative, smartly modern, a pattern always in good taste, for your year 'round enjoyment for years to come.

Year 'Round: 1958 brochure.

V 810 Tickled Pink, V 820 Heavenly Days, V 830 Anytime, V 840 Tisket-A-Tasket, V 850 Sherwood, V 870 Rose-A-Day, V 880 Year 'Round

No.	Item	Price	No.	Item	Price
00	Cup	$8 – 9	34	Pepper	$10 – 12
02	Saucer	$2 – 3	35	Tumbler, 14 oz.	$22 – 25
03	Bread & Butter, 6¼"	$6 – 7	37	Pitcher, lg., 2 qt.	$35 – 40
04	Salad Plate, 7½"	$8 – 9	40	Coffee Pot & Lid, 8 cup	$55 – 60
06	Dinner Plate, 10"	$11 – 12	40W	"Coffee Hot," metal stand	$18 – 20
07	Soup, 8½"	$12 – 14	42	Chowder, 6"	$10 – 12
08	Vegetable, sm., rnd., 7½"	$20 – 25	43	Pitcher, med., 1 qt.	$30 – 35
13	Butter & Lid	$40 – 45	60	Casserole & Lid, 1½ qt.	$45 – 50
15	Vegetable, med., rnd., 9"	$25 – 30	60W	"Casserole Hot," metal stand	$18 – 20
16	Platter, med., oval, 11"	$25 – 30	70	Teapot & Lid, 7 cup	$55 – 60
17	Platter, lg., oval, 13½"	$30 – 35	76	Mug, 12 oz.	$18 – 20
18	Sugar & Lid	$18 – 20	88	Pitcher, sm., 1 pt.	$22 – 25
19	Creamer	$16 – 18	—	2-Tier Server (except Year 'Round)	$45 – 50
21	Fruit, 5½"	$8 – 9	—	3-Tier Server (except Year 'Round)	$40 – 45
23	Gravy Boat, 1 pt.	$20 – 25	**V 810 Tickled Pink, V 820 Heavenly Days Additions**		
23W	"Gravy Hot," metal stand	$12 – 15	10	Salad Bowl, 12"	$45 – 50
24	Platter, sm., oval, 9½"	$22 – 25	22AB	Salad Fork & Spoon Set	$40 – 45
28	Relish Dish, 3-section, 12¾"	$30 – 35	26	Vegetable & Lid, 9"	$45 – 50
29	Vegetable, div., med., rnd., 9½"	$30 – 35	63	Oval Baker, 10¼"	$30 – 35
30	Chop Plate, 13"	$30 – 35			
33	Salt	$10 – 12			

(Although it cannot be documented from brochure materials, these additions may have been produced in the other patterns as well.)

San Fernando Shape

V 930 True Blue (1959)

V 960 Patrician White (1959)

V 940 Pink Lady (1960)

V 950 Vineyard (1960)

V 970 Autumn Leaves (1960)

V 980 Fruit Basket (1961)

V 910 Castile (1964)

V 790 Vernon Rose (1965)

V 920 San Fernando (1966)

V 981 Blue Fascination (1967)

V 982 Caprice (1967)

V 921 Vernon Nasturtium (1972)

V 627 White Rose (1977)

V 664 Meadow (1980)

V 668 Marissa (1980)

V 941 Laura (early 1980s)

FRUIT BASKET

Included in Evan K. Shaw's 1958 purchase of a limited number of Vernon Kilns patterns were the production rights to Vernon's San Fernando shape. The original Vernon San Fernando patterns appeared in 1944. The scalloped rims, fluted detailing, and scroll handles of the shape were adapted from English dinnerware designs. While English and European imports were curtailed by World War II, the demand for English style dinnerware was still very high in the United States. The Vernon patterns were immediately popular and sold very well through the early 1950s. When Shaw, who had always felt an affinity for traditional English style dinnerware, first purchased Metlox, he seriously considered, then rejected, only fashioning dinnerware sets after those of Spode and other English companies. Vernon's San Fernando shape offered him the perfect one on which to develop a series of English look-alike dinnerware patterns.

As was typical of his personality and character, Shaw was not content to merely release patterns that were similar to Vernon's and included the same number and kinds of items. He immediately requested that Allen and Shaw develop San Fernando into a distinctive Metlox shape. The original Vernon sets had only 30 items. Vernon's R.F.D., introduced in 1951, included these plus 16 additional ones made expressly for it. Metlox increased the number of open stock items, discontinuing some of the original set's pieces and including many of R.F.D.'s as standard items. Thirteen new items were added to the line. Several pieces were redesigned, including a soup tureen now seated on a large fluted pedestal. Handles were added to the salt and pepper shakers. Most Metlox items were produced with slightly larger dimensions and a heavier body than their Vernon counterparts. Metlox's patterns were also very different. The Vernon patterns were either plain or hand-tinted transfer prints with a gloss glaze. The Metlox patterns were hand-painted and many used satin glazes.

The early Metlox San Fernando patterns — V 930, V 940, V 950, V 970, and V 980 — were the first successes of the Vernonware Division and enjoyed lengthy production runs. Various other patterns were introduced on the shape through the early 1980s, including two sculptured designs, Vernon Rose and its all-white counterpart White Rose, and two decal decorated patterns, Meadow and Marissa. The longstanding popularity of San Fernando patterns proved that Shaw's instincts and astute judgment were correct when he purchased and revitalized this shape.

True Blue: 1974 brochure.

True Blue

A delightful pattern featuring scalloped edges and fluted detail. The soft blue floral, hand-painted with 48 brush strokes, on an off-white background, is accented with all-blue cups and serving pieces. Perfect for provincial or traditional decor...dainty and decorative for your nicest parties.

Pink Lady

Dinnerware with an 'heirloom' look for gracious living. A design rich in tradition with graceful, scalloped edges and fluted detail. A charming floral pattern with pink and purple posies and tiny green leaves on an off-white background...accented with all-pink cups and serving pieces.

Pink Lady: 1965 brochure.

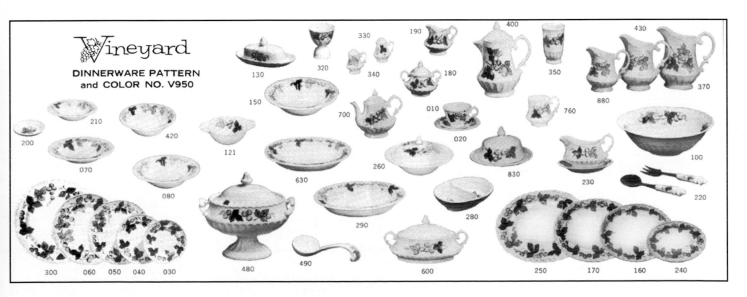

Vineyard: 1974 brochure.

Vineyard
A colorful California design with an 'old world' touch. A graceful pattern of blue-green grapes with soft green and golden brown leaves, hand-painted with 150 brush strokes, on an antique finish, off-white background. The scalloped edges and fluted detail create a handsome provincial-traditional effect.

Vineyard: 1974 brochure.

Vineyard: sugar and lid, creamer, dinner plate, and teapot and lid.

Vineyard: tumbler and coaster.

Vineyard: medium vegetable bowl and divided vegetable.

Vineyard: cup and saucer, salad plate, and bread and butter plate.

Vineyard: gravy with fastand, medium platter, and medium one quart pitcher.

Fruit Basket

Brings old-world charm to your table with its antique white scalloped edges and fluted detail. The central motif is a basket of fruit and flowers, hand-painted with 152 brush strokes, in warm tones of yellow, green and brown.

Fruit Basket: Metlox brochure.

Fruit Basket: sugar and lid, cereal bowl, creamer, and fruit bowl.

Fruit Basket: dinner plate, salad plate, bread and butter plate, cup and saucer, and pepper shaker.

Autumn Leaves

For the colorful sparkle of Indian summer on your table...Leaves and flowers hand-painted in warm tones of brown, green and yellow, form a rich border on a graceful, antique-white traditional shape with scalloped edges and fluted detail...168 hand-painted brush strokes.

San Fernando: salt and pepper shakers, buffet server, cup and saucer, and coffee pot and lid.

San Fernando
Sets a mood of old-world hospitality! It brings Mediterranean warmth, charm and subtle elegance to your table, with a delicate Spanish scroll design in warm brown tones on a blended golden amber, provincial-traditional shape.

San Fernando:
Metlox brochure.

V 920 San Fernando, V 930 True Blue, V 940 Pink Lady, V 950 Vineyard, V 970 Autumn Leaves, V 980 Fruit Basket

010	Cup, 6 oz.	$9 – 10
020	Saucer, 6¼"	$3 – 4
030	Bread & Butter, 6⅝"	$7 – 8
040	Salad Plate, 7½"	$9 – 10
060	Dinner Plate, 10¾"	$12 – 13
070	Soup, 8⅛"	$16 – 18
080	Vegetable, sm., rnd., 8¼"	$30 – 35
100	Salad Bowl, 12½"	$60 – 65
130	Butter & Lid, oval	$50 – 55
150	Vegetable, med., rnd., 9¼"	$35 – 40
160	Platter, med., oval, 12⅜"	$30 – 35
170	Platter, lg., oval, 13¾"	$35 – 40
180	Sugar & Lid, 8 oz.	$22 – 25
190	Creamer, 8 oz.	$20 – 22
210	Fruit, 6"	$11 – 12
220	Salad Fork & Spoon Set	$50 – 55
230	Gravy, Fastand, ¾ pt.	$32 – 35
236	Gravy Server, ¾ pt. (except Pink Lady)	$25 – 28
237	Gravy Server Stand (except Pink Lady)	$10 – 12
240	Platter, sm., oval, 9¾"	$28 – 30
280	Jam & Jelly, 8¼"	$40 – 45
290	Vegetable, div., med., oval, 11¼"	$45 – 50

300	Buffet Server, rnd., 14¼"	$50 – 55
330	Salt	$10 – 12
340	Pepper	$10 – 12
350	Tumbler, 10 oz.	$22 – 25
370	Pitcher, lg., 2 qt.	$55 – 60
400	Coffee Pot & Lid, 8 cup	$80 – 90
420	Cereal, 6⅞"	$13 – 14
430	Pitcher, med., 1 qt.	$40 – 45
480	Soup Tureen & Lid, 3 qt.	$120 – 135
490	Soup Tureen Ladle	$20 – 25
600	Casserole & Lid, oval, 1¼ qt.	$75 – 80
630	Oval Baker, 11¼"	$40 – 45
700	Teapot & Lid, 6 cup	$80 – 90
760	Mug, 8 oz.	$18 – 20

V 920 San Fernando Addition

050	Luncheon Plate, 9¾"	$14 – 15

V 930 True Blue, V 940 Pink Lady, V 970 Autumn Leaves Additions

121	Individual Soup Server, lug, 5¼"	$16 – 18
200	Coaster, 4"	$12 – 14

(continued)

250	Platter, ex. lg., oval, 16⅛"	$45 – 50
260	Vegetable & Lid, med., 9¼"	$65 – 70
320	Egg Cup	$25 – 28
830	Cheese Server & Lid, rnd. (aka Butter & Lid, rnd.)	$60 – 65
880	Pitcher, sm., 1½ pt.	$30 – 35

V 950 Vineyard Additions

050	Luncheon Plate, 9¾"	$14 – 15
121	Individual Soup Server, lug, 5¼"	$16 – 18
200	Coaster, 4"	$12 – 14
250	Platter, ex. lg., oval, 16⅛"	$45 – 50
260	Vegetable & Lid, med., 9¼"	$65 – 70

320	Egg Cup	$25 – 28
830	Cheese Server & Lid, rnd. (aka Butter & Lid, rnd.)	$60 – 65
880	Pitcher, sm., 1½ pt.	$30 – 35

V 980 Fruit Basket Additions

050	Luncheon Plate, 9¾"	$14 – 15
200	Coaster, 4"	$12 – 14
250	Platter, ex. lg., oval, 16⅛"	$45 – 50
260	Vegetable & Lid, med., 9¼"	$65 – 70
320	Egg Cup	$25 – 28
880	Pitcher, sm., 1½ pt.	$30 – 35

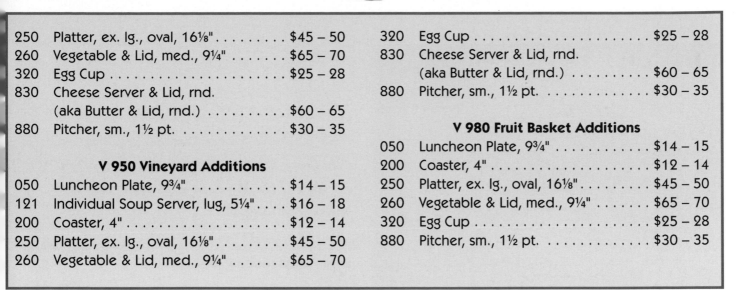

Vernon Rose
A garland of delicate pink roses and green foliage, hand-carved and hand-painted with 251 brush strokes, forms a graceful border on a fluted and scalloped traditional shape.

Vernon Rose:
1974 brochure.

Vernon Rose:
cup and saucer,
soup bowl,
and salad plate.

Castile: bread and butter plate and cup and saucer.

Castile
'Castles in Spain' exemplified by a wrought iron design in delicate blue over a soft Spanish silver blue band. All of this is combined with a subtle beige swirl effect to give that warm Mediterranean feeling. Something soft, something blue, something delicate, and something true.

Blue Fascination
...a sophisticated floral in a tropical mood on a graceful traditional shape. Dramatic blossoms in House & Garden tones of Persian Blue, Curry and Fern Green, accented with green holloware, create a pattern of California charm, elegance. 526 hand painted brush strokes.

Blue Fascination: 1968 brochure.

Blue Fascination: salad plate.

Caprice
Yellow Blossoms in Gay Abandon to Form a Sunny Floral.

Meadow:
Metlox brochure.

Meadow

Vernon Nasturtium

The warm, friendly charm of your dream garden comes to life on your table with Vernon's Nasturtium. Happy flowers and leaves are hand-painted in tones of gold, yellows and greens on a traditional shape with a scalloped edge rim and fluted detail.

Vernon Nasturtium: 1974 brochure.

Vernon Nasturtium: large platter and teapot and lid.

V 627 White Rose, V 664 Meadow, V 790 Vernon Rose, V 910 Castile, V 921 Vernon Nasturtium, V 960 Patrician White, V 981 Blue Fascination, V 982 Caprice

Add 15 – 20% for V 627 White Rose and V 790 Vernon Rose.

010	Cup, 6 oz.	$8 – 9
020	Saucer, 6¼"	$2 – 3
030	Bread & Butter, 6⅝"	$6 – 7
040	Salad Plate, 7½"	$8 – 9
060	Dinner Plate, 10¾"	$10 – 11
070	Soup, 8⅛"	$14 – 16
130	Butter & Lid	$45 – 50
150	Vegetable, med., rnd., 9¼"	$25 – 30
170	Platter, lg., oval, 13¾"	$30 – 35
180	Sugar & Lid, 8 oz.	$20 – 22
190	Creamer, 8 oz.	$18 – 20
210	Fruit, 6"	$9 – 10
230	Gravy, Fastand, ¾ pt.	$28 – 30
290	Vegetable, div., med., oval, 11¼" (except V 960 Patrician White)	$35 – 40
330	Salt	$9 – 10
340	Pepper	$9 – 10
400	Coffee Pot & Lid, 8 cup	$70 – 80

420	Cereal, 6⅞"	$11 – 12
700	Teapot & Lid, 6 cup	$70 – 80

V 664 Meadow Additions

236	Gravy Server, ¾ pt.	$22 – 25
237	Gravy Server Stand	$8 – 10
760	Mug, 8 oz.	$16 – 18

V 790 Vernon Rose Addition

760	Mug, 8 oz.	$18 – 20

(A brochure dated December 1, 1980, lists this item as scheduled for production during spring 1981. Its appearance has not been verified from subsequent brochure material.)

V 921 Nasturtium Additions

236	Gravy Server, ¾ pt.	$22 – 25
237	Gravy Server Stand	$8 – 10

Marissa: creamer, large platter, and coffee pot and lid.

Marissa: Metlox brochure*.

Laura: Metlox brochure*.

*Poor quality, only photo available.

V 668 Marissa, V 941 Laura

010	Cup, 6 oz..	$8 – 9	400	Coffee Pot & Lid, 8 cup	$70 – 80
020	Saucer, 6¼".	$2 – 3	420	Cereal, 6⅞".	$11 – 12
040	Salad Plate, 7½"	$8 – 9			
060	Dinner Plate, 10¾"	$10 – 11		**V 941 Laura Additions**	
150	Vegetable, med., rnd., 9¼"	$25 – 30	030	Bread & Butter, 6⅝"	$6 – 7
170	Platter, lg., oval, 13¾"	$30 – 35	070	Soup, 8⅛".	$14 – 16
180	Sugar & Lid, 8 oz.	$20 – 22	210	Fruit, 6".	$9 – 10
190	Creamer, 8 oz.	$18 – 20	760	Mug, 8 oz.	$16 – 18

Early Original Vernonware Shapes

V 710 Butterscotch (1960)

Town and Country Series (1961)

V 720 Nutmeg Brown

V 730 Clover Green

V 740 Larkspur Blue

V 750 Buttercup Yellow

V 760 Springtime (1961)

V 610 Accents (1961)

V 620 Sierra Flower (1962)

V 630 Sun 'N Sand (1962)

V 640 Blue Zinnias (1963)

Two years after its creation, the Vernonware Division began to release patterns on shapes that were original designs and not merely continuations or adaptations of Vernon Kilns shapes. The first two shapes (company names and designer/designers unknown) are grouped as above.

Both shapes were rather simple, commonplace, and utilitarian, lacking the originality and distinctiveness of earlier Poppytrail shapes and the ornate traditionalism of the San Fernando shape. Items in the first group were characterized by their unusual thickness and heaviness. Three patterns were noteworthy. Butterscotch copied the popular Vernon Organdie plaid design but colored it with shades of browns and rust only. Several serving pieces were dark brown. Bob Allen's Sierra Flower and Blue Zinnias featured beautiful, elaborate floral designs that covered the entire surface of the coupe shape flatware. None of the patterns were particularly successful, and both shapes and their patterns were discontinued by 1965.

Blue Zinnias
A year round pattern of color harmony in beautiful shades of blue, magenta and dusty rose pinks, touches of lemon yellow, variations in olive green, all harmonizing with a soft green theme throughout the serving pieces.

Blue Zinnias: large platter.

Town & Country (V 720 Nutmeg Brown, V 730 Clover Green, V 740 Larkspur Blue, V 750 Buttercup Yellow), V 710 Butterscotch, V 760 Springtime

Add 10 – 15% for V 710 Butterscotch and V 760 Springtime.

00	Cup	$5 – 6	29	Vegetable, div.	$20 – 22
02	Saucer	$2 – 3	30	Chop Plate	$22 – 25
03	Bread & Butter	$3 – 4	33	Salt	$7 – 8
04	Salad Plate	$5 – 6	34	Pepper	$7 – 8
06	Dinner Plate	$7 – 8	40	Coffee Pot & Lid	$40 – 45
07	Soup	$10 – 11	42	Chowder	$8 – 9
13	Butter & Lid	$25 – 28	70	Teapot & Lid	$40 – 45
15	Vegetable, med., rnd.	$18 – 20			
16	Platter, med., oval	$18 – 20		**V 710 Butterscotch Addition**	
17	Platter, lg., oval	$20 – 22	76	Mug	$14 – 15
18	Sugar & Lid	$14 – 16			
19	Creamer	$12 – 14		**V 760 Springtime Additions**	
21	Fruit	$6 – 7	60	Casserole & Lid	$35 – 40
23	Gravy	$16 – 18	76	Mug	$14 – 15

Town and Country: coffee pot and lid.

Sierra Flower

A lovely floral design with a modern flair . . . hand-painted in soft, warm tones of brown, bronze and green on a textured beige background. Serving pieces combine pattern and solid color for a refreshing change of pace.

Sun 'N Sand

Hand-painted abstract forms in vivid earth tones create a striking border design on a creamy textured background. Serving pieces combine pattern and solid color in gold, beige and brown tones.

V 610 Accents, V 620 Sierra Flower, V 630 Sun 'N Sand, V 640 Blue Zinnias

Add 25% for V 620 Sierra Flower and V 640 Blue Zinnias.

00	Cup	$5 – 6	19	Creamer	$12 – 14
02	Saucer	$2 – 3	21	Fruit, 5¼"	$6 – 7
03	Bread & Butter, 6¼"	$3 – 4	23	Gravy (Sauce Boat), 1 pt.	$16 – 18
04	Salad Plate, 8"	$5 – 6	29	Vegetable, div., rect., 11"	$20 – 22
06	Dinner Plate, 10¼"	$7 – 8	33	Salt	$7 – 8
07	Soup, 6½"	$10 – 11	34	Pepper	$7 – 8
13	Butter & Lid	$25 – 28	40	Coffee Pot & Lid, 10 cup	$40 – 45
15	Vegetable, med., rnd., 9"	$18 – 20	42	Chowder, 5¾"	$8 – 9
17	Platter, lg., oval, 14½"	$20 – 22	70	Teapot & Lid, 7 cup	$40 – 45
18	Sugar & Lid	$14 – 16			

Classic Shape

V 680 Classic Antique (1963)

V 670 Classic Flower (1964)

V 690 Classic Roma (1964)

V 605 Flower Basket (1976)

V 606 Classic Blue (1977)

V 609 Classic Wheat (1977)

The Classic shape was inspired by ancient Greco-Roman art styles. All items featured a circular band composed of many sculptured flutes. A smaller circular lotus band was also incorporated into the designs. The fluting covered the wide rims of the flatware and bowls and all or part of the sides of the holloware. A streamlined impression was created by the straight-sided design of the cup and several of the serving pieces, the simple curvature of the unadorned handles, and the straight spouts of the coffee pot and teapot. A pedestal base anchored the sugar bowl. The visual effect of the entire set was classic yet very contemporary.

The shape was designed by Bob Allen and modeled by Frank Irwin. Evan K. Shaw was not consulted during the planning or development stages. When shown the completed set for the first time, Shaw reportedly quipped, "Do we really need a Classic shape?" His immediate negative response was probably attributable more to hurt feelings created by being excluded from the set's development than a total critical rejection of the design. In time he mellowed and grew to like the shape.

Three Classic patterns were initially released in 1963 – 64 in the Vernonware division. Sales did not meet Shaw's expectations. Retailers complained that the shape was too masculine looking for their female clientele. Another criticism was that the space allowed for the pattern designs was too limited by the wide fluted rims of the flatware. The shape was revived for a second series of three patterns in 1976 – 77. The Classic shape proved to be very important to the Vernonware Division because it later served as the model for the immensely successful Della Robbia shape.

Classic Flower: large platter, sugar and lid, creamer, cup and saucer, and butter and lid.

181

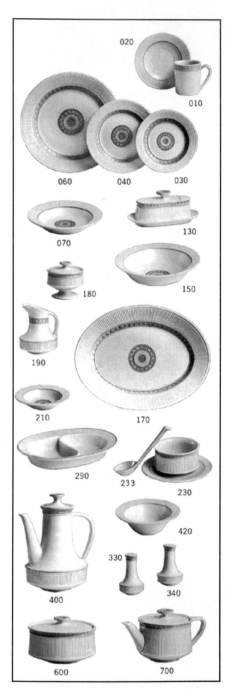
Classic Flower

Classic harmony pictured in an authentic rosette hand col-ored in a delicate green-gold tone to bring elegance to your table. Something distinctive and beautiful for many different occasions. Delightful sophistication in the true tradition of the 18th Century Classic Revival Period... smartly styled with classic carved fluting.

Classic Flower: medium vegetable bowl.

Classic Flower: 1968 brochure.

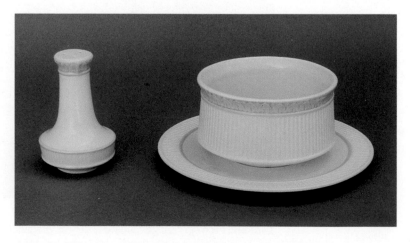

Classic Flower: salt shaker and gravy with fastand.

Classic Antique
Stately magnificence in white splendor with a pinkish beige color . . . under an antique white glaze . . . in the carved lines of the new sculptured classic shape. Both traditional and contemporary.

Classic Roma
Classic shapes, available in Roma Yellow, Roma Blue, Roma Green, Roma Orange.

Flower Basket
Basket of mixed coral, yellow, blue and white flowers delicately hand decorated on Classic Shapes.

Classic Blue
A heavenly blue tone on the outer edge and inner lotus border, enhancing the classic fluted ridges of the wide rim. Simple, yet sophisticated, a pattern for your most elegant entertaining, sturdy and lovely for everyday use.

Classic Wheat
The warm golden color of ripe wheat on the carved lotus inner band and outer edge of the classic fluted rim. Elegantly understated for your formal or informal entertaining and everyday enjoyment.

V 605 Flower Basket, V 606 Classic Blue, V 609 Classic Wheat, V 670 Classic Flower, V 680 Classic Antique, V 690 Classic Roma

No.	Item	Price	No.	Item	Price
010	Cup, 6 oz.	$9 – 10	230	Gravy, Fastand, 1 pt.	$30 – 32
020	Saucer, 6⅜"	$3 – 4	290	Vegetable, div., med., 11⅝"	$35 – 40
030	Bread & Butter, 6½"	$7 – 8	330	Salt	$10 – 12
040	Salad Plate, 7⅝"	$9 – 10	340	Pepper	$10 – 12
060	Dinner Plate, 10½"	$12 – 13	400	Coffee Pot & Lid, 8 cup	$80 – 90
070	Soup, 8½"	$16 – 18	420	Cereal, 7⅛"	$13 – 14
130	Butter & Lid	$45 – 50	700	Teapot & Lid, 6 cup	$90 – 100
150	Vegetable, med., rnd., 9⅝"	$30 – 35			
170	Platter, lg., oval, 14⅜"	$35 – 40		**V 670 Classic Flower, V 680 Classic Antique,**	
180	Sugar & Lid	$22 – 25		**V 690 Classic Roma Additions**	
190	Creamer, 9 oz.	$20 – 22	233	Gravy Ladle	$15 – 20
210	Fruit, 6⅛"	$11 – 12	600	Casserole & Lid, 2 qt.	$75 – 80

Della Robbia Shape

V 780 Vernon Della Robbia (1965)
V 770 Vernon Antiqua (1966)
V 781 Vernon Florence (1969)

The Della Robbia shape, designed by Allen and Shaw, was a sculptured series based on the earlier Classic shape. It highlighted an elaborately carved arrangement of fruit, flowers, and foliage encircling items like an ornamental wreath. The shape was named after the famous Della Robbia family of artists from Florence, Italy, who frequently incorporated this design into their sculptures. The inspiration and model for the wreath was an Italian wall plaque, depicting a cherub surrounded by the border garland. The plaque was part of a collection of artistic examples at the factory. Although Allen and Shaw retained the basic shapes of the Classic items, they changed several design details and slightly modified some shapes, thereby altering the austere, Greco-Roman appearance of the Classic shape into a more adorned, Renaissance transformation. The major change was the substitution of the wreath design for the carved fluting on the rim and/or exteriors of every piece. The coffee pot, teapot, and creamer received curved spouts and ornate handles while the sugar bowl lost its pedestal base. The cup was completely redesigned

and seven new open stock items were added. Antique glazes were used that darkened the recesses of the carvings, bringing the wreath design into sharp relief and imparting a feeling of age.

After the disappointing sales record of the Classic shape patterns, Shaw felt the Vernonware Division needed a popular shape to boost its profits and image. He was convinced that the Della Robbia shape would be as successful as the Poppytrail Division's Sculptured Grape design. Only three patterns were ever released on the Della Robbia shape. V 780 Vernon Della Robbia and V 770 Vernon Antiqua were immediate bestsellers, and V 781 Vernon Florence also sold well. The Della Robbia salad plate was later used as the template for the Songs of Christmas limited edition collector plate series, the only artware line assigned to the Vernonware Division. The popularity of the Della Robbia patterns exceeded even Shaw's expectations, elevating the Vernonware Division to a stature equal to the Poppytrail Division.

Vernon Della Robbia: dinner plate and soup bowl.

Vernon Della Robbia: salt and pepper shakers, small platter, butter and lid, and mug.

Vernon Della Robbia: cup and saucer, medium platter, and gravy with fastand.

Vernon Della Robbia: sugar and lid, coffee pot and lid, and creamer.

Vernon Della Robbia: 1974 brochure.

Vernon Della Robbia
. . .the richness of a California harvest!
A luxuriously carved border of fruit, flowers and foliage, hand-painted with 531 brush strokes in green, yellow, brown and orange on an antique white background. A truly handsome pattern for your most elegant party tables. . .adds a 'special' look to simple family meals.

Vernon Della Robbia:
1974 brochure.

Vernon Della Robbia: oval divided vegetable and oval baker.

Vernon Florence
. . . younger than springtime. Exquisitely cool tints of House & Garden colors: rich Ultramarine Blue, Chartreuse Yellow, Green Almond and tinted White. . .hand-painted with 531 strokes on a border of enchantingly luxurious carved flowers, foliage and fruit. . .Smart, and oh, so elegant for your loveliest parties.

Vernon
FLORENCE

Vernon
ANTIQUA

Vernon
DELLA ROBBIA

Vernon Florence: salt and pepper shakers, dinner plate, cup and saucer, and coffee pot and lid.

Vernon Florence, Antiqua, and Della Robbia: Metlox brochure.

Vernon Antiqua:
creamer, dinner plate,
sugar and lid, and
coffee pot and lid.

Vernon Antiqua:
cup and saucer,
large platter,
and teapot and lid.

Vernon Antiqua:
two quart casserole and lid
and gravy with fastand.

Vernon Antiqua:
medium platter and
cereal bowl.

Vernon Antiqua: bread and butter plate and butter and lid.

Vernon Antiqua

A handsomely carved border of fruit, foliage and flowers subtly shaded in beige tones to accent the carving under an antique-white glaze. A pattern of unsurpassed beauty that will complement modern, provincial or traditional decor . . . sets a theme of dining elegance for years to come.

Vernon Antiqua: round divided vegetable and salad plate.

V 770 Vernon Antiqua, V 780 Vernon Della Robbia, V 781 Vernon Florence

010	Cup, 8 oz.	$10 – 12
020	Saucer, 6½".	$3 – 4
030	Bread & Butter, 6½"	$8 – 9
040	Salad Plate, 7⅝"	$10 – 11
060	Dinner Plate, 10⅝"	$13 – 14
070	Soup, 8⅜"	$18 – 20
080	Vegetable, sm., rnd., 9⅜"	$35 – 40
090	Vegetable, div., sm., rnd., 9⅜"	$40 – 45
130	Butter & Lid	$55 – 60
150	Vegetable, med., rnd., 10⅝"	$40 – 45
160	Platter, med., oval, 11⅛"	$40 – 45
170	Platter, lg., oval, 14⅜"	$45 – 50
180	Sugar & Lid, 10 oz.	$25 – 28
190	Creamer, 10 oz.	$22 – 25
210	Fruit, 6½"	$12 – 14
230	Gravy, Fastand, 1 pt.	$30 – 35
240	Platter, sm., oval, 9⅝"	$35 – 40
290	Vegetable, div., med., oval, 12⅛"	$50 – 55
300	Buffet Server, rnd., 12¼"	$65 – 75
330	Salt	$12 – 13
340	Pepper	$12 – 13
400	Coffee Pot & Lid, 8 cup	$90 – 100
420	Cereal, 7⅛"	$14 – 16
600	Casserole & Lid, 2 qt.	$90 – 95
630	Oval Baker, 12⅛"	$45 – 50
700	Teapot & Lid, 4½ cup	$100 – 110
760	Mug, 10 oz.	$20 – 22
050	Luncheon Plate.	$15 – 18

(A brochure dated December 1, 1980, lists this item as scheduled for production both in Della Robbia and Antiqua during spring 1981. Its appearance has not been verified from subsequent brochure material.)

Vernonware Shape

V 631 Vernon Pueblo (1972)
V 601 Mesa (1976)
V 604 Old Cathay (1976)
V 619 Painted Desert (1977)
California Collection
    V 633 Monterey (1977)
    V 634 Big Sur (1978)
    V 635 Catalina (1978)
    V 636 Capistrano (1978)
V 637 Cognac (1978)

V 620 Petalburst (1968)
V 621 Golden Amber (1968)
V 623 Margarita (1969)
V 624 Vernon Gaiety (1970)
V 625 Vernon Tulips (1971)
V 626 Vernon Calypso (1971)
V 628 Vernon Pacific Blue (1971)

The Vernonware shape was created to provide the Vernonware Division with a contemporary shape similar to the Poppytrail Division's Studio Potter. It was not conceived as a totally new, original set of designs. Rather, it was constructed of borrowed Vernonware and Poppytrail items that were modified or redesigned to produce a new shape unified in style and design. Metlox's concept was to produce simple, commonplace forms that stressed practicality and function over design brilliance and ornateness. Therefore, the Vernonware shape was the antithesis of the Della Robbia and San Fernando shapes.

The first eight patterns, issued from 1968 to 1972, featured brightly colored designs. Simple, childlike abstract floral patterns were the dominant themes. A notable exception is Tulips, a graceful, beautifully detailed pattern created by Bob Allen.

The later patterns, dating from 1976 to 1978, are more original and important. Mesa featured intricate American Indian designs on most items. In typical Metlox fashion each decorated item had its own design that was not repeated on other pieces. Painted Desert, a simple geometric design decorated with the contrasting desert landscape hues of brown, sky blue, and cream white on the flatware and caramel accessories, was a modernistic pattern ideally suited for the shape. The California Collection series, created by Robert McIntosh, consisted of four patterns named after well-known California locales. Each was represented by a hand-painted, impressionistic scene on the dinner plate, salad plate, and buffet server, an item which was added to showcase the painting. The unimpressive Cognac offered the item selection of the California Collection as a solid dark brown pattern. Old Cathay, an Oriental-inspired pattern depicting a bird landing on a flowered branch, redesigned the shape of the flatware, platter, and bowls. Rim shapes were used for these slightly enlarged items. All other pieces were repeated unchanged. Metlox produced Vernonware shape patterns to compete with other manufacturers' contemporary-styled lines. It was the dominant Vernonware Division shape of the 1970s.

Petalburst

A young, exciting dinnerware that combines dramatic serving pieces with decorated plates. The stunning flower design in rust, olive green and brown...created with 84 hand-painted brush strokes, blends smartly with its amber-gold background of plates, lids and serving piece interiors.

PETALBURST

Petalburst: Metlox brochure.

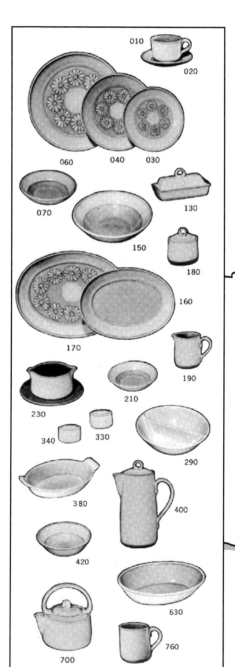

Margarita: 1971 brochure.

Margarita: 1971 brochure.

Margarita

...sets a fiesta table! Perfect for Spanish, Mediterranean, Mexican or modern decor. A little mad, a little mod, to brighten your dining, make every meal a pleasure. A gay circlet of golden yellow margaritas, hand painted by 117 strokes on a burnt orange background, with a brushed yellow border. Plain brushed yellow and orange serving pieces provide a warmly colorful accent.

Margarita: coffee pot and lid.

Vernon Gaiety

Lively, white daisies, yellow centers and green leaves...dance across a smashing sunburnt-yellow background to create the happiest pattern you've ever seen.

Vernon Gaiety:
Metlox brochure.

Vernon Tulips

Almost oriental with its free-flowing, graceful lines...hand-painted with 175 strokes... A misty aqua background is the subtle setting for free-flowing tulips in blue opaline and touches of lavender with parrot green leaves. Hand painted in the manner of the studio potter.

Vernon Tulips:
1972 brochure.

Vernon Tulips:
salad plate and
teapot and lid.

Vernon Calypso

Rich golden orange and yellow spray of wild flowers make their majestic appearance from parrot green leaves. Surrounded by bands of yellow, green and brown, the flowers are hand painted on a background of deep dark brown. Cruise the Caribbean and pick yourself a bouquet, or choose Vernon Calypso dinnerware where the feel of the South Sea Islands is yours each time you dine on its hand painted beauty.

Vernon Calypso: Metlox brochure.

191

Vernon Pacific Blue: Metlox brochure.

Vernon Pacific Blue

Here, a crisp and happy pattern breathes a salt spray of fresh sea flowers. Petals of gleaming 'Pacific Blue' and misty sea foam white surround sun speckled centers. Dot etched leaves formed in rich moss green are splashed around the flowers on a background of deep toned velvet brown, and bordered with a wide band of blue, edged in green and brown. Those sharing the magnificent blue waves of the Pacific know their breathtaking beauty. You will experience the same feeling of pride and joy when you possess 'Pacific Blue' by Vernonware.

Vernon Pueblo

Symbol of a happy home...Today's California hand-crafted look in a timeless pattern of warm, mother-earth colors. A crown of graceful dark-brown swirls on rich henna, contrast dramatically with the desert-sand tone of the plate background, serving piece interiors and tops.

Golden Amber

The golden amber glaze of these pieces give the pattern its name. Calculated to enrich the sophisticated yet simple hand thrown shape, the banding of Van Dyke brown, and the solid-color holloware give the pattern classic beauty.

V 620 Petalburst, V 621 Golden Amber, V 623 Margarita, V 624 Vernon Gaiety, V 625 Vernon Tulips, V 626 Vernon Calypso, V 628 Vernon Pacific Blue, V 631 Vernon Pueblo

Add 25% for V 625 Vernon Tulips.

Code	Item	Price		Code	Item	Price
010	Cup, 6 oz.	$6 – 7		290	Vegetable, div., med., rnd., 9"	$22 – 25
020	Saucer, 5¾"	$2 – 3		330	Salt	$7 – 8
030	Bread & Butter, 6⅜"	$4 – 5		340	Pepper	$7 – 8
040	Salad Plate, 7¾"	$6 – 7		400	Coffee Pot & Lid, 7 cup	$45 – 50
060	Dinner Plate, 10¼"	$8 – 9		420	Cereal, 6¼"	$9 – 10
070	Soup, 7"	$11 – 12		700	Teapot & Lid, 6 cup	$45 – 50
130	Butter & Lid	$28 – 30				
150	Vegetable, med., rnd., 9"	$20 – 22			**V 620 Petalburst, V 623 Margarita,**	
170	Platter, lg., oval, 13"	$22 – 25			**V 624 Gaiety Additions**	
180	Sugar & Lid, 8 oz.	$16 – 18		160	Platter, med., oval, 11"	$20 – 22
190	Creamer, 10 oz.	$14 – 16		380	Oval Baker, individual, 9⅜"	$20 – 22
210	Fruit, 5½"	$7 – 8		630	Oval Baker, 9⅞"	$22 – 25
230	Gravy, Fastand, 1¼ pt.	$18 – 20		760	Mug, 8 oz.	$14 – 15

Old Cathay:
cereal bowl,
dinner plate,
and fruit bowl.

Old Cathay
A modern adaptation of oriental art hand decorated
in warm golds, rusts, blues and greens.

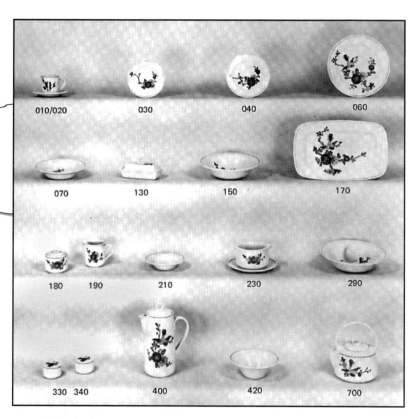

Old Cathay:
1979 brochure.

V 604 Old Cathay

Code	Item	Price	Code	Item	Price
010	Cup, 7 oz.	$8 – 9	190	Creamer, 10 oz.	$18 – 20
020	Saucer, 6⅞"	$2 – 3	210	Fruit, 6"	$9 – 10
030	Bread & Butter, 6⅞"	$6 – 7	230	Gravy, Fastand, 1¼ pt.	$22 – 25
040	Salad Plate, 8"	$8 – 9	290	Vegetable, div., med., rnd., 9"	$30 – 35
060	Dinner Plate, 10¾"	$10 – 11	330	Salt	$9 – 10
070	Soup, 7¼"	$13 – 15	340	Pepper	$9 – 10
130	Butter & Lid	$35 – 40	400	Coffee Pot & Lid	$55 – 60
150	Vegetable, med., rnd., 9"	$25 – 30	420	Cereal, 7"	$11 – 12
170	Platter, lg., rect., 13¼"	$30 – 35	700	Teapot & Lid	$55 – 60
180	Sugar & Lid, 8 oz.	$20 – 22			

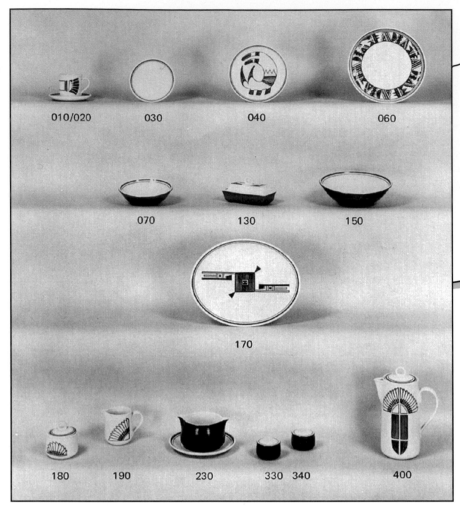

Mesa:
1979 brochure.

Painted Desert:
1977 brochure.

Monterey: 1979 brochure.

Monterey
The windswept loveliness of a Monterey Cypress...a silhouette impression against an indigo sky. Subtle, sophisticated, a collector's item, an heirloom in the making. The striking scene in blues and browns, on sand-tone background, decorate the dinner, salad plate and dramatic buffet server. Other pieces are plain sand-tone, two-tone, or striped.

California Collection: V 633 Monterey, V 634 Big Sur, V 635 Catalina, V 636 Capistrano; V 601 Mesa, V 619 Painted Desert, V 637 Cognac

Deduct 10% for V 637 Cognac.

010	Cup	$7 – 8	230	Gravy, Fastand, 1¼ pt.	
020	Saucer, 6"	$2 – 3		(except *California Collection*)	$20 – 22
030	Bread & Butter, 6⅜"	$5 – 6	290	Vegetable, div., med., rnd., 9"	$25 – 30
040	Salad Plate, 8"		330	Salt	$8 – 9
	(except *California Collection*)	$7 – 8	340	Pepper	$8 – 9
060	Dinner Plate, 10⅛"		400	Coffee Pot & Lid	$50 – 55
	(except *California Collection*)	$9 – 10	420	Cereal, 6¼"	$10 – 11
070	Soup, 6¾"	$12 – 13	700	Teapot & Lid	$50 – 55
130	Butter & Lid	$30 – 35		***California Collection* Additions**	
150	Vegetable, med., rnd., 9"	$22 – 25	040	Salad Plate, 8"	$12 – 13
170	Platter, lg., oval, 13"	$25 – 30	060	Dinner Plate, 10⅛"	$14 – 15
180	Sugar & Lid, 8 oz.	$18 – 20	236	Gravy Server, 1¼ pt.	$15 – 17
190	Creamer, 10 oz.	$16 – 18	237	Gravy Server Stand	$7 – 8
210	Fruit, 5½"	$8 – 9	300	Buffet Server, rnd., 13"	$45 – 50

Country French Shape

V 641 Cinnamon (1973)

V 642 Vernon Bouquet (1974)

V 643 Lemon Tree (1975)

V 644 Lime Tree (1975)

V 648 Antique Blue (1975)

V 602 Brookside (1976)

V 603 Cinnamon Green (1976)

V 655 Gigi (1978)

V 656 Happy Days (1978)

V 660 Italian Delight (1979)

V 661 Spring Garland (1979)

V 666 Morning Glory (1980)

Gigi

In the early 1970s Evan K. Shaw decided the Vernonware Division needed an elegant, European-style shape that was similar to the Poppytrail Division's American Tradition shape, but softer and more feminine. He was familiar with the dinnerware creations of Vreni Wawra, a local ceramicist who specialized in handcrafted, French-inspired designs. Her dinnerware lines, known as Vreni Ware, were carried in finer department stores throughout Southern California. The Country French shape was based on the idea, style, and look of her designs. Shaw purchased from her one dinner plate, a sugar and lid, a creamer, and a teapot along with the right to create a shape styled after these items. Molds, blocks, and cases were not included in the purchase.

Country French was characterized by widely spaced ridges on the rims of the flatware and grooves in the body of the holloware. The distinctive salad/dessert plate, a rounded square design slightly larger than the salad plate, was produced only in Antique Blue and Spring Garland. A majority of the patterns were floral designs. The two solid color exceptions were the all-yellow Lemon Tree and the all-green Lime Tree. Antique Blue and Morning Glory were decal decorated patterns.

Country French was the last major shape developed by the Vernonware Division. Unfortunately it was introduced at a time when the popularity of hand-painted designs on beautiful shapes was beginning to wane. Therefore, none of these patterns were bestsellers for the company.

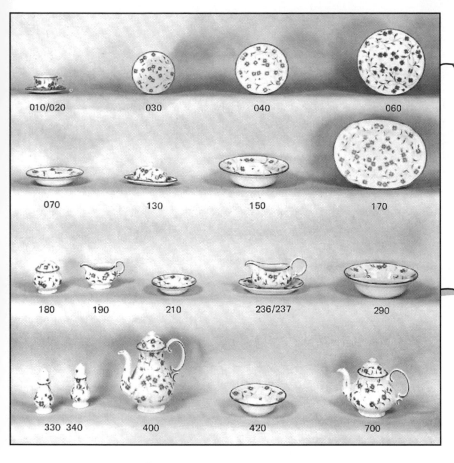

Cinnamon: 1979 brochure.

Cinnamon
New...Country French, hand-crafted shapes, with graceful rounded curves, create a perfect background for an all-over floral in warm cinnamon tones. The hand-painted swirl-texture under the pattern, gives a distinctive individuality to every piece.

Vernon Bouquet
A charming provincial bouquet of flowers and foliage in today's favorite colors of warm henna, burgundy and brilliant, electric blue, with soft, light green leaves. Hand-painted with a rich, hand-crafted look on a Country French shape.

Vernon Bouquet: Metlox brochure.

Gigi

Gigi: 1979 brochure.

V 602 Brookside, V 603 Cinnamon Green, V 641 Cinnamon, V 642 Vernon Bouquet, V 643 Lemon Tree, V 644 Lime Tree, V 648 Antique Blue, V 655 Gigi, V 656 Happy Days, V 660 Italian Delight, V 661 Spring Garland

010	Cup, 7 oz.	$8 – 9
020	Saucer, 6⅞".	$2 – 3
030	Bread & Butter, 6⅞"	$6 – 7
040	Salad Plate, 8" (except Antique Blue).	$8 – 9
060	Dinner Plate, 10¾"	$10 – 11
070	Soup, 7¼".	$13 – 15
130	Butter & Lid	$45 – 50
150	Vegetable, med., rnd. 9".	$25 – 30
170	Platter, lg., oval, 13¼".	$30 – 35
180	Sugar & Lid, 8 oz.	$20 – 22
190	Creamer, 8 oz.	$18 – 20
210	Fruit, 5½" .	$9 – 10
236	Gravy Server, 1 pt.	$22 – 25
237	Gravy Server Stand	$8 – 10
290	Vegetable, div., med., rnd., 9"	$30 – 35
330	Salt	$9 – 10
340	Pepper	$9 – 10
400	Coffee Pot & Lid, 8 cup	$70 – 80
420	Cereal 6½"	$11 – 12
700	Teapot & Lid, 4½ cup	$70 – 80

V 641 Cinnamon, V 642 Vernon Bouquet, V 643 Lemon Tree, V 644 Lime Tree Addition

760	Mug, 8 oz.	$16 – 18

V 648 Antique Blue Addition

110	Salad/Dessert Plate, 8¼"	$8 – 9

V 655 Gigi Additions

080	Vegetable, sm., rnd., 8¼"	$22 – 25
160	Platter, med., oval, 12⅜".	$25 – 30
620	Casserole & Lid, 2 qt.	$65 – 70
760	Mug, 8 oz.	$16 – 18
—	Candleholder	$25 – 28

V 661 Spring Garland Additions

080	Vegetable, sm., rnd., 8¼"	$22 – 25
110	Salad/Dessert Plate, 8¼"	$8 – 9
160	Platter, med., oval, 12⅜".	$25 – 30
620	Casserole & Lid, 2 qt.	$65 – 70
760	Mug, 8 oz.	$16 – 18

Spring Garland: Metlox brochure.

Morning Glory: Metlox brochure*.

*Poor quality, only photo available.

V 666 Morning Glory

010	Cup, 7 oz..	$8 – 9
020	Saucer, 6⅞"	$2 – 3
040	Salad Plate, 8"	$8 – 9
060	Dinner Plate, 10¾"	$10 – 11
150	Vegetable, med., rnd., 9"	$25 – 30
170	Platter, lg., oval, 13¼"	$30 – 35
180	Sugar & Lid, 8 oz.	$20 – 22
190	Creamer, 8 oz.	$18 – 20
400	Coffee Pot & Lid, 8 cup	$70 – 80
420	Cereal, 6½"	$11 – 12

Hermosa Collection

Hermosa Collection
V 651 Uno (1978)
V 652 Dos (1978)
V 653 Tres (1978)
V 654 Mucho (1978)
V 657 Mount Whitney (1978)
V 658 Rattan (1979)

Rattan

The Hermosa Collection was composed of four abstract patterns with simple shapes redesigned from existing Vernonware shapes. These small gourmetware patterns featured three casseroles and two oval bakers. The dinner plate and the salad plate were decorated with the pattern's design. Uno offered a single large flower encircled by three solid color bands; Dos a single group of two petals with two solid color bands; Tres three groups of three petals with two solid color bands; and Mucho a wide circular band of many petals with four solid color bands. Each of the remaining items was identically decorated in all four patterns with either one of the four designs or the solid color bands.

Mount Whitney, referred to as "Hermosa White" in the Metlox company files, was a solid white pattern consisting of place setting and completer items only. The size of most items was slightly different from similarly shaped Hermosa Collection pieces. The coffee pot, casseroles, and oval bakers of the Hermosa patterns were intended to combine with Mount Whitney and provide contrasting, patterned items.

Rattan, a beautiful pattern featuring embossed rattan stems and leaves, evolved from the shapes of Mount Whitney. It included more dinnerware items than the other patterns but lacked the gourmetware.

Hermosa Collection — Uno: 1979 brochure.

760   040   060   150
170   180 190   400
420   600   610
630   631   640

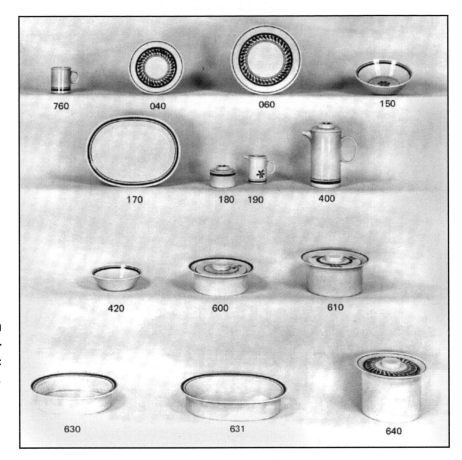

Hermosa Collection — Mucho: 1979 brochure.

Hermosa Collection: V 651 Uno, V 652 Dos, V 653 Tres, V 654 Mucho

040	Salad Plate, 8½"	$5 – 6	420	Cereal, 7¼"	$8 – 9
060	Dinner Plate, 10⅛"	$7 – 8	600	Casserole & Lid, 1 qt.	$30 – 35
150	Vegetable, med., rnd., 9⅛"	$18 – 20	610	Casserole & Lid, 2 qt.	$35 – 40
170	Platter, lg., oval, 13½"	$20 – 22	630	Oval Baker, 1 qt.	$25 – 30
180	Sugar & Lid	$14 – 16	631	Oval Baker, 2 qt.	$30 – 35
190	Creamer, 6½ oz.	$12 – 14	640	Casserole & Lid, 3 qt.	$40 – 45
400	Coffee Pot & Lid, 44 oz.	$35 – 40	760	Mug, 8 oz.	$8 – 9

V 657 Mount Whitney

010	Cup, 8 oz.	$5 – 6	170	Platter, lg., oval, 14¾"	$20 – 22
020	Saucer, 6¼"	$2 – 3	180	Sugar & Lid	$14 – 16
040	Salad Plate, 7½"	$5 – 6	190	Creamer, 6½ oz.	$12 – 14
060	Dinner Plate, 10½"	$7 – 8	420	Cereal, 7¼"	$8 – 9
150	Vegetable, med., rnd., 10"	$18 – 20	760	Mug, 8 oz.	$7 – 8

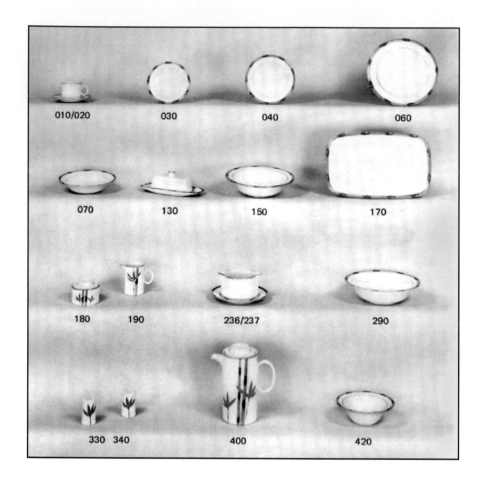

Rattan:
1979 brochure.

V 658 Rattan

010	Cup, 8 oz..	$8 – 9	290	Vegetable, div., med., 10"..	$30 – 35
020	Saucer, 6¼"..	$2 – 3	330	Salt..	$9 – 10
030	Bread & Butter, 6½"	$6 – 7	340	Pepper..	$9 – 10
040	Salad Plate, 7½"..	$8 – 9	400	Coffee Pot & Lid, 44 oz..	$65 – 75
060	Dinner Plate, 10½"..	$10 – 11	420	Cereal, 7¼"..	$11 – 12
070	Soup, 8½"..	$14 – 16			
130	Butter & Lid	$45 – 50			
150	Vegetable, med., rnd., 10"	$25 – 30			
170	Platter, lg., rect., 14¾"	$30 – 35			
180	Sugar & Lid..	$20 – 22			
190	Creamer, 6½ oz..	$18 – 20	210	Fruit..	$9 – 10
236	Gravy Server, 1 pt..	$22 – 25	700	Teapot & Lid..	$65 – 75
237	Gravy Server Stand..	$8 – 10	760	Mug, 8 oz..	$16 – 18

A brochure dated December 1, 1980, lists the following items as scheduled for production during spring 1981. Their appearance has not been verified from subsequent brochure material.

Vernonware Gourmet Patterns

Blue Bird

V 760 Blue Bird
V 761 Country Floral
V 762 Chesapeake
P 054 American Heritage (Gourmet Set)

These early 1980s patterns, listed together as "decorated gourmet" sets in brochure material, were composed of borrowed items from other shapes. The items were classified in dinnerware, gourmetware, and giftware categories. Most of the gourmetware came from Colorstax and the gourmet artware lines. The giftware items were primarily Provincial shapes. P 054 American Heritage (Gourmet Set) is included here because it offered identical items and was always listed with the three other patterns. It should not be confused with P 054 American Heritage, a pattern on the Poppytrail Division American Tradition shape that included only dinnerware items. Both patterns shared the same design. The dinnerware items are listed in the American Tradition shape chapter.

American Heritage:
Metlox brochure.

V 760, V 761, and V 762 were the last patterns released by the Vernonware Division. Although some Vernonware patterns continued to be produced, shortly after Shaw's death the division was formally dissolved.

American Heritage

Country Floral and Chesapeake: Metlox brochure.

V 760 Blue Bird, V 761 Country Floral, V 762 Chesapeake, P 054 American Heritage (Gourmet Set)

Dinnerware (except P 054 American Heritage)

010	Cup.	$7 – 8
020	Saucer	$2 – 3
040	Salad Plate	$7 – 8
060	Dinner Plate	$9 – 10
150	Vegetable, med.	$22 – 25
170	Platter, lg., rnd.	$25 – 30
180	Sugar & Lid	$20 – 22
190	Creamer	$18 – 20
400	Coffee Pot & Lid	$50 – 55
420	Cereal	$10 – 11

Gourmetware

101	Mixing Bowl, sm., 16 oz.	$25 – 30
102	Mixing Bowl, med., 44 oz.	$30 – 35
103	Mixing Bowl, lg., 84 oz.	$35 – 40
230	Sauce Server, 1 pt.	$22 – 25
383	Souffle, lg., 8 cup	$25 – 28
384	Ramekin, 6 oz.	$14 – 15
385	Au Gratin	$20 – 22
387	Quiche Server, 10½"	$30 – 32
640	Casserole & Lid, 4 qt.	$50 – 55
781	Lasagna Server, med., 13"	$35 – 40

V 761 Country Floral and V 762 Chesapeake Gourmetware Additions

440	Canister & Lid, ex. lg., 2¾ qt.	$25 – 30
450	Canister & Lid, lg., 2 qt.	$20 – 25
460	Canister & Lid, med., 1 qt.	$18 – 20
470	Canister & Lid, sm., 1 pt.	$15 – 18
620	Casserole & Lid, 2 qt.	$40 – 45

Giftware

330	Salt	$9 – 10
340	Pepper	$9 – 10
350	Tumbler, 11 oz.	$22 – 25
360	Candleholder	$20 – 22
370	Pitcher, lg., 2 qt.	$45 – 50
710	Bread Server, 9½"	$35 – 40
720	Mug, lg., 1 pt.	$22 – 25
760	Mug, 8 oz.	$16 – 18
880	Pitcher, sm., 1½ pt.	$30 – 35

V 760 Blue Bird Giftware Addition

—	Clock	$100 – 110

Artware Lines

The Prouty Years

Willis Prouty began to focus Metlox's attention on the creation of artware lines after he was encouraged by the success of the dinnerware lines introduced in the mid-1930s. Prouty recognized the sales potential of decorative pottery artware items which were very popular in the 1930s. Most of the Prouty artware was produced from 1938 to 1942. To his credit, Prouty obviously set high standards for his artware lines; his was some of the finest artware produced in the pre-World War II period. His emphasis on quality, craftsmanship, and beauty established the Metlox artware tradition which Evan K. Shaw inherited and continued.

Documentation of the Prouty artware lines is difficult due to the scarcity of brochure material. The only available printed source for the listings below is a lengthy, comprehensive Poppy Trail Pottery Dinnerware and Artware brochure dated January 1, 1942. It presents a photograph of each item with its item number and a dimension, usually the height, but without the company item name or description. The items are arranged by artware lines. Although each line's list shows only the items offered for sale in 1942, it is representative of the selection and includes the items most commonly found. The identification of items not listed in the 1942 brochure was provided by interested collectors.

Additional information about the artware lines was obtained from several sources. Jack Chipman, noted authority on Southern California pottery, shared his intimate knowledge of the Prouty artware lines and helped to name and describe items. Author-historian Harvey Duke supplied copies of advertising material and trade articles from the late 1930s and early 1940s which contained excellent descriptions. Devoted collectors contributed useful facts concerning the artware's marks, color selection, and glazes.

Carl Romanelli

The reputation of Prouty's artware would be greatly diminished if it lacked the extraordinary creations of brilliant designer Carl Romanelli. The American-born progeny of seven generations of family-trained sculptors from the Romanelli Studio in Florence, Italy, Carl Romanelli utilized his background and artistry to create artware that was, and still is today, recognized as truly outstanding.

Romanelli's mystique in the collecting world has been enhanced by the enigmatic nature of his career at, and abrupt disappearance from, Metlox. He first joined Metlox's design department around 1938 and

Modern Masterpieces: No. 1814 Angelfish Vase, 8½"; No. 1809 Sea Horse Vase, 9¼"; and No. 1801 Swordfish Vase, 9".

Romanelli's Artware for Prouty

Romanelli's Modern Masterpieces was a high point in American art pottery design. Although primarily composed of vases and flower holders, this large line also included busts, figures, bookends, and a wall plaque. Extreme attention to detail, a flowing sense of line, a feeling of suspended movement, a sensitive awareness of balance, and a carved, rather than molded, look characterized these distinctive sculptures in clay. The florid, ornate styling and statuesque poses of many designs reflected Romanelli's Florentine heritage. His love of figures in suspended animation manifested itself in designs of birds in flight, ladies dancing, and fish swimming. Nudes were a frequent subject. The risque hands-on-holster stance of the topless cowgirl undoubtedly was quite shocking for its time. The 12 Zodiac vases, incorporated as a distinct series in the line, featured the motifs of each astrological sign in bas-relief. One side of the vase showed the symbol of the sign while the other depicted its corresponding element. According to trade articles, the Zodiac Series was introduced in 1940, as probably were the other initial offerings of

worked there until 1942. During this period he created the Modern Masterpieces line and worked on the Metlox Miniatures series. Although it is not known if he helped with the other artware lines, he certainly had no involvement with dinnerware designs. He reappeared briefly at Metlox in the 1950s, assisting Bob Allen with the designs of the Art Treasures of the World series. A tall, big man remembered by employees for his unassuming nature as much as his artistic temperament, Romanelli had a definite personality clash with Evan K. Shaw. Romanelli's rapid departure from Metlox resulted from artistic disagreements with Shaw and Shaw's refusal to give Romanelli, or any designer, royalties.

Romanelli also had an active, productive career outside of Metlox. As a young man, he was trained by his father, who, at the beginning of this century, was the first noted sculptor to settle in the Los Angeles area. After serving in World War II, the reason for his first departure from Metlox, he opened a studio at 3944 Wilshire Boulevard in Los Angeles. There he devoted his creative efforts to various forms of sculpture including plaques, heads, and figures of famous personalities and movie stars. Noted for his action and portrait sculptures, Romanelli benefitted from numerous commissions. His well-known works include the Al Jolson Memorial at Hillside Memorial Park in Inglewood, California; a bronze of John Henry Cardinal Newman which won a national competition and was presented to Pope John XXIII on his eightieth birthday in 1962; a statue of John F. Kennedy for the Bell, California Civic Center in 1969; a bronze bust of Alaskan artist Sydney Laurence unveiled in the Civic Center in Anchorage, Alaska, in 1975; and a life-size statue of Elvis Presley introduced in Las Vegas, Nevada, in 1978.

Modern Masterpieces: Indian Squaw and Indian Brave.

Modern Masterpieces: No. 1803 Mermaid and Fish Vase.

Modern Masterpieces. Succeeding items in the line were added through the beginning of 1942.

Metlox assigned the Modern Masterpieces "1800" series item numbers in numerical order. Since the lowest and the highest numbers were 1801 and 1833 respectively in the 1942 brochure, and since the line was discontinued in 1942, it is assumed that the Modern Masterpieces were numbered from 1801 to 1833 inclusively. Counting each of the 12 Zodiac vases separately, the number of items would logically total 44. In the list below, ten item numbers are skipped. If six of these belong to the six additional items without a known number, the list should be nearly complete.

Most of the Modern Masterpieces were very well marked. Often the incised artist signature "C Romanelli" appeared on the design. Several forms of incised, underside marks included:
1. "Poppy trail" — the item number — "MADE IN CALIFORNIA" — "U.S.A." — "C Romanelli";
2. "Poppy trail" — "C Romanelli" — the item number — "METLOX" — "MADE IN U.S.A.";
3. "Poppy trail" — the item number — "MADE IN U.S.A."
"C Romanelli" and "Poppy trail" appeared as script signatures with "Poppy trail" in quotation marks. Items also bore paper labels, including a flower-shaped sticker reading "The Famous Poppytrail POTTERY BY METLOX." Many of the designs were patented. A six-digit design patent number, not to be confused with the "1800" item numbers, was sometimes ink-stamped on the underside of some items.

Metlox Miniatures (c. 1939 – 42), was a large collection of small, mostly animal-shaped figurines. While many presented the subject in a realistic fashion, others featured a comical rendering, and a few were decidedly modernistic in style. Although several, such as the flamingos and the heron, are easily found, many are seen infrequently. Metlox advertised the larger miniatures as centerpieces for the low flower bowls. Although never officially credited to Romanelli in the 1942 brochure, in advertising, or in trade articles, the idea for the line and most of the designs were unmistakably his. The Miniatures are first mentioned in trade articles from 1939, probably the year the series was introduced.

Some subject-related items were released in small groups of three or four. Various sizes of the Chinese Lady, Chinese Man, and Japanese Lady were produced. One large group, labeled "AUTHENTIC MINIATURES OF ODDITIES OF THE ANIMAL KINGDOM BY METLOX," included a name card with an elaborate description attached to each animal figurine. The card listed the group's members — a chimpanzee, dinosaur, nine-banded armadillo, aardvark, otter, giraffe, Indian rhinoceros, plated lizard, giant anteater, bactrian camel, hippopotamus, and three versions of "Baby" the Indian elephant — as copyrighted designs. The following description of the bactrian camel appeared on its name card.

> *Bactrian Camel*
> *This variety of camel has two humps and is a native of Asia. It is capable of carrying nearly six hundred pounds for as much as four days between drinks. It stores water in extra cavities in its stomach.*
> *It is slow of pace and ungainly in carriage but has served mankind from the earliest ages under conditions which no other creature could withstand.*

The 1942 brochure assigned the series item numbers ranging from 53-G to 135-G. The meaning of the "G" is unknown. It seems probable that an item was assigned to each number in this range. If the items without known numbers, including those produced in various sizes, are included in the range, then the following listing is nearly complete.

Metlox marked the series with paper labels and ink backstamps. Probably no incised markings were used because the small size of the items precluded it. The earliest items bore a sticker in the shape of an "M." Another common label was a square with rounded cor-

Miniatures Series: Bactrian Camel with AUTHENTIC MINIATURES OF ODDITIES OF THE ANIMAL KINGDOM name card.

ners. Both labels read "Miniatures by METLOX" — "MANHATTAN BEACH" — "CALIFORNIA." The various ink backstamps included "METLOX" — "MADE IN U.S.A.," "METLOX," "U.S.A.," and a "Made in U.S.A." confusingly similar to a stamp used by Franciscan Ceramics.

Both the Modern Masterpieces and the Metlox Miniatures were decorated in the following ways:
1. A pastel color with a satin matte glaze (very common);
2. A vivid color with a high-gloss glaze (common);
3. Hand decorated with a high-gloss glaze;
4. Blended colors with a high-gloss glaze;
5. Blended colors with a high-gloss and a satin matte glaze together (rare); and
6. Two-tone colors (probably a few Modern Masterpieces items only).
The hand-decorated and blended colors are harder to find. Ivory with a satin matte glaze is the most common color. Black with a high-gloss glaze and white with a high-gloss glaze are probably the most rare.

Other Prouty Artware

The remainder of Prouty's artware was divided into separate lines in the 1942 brochure. Lines, such as the "700" series Low Flower Bowls and the "100" series Bud Vases and Vases, followed a distinct item numbering system. It could not be ascertained whether or not skipped item numbers in a series indicate a missing item. Trade articles date the lines from 1939 to 1942. The designer or designers are unknown.

The Low Flower Bowls presented a variety of geometrical, leaf, and shell shapes. Many featured a ruffled, ribbed, irregular, or crimped styling. Two sizes of the same design often were produced. Numbers 779, 780, 781, and 782 were variations of the same round design with different sides and handles. A variety of incised, underside marks included the following:

1. "Poppy trail" — the item number — "MADE IN CALIFORNIA U.S.A.";
2. "Poppy trail " — "BY METLOX" — the item number — "MADE IN U.S.A.";
3. the item number — "Poppy trail" — "MADE IN CALIFORNIA U.S.A.";
4. "Hand made" — "Poppy trail" — "MADE IN CALIFORNIA U.S.A.";
5. "METLOX" — the item number — "MADE IN U.S.A."

"Poppy trail" appeared as a two-word script signature in quotation marks. Some items were ink-stamped "MADE IN U.S.A." or "METLOX" — "MADE IN U.S.A." in addition to the incised mark. Others used one of the ink-stamps instead of an incised marking. Ink-stamped, six-digit design patent numbers were common.

Prouty produced a diverse assortment of Bud Vases, Vases, and Cactus Containers. The lists below distinguish each item by describing its type, shape, and/or styling, and by giving the height. Most had paper labels or the common, incised, underside marking "METLOX" — the item number — "MADE IN U.S.A." Although bud vases have been found with the "M"-shaped Miniatures sticker, these were not designated as members of that series by Metlox in the 1942 brochure.

The Low Flower Bowls, Bud Vases, Vases, and Cactus Containers were produced in a variety of colors. By far the most common was a pastel color with a satin matte glaze. A vivid color with a high-gloss glaze was less frequent. Blended colors were rare. Two-tone colors often were used for the Low Flower Bowls.

The Console Bowls and Candle Holders were merchandised both separately and together as matching console sets. Numbers 20, 21, and 22 were the same design in three sizes. Number 20 was paired with the number 30 candle holder and number 22 with the number 31 candle holder. The footed sea shell items complemented each other as did the Yorkshire designs. The Ashtrays could also be used with the console sets, especially the sea shell and the Yorkshire designs.

Low Flower Bowl: No. 736 round 11" ruffled rim low flower bowl with sea horse miniature.

The round, number 51 ashtray frequently appeared with advertising designs of various companies.

Garden Pottery consisted of flower pots, planters, jardinieres, and a set of three saucers. All were produced in vivid colors with a high-gloss glaze and pastels with a satin matte glaze.

The lovely, 12¼" deco wine bottles, marked "METLOX," came in pastel colors with a satin matte glaze.

Collectors should also be aware of artware marked "Mission Bell" — "California." This was most likely a complementary artware line to Metlox's Mission Bell dinnerware pattern.

The artware of the Prouty years is even more impressive when one considers the short period of time in which it was created. Production began in 1938 and ceased when the United States entered World War II. By the time the war ended, American tastes had changed, encouraged by an abundance of new design concepts, trends, and looks fashioned for a modern lifestyle. Prouty's designs were passé. Willis Prouty himself had decided to sell the company and to move on to other endeavors. After Evan K. Shaw purchased Metlox, his Poppytrail Artware Division, staffed by designers with very different, fresh ideas, would create artware lines as distinctive as those of the Prouty years.

Modern Masterpieces: No. 1805 Nude Figurine Flower Holder, 8¾"; No. 1817 Nude with Flamingo Vase; and No. 1806 Nude Figurine Flower Holder, 10".

Modern Masterpieces: No. 1826 Two Birds on a Branch, 8"; No. 1825 Nude Figure Holding Birds, 11"; and Single Bird on Branch.

Modern Masterpieces:
Bookends — Nude with Hounds.

Modern Masterpieces: No. 1820 Double Angelfish Vase, 14"; and No. 1814 Angelfish Vase, 8½".

Modern Masterpieces: Victory Vase with Eagle.

Modern Masterpieces: No. 1833 Hawaiian Girl Flower Holder, 9".

Modern Masterpieces: No. 1827 Rooster, 8¼"; No. 1826 Two Birds on Branch, 8"; No. 1805 Nude Figurine Flower Holder, 8¾"; and No. 1822 Birds and Clouds, 9".

Modern Masterpieces: No. 1804-8 Scorpio Vase and No. 1804-2 Taurus Vase from the Zodiac Series (front and back views).

Modern Masterpieces: No. 1819 Cowgirl, 9½"'; and Cowboy.

Modern Masterpieces: No. 1818 Fan Dancer Vase, 13½".

Modern Masterpieces: No. 1803 Mermaid and Fish Vase.

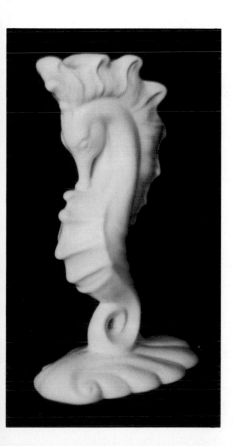

Modern Masterpieces: No. 1823 Deer, 7" and No. 1808 Water Bearer Bud Vase, 6⅜".

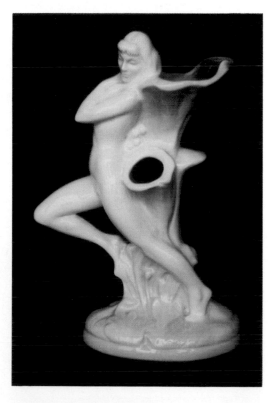

Modern Masterpieces: No. 1809 Sea Horse Vase, 9¼".

Modern Masterpieces: No. 1806 Nude Figurine Flower Holder, 10".

"Modern Masterpieces" Designed by Carl Romanelli

1801	Swordfish Vase, 9"	$100 – 125
1803	Mermaid & Fish Vase	$110 – 125
1804	Zodiac Vase Series, 4" x 3" x 8"	
	1804-1	Aries	$95 – 110
	1804-2	Taurus	$95 – 110
	1804-3	Gemini	$95 – 110
	1804-4	Cancer	$95 – 110
	1804-5	Leo	$95 – 110
	1804-6	Virgo	$95 – 110
	1804-7	Libra	$95 – 110
	1804-8	Scorpio	$95 – 110
	1804-9	Sagittarius	$95 – 110
	1804-10	Capricorn	$95 – 110
	1804-11	Aquarius	$95 – 110
	1804-12	Pisces	$95 – 110
1805	Nude Figurine Flower Holder, 8¾".	$175 – 200
1806	Nude Figurine Flower Holder, 10".	$225 – 250
1808	Water Bearer Bud Vase, 6⅜"	$100 – 125
1809	Sea Horse Vase, 9¼"	$150 – 175
1814	Angelfish Vase, 8½"	$75 – 90
1816	Water Bearer Bud Vase, 9¼"	$175 – 200
1817	Nude with Flamingo Vase	$225 – 250
1818	Fan Dancer Vase, 13½"	$250 – 275
1819	Cowgirl, 9½"	$225 – 250
1820	Double Angelfish Vase, 14"	$175 – 200
1822	Birds & Clouds, 9"	$100 – 125
1823	Deer, 7"	$85 – 100
1824	Bird in Flight, 9½"	$85 – 100
1825	Nude Figure Holding Birds, 11"	$175 – 200
1826	Two Birds on Branch, 8"	$75 – 90
1827	Rooster, 8¼"	$75 – 90
1828	Female Bust, 11"	$200 – 225
1829	Wall Plaque — Woman's Head & Arms, 14½"	$275 – 300
1832	Dancing Lady, 9¼"	$150 – 175
1833	Hawaiian Girl Flower Holder, 9".	$175 – 200

Additional items

—	Bookends — Nude with Hounds, ea.	$175 – 200
—	Cowboy	$325 – 350
—	Indian Brave, 9"	$250 – 275
—	Indian Squaw	$325 – 350
—	Single Bird on Branch	$150 – 175
—	Victory Vase with Eagle	$125 – 150

Miniatures Series: comical standing duck with oversized head, heron, flamingo (head upright), 5½" fawn, 4¼" fawn, circus horse with front legs raised, Scottie dog, goofy horse, dinosaur, sitting bird with tail up, nine-banded armadillo, and shark. The rooster is from Romanelli's Modern Masterpieces series.

Miniatures Series: three versions of "Baby" the Indian elephant from the Authentic Miniatures of Oddities of the Animal Kingdom series. "Baby" was brought by MGM from the forests of south India to appear in the popular Tarzan movies with Johnny Weissmuller. These three poses — walking, sitting, and balancing on a ball — were originally modeled by H. Loud. Metlox obtained the exclusive rights to reproduce them as members of the Miniatures series.

Miniatures Series: bactrian camel, hippopotamus, "Baby" the Indian elephant walking, Indian rhinoceros, chimpanzee on all fours, "Baby" the Indian elephant sitting, and otter — all members of the Authentic Miniatures of Oddities of the Animal Kingdom Series.

Miniatures Series: giraffe, plated lizard, dinosaur, giant anteater, aardvark, and nine-banded armadillo — all members of the Authentic Miniatures of Oddities of the Animal Kingdom Series.

Miniatures Series: stylized small elephant with trunk up, chimpanzee ashtray, chimpanzee scratching head, cubistic dog sitting, cubistic dog prone, and stylized little pig.

Miniatures Series: chimpanzee scratching head, sailboat, abstract dog running, aardvark, and cubistic dog prone.

Miniatures Series: standing burro, sitting burro, goofy horse, squirrel, bird on branch, bird with wings tucked, and stylized horse.

Miniatures Series: 4¼" fawn, 5½" fawn, heron, goose with head forward, duck with head tilted forward, and duck with head down.

Miniatures Series: Chinese man, Chinese lady, and young man playing a mandolin.

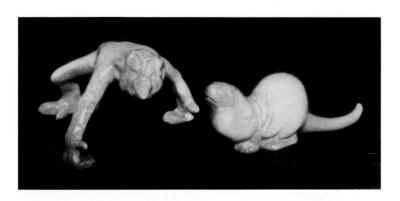

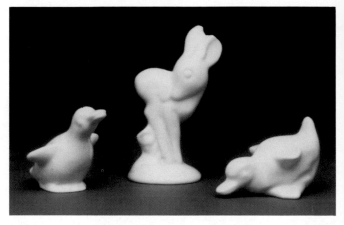

Miniatures Series: chimpanzee on all fours and otter — both from the Authentic Miniatures of Oddities of the Animal Kingdom series.

Miniatures Series: duck with head tilted forward, fawn (looking back), and duck with head down.

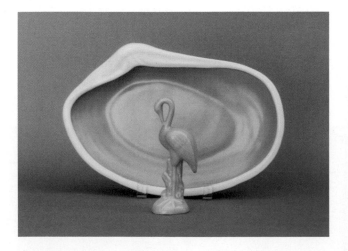

Low Flower Bowl: No. 737 round 11" crimped rim low flower bowl with flamingo (head upright) miniature.

Low Flower Bowl: No. 746 12¼" clam shell low flower bowl with flamingo (head down) miniature.

Metlox Miniatures

—	Aardvark	$80 – 85
—	Giant Anteater	$80 – 85
—	Nine-Banded Armadillo, 1¾"	$80 – 85
108-G	Bear, Paw Upraised, 5"	$60 – 65
109-G	Reclining Bear, 5½"	$60 – 65
112-G	Standing Bear, 6½"	$70 – 75
118-G	Bee	$20 – 25
110-G	Bird on Branch, 4⅝"	$65 – 70
98-G	Bird, Wings Tucked, 4"	$30 – 35
134-G	Bird, Wings Up, 5"	$40 – 45
132-G	Little Bird, Wings Outstretched	$25 – 30
131-G	Little Bird, Wings Tucked	$25 – 30
133-G	Little Bird, Wings Up	$25 – 30
107-G	Sitting Bird, Tail Up, 6¼"	$30 – 35
71-G	Sitting Burro, 3"	$40 – 45
72-G	Standing Burro, 3"	$40 – 45
92-G	Bactrian Camel, 5"	$90 – 95
117-G	Caterpillar	$20 – 25
82-G	Chimpanzee on All Fours, 4½"	$80 – 85
—	Chimpanzee Ashtray	$70 – 75
—	Chimpanzee Scratching Head, 3½"	$70 – 75
62-G	Crocodile, 9"	$80 – 85
—	Dinosaur, 4½"	$130 – 140
—	Abstract Dog, Running	$50 – 55
—	Cubistic Dog, Prone, 5"	$70 – 75
—	Cubistic Dog, Sitting, 3½"	$60 – 65
—	Scottie Dog, two sizes	$45 – 65
135-G	Terrier, 12½"	$85 – 95
—	Comical Standing Duck, Oversized Head, 5½"	$40 – 45
53-G	Duck, Head Down, 3"	$30 – 35
54-G	Duck, Head Tilted Forward, 3½"	$30 – 35
56-G	Duck, Head Upright, 3"	$30 – 35
55-G	Laughing Duck, Head Skyward, 3"	$30 – 35
76-G	"Baby" the Indian Elephant, Balancing on a Ball, 6½"	$115 – 125
—	"Baby" the Indian Elephant, Sitting, 3¾"	$75 – 85
75-G	"Baby" the Indian Elephant, Walking, 6½"	$90 – 95
—	Stylized Small Elephant, Trunk Up	$45 – 50
114-G	Fawn, 4¼"	$35 – 40
115-G	Fawn, 5½"	$45 – 50
—	Fawn, Looking Back	$35 – 40
—	Centerpiece with Three Highly Stylized Fish	$115 – 125
68-G	Fish, 3"	$30 – 35
103-G	Flamingo, Head Down, 6¼"	$45 – 50
104-G	Flamingo, Head Upright, 6¼"	$45 – 50
116-G	Frog, Head Down	$30 – 35
80-G	Frog, Head Up, 3"	$30 – 35
88-G	Giraffe, 5¾"	$80 – 85
101-G	Goose, Head Back, 3¾"	$40 – 45
102-G	Goose, Head Forward, 6½"	$40 – 45
100-G	Goose, Head Upright, 5"	$40 – 45
105-G	Heron, 6½"	$40 – 45
—	Hippopotamus	$80 – 85
—	Circus Horse, Front Legs Raised, 6"	$95 – 100
59-G	Goofy Horse, 4½"	$60 – 65
—	Abstract Prancing Horse	$50 – 55
—	Prancing, Saddled Horse	$50 – 55
69-G	Stylized Horse, 3"	$60 – 65
—	Chinese Lady, various sizes	$65 – 125
—	Japanese Lady, various sizes	$65 – 125
77-G	Lizard, 9½"	$80 – 85
—	Plated Lizard	$140 – 150
—	Chinese Man, various sizes	$65 – 125
—	Young Man Playing a Mandolin	$100 – 110
—	Otter	$70 – 75
58-G	Penguin, 3"	$45 – 50
73-G	Penguin, One Wing Outstretched, 2½"	$40 – 45
—	Stylized Little Pig	$40 – 45
—	Indian Rhinoceros	$80 – 85
57-G	Sailboat, 2½"	$30 – 35
78-G	Sea Horse, 4½"	$70 – 75
—	Shark, 6"	$70 – 75
79-G	Squirrel, 2"	$30 – 35
99-G	Swan, 3"	$40 – 45
—	Standing Turtle	$45 – 50

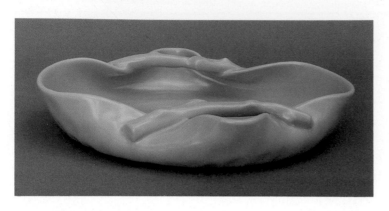

Low Flower Bowl: No. 782 round 11" low flower bowl with double handle.

Low Flower Bowl: No. 728 12" conch shell low flower bowl.

Low Flower Bowl: No. 779 round 11" low flower bowl with a bird on a single branch.

Low Flower Bowl: No. 784 15" leaf shape and no. 741 14¾" oval with horizontal ribbed sides low flower bowls.

Low Flower Bowls

728	Conch Shell, 12"	$30 – 35
736	Round, Ruffled Rim, 11"	$18 – 20
737	Round, Crimped Rim, 11"	$18 – 20
738	Oval, Horizontal Ribbed Sides, 11¼".	$25 – 30
741	Oval, Horizontal Ribbed Sides, 14¾".	$35 – 40
743	Oval, Smooth Irregular Sides, 11½" .	$18 – 20
744	Oval, Smooth Irregular Sides, 14¾" .	$20 – 25
746	Clam Shell, 12¼"	$25 – 30
747	Clam Shell, 15"	$35 – 40
748	Fluted, Straight Sides, 10½"	$20 – 25
756	Round, Shallow, 12¾"	$25 – 30
772	Oval, Irregular Sides, 15½"	$18 – 20
779	Round, Single Branch with Bird, 11".	$40 – 45
780	Round, Single Branch with Frog, 11".	$40 – 45
781	Round, Single Handle, 11"	$20 – 25
782	Round, Double Handle, 11"	$25 – 30
784	Leaf Shape, 15"	$30 – 35
785	Leaf Shape, 18"	$40 – 45
950	Rectangular, Crimped Rim, 12"	$18 – 20

(Brochure listing possibly wrong; item number may be 750.)

Garden Pottery: No. F-6 large ringed "Bauer" style flower pot.

Bud Vases: No. 106 5" horizontal ribbed pitcher, miniature flamingo (head down), and no. 112 5½" smooth-sided pitcher.

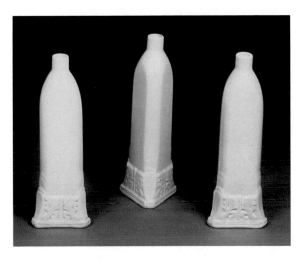

Miscellaneous: three 12¼" Deco style wine bottles.

Console Bowls: footed sea shell console bowl and candle holders.

Miscellaneous Artware

—	Deco Style Wine Bottle, 12¼"	$60 – 65

Garden Pottery

	Flower Pots, Ringed "Bauer" Style, Cone-Shaped				
F-2	Miniature	$20 – 25	6-S	Medium	$8 – 10
F-3	Very Small	$12 – 15	8-S	Large	$12 – 15
F-4	Small	$18 – 20			
F-5	Medium	$20 – 25		**Jardinieres, Ball-Shaped**	
F-6	Large	$25 – 30	760	Small	$18 – 20
F-7	Extra Large	$30 – 35	761	Medium	$25 – 30
F-8	Jumbo	$40 – 45	762	Large	$35 – 40
	Planters, Ringed "Bauer" Style, Bowl-Shaped			**Jardinieres, Rectangular**	
P-55	Small	$20 – 25	766	Small	$18 – 20
P-56	Medium	$30 – 35	767	Medium	$25 – 30
P-57	Large	$40 – 45	768	Large	$35 – 40
	Saucers/Underplates			**Jardinieres, Gourd-Shaped**	
			769	Medium	$20 – 25
4-S	Small	$4 – 5	770	Large	$30 – 35

Bud Vases

105	Cowboy Boot, 5¼"	$20 – 25
106	Horizontal Ribbed Pitcher, 5"	$20 – 25
108	Urn Shape, Double Handle, 4¼"	$18 – 20
109	Mexican Gourd Shape, 4¼"	$18 – 20
110	Smooth, Flared Rim, 5"	$18 – 20
111	Double Handle, 4½"	$18 – 20
112	Smooth-Sided Pitcher, 5½"	$20 – 25
114	Angular Ewer, 6"	$30 – 35
118	Fancy Victorian Ewer, 5½"	$30 – 35
119	Straight-Sided Pitcher, Rectangular Handle, 4¾"	$30 – 35
120	Pitcher, Bulbous Shape, 4½"	$25 – 30

Vases

121	"V for Victory" Vase on Pedestal, 6"	$40 – 45
130	Urn Shape, Chinese Style, 4½"	$30 – 35
131	Angular Shape, Chinese Style, 5¼"	$35 – 40
132	Bulbous Shape, Chinese Style, 5½"	$35 – 40
134	Urn Shape, with Oriental Style Blossoms, 5½"	$45 – 50
136	Horizontal Ribbed Pitcher, 7¾"	$40 – 45
137	Cylindrical, Horizontal Ribbed Lower Half, 8"	$55 – 60
160	Footed, Flared Rim, 8½"	$40 – 45
166	Rectangular, Embossed Deco Flowers, 10¼"	$60 – 65
751	Fan-Shaped Shell, 12¼"	$40 – 45

Console Bowls

20	Round, 12"	$55 – 60
21	Round, 5½"	$18 – 20
22	Round, 8¾"	$30 – 35
532	Yorkshire, Vertical Ribs	$40 – 45
733	Footed Sea Shell, 11"	$40 – 45
735	Round, Ruffled Rim, 11"	$40 – 45

Cactus Containers

46-C	Fawn, 7"	$30 – 35
47-C	Baby Shoe, 4¾"	$20 – 25
49-C	Small Dutch Shoe, 4"	$18 – 20
50-C	Large Dutch Shoe, 6½"	$25 – 30

Ashtrays

51	Round, often including advertising	$12 – 15
53	Sea Shell	$18 – 20
54-A	Round, Deep, with 3 Cigarette Rests	$20 – 25
551	Yorkshire, Round, Low	$18 – 20

Candle Holders

30	Ribbon Twist Shape, Footed	$40 – 45
31	Ball Shape, Footed	$20 – 25
581	Yorkshire, Vertical Ribs	$20 – 25
734	Footed Sea Shell	$20 – 25

Poppytrail Artware Division

Metlox Poppytrail Artware offers the most complete selection of artware items manufactured in the United States. They come in whimsical, elegant, and functional designs. We design with beauty and flexibility in mind. We are forever aware of function and serving elegance.

Research and design are the keynote of our success. Here at Metlox, master craftsmen work hand in hand with industry-trained designers to perfect our lovely designs. These designers often work for months on a project, experimenting with glazes and shapes until they achieve the perfect effect. Artware techniques are often used in our dinnerware. Because of this, our dinnerware and artware can often be coordinated, which is a source of joy to the fashion-conscious consumer.

Poppytrail's famous Dinnerware Quality Standard applies to our artware line. It has the same durable, sealed-under-glaze dinnerware body. This assures the customer of uniform high quality and design. The ware has been thoroughly tested in our own well-staffed laboratory. Poppytrail Artware is hand-crafted, hand-decorated, hand-painted, and hand-carved. It is not only functional and strong, but one of the most beautiful ceramic artware lines in the world.

— Quote from a 1969 Poppytrail Artware Catalogue

In what came to be designated as the Poppytrail Artware Division, Evan K. Shaw continued the Metlox artware tradition. At first, Shaw's treatment of and attitude toward the division was characterized by a degree of ambivalence. Shaw felt artware lines enhanced the company's credibility and reputation. If he believed strongly in a line's worth, he would spare no expenditure of time or money; expensive research, design, modeling, and production resources were readily committed in pursuit of the desired quality and beauty of each finished item. However, where production and merchandising were concerned, his attitude changed considerably. Unless a line sold extremely well, only a one-time production run in limited numbers was allowed. Artware lines in general were not marketed as aggressively as the dinnerware patterns. To Shaw, dinnerware, the financial backbone of the company, came first, and artware lines were secondary. Instead of intensifying the advertising and promotion of existing artware lines, he tended to replace them quickly with newly developed lines. In Shaw's defense, many of the artware lines of the 1950s were not financially successful. This also may explain Shaw's reticence in the late 1950s to support Allen and Shaw's preference for producing even more lines best classified as art pottery. Therefore, many experimental models in the vein of Art Treasures of the World and Ceramic Art Traditions, as well as designs resembling the style of Sascha Brastoff and Howard Pierce, were never developed or produced.

Shaw changed the emphasis of the Artware Division in the late 1950s and early 1960s. Lines coordinating with dinnerware and related to food service, as well as cookie jars and canister sets, were favored over art pottery. This proved quite profitable for the company and justified, in an economic sense, Shaw's decisions. Throughout the 1970s, the Artware Division continued to thrive. During the 1980s the cookie jars and giftware groups greatly helped to sustain the company financially.

It is sometimes difficult to identify Metlox artware because much of it — especially from the late 1940s and 1950s — was not signed with in-mold or ink-stamped marks. Instead, easily removed paper labels were used. Rationales for this procedure have been offered by modeler Frank Irwin. Artware was cast in plaster of Paris production molds. Every time an item was cast, a minute portion of the production mold would come off, thus gradually diminishing the detailing of the design. A typical production mold tended to last for a maximum of 20 casts. If in-mold marks were used, after ten casts the marking would be hardly discernible. In addition, the thick glaze sometimes filled the in-mold marks so completely that they could not be read.

Ink-stamping also had its drawbacks. Since it had to be applied to artware items by hand rather than by automation, it was more time-consuming and expensive than the application of paper labels. It also risked damaging the items, especially the smaller ones. To aid in the identification of Metlox's artware, an abundant amount of brochure reprints and archive photographs accompany the text.

After purchasing Metlox in 1946, Shaw continued the profitable Walt Disney Figurine line begun at his American Pottery in 1942. Shortly afterwards, Metlox introduced California Ivy Artware and the Nostalgia Line. Other lines, dating through the mid-1950s and almost exclusively of an art pottery style, were Ceramic Art Traditions, Art Treasures of the World, Tropicana, Mosaic Originals, California Contemporary Artware, Colonial Series, and Leaves of Enchantment. According to dated brochure materials in the late 1950s, food accessory lines began to dominate with the introduction of Sea Servers, Chip 'N Dips, Jam and Jellies, and the first cookie jars in 1959; Bake and Serve Casserolettes, Cabbage and Tomato Decorative Serving Accessories, Casual Serving Accessories, Twin and Triple Servers, and Animal Keepers in 1960; Smorgasboat Line and the first canisters in 1961; and Pebbline, Gold Nugget, Cock-A-Doodle-Do, and Directional Flower Arrangers in 1962. All of these lines were assigned a series of numbers within a range from 1 to 999. A skipped number in a line's series does not indicate a missing item. As an individual item or entire line was discontinued, numbers were often used again. By 1963 this numbering system was abandoned.

In the mid to late 1960s important introductions were the Eagle Provincial Accessories, 040 Strawberry Accessories, 050 Daisy Accessories, 070 Poppets, 071 Toppets, 081 1776 Line, and 120 Owl Line. The Vegetable Line and various gourmetware lines date from the late 1960s. The production of cookie jars and canister sets continued to increase during this period. From 1967 until the company's close, six-digit item numbers were assigned to items in the artware lines. The first three digits indicated the line number and the second three were the item numbers.

In the 1970s and 1980s, Metlox stressed the continuation and augmentation of existing successful lines rather than the introduction of new artware lines. A major exception was the Songs of Christmas, a 1971 – 79 holiday decorative plate series uniquely assigned to the Vernonware Division. Cookie jars and giftware groups dominated during the 1980s. Although dissimilar in style to the outstanding artware of the Prouty years, the Poppytrail Artware Division's total output, characterized by variety, originality, quality, and beauty, is just as impressive.

Walt Disney Figurines

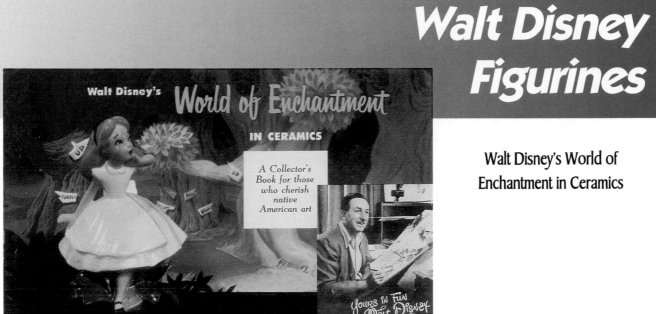

Walt Disney's World of
Enchantment in Ceramics

This large group includes planters, cookie jars, toothbrush holders, miniature teapots, and a child's dinnerware set as well as numerous figurines. Each item is a meticulously produced ceramic replica of a character or object from a Disney animated feature or cartoon. Referred to as "Walt Disney Original Art in Ceramics" in advertising material, they were intended to be used as fine art decoration for the home.

The history of Evan K. Shaw's Disney line is complex, involving four companies from 1940 to 1955. During the late 1930s Kay Kamen, the sole licensing agent for Disney character merchandise and the individual most responsible for its development, convinced Disney that it would be good advertising to allow select companies to produce and sell lines of ceramic character figurines. On October 10, 1940, a license was issued to Vernon Kilns. Over a one-and-a-half year period Vernon manufactured 36 figures from the film *Fantasia*, five from *Dumbo*, and one "Baby Weems" from *The Reluctant Dragon*. Eight dinnerware patterns, five bowls, and three vases, all based on *Fantasia* motifs, were also made. Due to the high production cost of these lines, Vernon decided to discontinue all of them. On July 22, 1942, with Disney's consent, Vernon assigned its contract to Shaw's fledgling American Pottery Company. Shaw also purchased the remaining Disney figurine inventory and the line's molds, blocks, and cases.

Shaw immediately continued to manufacture a limited number of Vernon's figures as well as develop his own designs. Production ceased temporarily when a devastating fire destroyed American Pottery in 1946. It resumed shortly after his purchase of Metlox in the same year. Reportedly, Shaw paid Disney only 5 percent of the sales profit. During the 1950s, other companies began to offer Disney a larger percentage and a higher production volume. When Shaw's license expired in 1955, it was not renewed.

The particular way Shaw's Disney line was licensed, labeled, and merchandised is confusing. The paper foil label used for identification on each figure reads either "American Pottery Company" or "Evan K. Shaw Company," never "Metlox Potteries." The most probable explanation is that Metlox was never licensed by Disney to manufacture the figurines. For some unknown reason, Disney issued Shaw two licenses. Both ran concurrently at the same address from 1945 to 1950. The first — for American Pottery located at 527 W. 7th Street, Los Angeles — was in effect from 1943 to 1950. The second — for Evan K. Shaw Company at 527 W. 7th Street, Los Angeles — lasted from 1945 to 1955. Although many collectors assume that figurines were manufactured at Evan K. Shaw Company, this company, in existence prior to Shaw's purchase of American Pottery and located at the above address, was never anything more than a distributorship. Shaw's Disney line, therefore, was produced only at American Pottery and Metlox.

Shaw valued his association with the Disney name and the status and credibility it added to the reputation of his companies. Additions to the line were carefully planned and developed. They were not timed to coincide with the release date of a new film. Rather they were determined by a character's established popularity. Frank Irwin modeled nearly all of the figures at American Pottery. Disney Studios provided him with animator's model sheets as examples of how each character should be designed. Brad Keeler, famed California ceramicist, was involved with the glazing and firing process at Shaw's American Pottery. Bob Allen and Mel Shaw, both experienced animators very familiar with Disney characters, designed their own figures at Metlox. Frank Irwin again was the chief modeler. Every new design was subject to approval by Evan K. Shaw and Disney Studios prior to production.

The accompanying list of Shaw Disney figurines and the "Walt Disney's World of Enchantment in Ceramics" brochure reprinted here were provided by David R. Smith of the Walt Disney Archives. His assistance is sincerely appreciated. Each entry has been positively identified either by its labeling or its appearance in company literature. A special thanks also to Stan Pawlowski, an avid collector of Disneyana, who helped to verify the inclusion of a few rare items and shared his extensive knowledge of the line.

Every figurine is listed and priced separately. For the most part, names, spellings, and descriptive words are exactly as they appear in

brochure material. Occasionally, words have been rearranged or added to identify a figure more clearly and distinguish it from similar ones. All item numbers are those used at American Pottery or Metlox. A majority of the figurines were assigned a "200 series" number. The Miniature Series, the last large group produced at Metlox, had its own numbering system. Although a listing of the figurines in numerical order seems to indicate somewhat accurately the order of production, the resulting jumbled listing would be confusing and inconvenient to the reader. Instead, the feature film character figures are grouped by the movie in which each appeared. The movies are arranged in chronological order according to the year of release. A large miscellaneous group lists all other cartoon character figures. If several versions of the same character were produced, they are arranged together by size from large to small. Unfortunately, company measurements were given only for the Miniature Series. Brochure listings, however, frequently used the adjectives small, medium, and large to indicate relative and proportionate size. For example, the large "Flower" is smaller than the large "Bambi" but larger than the medium and small "Flower."

It is impossible to determine exactly which figurines were made only at American Pottery, only at Metlox, or at both companies. Some were designed at American Pottery but not produced until after the move to Metlox. Some were manufactured at both companies. Paper foil labels are no help because American Pottery labels were used for several years at Metlox. Metlox labels were never used. One conclusion is certain: if a film was released after 1946, the year Shaw purchased Metlox, its character figurines were produced only at Metlox.

Walt Disney Figurines: Cinderella's Coach cookie jar/candy dish. *Photo courtesy of Stan Pawlowski.*

The known Vernon Kilns figures that Shaw produced are indicated in the list by the initials "VK" in parentheses after each entry. Frank Irwin confirms that only a limited number of the 42 Vernon figurines were continued at American Pottery. To date, nine have been identified. They are all of the *Fantasia* figures listed plus three from *Dumbo*. There are significant differences between the Vernon and American Pottery version. Vernon figures were signed and numbered on the unglazed bisque bottom of each piece. American Pottery always used identifying labels, and figures were glazed underneath and inside. American Pottery figures are usually slightly larger than Vernon's due to the fact that American's clay body tended to shrink less than Vernon's when fired.

In 1955, Metlox produced a group of 45 figures referred to as the Miniature Series. Issued as a group, they included all the *Lady and the Tramp* figurines plus very small versions of earlier figurines.

Walt Disney Figurines:
boy and girl versions of Potty.
Photo courtesy of Stan Pawlowski.

Collectors often confuse the miniatures with other small figures. To differentiate them in the list, a small "m" has been added before the item number and the word "miniature" before the entry's name. Sizes from brochure material are also given that can help to identify them.

The list does not include a series of small figurines made in Mexico that are commonly attributed to Metlox. They are poor replicas of the original "Jose," "Panchito," "Donald Duck," "Mickey Mouse," "Minnie Mouse," "Thumper," "Thumper's Girl Friend," "Flower," and "Bambi" by Metlox. Reportedly Evan K. Shaw was quite upset when he learned of them and was concerned that collectors would assume they were produced by Metlox. He considered their clay body, detail, and color very inferior in quality. Fortunately, some are marked "Made in Mexico." Collectors should also be aware of a series of figures made in Australia that closely resemble those made by Evan K. Shaw.

Two extremely rare items deserve special mention. The "Cinderella's Pumpkin Coach" cookie jar is quite small and could be used more fittingly as a candy jar. Less than a hundred were ever made. "Potty," actually a planter, was made especially for Walt Disney himself and was never offered for sale to the general public. Disney used "Potty" as a baby gift for company employees. There was a pink version for girls and a blue one for boys. It was manufactured in groups of 50. Probably only 200 and certainly no more than 300 were ever made.

In recent years the worth of Shaw's Disney figures has increased dramatically. This book's valuations are based on the West Coast market where collector interest is greatest. Recent auction sales for very rare items were considered too. It should be noted that the January 17, 1994, Northridge earthquake also influenced values. When several large collections sustained substantial damage, there was a sudden increase in demand and price as collectors attempted to replace items. Figurines with the original label are at the high end of the scale.

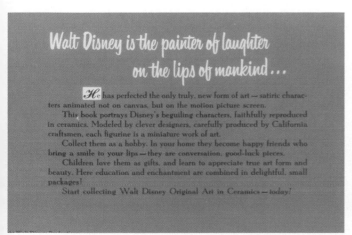

Walt Disney Figurines: Alice in Wonderland figures from Disney brochure.

Walt Disney Figurines: Cinderella figures from Disney brochure.

Walt Disney Figurines: Snow White figures from Disney brochure.

    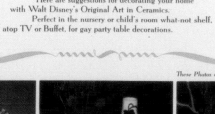 

Walt Disney Figurines: Disney brochure.

BAMBI

Here Bambi and Faline,
the deer.
    Meet Thumper and his gal —
And Flower, striped in
white on black
Shyly joins his pals.

They come in several sizes —
    And they're authentic, too.
Friend Owl, atop his
tree-stump vase
    Says they're in his
    Who's Whooooo.

SHOWN ON LEFT-HAND PAGE:
(left to right) Small Bambi
(tail up), Bambi, Small Bambi
(tail down), Faline,
Small Bambi (with butterfly)
Bambi (with butterfly)

SHOWN ON THIS PAGE:
Owl, Stump, Small Flower
Small Thumper, Minnie (girl
friend), Thumping Thumper
(eyes open)

Pages 8 - 9

Walt Disney Figurines: Bambi figures from Disney brochure.

DISNEY LAND

The little figures pictured here
    Thrill a collector's heart
They reproduce so faithfully
    The famed Walt Disney art.

Good Pluto, Dumbo and
the ducks,
    Pinocchio and his kitten —
Now that you've seen them,
don't you feel
    You, too, are also smitten?

SHOWN ON LEFT-HAND PAGE:
(left to right) Pluto (walking),
Pinocchio, Figam (standing)

SHOWN ON THIS PAGE:
(left to right) Pluto (sniffing),
Small Dumbo, Huey (with bat),
Louie (with mitt),
Dewey (with ball)
Frog

Pages 10 - 11

Walt Disney Figurines: Disney Land figures from Disney brochure.

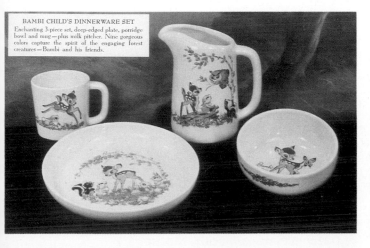

BAMBI CHILD'S DINNERWARE SET
Enchanting 3-piece set, deep-edged plate, porridge
bowl and mug — plus milk pitcher. Nine gorgeous
colors capture the spirit of the engaging forest
creatures — Bambi and his friends.

Walt Disney Figurines: Bambi child's dinnerware set from Disney brochure.

Walt Disney Figurines: Alice in Wonderland figures from Disney brochure.

Three Little Pigs (1933)

m 0025	miniature Pig #1, 1¼"	$150 – 200	m 0027	miniature Pig #3, 1¼"	$150 – 200
m 0026	miniature Pig #2, 1¼"	$150 – 200	228A	3 Pigs toothbrush holder	$350 – 400

Snow White and the Seven Dwarfs (1937)

220	Snow White	$425 – 500	m 0030	miniature Snow White, 3"	$550 – 600
221	Bashful	$200 – 250	m 0031	miniature Bashful, 2"	$200 – 250
222	Dopey	$200 – 250	m 0032	miniature Dopey, 2"	$200 – 250
223	Doc	$200 – 250	m 0033	miniature Doc, 2"	$200 – 250
224	Grumpy	$200 – 250	m 0034	miniature Grumpy, 2"	$200 – 250
225	Happy	$200 – 250	m 0035	miniature Happy, 2"	$200 – 250
226	Sleepy	$200 – 250	m 0036	miniature Sleepy, 2"	$200 – 250
227	Sneezy	$200 – 250	m 0037	miniature Sneezy, 2"	$200 – 250

Pinocchio (1940)

234	Pinocchio	$400 – 450	239	Figaro standing	$175 – 225
m 008	miniature Pinocchio, 2"	$200 – 250	—	Figaro standing, one foot up	$175 – 225
—	Jiminy Cricket	$550 – 600	—	Figaro sitting	$175 – 225
m 0024	miniature Jiminy Cricket, 1¼"	$175 – 225	m 0017	miniature Figaro, 1¼"	$175 – 225

Fantasia (1940)

—	Sprite (VK)	$175 – 250	—	Hippo (VK)	$325 – 400
—	Unicorn (VK)	$250 – 325	—	Mushroom pepper shaker (VK)	$70 – 90
—	Elephant (VK)	$350 – 425	—	Mushroom salt shaker (VK)	$70 – 90

Dumbo (1941)

—	Dumbo standing	$200 – 225	m 006	miniature Dumbo, 1¾"	$175 – 200
—	Dumbo seated w/bonnet, front legs down (VK)	$125 – 150	277	Dumbo cookie jar (circus drum)	$1,500 – 2,000
—	Dumbo seated w/bonnet, front legs up	$200 – 225	—	Timothy Mouse (VK)	$175 – 250
—	Dumbo lying on ear (VK)	$125 – 150	m 0016	miniature Timothy Mouse, 1¼" (aka Dumbo Mouse)	$200 – 250
260	small Dumbo	$150 – 175			

Bambi (1942)

No.	Item	Price
210	jumbo Bambi	$1,000 – 1,500
—	large Bambi, blue butterfly	$150 – 185
—	large Bambi looking left	$140 – 165
207	medium Bambi	$140 – 165
202	Bambi	$140 – 165
203	Bambi with butterfly	$225 – 250
216	small Bambi, tail down	$200 – 225
217	small Bambi, tail up	$200 – 225
218	small Bambi with butterfly	$225 – 250
m 033	miniature Bambi w/butterfly, 2½"	$250 – 285
m 298	miniature Bambi, 2½"	$240 – 265
m 002	miniature prone Bambi, 1½"	$240 – 265
257	large Bambi planter	$400 – 450
212	Bambi planter	$275 – 325
206	small Bambi planter	$225 – 250
250 – 253	Bambi Child's Set	
250	Bambi cup	$65 – 75
251	Bambi bowl	$75 – 100
252	Bambi plate	$70 – 85
253	Bambi pitcher	$75 – 100
—	large Faline looking straight ahead	$140 – 165
204	Faline	$140 – 165
—	small Faline	$200 – 225
200	large Thumper	$85 – 95
259	medium Thumper	$75 – 100
262	small Thumper	$100 – 125
271	Thumper thumping, eyes open	$100 – 125
274	Thumper thumping, eyes closed	$100 – 125
m 241	miniature Thumper, 1¾"	$150 – 185
258	large Thumper planter	$250 – 275
213	Thumper planter	$200 – 225
201	large Thumper's girl friend	$50 – 65
272	small Thumper's girl friend	$100 – 125
299	large Flower	$60 – 75
258	medium Flower	$75 – 100
263	small Flower	$100 – 125
m 299	miniature Flower, 1½"	$150 – 185
256	large Flower planter	$650 – 700
229	Flower planter	$200 – 225
205	Stag	$1,250 – 1,500
273	Owl	$175 – 200
275	Stump	$75 – 100

The Three Caballeros (1945)

No.	Item	Price
210	Jose	$325 – 350
211	Panchito	$325 – 350
—	Donald Duck	$325 – 350
1210	small Jose	$150 – 175
1211	small Panchito	$325 – 350
1214	small Donald Duck	$350 – 375

Cinderella (1950)

No.	Item	Price
278	formal Cinderella	$400 – 450
283	peasant Cinderella	$450 – 500
279	Gus	$225 – 250
280	Jaq	$225 – 250
282	Prince Charming	$350 – 400
284	Baby Mouse	$475 – 500
285	Mamma Mouse	$175 – 200
286	Boy Bird	$225 – 250
287	Girl Bird	$225 – 250
288	Bruno sitting	$175 – 200
289	Bruno lying down	$175 – 200
—	Cinderella's Coach cookie jar/ candy dish (pumpkin)	$5,000+

Alice in Wonderland (1951)

No.	Item	Price
254	Disney Teapot — Tea 'n Cream	$300 – 400
255	Disney Teapot — Tea for 3	$300 – 400
256	Disney Teapot — Tea 'n Sugar	$300 – 400
257	Disney Teapot — Magic Tea	$300 – 400
290	Tweedle Dee	$225 – 250
291	Tweedle Dum	$225 – 250
292	Alice in Wonderland	$350 – 400
293	The White Rabbit	$250 – 275
294	The Mad Hatter	$250 – 275
295	The March Hare	$325 – 350
296	The Walrus	$300 – 325
297	The Dormouse	$450 – 500

Peter Pan (1953)

243	Tinker Bell	$450 – 500
244	Peter Pan	$400 – 450
249	Peter Pan standing	$400 – 450
245	Mermaid	$450 – 475

246	Michael	$150 – 180
247	Wendy	$350 – 400
248	Nana	$225 – 250

Lady and the Tramp (1955)

m 238	miniature Lady sitting, 1¾"	$85 – 125
m 240	miniature Lady standing, 1¾"	$85 – 125
m 242	miniature Jock, 1¾"	$200 – 250
m 001	miniature Trusty, 3"	$200 – 250
m 005	miniature Tramp, 2½"	$200 – 250
m 0010	miniature Dachshund, 1¼"	$200 – 250
m 0014	miniature Limey, 1½"	$200 – 250

m 0015	miniature Peg, 1½"	$200 – 250
m 0028	miniature Si, 2½"	$200 – 250
m 0029	miniature Am, 2¼"	$200 – 250
m 0040	miniature Pup #1, 1"	$200 – 250
m 0041	miniature Pup #2, 1"	$200 – 250
m 0042	miniature Pup #3, ¾"	$200 – 250
m 0043	miniature Scamp Pup, ¾"	$200 – 250

Miscellaneous

267	Donald Duck with guitar	$275 – 300
—	prone Donald Duck	$275 – 300
m 009	miniature Donald Duck waving, 2"	$225 – 250
211B	Donald Duck wall planter	$350 – 400
—	Donald Duck planter (boat)	$1,500 – 1,800
—	Donald Duck planter (beehive)	$2,000 – 2,500
228B	Donald Duck toothbrush holder	$350 – 400
215	Donald Duck cookie jar	$5,000+
	a: holding hat in front	
	b: holding cookie in front	
268	Huey with bat	$250 – 275
269	Dewey with ball	$250 – 275
270	Louie with mitt	$250 – 275
m 0018	miniature Huey with mitt, 1¼"	$250 – 275
m 0019	miniature Dewey with bat, 1¼"	$250 – 275
m 0020	miniature Louie with ball, 1"	$250 – 275
—	Huey waving	$150 – 175
—	Dewey waving	$150 – 175
—	Louie waving	$150 – 175
232	Pluto sitting	$225 – 250
233	Pluto walking	$300 – 350
264	Pluto sniffing	$225 – 250

265	Pluto prone	$225 – 250
235	small Pluto	$200 – 250
m 007	miniature Pluto, 1¾"	$225 – 275
255	Pluto planter (dog house)	$500 – 600
266	Frog	$225 – 250
m 0013	miniature dog house, 2½"	$125 – 150
m 004	miniature fire plug, 1¾"	$100 – 125
212	Mickey Mouse	$350 – 400
276	small Mickey Mouse with hat	$250 – 275
m 0011	miniature Mickey Mouse waving, 2½"	$275 – 300
211A	Mickey Mouse wall planter	$325 – 350
213	Minnie Mouse	$275 – 300
—	Minnie Mouse planter (bassinet)	$700 – 750
m 0022	miniature Stormy, 2"	$175 – 200
m 0023	miniature Stormy prone, 1¼"	$125 – 150
242	Little Toot	$2,000 – 2,500
—	Brer Rabbit planter	$4,000 – 4,250
219	Potty	$6,000+
	a: pink — girl	
	b: blue — boy	

California Ivy Artware

California Ivy Artware:
Metlox archive photo.

California Ivy Artware, mentioned as early as December, 1948, in brochure material, was a series of flower vases, console bowls, planters, and miscellaneous items that complemented the extremely popular P 170 California Ivy dinnerware pattern. All pieces were decorated with the hand-painted ivy vine design. The shapes of the vases, planters, and console bowls were the simple, common ones of the period. The creamer, gravy, and round plate, all taken directly from the dinnerware pattern, probably were intended to be used as decorative pieces and a liner respectively. The pitcher and mug were quite different from their dinnerware counterparts. Both were simpler, thicker shapes with a plain white handle instead of a brown twig one. The candle holder, creamer, and gravy, however, did have a twig handle. Although they used the ivy design, the 604 ivy hurricane lamp and 607 ivy harp from the Nostalgia Line were never included by Metlox in California Ivy Artware. Exact measurements were not given in company material. Designed by Allen and Shaw.

California Ivy Artware

300	Cigarette Box & Lid	$60 – 65	319	Creamer	$20 – 22
306	Cylinder Flower Vase, lg.	$30 – 35	320	Coaster/Ashtray	$16 – 18
307	Cylinder Flower Vase, med.	$25 – 30	321	Shallow Console Bowl	$40 – 45
308	Cylinder Flower Vase, sm.	$20 – 25	322	Fan Flower Vase	$35 – 40
309	Planter Box, lg.	$22 – 25	326	Candle Holder	$35 – 40
310	Planter Box, med.	$20 – 22	349	Dutch Shoe Planter, sm.	$25 – 30
311	Planter Box, sm.	$18 – 20	350	Dutch Shoe Planter, lg.	$30 – 35
312	Flower Bowl	$30 – 35	360	Mug, straight-sided	$18 – 20
313	Curved Planter	$30 – 35	361	Bowl, med.	$15 – 18
314	Planter Box, ex. lg.	$25 – 30	362	Service Plate, rnd.	$13 – 15
315	Cylinder Flower Vase, ex. lg.	$35 – 40	363	Pitcher	$40 – 45
316	Console Bowl, lg.	$45 – 50	—	Gravy-Shaped Wall Pocket	$40 – 45
318	Gravy	$28 – 30			

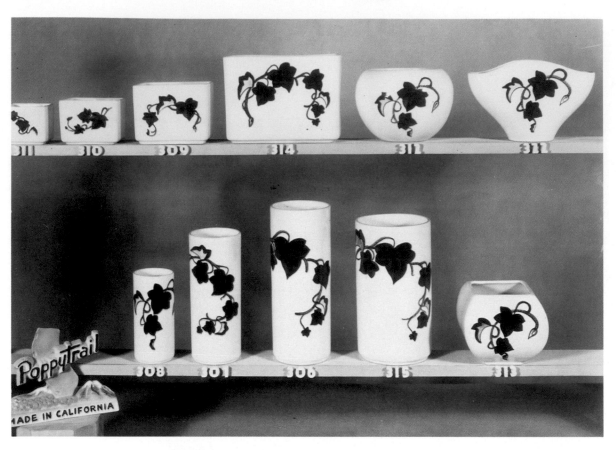

California Ivy Artware:
Metlox archive photos.

Nostalgia Line

Nostalgia Line:
Metlox archive photo.

*Nostalgia Line
Each piece of Nostalgia Artware captures the feeling of the late 19th Century yet is ultra modern in line and color... A touch of Americana that revives old memories of an era long since passed...*

The Nostalgia Line sought to recall the spirit, look, and feel of nineteenth and early twentieth century America by precisely recreating familiar reminders of that period. This large line, produced from the late 1940s through the 1960s, consisted of several groups — miscellaneous Americana items, antique automobiles, The Carriage Collection, Americana figures, and the American Royal Horses. Besides their decorative appeal, many were also designed for practical use as planters, holders, and containers.

Interestingly, the idea for the line originated outside of Metlox. Immediately after Allen and Shaw became a design team in 1946, they worked briefly for a small ceramics company named Helen's Ware, owned by Helen Hutula and located on San Fernando Road. Along with a few miscellaneous artware items, Allen and Shaw designed a line of Americana-related items that included the following: a wall telephone planter, "old shoe" house planter, locomotive and tender planter, 1925 Ford Coupe planter, antique grand piano cigarette box, old-fashioned Victrola with horn planter, antique grandfather's clock vase and planter, old farm pump and bucket lamp and planter, cigar store Indian, and the three-piece street vendor, horse, and wagon set. When Allen and Shaw joined Metlox, they left Helen's Ware because their contractual agreement with Evan K. Shaw disallowed designing for other ceramics companies. Evan K. Shaw admired Helen's Ware Americana

line. When Hutula lost her financial backing in the late 1940s, Evan K. Shaw purchased the molds, blocks, and cases of the Allen and Shaw designs. This was the beginning of Metlox's Nostalgia Line. As production continued on most of the Helen's Ware items, Allen and Shaw augmented the line with new additions.

Nostalgia Line: Metlox archive photo.

Nostalgia Line: Metlox archive photo.

painstakingly modeled. Most items were hand decorated in varied color schemes which frequently employed the use of liquid gold. Retail cost was high because the line was very expensive and time-consuming to produce. Most pieces had a limited production run and were marked with a Metlox Poppytrail or Evan K. Shaw sticker.

The ceramic body of each Carriage Collection item fit into a brass holder designed as the frame, harness, and wheels of the vehicle. These holders were manufactured by Mel David's wire company, Melco, to the exact specifications of each item. The brass holders were painted a more realistic black or dark brown on some of the later models. Although they were merchandised separately, the carriages and horses were intended to be joined together by placing the carriage harness on the back of a horse.

The Budweiser Beer Wagon was commissioned by the Anheuser-Busch Company exclusively for its use as an advertising display piece and as a gift for valued company employees. It was larger than the other vehicles and had ceramic wheels. Several Metlox versions with minor variations have been reported. The Clydesdale horse and the wagon master figurine, each usually paired with the wagon, were merchandised by Metlox while the beer wagon was not. A small dalmatian figurine may have been produced for the assembly. Collectors should be wary of recent reproductions of the beer

It was Evan K. Shaw's idea to include The Carriage Collection and the American Royal Horses in the line. Shaw loved horses and always enjoyed equestrian activities such as polo and horseback riding. His hobby, indeed his passion as a collector, became finding and restoring antique carriages, buggies, surreys, wagons, and sleighs. Shortly after purchasing Metlox, he began to assemble his collection, searching for classics throughout the country. Several Pennsylvania Amish carriage restoration experts served as consultants. The collection, finally numbering nearly 80 vehicles, was stored in several warehouses. Shaw loaned carriages for charity benefits, horse shows, civic events, and parades in the Southern California area and nationwide. Since they were such an important part of America's past, Shaw felt it was appropriate to incorporate antique carriages, along with the horses that drew them, into the Nostalgia Line.

Nostalgia was undoubtedly one of Shaw's favorite artware lines. He insisted that every item be recreated as authentically and realistically as possible with no cost spared. After each subject was thoroughly researched and studied, its dimensions, scale, styling, and look were precisely duplicated during each stage of the design and production process. Allen and Shaw created all of the designs which Bob Chandler, Frank Irwin, and Bernie Hassenstab

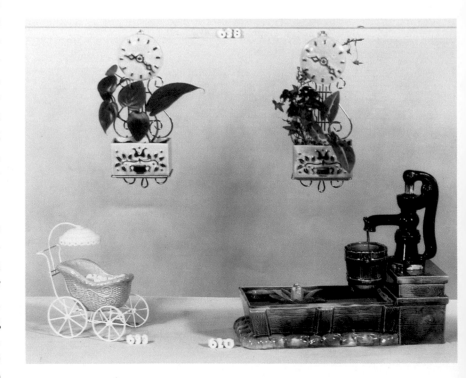

Nostalgia Line: Metlox archive photo.

wagon and the Clydesdale which are excellent replicas of the Metlox orginals.

The figurines were created as companion pieces for The Carriage Collection. The four-piece Coachman, Mama, Papa, and Mary Jane set, and the three-piece Amish family set were designed as groups for the two-seaters. The sulky driver was intended for the racing sulky, the doctor for the buggies, and Santa and the two reindeer for the one-seat cutter sleigh. Many of the reindeer were returned to the factory and destroyed because, despite careful packaging, the fragile antlers tended to break during shipping.

Many Nostalgia items, designed as planters, could also serve as holders for nuts, candy, cigarettes, and small flower arrangements. A few had specific functions, e.g., the ice wagon was an ice bucket and the mail wagon was a letter holder. The Old Mill Ensemble and the Roman Fountain Bowl and Centerpiece were installed with a motor and pump to circulate water. The Old Mill, often used as a Poppytrail Artware display item in department stores, had a working mill wheel. The centerpiece of the elaborately carved Roman Fountain set was crowned with a cherub holding a fish. Water circulated up the centerpiece and spouted out of the fish's upturned mouth. Although

Nostalgia Line: Metlox archive photo.

The Carriage Collection items were frequently shown with lighting attachments in archive photographs, they were never merchandised as lamps by Metlox.

The Nostalgia Line was one of the finest achievements of the Poppytrail Artware Division. With very few exceptions, similar lines from other companies and foreign copycat imitations were invariably poor rivals to the artistry and craftsmanship of the Nostalgia Line. Identification of the items by collectors has been difficult due to the use of easily removed paper labels and the lack of documentation. The extensive listing on page 239 and the accompanying archive photographs hopefully will correct this situation.

Nostalgia Line: Metlox archive photo.

Nostalgia Line:
Metlox archive photo.

Nostalgia Line:
Metlox archive photo.

Nostalgia Line:
Metlox archive photo.

Nostalgia Line:
Metlox archive photo.

Nostalgia Line:
Metlox archive photo.

Nostalgia Line:
Metlox archive photo.

Nostalgia Line:
Metlox archive photo.

Nostalgia Line:
Metlox archive photo.

Nostalgia Line:
Metlox archive photo.

Nostalgia Line: Metlox archive photo.   **Nostalgia Line:** Metlox archive photo.

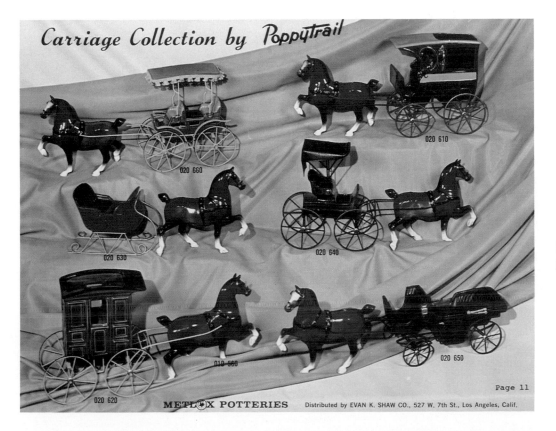

Nostalgia Line:
Metlox brochure.

675 • LARGE SADDLE BRED
Chestnut — 9" high, 8" long
686 • MEDIUM SADDLE BRED
Chestnut — 6" high, 6" long

643 • LARGE CIRCUS HORSE
Palomino — 8" high, 11" long

644 • LARGE HACKNEY
Bay — 8¾" high, 8¾" long
679 • MEDIUM HACKNEY
Bay — 6½" high, 6¼" long

645 • CLYDESDALE
Bay — 9" high, 9" long

American Royal Horses

Here is a proven, repeat, collectors' item. Stores find that after a customer's first purchase, he returns time after time to add to the collection. They're conversation pieces — authentic conformations — have been captured in realistic detail true-to-life, pleasing ceramic figures.

Here is your RE-ORDER LINE. Stock and sell every number — if you want volume business. Individually boxed.

ORDER TODAY BY NUMBER, SIZE AND COLOR

646 • ARABIAN
Palomino — 8¾" high, 7¼" long

641 • DOBBIN
Grey — 9" high, 11" long

671 • LARGE MARE
Chestnut — 7¼" high, 8½" long
682 • MEDIUM MARE
Chestnut — 5" high, 6½" long

649 • LARGE THOROUGHBRED
Bay — 8½" high, 8¾" long
666 • MEDIUM THOROUGHBRED
Chestnut — 6¼" high, 6¾" long

684 • MEDIUM CIRCUS HORSE
Palomino & Blue Trim — 6" high, 6" long
White & Red Trim — 6" high, 6" long
Both available in black and white

685 • PALOMINO
6" high, 6" long

674 • LARGE GAITED
Palomino — 9" high, 11" long
667 • MEDIUM GAITED
Palomino — 4" high, 3" long

673 • LARGE MUSTANG
Pinto — 8" high, 10" long
678 • MEDIUM MUSTANG
Pinto — 5¼" high, 7" long
Both available in black and white

640 • CURRIER & IVES
Grey — 7¾" high, 11" long

648 • MORGAN
Grey — 7¾" high, 8½" long

642 • PONY
Pinto — 6" high, 7½" long

670 • PRONE COLT
Bay — 3" high, 4¼" long

672 • LARGE STANDING COLT
Bay — 5½" high, 4½" long
681 • MEDIUM STANDING COLT
Bay — 4" high, 3" long

6

Nostalgia Line: Metlox brochure.

Nostalgia Line

Miscellaneous Americana Items

601	Locomotive	$60 – 65
603	Piano & Lid	$75 – 80
604	Ivy Hurricane Lamp	$115 – 125
605	Victrola	$60 – 65
606	Bathtub, 7½ x 4½ x 3¼"	$55 – 60
607	Ivy Harp	$90 – 100
608	Grandmother Clock	$55 – 60
609	Dormer Window	$85 – 95
610	Old Cannon	$50 – 55
611	Drum (has also been listed as #612)	$30 – 35
613	Drum Table	$40 – 45
614	Powder Horn with Strap	$45 – 50
615	Flower Vendor Set, 3-piece	$160 – 175
	Standing Man Holding a Pot	$40 – 45
	Burro	$55 – 60
	Wagon	$65 – 70
616	Train Set, 3-piece	$150 – 165
	Locomotive	$60 – 65
	Train Car	$35 – 40
	Caboose & Lid	$55 – 60
620	Watering Trough, 15 x 13 x 6½"	$90 – 100
621	Roman Fountain Bowl & Centerpiece	$175 – 200
622	Old Mill Ensemble, 2-piece	$200 – 225
	Mill, 12 x 6 x 8½"	$140 – 155
	Base, 16 x 1½ x 15"	$60 – 70
633	Perambulator	$60 – 65
634	Trolley Car	$85 – 95
638	Lyre Clock	$100 – 110

Antique Automobiles

602	Old Ford	$75 – 85
612	Cadillac	$75 – 85
618	Merrie Oldsmobile	$75 – 85
619	Chevrolet	$75 – 85
636	Olds, 7¾ x 5¾ x 5¾"	$75 – 85

The Carriage Collection

617	Stage Coach	$90 – 100
623	Old Fashioned Buggy, 9 x 9¼ x 6"	$65 – 70
624	Surrey with Metal Fringe, 10¼ x 9 x 5¾"	$80 – 90
625	Victorian Carriage, 11 x 5 x 5½"	$90 – 100
626	Bob Sleigh, 12"	$90 – 100
627	Cutter Sleigh, 8½"	$75 – 85
628	Hansom Cab, 13 x 7 x 5¼"	$70 – 80
629	Pony Cart	$55 – 60
630	Mail Wagon	$70 – 80
631	Delivery Wagon	$75 – 85
632	Ice Wagon	$70 – 80
637	Barrel Wagon, 11 x 8"	$90 – 100
658	Racing Sulky	$50 – 55
659	Fire Wagon	$90 – 100
691	Buggy	$65 – 70

020	610	Package Wagon, 9"	$80 – 90
020	620	R.F.D. Mail Wagon, 11"	$80 – 90
020	630	Vanderbilt Sleigh, 9"	$65 – 70
020	640	Doctor's Buggy, 9"	$65 – 70
020	650	Victoria Carriage, 10½"	$90 – 100
020	660	Surrey with Fabric Fringe, 9½"	$80 – 90
—		Budweiser Beer Wagon, 12½"	$275 – 300
—		1-seat Sleigh w/Back Cargo Space, 8½"	$55 – 60

Americana Figures

650	Hitching Post Boy	$50 – 55
651	Coachman	$40 – 45
652	Mama	$40 – 45
653	Papa	$40 – 45
654	Mary Jane	$40 – 45
655	Santa	$60 – 65
656	Donder	$125 – 135
657	Blitzen	$125 – 135
660	Wagon Master	$40 – 45
—	Sulky Driver	$40 – 45
	Amish Set, 3-piece	
—	Father	$40 – 45
—	Mother	$40 – 45
—	Child	$40 – 45
—	Doctor	$40 – 45

American Royal Horses

640	Currier & Ives, 11 x 7¾"	$115 – 125
641	Dobbin, 11 x 9"	$95 – 105
642	Pony, 7½ x 6"	$85 – 95
643	Large Circus/Draft Horse, 11 x 8"	$125 – 135
644	Large Hackney, 8¾ x 8¾"	$115 – 125
645	Clydesdale, 9 x 9"	$175 – 185
646	Arabian, 7¾ x 8¾"	$105 – 115
647	Morgan, 8½ x 7¾"	$105 – 115
648	Large Circus/Draft Horse with Clydesdale Harness	$125 – 135
649	Large Thoroughbred, 8¾ x 8½"	$105 – 115
666	Medium Thoroughbred, 6¾ x 6¼"	$85 – 95
667	Medium Gaited, 3 x 4"	$75 – 85
670	Prone Colt, 4¼ x 3"	$65 – 70
671	Large Mare, 8½ x 7¼"	$95 – 105
672	Large Standing Colt, 4½ x 5½"	$85 – 95
673	Large Mustang, 10 x 8"	$115 – 125
674	Large Gaited, 11 x 9"	$115 – 125
675	Large Saddle Bred, 8 x 9"	$115 – 125
678	Medium Mustang, 7 x 5¼"	$85 – 95
679	Medium Hackney, 6¼ x 6½"	$85 – 95
681	Medium Standing Colt, 3 x 4"	$65 – 70
682	Medium Mare, 6½ x 5"	$70 – 80
684	Medium Circus Horse, 6 x 6"	$105 – 115
685	Palomino, 6 x 6"	$105 – 115
686	Medium Saddle Bred, 6 x 6"	$85 – 95

Ceramic Art Traditions

Ceramic Art Traditions:
Metlox archive photo.

This important line, designed solely by Harrison McIntosh, consisted of only 13 items. Although McIntosh was listed as a "Consulting Ceramics Designer" in one Metlox artware catalog, Ceramic Art Traditions was the only series he actually created for the company. The line was based on McIntosh's hand-thrown stoneware models rather than drawn designs. Evan K. Shaw decided which items would be produced. Master molds were then made at Metlox. Special matte glazes and unusual colors were created for the pieces as follows: the cachepotes with saucer, cylinder vases, and low bowls were either melon gray, avocado green, brown gray, or melon gold; the bottle vases gray, melon, or white gloss; and the compotes white speck, white gloss, melon gold, brown gray, or melon gray. The entire line, resembling stoneware vessels of the past, had an ancient yet very contemporary look. Ceramic Art Traditions did not sell well and had only a limited production run.

Ceramic Art Traditions

701	Bottle Vase, 5½"	$100 – 110
702	Bottle Vase, 9½"	$125 – 135
703	Bottle Vase, 12½"	$140 – 150
704	Cylinder Vase, 6"	$110 – 120
705	Cylinder Vase, 10"	$130 – 140
706	Low Bowl, 12 x 2"	$65 – 75
708	Compote, 8½ x 4"	$115 – 125
709	Cachepote with Saucer, 5"	$65 – 75
710	Cachepote with Saucer, 6"	$75 – 85
711	Cachepote with Saucer, 7½"	$85 – 95
712	Low Bowl, 10 x 2"	$60 – 70
713	Compote, 6 x 3"	$100 – 110
714	Compote, 12 x 4½"	$130 – 140

Ceramic Art Traditions
Contempo-Interpreted. Graceful curves — soft colors — subdued glazes — Conceived in the casual atmosphere of California by famed ceramic artist, Harrison McIntosh. Inspired by the arts of antiquity — Greco-Roman, Egyptian, Chinese, and Byzantine. A trend in fine decor!

Art Treasures of the World:
Metlox archive photo.

Art Treasures of the World
In each era of antiquity until this day, a work of art bespoke a people's history or tradition. Now Metlox - Poppytrail creates for today's decor, the Heirlooms of Tomorrow.

Art Treasures of the World offered extremely detailed replicas of artwork from various past civilizations. Each human or animal figure was molded after the prevailing artistic style of a particular culture or period. Bob Allen conceived the idea and designed the Corinthian horse, rooster, llama, and pair of small birds. Allen asked Carl Romanelli, who worked again at Metlox for a brief period in the Research, Design, and Development Department on a contract basis, to assist with the line. Romanelli contributed the Tang horse, Eastern princess head, the two Egyptian head wall plaques, and the two Indonesian dancer wall plaques. Both wall plaque sets included one male and one female design and were suitable for framing. Bill Selby, an employee of Allen-Shaw and Associates, created the Trojan horse bookends. It was Allen's idea to decorate each piece with numerous small in-mold mosaics that created a tile effect.

Art Treasures of the World was produced in two color schemes. Both required three instead of the usual two firings. The first was a deep satin-finished brown with turquoise, ivory, and gold mosaics. The second utilized a special white crackle glaze, reminiscent of old Chinese techniques and invented by John Johnson specifically for this line. After the initial firing changed the green ware into bisque, it was painted entirely with a white glaze and fired again. Then, a dark stain was hand rubbed into the many cracks and indentations of the design and mosaics. This was sealed with a clear glaze and the piece was fired a third time. Crackle glaze item numbers included a "C" after the item number. Both decorations, although time consuming and therefore expensive to produce, enhanced the "aura of the past" look of the series.

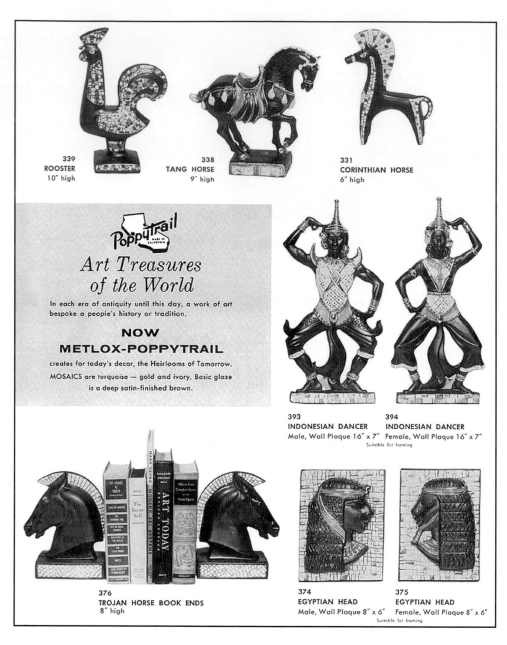

Art Treasures of the World: Metlox brochure.

Art Treasures of the World

331 Corinthian Horse, 6" . . . . $65 – 75	376 Trojan Horse Bookends, 8⅛". . . pr. $160 – 170
338 Tang Horse, 9". . . . . $100 – 110	(This item has also been listed as no. 380.)
339 Rooster, 10" . . . . $85 – 95	393 Indonesian Dancer, Male, wall plaque,
361 Eastern Princess Head . . . . $115 – 125	16 x 7" . . . . $125 – 150
374 Egyptian Head, Male, wall plaque, 8 x 6". $90 – 100	394 Indonesian Dancer, Female, wall plaque,
375 Egyptian Head, Female, wall plaque,	16 x 7" . . . . $125 – 150
8 x 6". . . . . $90 – 100	— Llama. . . . . $50 – 60
	— Pair of Birds, 4½" . . . . pr. $65 – 75

Mosaic Originals and Tropicana

Tropicana:
Metlox archive photo.

Mosaic Originals
Artistic beauty of the 'ages' contempora interpreted
for modern living. Mosaic combinations of blue-
turquoise and gold...

Inspired by the artwork of past cultures, Mosaic Originals was a series of satin white decorative pieces featuring mosaic patterns that were composed of many small blue, turquoise, ivory, and gold squares. Tropicana items were available in a hand-painted pineapple or tropical fish motif on a white satin glaze background. The pineapple was colored reddish brown and yellow with dark green and chartreuse leaves and additional gold decoration. The tropical fish was dark blue and turquoise with gold highlighting. Tropicana, the larger of the two lines, included all of the Mosaic items except the hour glass vase and lip vase. In addition, Tropicana added nine hostess serving accessories, four sizes of flower pots, and five square ashtrays.

Allen and Shaw designed most of the decorative items in both lines. The food serving accessories and flower pots were shapes adapted from Allen and Shaw's Confetti and Navajo and Frank Irwin's Freeform dinnerware patterns. Bob Allen conceived the in-mold mosaic patterns that were also used on the Art Treasures of the World line. Helen McIntosh designed the pineapple and tropical fish motifs. Naturally, the use of gold in both lines added to production costs. Both series, created with the highly stylized 1950s contemporary look popularized by Sascha Brastoff, were moderately successful lines.

Mosaic Originals and Art Treasures of the World:
Metlox archive photo.

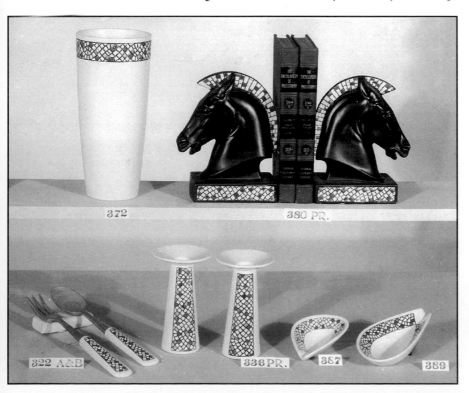

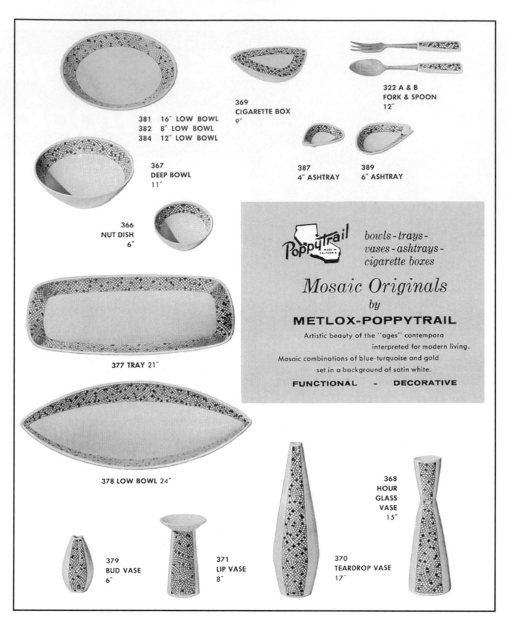

Mosaic Originals: Metlox brochure.

Mosaic Originals

No.	Item	Price	No.	Item	Price
308	Ashtray, rnd., 8"	$30 – 35	372	Vase, 10"	$55 – 60
322A-B	Salad Fork & Spoon Set, 12" . . pr.	$60 – 65	377	Large Tray, rect., 21"	$80 – 90
336	Candle Holder, 6"	$40 – 45	378	Low Bowl, 24"	$90 – 100
366	Nut Dish, 6"	$25 – 30	379	Bud Vase, 6"	$35 – 40
367	Deep Bowl, 11"	$60 – 65	381	Low Bowl, 16"	$65 – 70
368	Hour Glass Vase, 15"	$80 – 90	382	Low Bowl, 8"	$45 – 50
369	Cigarette Box, 9"	$85 – 95	384	Low Bowl, 12"	$55 – 60
370	Teardrop Vase, 17"	$85 – 95	387	Ashtray, 4"	$20 – 25
371	Lip Vase, 8"	$50 – 55	389	Ashtray, 6"	$25 – 30

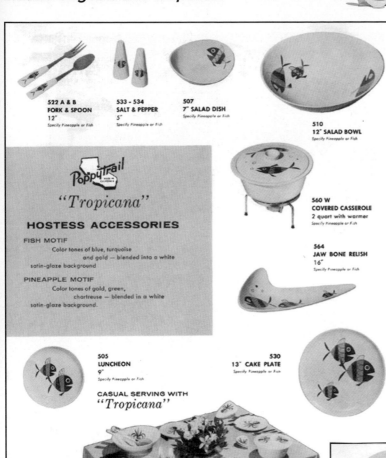

Poppytrail

"Tropicana"

HOSTESS ACCESSORIES

FISH MOTIF
Color tones of blue, turquoise
and gold — blended into a white
satin-glaze background

PINEAPPLE MOTIF
Color tones of gold, green,
chartreuse — blended in a white
satin-glaze background.

522 A & B
FORK & SPOON
12"
Specify Pineapple or Fish

533 - 534
SALT & PEPPER
5"
Specify Pineapple or Fish

507
7" SALAD DISH
Specify Pineapple or Fish

510
12" SALAD BOWL
Specify Pineapple or Fish

560 W
COVERED CASSEROLE
2 quart with warmer
Specify Pineapple or Fish

564
JAW BONE RELISH
16"
Specify Pineapple or Fish

505
LUNCHEON
9"
Specify Pineapple or Fish

530
13" CAKE PLATE
Specify Pineapple or Fish

CASUAL SERVING WITH
"Tropicana"

Tropicana: Metlox brochure.

Tropicana
Pineapple and Tropical Fish Motif
Functional ceramics created in California by Pop-
pytrail craftsmen, Tropicana hand painted designs
are brilliant — blues of the ocean — yellows of
an equatorial sun — greens of lush palms —
red-browns of the ripest fruits. Ornamental gold
bands glisten . . .

Tropicana: Metlox brochure.

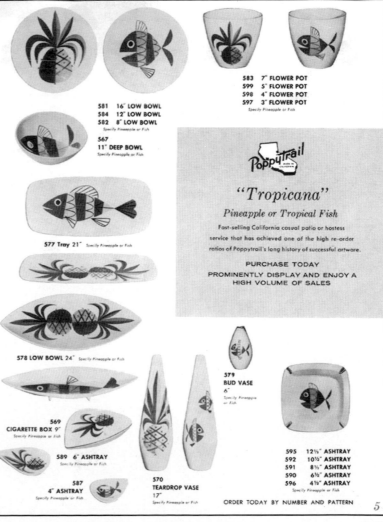

581 16" LOW BOWL
584 12" LOW BOWL
582 8" LOW BOWL
Specify Pineapple or Fish

567
11" DEEP BOWL
Specify Pineapple or Fish

583 7" FLOWER POT
599 5" FLOWER POT
598 4" FLOWER POT
597 3" FLOWER POT
Specify Pineapple or Fish

577 Tray 21" Specify Pineapple or Fish

578 LOW BOWL 24" Specify Pineapple or Fish

569
CIGARETTE BOX 9"
Specify Pineapple or Fish

589 6" ASHTRAY
Specify Pineapple or Fish

587
4" ASHTRAY
Specify Pineapple or Fish

579
BUD VASE
6"
Specify Pineapple or Fish

570
TEARDROP VASE
17"
Specify Pineapple or Fish

595 12½" ASHTRAY
592 10½" ASHTRAY
591 8½" ASHTRAY
590 6½" ASHTRAY
596 4½" ASHTRAY

Poppytrail

"Tropicana"

Pineapple or Tropical Fish

Fast-selling California casual patio or hostess
service that has achieved one of the high re-order
ratios of Poppytrail's long history of successful artware.

PURCHASE TODAY
PROMINENTLY DISPLAY AND ENJOY A
HIGH VOLUME OF SALES

ORDER TODAY BY NUMBER AND PATTERN

Tropicana (Fish Motif):
5" flower pot, 6" bud vase,
7" flower pot,
and 4" flower pot.

Tropicana (Pineapple Motif): 6" and 4" ashtrays.

Tropicana (Fish Motif): large rectangular serving tile with holder.

Tropicana

All items were available in Pineapple and Tropical Fish Motif.

No.	Item	Price
505	Luncheon Plate, 9"	$22 – 25
507	Salad Dish, 7"	$30 – 35
508	Ashtray, rnd., 8"	$30 – 35
510	Salad Bowl, 12"	$75 – 85
522A-B	Salad Fork & Spoon Set, 12" . . pr.	$60 – 65
530	Cake Plate, 13"	$55 – 60
533	Salt, 5"	$22 – 25
534	Pepper, 5"	$22 – 25
536	Candle Holder, 6"	$40 – 45
560	Casserole & Lid w/Warmer, 2 qt.	$115 – 125
564	Jaw Bone Relish, footed, 16"	$85 – 95
566	Nut Dish, 1¾"	$25 – 30
567	Deep Bowl, 11"	$60 – 65
569	Cigarette Box, 9 x 1½"	$85 – 95
570	Teardrop Vase, 17"	$85 – 95
572	Vase, 10"	$55 – 60
577	Large Tray, rect., 21 x 9½"	$80 – 90
—	Large Rectangular Serving Tile with Holder	$115 – 125
578	Footed Low Bowl, 24 x 10 x 3½"	$90 – 100
579	Bud Vase, 6"	$35 – 40
581	Footed Low Bowl, 16 x 3"	$65 – 70
582	Low Bowl, 8 x 1¾"	$45 – 50
583	Flower Pot, 7"	$75 – 80
584	Footed Low Bowl, 12 x 2"	$55 – 60
587	Ashtray, 4"	$20 – 25
589	Ashtray, 6"	$25 – 30
590	Ashtray, sq., med., 6½"	$25 – 30
591	Ashtray, sq., med., 8½"	$30 – 35
592	Ashtray, sq., lg., 10½"	$35 – 40
595	Ashtray, sq., lg., 12½"	$40 – 45
596	Ashtray, sq., sm., 4½"	$20 – 25
597	Flower Pot, 3"	$40 – 45
598	Flower Pot, 4"	$50 – 55
599	Flower Pot, 5"	$60 – 65

California
Contemporary Artware

Keeping in step with the trends of tomorrow a completely new California Contemporary group has been created... Refreshing, accessory pieces for modern and contemporary decor.

California Contemporary Artware, designed by Frank Irwin, was intended primarily as a patio line. Most of the individual items, however, could be used indoors as well as outdoors. Its modernistic shapes, abstract and simple, were inspired by the contemporary styling of the Freeform dinnerware patterns also created by Irwin. A special feature of the line was the inclusion of four black metal stands and two wire bases made by Mel David's wire company. The lawn planter stand, a metal rod with three prongs for holding a pot at one end and a sharp point for easy insertion into the ground at the other end, was sold by itself without a pot. Each of the other three stands had four feet and came with the appropriate number of fitted ceramic items. The 12" flower bowl and two-part hors d'oeuvre had a wire base. The two and three dish stands were useful as nut, candy, or food servers. The 10" flower bowl, flower urn, and free form dish had ceramic feet. The free form dish was identical to the jaw bone of the Freeform dinnerware patterns. Brochure material did not list measurements for the items. Although various color schemes were used, the most common one was a smooth blue interior with a rough, variegated dark olive and blue exterior. The line was commercially unsuccessful and had a limited production run. It was yet another example of Evan K. Shaw's willingness to produce experimental artware lines.

California Contemporary Artware:
Metlox archive photo.

247

California Contemporary Artware:
Metlox archive photo.

California Contemporary Artware:
Metlox archive photo.

California Contemporary Artware

160A	Planter Stand & Pot	$135 – 145	165	Three Dish Stand	$140 – 150
160B	Lawn Planter Stand	$80 – 90	166	Two Dish Stand	$130 – 140
161	10" Flower Bowl, footed	$45 – 55	167	Two-Part Hors D'Oeuvre & Wire Base	$75 – 85
162	Flower Urn, footed	$50 – 60	168	Hour Glass Vase	$60 – 70
163	12" Flower Bowl & Wire Base	$65 – 75	169	Tear Drop Vase	$60 – 70
164	Free Form Dish	$65 – 75	170	Spheriform Bowl	$45 – 55

Colonial Series:
Metlox archive photo.

This limited series consisted of five items taken from the Provincial dinnerware patterns. Each was decorated with a detailed scene of everyday life in Colonial America. In lieu of a known company name, the designation Colonial Series has been adopted by collectors and Metlox artists. Designed by Mel Shaw.

Colonial Series

741	Jam & Mustard — Woman with Spinning Wheel	$40 – 45
772	Large Mug, 1 pt. — Fife & Drum Corps	$28 – 30
781	Match Box — Fire Brigade	$50 – 60
782	Spice Box Planter — Stagecoach	$50 – 60
784	Sprinkling Can — Flower Girl	$55 – 65

Leaves of Enchantment

Leaves of Enchantment was created for a variety of functional as well as decorative uses. They could serve as centerpieces, ashtrays, flower bowls, television ornaments, and candy containers. Some were practical as serving pieces, trays, and platters for hors d'oeuvres, snacks, tidbits, and other food. The large ivy bowl, salad fork and spoon set, and smaller bowl-shaped leaves combined to make a salad serving set. The leaves were painted in several different green shades. Adapted versions of the banana leaves were included in the Lotus dinnerware pattern. The sizes given in the list below are approximate since the shapes tended to be very irregular. Leaves of Enchantment was one of the best-selling artware lines from the late 1950s. Designed by Allen and Shaw.

Leaves of Enchantment: Metlox archive photo.

Leaves of Enchantment

Metlox has borrowed the design and color of these leaves from Mother Nature herself. Unable to improve on the natural beauty of tropical plants we've copied them . . . Authentic reproductions of the forest and jungle molded into lovely ceramic leaves. Hand finished in matte green, the veins so strikingly lifelike, you sense a natural fragrance.

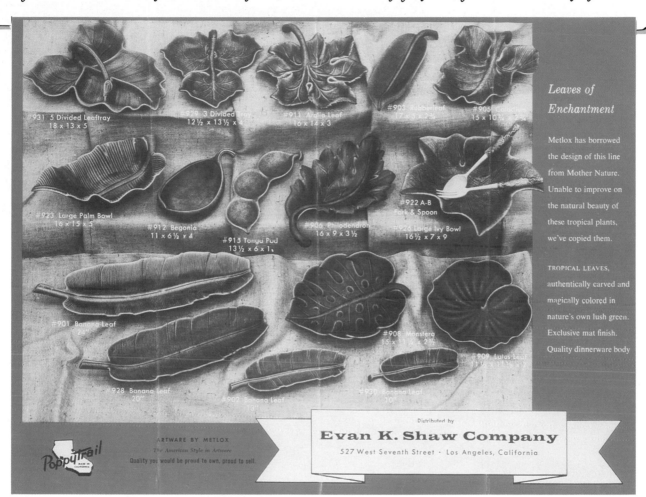

Leaves of Enchantment: Metlox brochure.

Leaves of Enchantment

No.	Item	Price
901	Banana Leaf, lg., 24 x 7¼ x 2"	$45 – 50
902	Banana Leaf, sm., 13 x 4 x 1¼"	$25 – 30
903	Rubber Leaf, 17 x 5 x 2¾"	$30 – 35
904	Ivy Leaf, lg., 9 x 7 x 1¾"	$20 – 25
905	Caladium, 15 x 10¾ x 2¾"	$30 – 35
906	Philodendron, lg., 16 x 9 x 3½"	$30 – 35
907	Philodendron, sm., 8 x 6½ x 1¼"	$20 – 25
908	Monstera, 15 x 11½ x 2½"	$30 – 35
909	Lotus Leaf, 11½ x 11½ x 2"	$25 – 30
911	Aralia Leaf, 16 x 14 x 3"	$35 – 40
912	Begonia, 11 x 6½ x 2¾"	$20 – 25
913	Ivy Leaf, sm., 4 x 4¾ x 1"	$12 – 15
914	Camellia Leaf, 6 x 4¼ x ¾"	$15 – 18
915	Tonga Pod, 13 x 4 x 1¼"	$25 – 28
922A-B	Salad Fork & Spoon Set, 12" pr.	$40 – 45
923	Large Palm Bowl, 16½ x 9 x 7"	$40 – 45
926	Large Ivy Bowl, 16 x 15 x 5"	$45 – 50
928	Banana Leaf, med., 20 x 6½"	$40 – 45
929	3-Section Leaf Tray, 12½ x 13½ x 4"	$35 – 40
930	Banana Leaf, 10 x 3"	$20 – 25
931	5-Section Leaf Tray, 18 x 13 x 5"	$45 – 50

Sea Servers

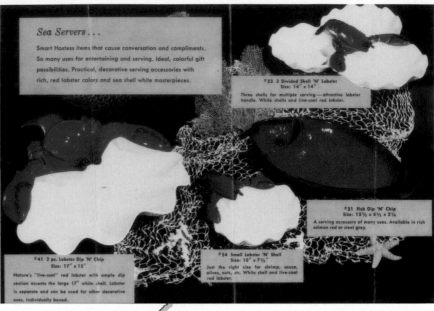

Sea Servers . . .

Smart Hostess items that cause conversation and compliments. So many uses for entertaining and serving. Ideal, colorful gift possibilities. Practical, decorative serving accessories with rich, red lobster colors and sea shell white masterpieces.

#53 3 Divided Shell 'N' Lobster
Size: 14" x 14"
Three shells for multiple serving — attractive lobster handle. White shells and live-coal red lobster.

#41 2 pc. Lobster Dip 'N' Chip
Size: 17" x 15"
Nature's "live-coal" red lobster with ample dip section accents the large 17" white shell. Lobster is separate and can be used for other decorative uses. Individually boxed.

#54 Small Lobster 'N' Shell
Size: 10" x 7½"
Just the right size for shrimp, sauce, olives, nuts, etc. White shell and live-coal red lobster.

#51 Fish Dip 'N' Chip
Size: 15½ x 8½ x 2¼
A serving accessory of many uses. Available in rich salmon red or steel gray.

Sea Servers
. . . smart serving pieces 'styled from the sea' . . .

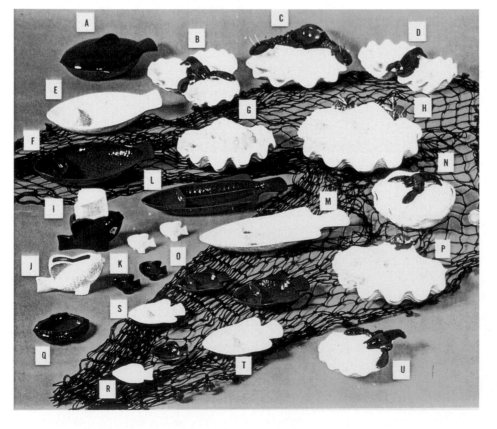

This series was an extensive accessory line designed primarily for serving food. Each item was shaped in the realistic form of a fish, lobster, crab, or seashell. The original colors were "live-coal red," "sea shell white," and "steel gray." Blue and green were used later. Both the fish and the shell susans revolved on an ebony finished wood base. The lobster on the lobster 'n shell chip 'n dip could be separated from the shell and used for decoration elsewhere. Four items — the shell chip 'n dip, the lobster 'n shell chip 'n dip, the twin shell 'n lobster server, and the triple shell 'n lobster server — were very popular and enjoyed extended production runs. The shell chip 'n dip appeared in various colors in the Lotus dinnerware series. Lobster Serveware (1989) consisted of four very popular items from the original line. Designed by Allen and Shaw.

Sea Servers: Metlox brochure.

Sea Servers

	14	Fish Canister & Lid, red or white, 9 x 11 x 6"	$90 – 100
[141]	41	2-Piece Lobster 'n Shell Chip 'n Dip, red & white, 16 x 4"	$40 – 45
	44	Small Fish Ashtray/Utility Dish, red, white, or gray, 4"	$5 – 7
	45	Medium Fish Ashtray, red, white, or gray, 6"	$8 – 10
	46	Large Fish Ashtray, red, white, or gray, 8½"	$10 – 12
	47	Small Crab Utility Dish, red, white, or gray, 6"	$8 – 10
	47	Small Fish Chip 'n Dip, red or white, 11 x 6 x 2"	$25 – 30
[151]	51	Fish Chip 'n Dip, red, white, or gray, 15½ x 8¾ x 2½"	$30 – 35
[152]	52	Twin Shell 'n Lobster Server, red & white, 14 x 10 x 5"	$40 – 45
[153]	53	Triple Shell 'n Lobster Server, red & white, 13¾ x 3"	$40 – 45
	54	Small Lobster 'n Shell Server, red & white, 10 x 7½"	$25 – 30
	55	Large Shrimp Server, red & white, 15 x 13 x 4"	$30 – 35
[156-Red] [160-White]	56	Fish Salt, red, white, or gray, 3½"	$10 – 12
[157-Red] [161-White]	57	Fish Pepper, red, white, or gray, 3½"	$10 – 12
[158-Red] [159-White]	58	Fish Tureen & Lid with Ladle, red or white, 2 qt.	$90 – 100
	60	Fish Casserole & Lid, red, white, or gray, 2 qt., 14 x 6"	$35 – 40
	61	Fish Susan with Wood Base, red or white, 16¾"	$40 – 45
	62	Shell Susan with Wood Base, red or white, 16"	$40 – 45
[170]	70	Shrimp Server, red & white, 12½"	$30 – 35
[172]	71	3-Section Fish Server, red or white, 17½ x 6 x 2½"	$30 – 35
	72A-B	Lobster Claw Fork & Spoon Set, red	pr. $40 – 45
[173]	73	Shell Chip 'n Dip, white, 12½"	$30 – 35
	74	Lobster 'n Shell Casserole & Lid, red & white	$45 – 50
	75	Lobster 'n Shell Seafood Platter, red & white, 17 x 14½ x 3½"	$40 – 45
	76	Shell Salad Bowl, white, 12¾ x 4½ x 11½"	$30 – 35
	77	Fish Napkin Holder, red or white	$20 – 25
	85	Crab Casserolette, red or white,	$8 – 10
	86	Fish Utility Dish, red or white, 8¼ x 5¼ x 2"	$10 – 12
	87	Shell Utility Dish, red or white, 5¾ x 1¾"	$8 – 10
	88	Small Shell Chip 'n Dip, white, 10 x 9 x 2"	$25 – 30

A giftware catalog dated Fall, 1963, lists the following additional items.

154	Fish Chip 'n Dip, white & blue	$30 – 35
166	Fish Chowder, white	$10 – 12
167	Fish Chowder, red	$10 – 12
171	3-Section Fish Server, white & blue	$25 – 30
192	Fish Casserole/No Lid, white & red	$15 – 20
193	Fish Casserole/No Lid, white & blue	$15 – 20

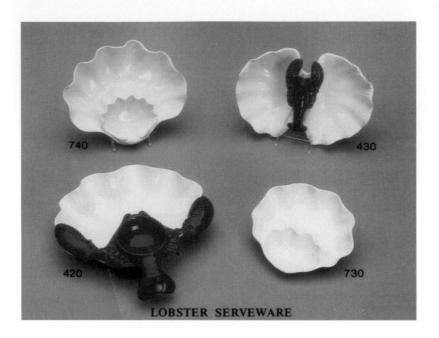

740   430

420   730

LOBSTER SERVEWARE

Lobster Serveware: Metlox catalog sheet.

Shell Line Serving Accessories

030 White

320	Fish Hors D'Oeuvre	$25 – 30
420	Lobster 'n Shell Chip 'n Dip (w/Red Lobster)	$40 – 45
430	Twin Shell 'n Lobster Server (w/Red Lobster)	$40 – 45
440	Triple Shell 'n Lobster Server (w/Red Lobster)	$40 – 45
730	Shrimp Server	$25 – 30
740	Shell Chip 'n Dip	$30 – 35
750	Fish Chip 'n Dip	$30 – 35

031 Green

320	Fish Hors D'Oeuvre	$25 – 30
740	Shell Chip 'n Dip	$30 – 35
750	Fish Chip 'n Dip	$30 – 35

032 Curry

320	Fish Hors D'Oeuvre	$25 – 30
740	Shell Chip 'n Dip	$30 – 35
750	Fish Chip 'n Dip	$30 – 35

198 Lobster Serveware

420	Lobster & Shell, 14½"	$40 – 45
430	Lobster & Twin Shell, 14"	$40 – 45
730	Shell Chip & Dip, 10"	$25 – 30
740	Shell Chip & Dip, 12½"	$30 – 35

Chip 'N Dips
and Casual Serving Accessories

This line, consisting of various serving accessories, offered realistic pineapple, watermelon, corn, and Mexican sombrero designs. Although all items were produced with natural full-color decoration, a number were also made in an all-white version. Several popular items, such as the sombrero pieces and the corn server, were manufactured for a long period and were included in later lines.

Chip 'N Dips: Metlox catalog sheet.

Chip 'N Dips:
Sombrero Chip 'N Dip.

Chip 'N Dips and Casual Serving Accessories

[340]	40	Sombrero Chip 'n Dip, 15 x 4"	$40 – 45
[342]	42	Sombrero Ashtray, sm., 6 x 2¾"	$20 – 25
[343]	43	Sombrero Ashtray, 9 x 3"	$25 – 30
	48	Pineapple Chip 'n Dip, white, 16 x 7¼ x 2"	$25 – 30
	48D	Pineapple Chip 'n Dip, decorated, 16 x 7¼ x 2"	$30 – 35
[349]	49	Watermelon Chip 'n Dip/Fruit Server, 15 x 8 x 3½"	$30 – 35
[350]	50	Corn Chip 'n Dip, white, 18 x 9½ x 3"	$25 – 30
	50D	Corn Chip 'n Dip, decorated, 18 x 9½ x 3"	$30 – 35
	58	Sombrero Casual Service Plate, div., 13 x 10¼"	$20 – 22
	59	Sombrero Casual Service Cup for Plate.	$10 – 12
	69	Watermelon Bowl, 6 x 3"	$12 – 15
	141	Pineapple Pitcher, decorated, 11"	$40 – 45
	142	Pineapple Tumbler, 10 oz.	$15 – 18
	143	Pineapple Chip 'n Dip, sm., white, 11½ x 6 x 2"	$20 – 22
	143D	Pineapple Chip 'n Dip, sm., decorated, 11½ x 6 x 2"	$22 – 25
	146	Pineapple Salt	$12 – 15
	147	Pineapple Pepper	$12 – 15
	148	Pineapple Individual Dish, white, 8¾ x 4 x 1¾"	$10 – 12
	148D	Pineapple Individual Dish, decorated, 8¾ x 4 x 1¾"	$12 – 15
	149	Watermelon Chip 'n Dip, sm., 10¼ x 6 x 2"	$22 – 25
[033 500]	150	Corn Individual Server, white, 11"	$15 – 16
	150D	Corn Individual Server, decorated, 11".	$18 – 20
	151	Corn Chip 'n Dip, sm., white, 12½ x 7½ x 2½"	$20 – 22
	151D	Corn Chip 'n Dip, sm., decorated, 12½ x 7½ x 2½"	$22 – 25
	156	Corn Salt	$12 – 15
	157	Corn Pepper.	$12 – 15
	170	Watermelon Cup	$8 – 10
	172	Watermelon Saucer	$4 – 5
	173	Watermelon Salt, 3 x 2½"	$12 – 15
	174	Watermelon Pepper, 3 x 2½"	$12 – 15
	175	Watermelon Plate, oval, 10½"	$12 – 15

Jam and Jellies

Jam and Jellies were covered, round 4½" tall jars attached to a small plate. They were designed with a basket weave texture except for the lid's finial which was the shape of the appropriate fruit. The lid was slotted for a serving spoon which was included with each jar. Each Jam and Jelly was produced in three different color schemes — a maple jar with full-color fruit, a white jar with full-color fruit, and an ironstone white jar with ironstone white fruit.

Jam and Jellies		
62A	Apple	$18 – 20
62B	Berry	$18 – 20
62C	Cherry	$18 – 20
62D	Orange	$18 – 20
62E	Strawberry	$18 – 20
62F	Peach	$18 – 20
62G	Grape	$18 – 20
62H	Honey Bee	$18 – 20

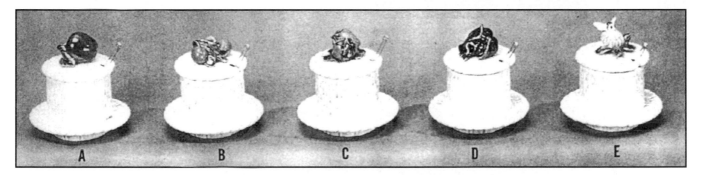

Jam and Jellies: Metlox brochure.

Twin and Triple Servers

These pieces were advertised as candy or nut servers. The twin server was oval shaped with a center divider. The triple server was three round bowl sections joined together. The exterior of both was a basket weave texture while the interior was smooth. The center finial was an apple, strawberries, or a grape cluster. Both types were decorated with a maple glaze and full-color fruit.

Twin and Triple Servers		
63A	Apple Twin Server	$20 – 25
63E	Strawberry Twin Server	$20 – 25
63G	Grape Twin Server	$20 – 25
64A	Apple Triple Server	$25 – 30
64E	Strawberry Triple Server	$25 – 30
64G	Grape Triple Server	$25 – 30

Twin and Triple Servers: Metlox brochure.

Baskets

The baskets resembled the small wood containers once used by grocery stores to hold fruit. The bottom was a box design featuring wood grain texture and a stapled rim. The lid was a pile of fruit — either strawberries, lemons, or tangerines. They were decorated with natural colors.

Baskets
040 480 Basket with Strawberry Lid, 1½ qt., 6 x 7½". $20 – 25
060 480 Basket with Lemon Lid, 1½ qt., 6 x 7½" . . . . $20 – 25
061 480 Basket with Tangerine Lid, 1½ qt., 6 x 7½". . $20 – 25

Baskets: Metlox catalog.

Bake and Serve Casserolettes

These multipurpose individual size casserolettes were useful for serving hot or cold dishes. Food could be baked in them if a foil cover was used. Glazed in brown or ironstone white, they were designed in five shapes — potato, beef, chicken, fish, and shell. Casserolettes were packed four units to a carton. A Hostess Hint Leaflet was enclosed in each carton.

Bake and Serve Casserolettes

80	Potato, brown only	$5 – 7
83	Beef, brown only	$8 – 10
84	Chicken, white or brown	$8 – 10
86	Fish, white or brown	$8 – 10
87	Shell, white or brown	$5 – 7

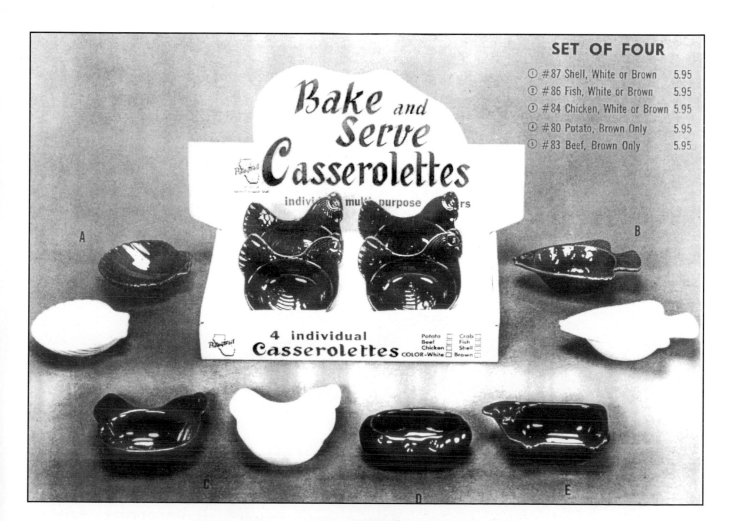

SET OF FOUR

① #87 Shell, White or Brown   5.95
② #86 Fish, White or Brown   5.95
③ #84 Chicken, White or Brown   5.95
④ #80 Potato, Brown Only   5.95
⑤ #83 Beef, Brown Only   5.95

Bake and Serve Casserolettes: Metlox catalog sheet.

Cabbage Lines

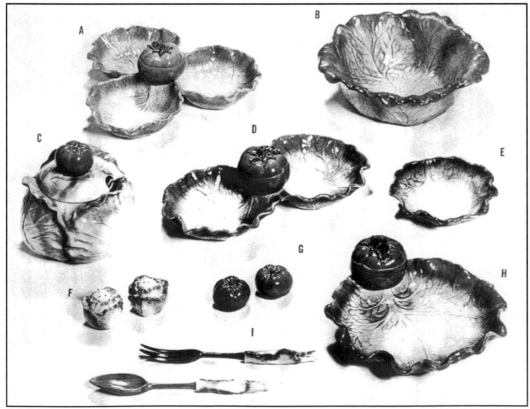

Metlox produced three accessory series which featured cabbage shapes. The first, Cabbage and Tomato Decorative Serving Accessories, was a large line dating from 1960. It "combined the chartreuse beauty of the cabbage and brilliant red of the tomato in large Hostess triumphs for serving that's unusual... Deeply carved, authentically duplicated, in both shape and color." All the flatware items, server sections, and bowls replicated a deeply veined cabbage leaf or leaves. The tomato served as the covered dip bowl on the leaf servers, the lid on the cabbage cruets, and the cabbage soup tureen lid finial. The mustard jar and the salt and pepper set were available in both cabbage and tomato shapes. Certain individual items were ingeniously designed to combine with others to form new pieces. For example, the cabbage four-section utility server could be used by itself, with the cruet set, or with the cruet set plus one pair of the salt and pepper sets.

The Cabbage Serving Line (White) was a much smaller series released in 1963. Items were produced only in the "striking new Roma White breakthrough glaze." No tomato shapes were included. The single leaf, twin server, and triple server had open cabbage bowls as dips. The cabbage tureen lid did not have a tomato finial.

The Cabbage Line was an updated version appearing in the late 1980s. It was composed of several items from the second series and the V 758 Vegetable Group (White), plus new additions, — a mug, 1½ quart casserole, large chip 'n dip, and 14" round platter. All items were produced in 300 Green (a rich evergreen color) and 303 White.

Cabbage and Tomato Decorative Serving Accessories: Metlox catalog.

Cabbage and Tomato Decorative Serving Accessories

100	Cabbage Leaf with Tomato & Lid, 12¼ x 5¼"	$20 – 25
101	Cabbage Serving Leaf, 7 x 3"	$10 – 12
102	Twin Cabbage Leaf with Tomato Center & Lid, 17 x 8½ x 5¼"	$25 – 30
103	Triple Cabbage Leaf with Tomato Center & Lid, 17 x 5¼"	$25 – 30
104	Cabbage Salad Bowl, 15 x 5½"	$55 – 60
105	Cabbage Soup Tureen & Lid with Tomato Finial, 11"	$110 – 120
105L	Cabbage Soup Tureen Ladle	$22 – 25
106	Cabbage Salt	$14 – 15
107	Cabbage Pepper	$14 – 15
108	Tomato Salt	$12 – 14
109	Tomato Pepper	$12 – 14
110	Cabbage Fruit/Dessert Cup, 3½"	$12 – 15
112	Cabbage Saucer, 7"	$4 – 5
114	4-Section Cabbage Leaf with Tomato Center & Lid, 13½ x 13½ x 4¾"	$25 – 30
115	Cabbage Luncheon Plate, 9½ x 1⅜"	$12 – 15
116	Tomato Mustard Jar & Slotted Lid with Glass Spoon, 4"	$18 – 20
117	Cabbage Mustard Jar & Slotted Lid with Glass Spoon, 4"	$18 – 20
118	Cabbage Oil & Vinegar Cruet Set with Tomato Lids, 6½"	$15 – 18 ea.
119	Cabbage 4-Section Utility Server, 12 x 8½ x ½"	$20 – 25
119/118	Cruet Set on Utility Server Base	$40 – 45
119/118C	Cruet Set & Cabbage Salt & Pepper on Utility Server Base	$50 – 55
119/118T	Cruet Set & Tomato Salt & Pepper on Utility Server Base	$50 – 55
120	Cabbage Relish Server, 13¾ x 8¼ x 1¼"	$20 – 25
120C	Cabbage Relish Server with Cabbage Salt & Pepper	$35 – 40
120T	Cabbage Relish Server with Tomato Salt & Pepper	$35 – 40
121	Tomato Soup Tureen & Lid, 2 qt.	$90 – 100
121L	Tomato Soup Tureen Ladle	$22 – 25
122A-B	Cabbage Fork & Spoon Set	$40 – 45 pr.

Cabbage Line
300 Green, 303 White
Deduct 20% for 303 White

040	Salad Plate, 8"	$12 – 14
050	Luncheon Plate, 9½"	$14 – 15
080	Soup Bowl, 7½"	$16 – 18
100	Salad Bowl, 14"	$55 – 60
250	Platter, rnd., 14"	$40 – 45
300	Leaf Plate, 11"	$35 – 40
330	Salt	$14 – 15
340	Pepper	$14 – 15
481-2	Soup Tureen & Lid, 3 qt.	$115 – 125
490	Soup Tureen Ladle	$22 – 25
620	Casserole & Lid, 1½ qt.	$70 – 75
740	Chip 'N Dip, lg., 12½"	$50 – 55
760	Mug, 8 oz.	$18 – 20

Cabbage Line: green cabbage soup tureen and lid.

Cabbage Serving Line (White)

360	Cabbage Leaf with Dip	$35 – 40
361	Cabbage Individual Bowl	$14 – 16
362	Cabbage Twin Server with Dip	$35 – 40
363	Cabbage Triple Server with Dip	$35 – 40
364	Cabbage Salad Bowl	$45 – 50
366	Cabbage Salt	$11 – 12
367	Cabbage Pepper	$11 – 12
368	Cabbage Soup Tureen & Lid w/Ladle	$115 – 125
372-3	Cabbage Fork & Spoon Set	pr. $40 – 45
375	Cabbage Jar & Lid	$20 – 25

Animal Keepers

Animal Keepers
an ideal place for the contents of his pockets. Color-
ful keepers at pocket-emptying time... Keeps his
dresser neat, all articles in one place.

Four Animal Keepers were designed — a roaring "Leo the Lion," a braying "Burrito the Burro," a panting "Watch Dog," and a bull. Each comical animal, seated with front legs spread, was attached to one side of a shallow dish with plenty of room for keys, change, a wallet, pencils, and pens. Wrist watches could be hung around the neck of each animal. Felt was attached to the bottom to protect furniture surfaces. Each came gift-boxed with an accompanying display insert.

Animal Keepers		
92	The Watch Dog	$25 – 30
93	Burrito, the Burro	$25 – 30
94	The Bull Pen	$25 – 30
95	Leo, the Lion	$25 – 30

Animal Keepers:
Metlox catalog sheet.

#315 Vege-
table Bowl
9¼" x 2½"
Retail $2.95

#310
Salad Bowl
12¾" x 3¼"
Retail $5.95

#330
Shield Platter
13½" x 1½"
Retail $4.95

#322A-B Fork
and Spoon
Pair
Retail $3.95

#333-34
Horn Salt
and Pepper
Retail $3.50

#304
Utility Plate
9¼" x 1"
Retail $2.50

Individual pieces featured hand-carved detail in authentic Viking period style. The "Smorgasboat," the three-part centerpiece of the set, resembled a Viking ship complete with shields on the side and dragonhead bows on each end section. Extra boat sections were available separately to increase the length as desired. A Viking shield design decorated the other serving pieces, bowls, and flatware. The salt and pepper shakers were shaped like small Viking horns. An ivory glaze was applied over a hand-rubbed burnt umber antique finish on each piece. Designed by Allen and Shaw.

Smorgasboat Line:
Metlox brochure.

Smorgasboat Line
The coordinated buffet serving line designed to supply every item needed for a complete Smorgasbord Party or Feast.

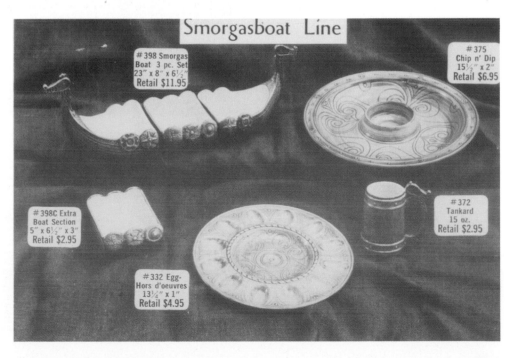

Smorgasboat Line

#398 Smorgas
Boat 3 pc. Set
23" x 8" x 6½"
Retail $11.95

#375
Chip n' Dip
15½" x 2"
Retail $6.95

#398C Extra
Boat Section
5" x 6½" x 3"
Retail $2.95

#372
Tankard
15 oz.
Retail $2.95

#332 Egg-
Hors d'oeuvres
13¾" x 1"
Retail $4.95

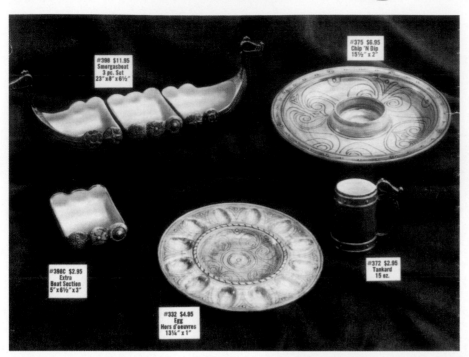

Smorgasboat Line: Metlox brochure.

Smorgasboat Line

304	Utility Plate, 9⅛ x 1".	$15 – 18	333	Horn Salt Shaker.	$15 – 18
310	Salad Bowl, 12¾ x 3¼"	$45 – 50	334	Horn Pepper Shaker	$15 – 18
315	Vegetable Bowl, 9⅛ x 2½"	$30 – 35	372	Tankard, 15 oz.	$18 – 20
322A-B	Salad Fork & Spoon Set	$40 – 45 pr.	375	Shield Chip 'N Dip, 15½ x 2"	$45 – 50
330	Shield Platter, 13½ x 1½"	$35 – 40	398	Smorgasboat 3-Piece Set, 23 x 8 x 6½".	$60 – 65
332	Egg Hors D'Oeuvres Plate, 13¼ x 1".	$45 – 50	398C	Smorgasboat Center Section, 5 x 6½ x 3".	$15 – 18

Pebbline and Gold Nugget
Ash trays, candy boxes, cigarette boxes with
authentically reproduced pebble motif — in moss
green with gray beige — nugget with a touch of
Sutters' gold and chocolate brown accent.

Pebbline and Gold Nugget featured a realistic pebble cluster design on the bottom or border of the ashtrays and on the lid of the cigarette boxes, candy box, and cigarette cup. Both lines included identical items. The only difference was the decoration — Pebbline in moss green and Gold Nugget in chocolate brown. A transparent gray beige glaze was applied to the cluster of both color versions. The glaze settled in the grooves enhancing the sparkling pebble look. For the Gold Nugget line several of the pebbles of each cluster were painted with gold to suggest gold nuggets discovered among the pebbles.

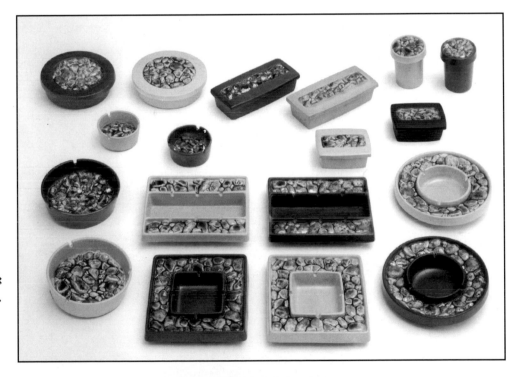

Pebbline and Gold Nugget:
Metlox archive photo.

Pebbline		
701	Pebble Candy Box, rnd., 7 x 2"	$25 – 28
702	Pebble Cigarette Box, sq., 5 x 3½ x 2".	$18 – 20
703	Pebble Cigarette Box, oblong,	
	8½ x 3¾ x 2"	$25 – 28
712	Pebble Cigarette Cup w/Lid, 4½ x 3¼".	$18 – 20
721	Pebble Deluxe Ashtray, rnd., 8 x 1¾".	$22 – 25
722	Pebble Deluxe Ashtray, sq., 8 x 1¾" .	$22 – 25
723	Pebble Deluxe Ashtray, oblong,	
	9 x 6½ x 1¾"	$25 – 28
731	Pebble Ashtray, rnd., 6½ x 1¾"	$20 – 22
732	Pebble Ashtray, sm., rnd., 4 x 1¾". . .	$15 – 16

Gold Nugget		
701G	Nugget Candy Box, rnd., 7 x 2"	$28 – 30
702G	Nugget Cigarette Box, sq., 5 x 3½ x 2".	$20 – 22
703G	Nugget Cigarette Box, oblong,	
	8½ x 3¾ x 2"	$28 – 30
712G	Nugget Cigarette Cup w/Lid, 4½ x 3¼".	$20 – 22
721G	Nugget Deluxe Ashtray, rnd., 8 x 1¾".	$25 – 28
722G	Nugget Deluxe Ashtray, sq., 8 x 1¾" .	$25 – 28
723G	Nugget Deluxe Ashtray, oblong,	
	9 x 6½ x 1¾"	$28 – 30
731G	Nugget Ashtray, rnd., 6½ x 1¾"	$22 – 25
732G	Nugget Ashtray, sm., rnd., 4 x 1¾" .	$16 – 18

Directional Flower Arrangers

This line, advertised as "the key to easy flower arranging," included four flower vase with holder sets, two flower bowls, and five sculptured flower arrangers. The vases were designed with a round directional arranger inside. The animal figurine arrangers — a white duck, a white swan, a green turtle, and a green frog — were intended for use in the low pebble bowl. The lotus arranger went with the lotus bowl. Each arranger was hollow on the inside, providing additional water for cuttings. A top and bottom set of holes, scientifically aligned and slanted to allow 25 possible different angles, held stems securely in place and prevented sliding.

Directional Flower Arrangers: Metlox catalog sheet.

Directional Flower Arrangers: Metlox catalog sheet.

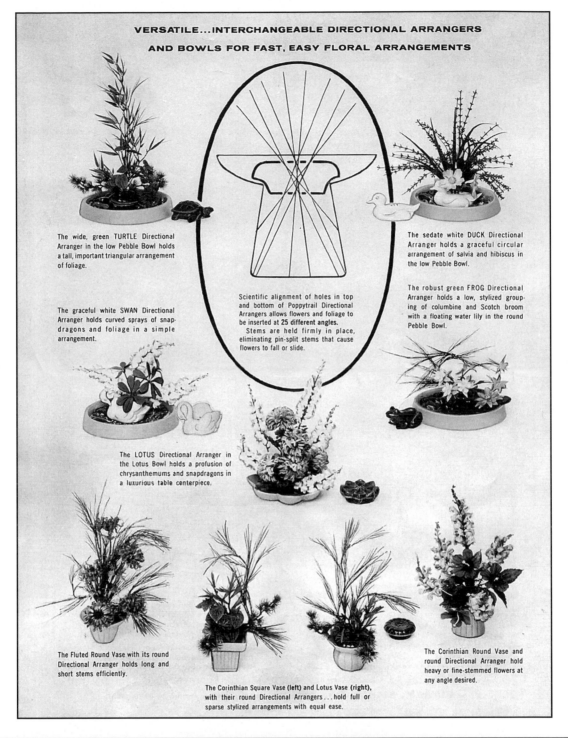

VERSATILE...INTERCHANGEABLE DIRECTIONAL ARRANGERS AND BOWLS FOR FAST, EASY FLORAL ARRANGEMENTS

The wide, green TURTLE Directional Arranger in the low Pebble Bowl holds a tall, important triangular arrangement of foliage.

The graceful white SWAN Directional Arranger holds curved sprays of snapdragons and foliage in a simple arrangement.

Scientific alignment of holes in top and bottom of Poppytrail Directional Arrangers allows flowers and foliage to be inserted at 25 different angles.
Stems are held firmly in place, eliminating pin-split stems that cause flowers to fall or slide.

The sedate white DUCK Directional Arranger holds a graceful circular arrangement of salvia and hibiscus in the low Pebble Bowl.

The robust green FROG Directional Arranger holds a low, stylized grouping of columbine and Scotch broom with a floating water lily in the round Pebble Bowl.

The LOTUS Directional Arranger in the Lotus Bowl holds a profusion of chrysanthemums and snapdragons in a luxurious table centerpiece.

The Fluted Round Vase with its round Directional Arranger holds long and short stems efficiently.

The Corinthian Square Vase (left) and Lotus Vase (right), with their round Directional Arrangers...hold full or sparse stylized arrangements with equal ease.

The Corinthian Round Vase and round Directional Arranger hold heavy or fine-stemmed flowers at any angle desired.

Directional Flower Arrangers

600	Fluted Round Vase & Directional Arranger, 6 x 5⅜" . . . . $15 – 18	
601	Corinthian Square Vase & Directional Arranger, 5¼ x 4⅜" . . . . $15 – 18	
602	Lotus Vase & Directional Arranger, 5¾ x 3⅞" . . . . $15 – 18	
603	Lotus Bowl, 11⅝ x 2" . . . . $18 – 20	
6032	Lotus Directional Arranger, 5⅛" . . . . $12 – 15	
605	Corinthian Round Vase & Directional Arranger, 6¾ x 4⅝" . . . . $18 – 20	
606	Pebble Bowl, 12½ x 2" . . . . $20 – 25	
630	"Frog" Directional Arranger, 5½" . . . . $15 – 18	
631	"Swan" Directional Arranger, 6⅞" . . . $15 – 18	
632	"Turtle" Directional Arranger, 6½" . . . $15 – 18	
633	"Duck" Directional Arranger, 7½" . . . $15 – 18	

Cock-A-Doodle-Do

Cock-A-Doodle-Do:
Metlox archive
photo.

This colorful line combined useful basket servers with stylized hen- and rooster-shaped serving pieces. All of the basket weave items were straw colored. The long-necked hen and rooster pieces were white with colored beaks, eyes, and combs. The rooster was crowing, beak open. The hen's tailfeathers were straight and standing up while the rooster's were curved. The hen design was used as the lid for all covered pieces. The rooster served as an attached toothpick holder on the egg hors d'oeuvres plate and the biscuit basket. The novel creamer used the rooster's neck and beak as a spout. Designed by Allen and Shaw.

Cock-A-Doodle-Do

[1018]	518	Hen Sugar & Lid, white, 4½ x 5"	$22 –	25
[1019]	519	Rooster Creamer, white, pours through beak, 5¾ x 5¼".	$22 –	25
[1023]	523	Hen Cranberry Server & Lid, white, 5½ x 6"	$25 –	28
[1029]	529	Twin Dip Biscuit Basket, straw color with white rooster, 11 x 6 x 5½"	$35 –	40
[1032]	532	Egg Hors D'Oeuvres, straw color with white rooster, 13½ x 5¼".	$40 –	45
[1050]	550	Round Basket 'N Chicken Chip 'N Dip, straw color with white hen, 14 x 8"	$45 –	50
[1053]	553	Rooster Salt, white, 4¼"	$15 –	18
[1054]	554	Hen Pepper, white, 3"	$15 –	18
[1055]	555	3-Section Basket Server & Lid, straw colored basket, white hen lid, 15½ x 8"	$45 –	50
[1056]	556	3-Section Basket Server without Lid, straw color, 15½ x 8"	$25 –	28
[1058]	558	Hen Soup Tureen & Lid with Ladle, white, 2½ qt., 10¾"	$90 –	100
[1060]	560	Hen Casserole & Lid, white, 1½ qt., 8½ x 8"	$60 –	65

First Series
080 Second Series
081 1776 Line

These related lines were created by Mel Shaw who styled their design after early American woodcuts. The color scheme for all three was blue on white. The American eagle was the primary decoration common to all three. Although the First Series (c. 1963) and the Second Series (c. 1967) of Eagle Provincial Accessories consisted of the same items, there was one important difference. One or more groups of three patriotic stars served as additional decoration on the First Series. The Second Series substituted the date "1776" for the groups of stars on most pieces. The First Series also had one extra item, the solid black matte finish Red Kampbell's kettle which was identical in shape to the bean pot kettle of both series.

Although similar to the 080 Second Series, the 081 1776 Line (c. 1972) was a much larger and more diverse line. The same eagle and "1776" date were used. The 1776 Line included all the items in the Second Series except the cookie jar and bean pot kettle and added many items from the Provincial dinnerware patterns, including the individual soup server, candle holder, bread server, match box, spice box, salt box, tankard, and two-piece cruet set on a wood base. The distinctive beverage server urn with warmer was adapted from the Studio Potter dinnerware patterns. The rims of many 1776 Line items were painted blue. Large patriotic stars were used singly or circularly on many of the items. The canister set and salt box lids were brown with white knobs.

1776 Line: Metlox archive photo.

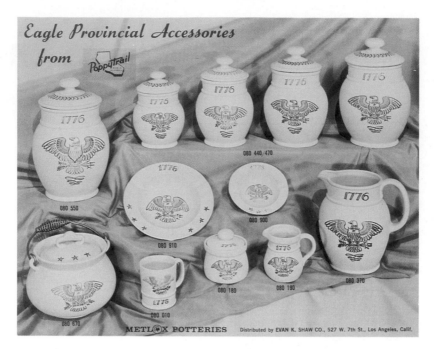

Eagle Provincial (Second Series):
Metlox catalog sheet.

Eagle Provincial Accessories

First Series

800	Cup/Soup Mug	$12 – 14
807	Cookie Canister & Lid	$35 – 45
818	Sugar & Lid	$20 – 22
819	Creamer	$18 – 20
837	Pitcher, 2 qt.	$35 – 40
867	Bean Pot Kettle & Lid	$40 – 45
868	Red Kampbell's Kettle & Lid	$40 – 45
890	Ashtray, med., 5¾"	$12 – 15
891	Ashtray, lg., 8½"	$15 – 18
931	Canister & Lid, ex. lg., 11"	$30 – 35
932	Canister & Lid, lg., 10"	$25 – 30
933	Canister & Lid, med., 9"	$20 – 25
934	Canister & Lid, sm., 7"	$18 – 20

080 Second Series

010	Cup/Soup Mug	$12 – 14
180	Sugar & Lid	$20 – 22
190	Creamer	$18 – 20
370	Pitcher, 2 qt.	$35 – 40
440	Canister & Lid, ex. lg., 3 qt.	$30 – 35
450	Canister & Lid, lg., 2½ qt.	$25 – 30
460	Canister & Lid, med., 1½ qt.	$20 – 25
470	Canister & Lid, sm., 1 qt.	$18 – 20
550	Cookie Jar & Lid	$35 – 45
670	Bean Pot Kettle & Lid	$40 – 45
900	Ashtray, med., 5¾"	$12 – 15
910	Ashtray, lg., 8½"	$15 – 18

081 1776 Line

010	Cup, 7 oz.	$ 9 – 10
020	Saucer, 6⅛"	$5 – 6
060	Dinner Plate, 10½"	$14 – 15
100	Salad Bowl, 11⅛"	$40 – 45
121	Individual Soup Server, 5"	$16 – 18
180	Sugar & Lid, 9 oz.	$20 – 22
190	Creamer, 9 oz.	$18 – 20
300	Buffet Plate, 12"	$35 – 40
360	Candleholder	$25 – 30
370	Pitcher, 2 qt.	$35 – 40
440	Canister & Lid, ex. lg., 3 qt.	$30 – 35
450	Canister & Lid, lg., 2½ qt.	$25 – 30
460	Canister & Lid, med., 1½ qt.	$20 – 25
470	Canister & Lid, sm., 1 qt.	$18 – 20
519	Cruet Set, 2-piece, complete	$70 – 75
510	Oil Cruet & Lid, 7 oz.	$25 – 28
515	Vinegar Cruet & Lid, 7 oz.	$25 – 28
518	Cruet Wood Base	$18 – 20
710	Bread Server, 9½"	$40 – 45
720	Tankard, 1 pt.	$22 – 25
760	Mug, 8 oz.	$12 – 14
809	Beverage Server Urn, Lid, & Warmer, 4 qt.	$85 – 95
810	Match Box	$35 – 40
820	Spice Box	$35 – 40
860	Salt Box w/Wood Lid and Ceramic Knob	$40 – 45
900	Ashtray, med., 5¾"	$12 – 15
910	Ashtray, lg., 8½"	$15 – 18

Strawberry Accessories

Strawberry Accessories was created in the early 1960s as a complementary artware line for the popular P 590 California Strawberry dinnerware pattern. Although the sets were compatible, they were also strikingly different. Strawberry Accessories items were realistically designed strawberry and leaf shapes in vivid red and avocado green. The dinnerware set, however, only used strawberry fruit, bloom, and leaf shapes as lid finials. The strawberry vine design was hand painted on the non-sculptured flatware and bowls. Holloware was a solid tone avocado green. Several of the same types of items — canister set, plate, sugar & lid, creamer, salt, pepper, and mug — were produced in both the artware line and the dinnerware pattern. The difference was the strawberry shapes of the artware pieces as opposed to the familiar shapes of the dinnerware.

The dinnerware pattern, and especially the accessories, featured an innovative selenium red color that was inspired by Chinese oxblood red and invented by Metlox glaze expert John Johnson. This rich and luscious red, a very difficult color to duplicate on hand-painted earthenware, became the envy of the industry. The only negative factor was that this underglaze color occasionally separated when fired, sometimes causing white spots on items.

The three-divided server with strawberry jar and lid, the leaf server, and the two ashtrays were avocado green leaf shapes. The jam/jelly jar, twin server, and triple server, all adaptations from the earlier Jam and Jellies and Twin and Triple Servers lines, were green basket weave texture

Strawberry Accessories: triple server, leaf server, and strawberry sugar/jam jar and lid.

items. The basket was light brown with a red strawberry pile lid. The rest of the items were various red strawberry shapes with green leaves or green leaves and white blooms. The cookie jar and the large canister were identical in shape and size. The three-piece red strawberry canister set should not be confused with the four-piece avocado green canister set of the dinnerware. This very popular line was designed by Allen and Shaw.

Strawberry Accessories (Second Series) was issued in the early 1980s as an associated artware line to Wicker Strawberry, a dinnerware pattern very different from P 590 California Strawberry. Wicker Strawberry was white instead of honey-toned and used a new strawberry vine design. The Second Series was an updated version of the original Strawberry Accessories. A lighter shade of green replaced the darker avocado green of the earlier series. Selenium red was again used for the strawberry shapes. All six sectional servers, the chip and dip, and the small ashtray were discontinued. The salad plate and leaf buffet plate were new items. The luncheon plate was redesigned without the white blooms and green leaves. The basket and lid and jam/jelly jar were white with colored fruit. All other items from the original line were continued unaltered.

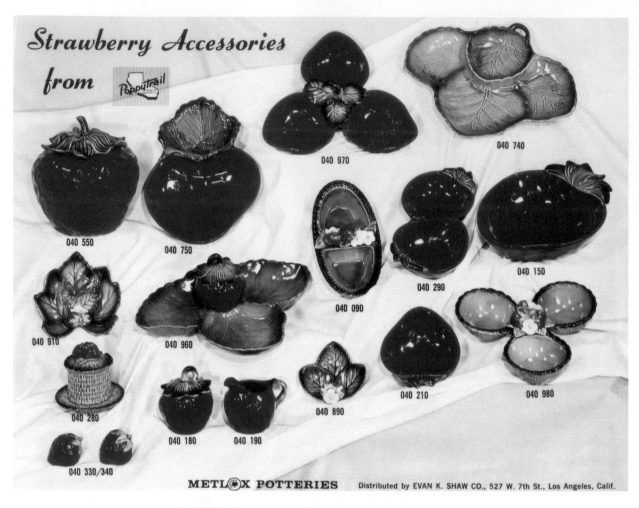

Strawberry Accessories: Metlox catalog sheet.

Strawberry Accessories: large 6½" ashtray, strawberry individual server, and small 4⅝" ashtray.

Strawberry Accessories: jam/jelly jar and lid, strawberry salt and pepper shakers, and 6 oz. mugs.

Basket & Lid, 1½ Qt. | Buffet Plate, Green, 11" | Canister, Large | Canister, Medium | Canister, Small | Cookie Jar & Lid

Leaf Dish, Green | Mug, 6 oz. | Serving Bowl, 11" | Sugar w/Lid, 6 oz.

Jam & Jelly Jar w/Lid | Salt & Pepper | Serving Bowl, Individual, 6½" | Creamer, 8 oz. | Luncheon Plate | Salad Plate

Strawberry Accessories (Second Series): Metlox catalog sheet.

040 Strawberry Accessories

	050 Luncheon Plate, 9⅜"	$20 – 22
[401]	090 Twin Berry Server, red, 9¼"	$25 – 30
[410]	150 Strawberry Fruit Bowl, 11"	$28 – 30
[418]	180 Sugar/Jam Jar & Lid, 6 oz.	$22 – 25
[419]	190 Creamer, 8 oz.	$22 – 25
[421]	210 Strawberry Individual Server, 6⅝".	$18 – 20
	280 Jam/Jelly Jar & Lid, 6 oz.	$22 – 25
	290 Twin Server, green, 11⅜"	$30 – 35
	330 Strawberry Salt Shaker	$14 – 15
	340 Strawberry Pepper Shaker	$14 – 15
	450 Strawberry Canister & Lid, lg., 3½ qt.	$60 – 70
	460 Strawberry Canister & Lid, med., 3 qt.	$45 – 55
	470 Strawberry Canister & Lid, sm., 2½ qt.	$30 – 40
	480 Strawberry Basket & Lid, 1½ qt.	$25 – 30
	550 Strawberry Cookie Jar & Lid, 3½ qt.	$60 – 70
[403]	740 Leaf Server, 13¾"	$30 – 35
[400]	750 Strawberry Chip & Dip, 13⅝"	$30 – 35
	760 Mug, 6 oz.	$20 – 22
	890 Ashtray, sm., 4⅝"	$22 – 25
	910 Ashtray, lg., 6½"	$25 – 28
[402]	960 3-Divided Server with Jar & Lid, 13½"	$45 – 50
[404]	970 3-Section Server with Handle, 11¾"	$40 – 45
	980 Triple Server, 9⅜"	$40 – 45

Strawberry Accessories (Second Series)

040	Salad Plate	$15 – 18
050	Luncheon Plate	$20 – 22
150	Strawberry Serving Bowl, 11"	$28 – 30
180	Sugar & Lid, 6 oz.	$22 – 25
190	Creamer, 8 oz.	$22 – 25
210	Strawberry Individual Serving Bowl, 6½"	$18 – 20
280	Jam/Jelly Jar & Lid, 6 oz.	$22 – 25
300	Leaf Buffet Plate, green, 11"	$30 – 35
330	Strawberry Salt	$14 – 15
340	Strawberry Pepper	$14 – 15
450	Strawberry Canister & Lid, lg., 3½ qt.	$60 – 70
460	Strawberry Canister & Lid, med., 3qt.	$45 – 55
470	Strawberry Canister & Lid, sm., 2½ qt.	$30 – 40
480	Strawberry Basket & Lid, 1½ qt.	$25 – 30
550	Strawberry Cookie Jar & Lid, 3½ qt.	$60 – 70
760	Mug, 6 oz.	$20 – 22
910	Leaf Dish, green	$25 – 28

Daisy Accessories

Daisy Accessories, begun in the mid-1960s, was the matching artware line for the P 270 Sculptured Daisy dinnerware pattern. Both were decorated with the same carved, raised daisy flowers — white petals surrounding wheat-yellow centers — and green leaves. Most of the accessory items, however, had more surface sculpturing than the dinnerware pieces. The cake plate, three daisy petal plates, individual bowl, luncheon plate, cup, and saucer were designed as a single, open daisy flower. The topiary cookie jar, soap dish, three square ashtrays, footed bowl and lid, and 6" bowl and lid were completely covered with numerous daisy blossoms. An elegant design feature was that many of the items were footed, including the cake plate, canister set, topiary cookie jar, and apothecary jar. Most of the lids had a single or multiple daisy finial. There were two cookie jars — the straight-sided cookie canister and the round, footed topiary jar designed in imitation of the gardening practice of trimming shrubs into ornamental shapes. The daisy petals, ashtrays, and canister set each consisted of three graduated sizes. The four-piece 095 Daisy Bouquet canister set, featuring a completely different shape and design, was never included in the line. The cake plate was the only item offered in both white and decorated versions. Daisy Accessories became a very popular artware line. Phyllis Ord created the cookie canister and topiary cookie jar. The other items were designed by Allen and Shaw.

Daisy Accessories: chip 'n dip.

Daisy Accessories: cake plate (decorated).

Daisy Accessories: large 8" daisy petal.

Daisy Accessories: Metlox catalog sheet.

050 Daisy Accessories

	010	Daisy Cup, 6 oz.	$15 – 18
	020	Daisy Saucer (Utility Dish), 5¾"	$6 – 8
[505]	050	Utility Plate, 8¼"	$18 – 20
	060	Luncheon Plate, 9¼"	$20 – 22
	210	Individual Bowl	$18 – 20
	280	Daisy Twin Server with Handle, 9⅞"	$35 – 40
	310	Cake Plate, 13"	$50 – 55
	051-310	Cake Plate, white, 13"	$45 – 50
[511]	320	Hors D'Oeuvres Server, 12½"	$40 – 45
	440	Daisy Cookie Canister & Lid, 3½ qt.	$35 – 45
	450	Daisy Canister & Lid, lg., 3½ qt.	$45 – 50
	460	Daisy Canister & Lid, med., 3 qt.	$40 – 45
	470	Daisy Canister & Lid, sm., 2½ qt.	$35 – 40
	550	Daisy Topiary Cookie Jar, 2¾ qt.	$65 – 75
	750	Chip & Dip, 12¼"	$50 – 55
[502]	830	Footed Bowl, 6½"	$30 – 35
[501]	840	Footed Compote, 8⅜"	$40 – 45
[503]	850	Footed Bowl & Lid, 4¾"	$35 – 40
[504]	860	Bowl & Lid, 6"	$35 – 40
[509]	870	Soap Dish, 5½"	$20 – 25
[510]	880	Apothecary Jar & Lid, 18 oz.	$45 – 50
[506]	890	Ashtray, sq., sm., 4¼"	$18 – 20
	891	Daisy Petal, sm., 4¾"	$15 – 18
[507]	900	Ashtray, sq., med., 5"	$20 – 22
	901	Daisy Petal, med., 6¼"	$18 – 20
[508]	910	Ashtray, sq., lg., 6½"	$22 – 25
	911	Daisy Petal, lg., 8"	$20 – 22

Poppets and Toppets

070 Poppets
071 Toppets
072 Poppet Accessories
073 Garden Sculpture Planters and Poppet Bowls

A Note from the Designer

"Poppets are for fun. They began as fun and as a whimsical departure from my serious ceramic work forms. They have many things about them that I like: smiles, high-fire glazes, natural clay finishes and fun. I hope they give your homes as many smiles and chuckles as they have given mine." — Helen Slater

Helen Slater was associated with Metlox only as the designer of the Poppets and Toppets lines, and several cookie jars. She was primarily an art potter whose medium was high-fired stoneware. Her originals were one-of-a-kind designs created by attaching various hand-thrown parts to a solid, heavy stoneware body. All of her unique pieces were signed in-mold "Slater." Besides serving as decorative items, individual Poppets, many with attached bowls, were useful as holders for pencils, pens, small brushes, candles, keys, change, cigarettes, or small dried flower arrangements. The charm and diversity of Slater's Poppet personalities, designed in a variety of stances, poses, and positions, attested to her inventiveness.

Evan K. Shaw was introduced to Slater by one of Metlox's financiers. Shaw asked her to design an extensive line of Poppets for Metlox. Several technical problems, however, had to be solved before the Poppets could be produced commercially. This assignment was entrusted to ingenious modeler Vincent Martinez who worked solely with Slater in the realization of the line. To lower production costs it was decided that only one master mold would be made for each Poppet design and that each Poppet would be fired only once. Slater submitted hand-thrown prototypes to Martinez who determined which ones could be produced as a one-mold design. This meant redesigning the original by cutting and refitting its parts while attempting to maintain the original's design concept and shape. To reproduce the original's stoneware look on Metlox's earthenware body, Martinez devised a clever decorating scheme. After the greenware figure was sprayed completely with a reddish iron oxide magnesium slip, it was sprayed in a hit-or-miss manner with yellowish slip to create a speckled effect. Then the hand-decorated colors were applied to the appropriate parts of the design and it was fired once. This involved process produced Metlox Poppets that closely resembled Slater's originals.

Eighty-eight Poppets were listed in available brochure materials and this is probably the number that was produced. Each Poppet was given an item number, a name, and an identifying description. A name tag, which accompanied each figure, gave a detailed, comical description. Many also bore a circular paper label. Some were backstamped with the Poppet's number, name, and the company name "METLOX" encircled by "POPPETS BY POPPYTRAIL" — "CALIF."

The Poppets were manufactured from the mid-1960s through the mid-1970s. Most had only one production run. An important exception was the seven-piece Salvation Army Group (numbers 329 – 389) commissioned by that organization. This group was very popular with the Salvation Army and the general public. The last 14 Poppets (numbers 799 – 929) were existing designs fitted with a 4" bowl.

The six Toppets, each with its own number, name, and description, featured a Poppet-like head with the neck serving as a base. Facial features were very simple and childlike. Arthur, Junior, Billy Bob, and Anne served as pencil and pen holders. Skipper and Lucy were candle holders.

Several other small Poppet-related lines were produced. The Poppet Accessories included three types of bottle vases with antique finishes that complemented the Poppet designs and coloring. The Marvin and Muriel bookends attached each figure to a larger bookend bowl. The shallow floral bowls were intended as flower or fruit bowls with a Poppet — not included with the bowl — to be placed in the middle. The three impressive Garden Sculpture Planters were large-scale Mexican Poppet designs with two or three planter bowls. The Zoopo's were designed by Vincent Martinez, not Helen Slater. Although these cute planters with comically grotesque animal designs were classified as small Garden Sculpture Planters, they, like the Poppets, could also be used as holders for a variety of items.

Poppets by Poppytrail are made of earthenware in much the same manner as fine dinnerware. Special clay formulas and decorative glazes give them their stoneware look and subtle colors.

Poppets:
Metlox catalog sheet.

Poppets and Garden Sculpture Planters:
Metlox catalog sheet.

070 Poppets

[701] 019 Casey, policeman . . . . $35 – 45
[702] 029 Grace, princess . . . . $35 – 45
[703] 039 Monica, nun, 8" . . . . $35 – 45
[704] 049 Elizabeth, queen . . . . $35 – 45
[705] 059 LeRoy, king . . . . $35 – 45
[706] 069 Louisa, girl with muff, 8½" . . . . $35 – 45
[707] 079 Angelina, angel, 7⅝" . . . . $45 – 55
[708] 089 Jenny, seated girl, 8¾" . . . . . . $35 – 45
[709] 099 Ralph, bather man, 11¾" . . . . . $35 – 45
[710] 109 Colleen, girl w/coiled hair, 7¼" . $35 – 45
[711] 119 Barney, bather boy, 8½" . . . . . $35 – 45
[712] 129 Mike, boy with pot, 5½" . . . . . $25 – 35
[713] 139 Pamela, girl in gown . . . . $35 – 45
[714] 149 Sally, girl with baby, 6¾" . . . . $25 – 35
[715] 159 Nancy, girl with dog, 6¾" . . . . $25 – 35
[716] 169 Nellie, girl with bird, 8⅝" . . . . $45 – 55
      179 Betsy, goose girl, 8½" . . . . $50 – 60
      189 Tina, costumed girl, 8½" . . . . . $45 – 55
      199 Johnnie, seated boy/sailor, 7⅛" . $35 – 45
      209 Minnie, mermaid . . . . $45 – 55
      219 St. Francis, 7¾" . . . . $50 – 60
      229 Eliza, flower vendor, 5⅝" . . . . $45 – 55
      239 Penelope, nursemaid, 7¾" . . . $25 – 35
      249 Schultz, tradesman/grocer, 8½" . $45 – 55
      259 Mary Lou, seated lady, 9" . . . . $35 – 45
      269 Sam, little boy, 5¾" . . . . $25 – 35
      279 Kitty, little girl, 6⅝" . . . . $25 – 35
      289 Suzie, girl with purse, 7" . . . . . $35 – 45
      299 Joe, street sweeper/cleaner, 7¼" . $35 – 45
      309 Conchita, Mexican girl, 8¾" . . . $50 – 60
      319 Lorna, standing girl, 7⅞" . . . . . $35 – 45
329 – 389 Salvation Army Group
      329 Molly, tambourine girl, 6⅜" . . . $25 – 35
      339 Grover, bass drum man, 6¾" . $45 – 55
      349 Chester, saxophone man, 8" . $45 – 55
      359 Sarah, choral lady no. 1, 7¾" . . $35 – 45
      369 Zelda, choral lady no. 2, 7⅝" . $35 – 45
      379 Rose, accordion lady, 8" . . . . . $35 – 45
      389 Effie, cymbal lady, 7¾" . . . . . . $35 – 45
      399 Cigar Store Indian, 8¾" . . . . . . $45 – 55
      409 Flora, girl w/flower basket, 7¾" . $35 – 45
      429 Herb Planter with Seeds, 8⅝" . $50 – 60
      439 Emma the Cook, 8" . . . . $35 – 45
      449 Bridget, maid with tray, 8⅛" . . . $35 – 45
      459 Myra & Mattie, mother &
            daughter, 8¼" . . . . $50 – 60

      469 Charlie, seated man, 5⅞" . . . . . $45 – 55
      479 Alaskan Girl, 5" . . . . $25 – 35
      489 Hawaiian Girl, 4¾" . . . . $25 – 35
      499 Mexican Boy, 5½" . . . . $25 – 35
      509 Dutch Girl, 5" . . . . $25 – 35
      519 American Boy, 5¾" . . . . $25 – 35
      529 British Boy, 5" . . . . $25 – 35
      539 Mickey, choir boy no. 1 . . . . . . $25 – 35
      549 Ronnie, choir boy no. 2 . . . . . $35 – 45
      559 Jackie, choir boy no. 3 . . . . . . $35 – 45
      569 Donald & David, group . . . . . . $45 – 55
      579 Dominique, nun, 7½" . . . . $35 – 45
      589 Joy, bell ringer, 6½" . . . . $25 – 35
      599 Pammy, baby, 4½" . . . . $35 – 45
      609 Huck, fishing boy, 6½" . . . . . . $35 – 45
      619 Arnie, golfer, 6½" . . . . $35 – 45
      629 Tony, cart peddler, 7⅛" . . . . . . $35 – 45
      639 Mother Nature, 6¾" . . . . $50 – 60
      649 Nick, organ grinder . . . . $45 – 55
      659 Babe, baseball player, 7¾" . . . $45 – 55
      669 Friar Tuck, 6½" . . . . $35 – 45
      679 Mother Goose, 8" . . . . $45 – 55
      689 Salty the Sea Captain, 5¼" . . . . $35 – 45
      699 Raymond the Barrister, 6¼" . . . $35 – 45
      719 Melinda, girl tennis player, 6¼" $35 – 45
      729 Elliot, boy tennis player, 6½" . . $25 – 35
      739 Doc, 7" . . . . $25 – 35
      749 Chimney Sweep, 7¾" . . . . $45 – 55
      759 School Marm, 6¾" . . . . $45 – 55
      789 Florence, nurse, 8¼" . . . . $35 – 45
      799 Monica with 4" bowl . . . . $45 – 55
      809 Sally with 4" bowl . . . . $35 – 45
      819 St. Francis with 4" bowl . . . . . $60 – 70
      829 Penelope with 4" bowl . . . . $35 – 45
      839 Grover with 4" bowl . . . . $55 – 65
      849 Elliot with 4" bowl . . . . $35 – 45
      859 Doc with 4" bowl . . . . $35 – 45
      869 School Marm with 4" bowl . . . $55 – 65
      879 Arnie with 4" bowl . . . . $45 – 55
      889 Babe with 4" bowl . . . . $55 – 65
      899 Mother Goose with 4" bowl . . $55 – 65
      909 Raymond, barrister with 4" bowl . $45 – 55
      919 Melinda, tennis girl with 4" bowl . $45 – 55
      929 Florence, nurse with 4" bowl . $45 – 55

Toppets: Metlox catalog sheet.

Zoopo's: Metlox archive photo.

Poppets and Toppets: Casey, Policeman Poppet; original Helen Slater Toppet; and Mother Goose Poppet.

071 Toppets, 072 Poppet Accessories, and 073 Garden Sculpture Planters and Poppet Bowls

071 Toppets

509	Arthur, knight	$45 – 55
519	Junior, apple boy	$45 – 55
529	Billy Bob, two-faced boy	$45 – 55
539	Skipper, sailor boy	$45 – 55
549	Lucy, sailor girl	$45 – 55
559	Anne, girl with flowers	$45 – 55

072 Poppet Accessories

609	Marvin, bookend boy, 5"	$45 – 55
619	Muriel, bookend girl, 5¾"	$45 – 55
629	Jack & Jill Couple with Bowl, 7¼"	$50 – 60
659	Carved Bottle Vase, antique bronze	$20 – 25
669	Embossed Bottle Vase, antique copper	$20 – 25
679	Hand Turned Bottle Vase, antique pewter	$20 – 25

073 Garden Sculpture Planters and Poppet Bowls

709	Floral Bowl, 9 x 2"	$20 – 25
719	Floral Bowl, 9¾ x 1½"	$20 – 25
729	Floral Bowl, 10½ x 1½"	$20 – 25
739	Juanita Bonita Planter	$350 – 375
749	Juan Planter	$350 – 375
759	Maria, girl with bird	$350 – 375
769	Zoopo's, turtle	$30 – 40
779	Zoopo's, duck	$30 – 40
789	Zoopo's, chicken	$30 – 40
799	Zoopo's, dragon	$30 – 40
019	Zoopo's, frog	$30 – 40

Owl Line

The Owl Line, dating from the mid-1960s, was the first giftware series designed with complementary items based on the subject or theme of a popular cookie jar. The original set was decorated in rich brown and gold shades. Each intaglio ashtray depicted the owl in an animated manner which contrasted to the stationary, figural poses of the holloware items. The ashtrays and canisters were both three-piece sets. The large canister and the cookie jar were identical pieces that shared the same item number. The Blue Owl and White Owl cookie jars, both later additions, were the same as the Brown Owl except for the color. They were also the only blue and white members of the set. Metlox never included the Owls on a Stump cookie jar in the series. Due to the popularity of the subject matter, the Owl Line was very successful and enjoyed a lengthy production run until the late 1970s. Designed by Helen McIntosh.

Owl Line: owl planter with figurine trio and small 6" ashtray.

	120 Owl Line	
330	Owl Salt, 5¼"	$20 – 25
340	Owl Pepper, 4⅞"	$20 – 25
450	Owl Cookie Jar, 2½ qt.	$40 – 45
450	Owl Canister & Lid, lg., 2½ qt. .	$40 – 45
460	Owl Canister & Lid, med., 2 qt. .	$ 35 – 40
470	Owl Canister & Lid, sm., 1½ qt.	$30 – 35
580	Owl Planter w/Figurine Trio, 5¾" .	$45 – 50
890	Ashtray, sm., 6".	$18 – 20
900	Ashtray, med., 7"	$20 – 22
910	Ashtray, lg., 8"	$22 – 25
121 450	Blue Owl Cookie Jar, 2½ qt. . . .	$65 – 75
122 450	White Owl Cookie Jar, 2½ qt. . .	$65 – 75

Southwest look with Terra Madre. The line was favorably received by both retailers and consumers. Unfortunately, it was discontinued after a short time because the Mexican factory was very unreliable and did not meet production demands.

Metlox created three distinct vegetable lines. The first, introduced in the late 1960s and simply named Vegetable Line; was composed of items that were realistic representations decorated in natural colors. The five canisters were not as evenly graduated in size as most Metlox canister sets. Though often regarded as cookie jars by collectors, these jars were classified only as canisters by Metlox. The four-quart wheat shock served as a cookie jar or a very large sixth canister. The purple cabbage tureen appeared in the Cabbage Lines colored solid chartreuse, white, or evergreen. The ladle for tureens came only in green. The large green leaf plate could be used as the liner for the tureens.

The V 758 Vegetable Group, dating from the early 1980s, was very different from the Vegetable Line. Its all-white color replaced the brilliant, contrasting hues of the earlier line. Only six items were repeated. The four vegetable plates, asparagus plate, and cabbage soup bowl were additions. The only decorated items were the embossed vegetable plates.

"Terra Madre" for Metlox — Hecho en Mexico, a 1988 line composed mostly of items from other artware lines and dinnerware patterns, was unique because it was the only Metlox line not manufactured at the factory in Manhattan Beach. The line was produced in a small plant in Tecate, Mexico, using molds, blocks, and cases originally made at Metlox. Pieces were then shipped back to California for merchandising. During this period of economic downturn for the company, Metlox thought production in Mexico might lower costs. Metlox hoped to capitalize on the popularity of the Mexican-

Made from red instead of white clay, Terra Madre — translated "Mother Earth" — resembled unglazed Mexican sandstone pottery. The corn, squash, broccoli, eggplant, bell pepper, and artichoke canisters were taken from the Vegetable Line. The pumpkin, egg basket, and Henrietta (chicken) canisters were produced originally as glazed cookie jars, not canisters. Margarita, a variation of the Dutch girl cookie jar, was created by Vincent Martinez specifically for this line. The round and square candlesticks appeared in several dinnerware patterns of the 1980s. The Grape Vineyard pitchers came from the sculptured grape dinnerware patterns.

Vegetable Line: squash canister and lid.

Vegetable Line: broccoli canister and lid.

Vegetable Line

[194 550] — —	Wheat Shock & Lid, 4 qt.	$100 – 125
[230 440] 301 440	Corn Canister & Lid, 2½ qt.	$90 – 100
[230 500] 301 500	Corn Server, individual, decorated, 11"	$18 – 20
[231 450] 302 450	Broccoli Canister & Lid, 1½ qt.	$120 – 135
[232 460] 303 460	Eggplant Canister & Lid, 1¼ qt.	$125 – 150
[233 470] 304 470	Red Pepper Canister & Lid, 1½ pt.	$100 – 125
[234 450] 305 450	Squash Canister & Lid, 2½ qt.	$150 – 175
[235 480] 306 480	Tomato Tureen & Lid, 3 qt.	$100 – 110
[235 490] 306 490	Tomato Tureen Ladle, 9½"	$22 – 25
[236 480] 307 480	Purple Cabbage Tureen & Lid, 3 qt.	$125 – 135
[236 490] 307 490	Purple Cabbage Tureen Ladle, 9½"	$22 – 25
[237 050] 308 050	Artichoke Plate, green, 9⅞"	$40 – 45
[237 470] 308 470	Artichoke Sauce Server & Lid, 1½ pt.	$65 – 70
[238 060] 309 060	Leaf Plate, lg., 11"	$35 – 40
[033 500] 311 500	Corn Server, individual, white, 11"	$15 – 16
— — 312 050	Artichoke Plate, white, 9⅞"	$30 – 35

Vegetable Line: purple cabbage tureen and lid.

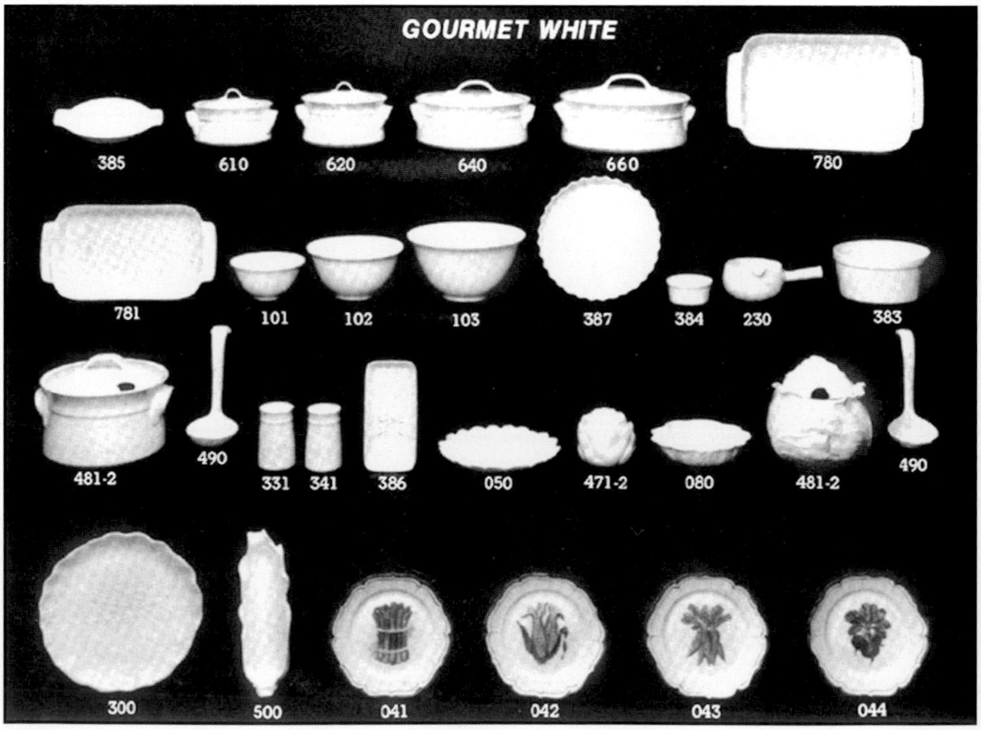

Vegetable Group (White) and Gourmet White Gourmetware: Metlox catalog sheet.

758 Vegetable Group (White)

041	Decorated Vegetable Plate, Asparagus .	$18 – 20	300	Cabbage Leaf Plate.	$28 – 30
042	Decorated Vegetable Plate, Corn. . . .	$18 – 20	386	Asparagus Plate	$25 – 28
043	Decorated Vegetable Plate, Carrot . .	$18 – 20	471-2	Artichoke Sauce Server & Lid. . . .	$45 – 50
044	Decorated Vegetable Plate, Beet. . . .	$18 – 20	481-2	Cabbage Soup Tureen & Lid, 3 qt.	$95 – 105
050	Artichoke Plate	$30 – 35	490	Cabbage Soup Tureen Ladle	$18 – 20
080	Cabbage Soup Bowl	$14 – 16	500	Corn Server	$15 – 16

"TERRA MADRE"
for Metlox
Hecho en Mexico

Terra Madre: Metlox catalog sheet.

Terra Madre for Metlox (Hecho en Mexico)

Canister Jars

005-470	Artichoke.	$55 – 65
005-571	Henrietta (Chicken)	$65 – 80
005-582	Egg Basket	$75 – 100
005-585	Pumpkin.	$95 – 110
005-647	Margarita	$200 – 225
005-702	Corn.	$70 – 80
005-703	Squash	$120 – 140
005-704	Broccoli	$95 – 110
005-705	Eggplant.	$100 – 120
005-706	Bell Pepper.	$80 – 100

Salt & Pepper Sets

003-235	Tomato.	$20 – 22
003-571	Baby Chicks	$28 – 30

003-702	Corn.	$22 – 24

Candlesticks

007-360	Round Candlestick, 5½"	$18 – 20
007-365	Square Candlestick, 8"	$20 – 22

Grape Vineyard

002-370	Large Pitcher, 2 qt.	$45 – 50
002-430	Medium Pitcher, 1 qt.	$35 – 40
002-880	Small Pitcher, 1 pt.	$30 – 35

The following Grape Vineyard items were listed as "not available" in all brochure material. It is uncertain that they were produced.

002-150	Fruit Bowl, 9"	$35 – 40
002-200	Vase, 10"	$40 – 45

Gourmetware Lines

Beginning in 1969, Metlox continuously produced gourmet lines that were marketed by the Poppytrail Artware Division until the company's close in 1989. Metlox used the word "gourmetware" primarily to designate items created for the cooking and serving of food. Gourmetware was advertised as durable oven-to-table earthenware, safe for use in the oven, freezer, dishwasher, and microwave. The larger gourmet lines were similar and shared many identical items (the covered casseroles, soup tureen, au gratin, and lasagna servers). The chief difference between these lines was the color — either solid or, in one instance, two-toned. Each line's name usually contained a description of its color. Various gourmetware items were included in several dinnerware patterns.

The first five lines — P 140 Gourmet, P 141 Flamenco Red Serving Accessories, P 142 Casual Cookery White, P 143 La Casa Brown Gourmet, and P 144 Casual Cookery Yellow (aka Gourmet Spanish Yellow) — were sold both as separate lines and as companion gourmet lines to all the Studio Potter shape dinnerware patterns begun at the same time (1969 – 70). Three lines — P 141, P 143, and P 144 — were named after corresponding dinnerware patterns: P 577 Flamenco Red, P 573 San Clemente La Casa Brown, and P 574 San Clemente Spanish Yellow. All of these lines were solid colored except P 140 Gourmet, a two-toned golden yellow and orange blend. Only P 140 and P 141 did not have side handles on the casseroles, soup

tureen, and lasagna servers. Although complete listings for P 143 and P 144 were unavailable, they included about the same number and kinds of items as the other lines. Most of the items in these five lines were also used in the P 001 California Brownstone and P 591 California Whitestone dinnerware patterns.

The P 145 Hand Forged Holders were black metal frames for the P 140 – 144 salad bowl, soup tureen, casseroles, bean pot, and lasagna servers. They were designed to protect furniture surfaces for direct oven-to-table use. The coffee service holder was especially elaborate. The bottom portion contained separate round holders for the Studio Potter shape coffee pot and mugs. Metal strips on which to hang coffee cups extended outward from a vertical rod attached to the bottom.

In the early 1980s, V 757 Gourmet White was released as an updated version of the earlier lines. Along with existing gourmet items there were several additions: a three-piece mixing bowl set, sauce server, souffle, and quiche server. Later a four-piece canister set, four large platters, a corn server, an artichoke plate, and an artichoke sauce server were added.

The Solid Color Serving Platters and Solid Color Mixing Bowls date from the late 1980s. Both used Colorstax dinnerware colors and numbering. Several of these items were included in V 757 Gourmet White and Colorstax. The beautiful turkey and steer platters, available only in white, featured each animal embossed in the center of the platter. The Mixing Bowls also were produced in four patterns. Two of these sets, True Blue and Laura, featured dinnerware pattern designs.

The following excerpt appeared in a 1975 P 591 California Whitestone leaflet. Its recommendations for the correct use of Metlox oven-to-table items is applicable to all of the gourmetware lines.

"Oven to Table...may be used in the oven; however, it should not be subjected to sudden or extreme temperature change. Ware should be at room temperature, and the oven temperature should not be in excess of 225 degrees when placed in the oven. If the oven is of a higher temperature, it would be advisable to first preheat under hot water. Maximum recommended oven temperature is 400 degrees. When removing dishes from the oven, do not place on a cold surface. Do not place dishes over direct heat such as gas burners or electric plates. Never place a cracked piece in the oven."

Flamenco Red Serving Accessories: 1976 catalog.

140 Gourmet, 141 Flamenco Red Serving Accessories, 142 Casual Cookery (White)

070	Salad/Chowder, ind., 7¼"	$12 – 13	780	Lasagna Server, lg., 15¾ x 10½ x 2⅝"	$40 – 45
100	Salad Bowl, 12⅛"	$35 – 40	[800/803] 809	Beverage Server Urn, Lid,	
150	Serving Bowl, med., 9¼"	$22 – 25		& Warmer	$85 – 95

141 Flamenco Red Serving Accessories Additions

160	Steak Plate/Medium Platter, oval, 10¾"	$22 – 25	300	Buffet Server, rnd., 13¼"	$30 – 35
170	Steak Plate/Large Platter, oval, 13¼"	$25 – 30	380	Individual Baker, 12 oz., 8⅜"	$18 – 20
180	Condiment/Sugar & Lid, 9 oz., 3½ x 4"	$18 – 20	385	Au Gratin, 9⅜"	$20 – 22
190	Sauce Jug/Creamer, 9 oz., 3¼ x 4"	$16 – 18	490	Soup Tureen Ladle, 11"	$18 – 20
220	Salad Fork & Spoon Set	$35 – 40	781	Lasagna Server, med., 13 x 8 x 2⅝"	$35 – 40

142 Casual Cookery (White) Additions

330	Salt	$8 – 9	130	Butter & Lid	$30 – 35
340	Pepper	$8 – 9	300	Buffet Server, rnd., 13¼"	$30 – 35
480	Soup Tureen & Lid, 5 qt., 9¾ x 8"	$55 – 60	380	Individual Baker, 12 oz., 8⅜"	$18 – 20
620	Casserole & Lid, 2 qt., 8 x 5½"	$40 – 45	385	Au Gratin, 9⅜"	$20 – 22
640	Casserole & Lid, 4 qt., 10¾ x 6"	$50 – 55	490	Soup Tureen Ladle, 11"	$18 – 20
660	Casserole & Lid, 6 qt., 12 x 7½"	$60 – 65	781	Lasagna Server, med., 13 x 8 x 2⅝"	$35 – 40
670	Bean Pot & Lid, 5 qt., 9¾ x 8"	$55 – 60			
760	Mug, 7 oz.	$14 – 15			

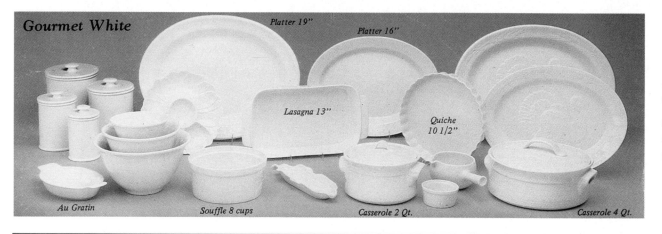

Gourmet White

Platter 19"
Platter 16"
Lasagna 13"
Quiche 10 1/2"
Au Gratin
Souffle 8 cups
Casserole 2 Qt.
Casserole 4 Qt.

Gourmet White: Metlox catalog sheet.

757 Gourmet White, aka Gourmet Group (White)

050	Artichoke Plate, 9⅞"	$30 – 35	470	Canister & Lid, sm., 1 pt.	$15 – 18
101	Mixing Bowl, sm., 16 oz.	$20 – 25	471-2	Artichoke Sauce Server & Lid	$45 – 50
102	Mixing Bowl, med., 44 oz.	$25 – 30	481-2	Soup Tureen & Lid, 5 qt.	$55 – 60
103	Mixing Bowl, lg., 84 oz.	$30 – 35	490	Soup Tureen Ladle	$18 – 20
230	Sauce Server, 1 pt.	$22 – 25	500	Corn Server	$15 – 16
250	Platter, lg., 16"	$35 – 40	610	Casserole & Lid, 1 qt.	$30 – 35
331	Salt, lg.	$14 – 15	620	Casserole & Lid, 2 qt.	$40 – 45
341	Pepper, lg.	$14 – 15	640	Casserole & Lid, 4 qt.	$50 – 55
383	Souffle, lg., 8 cup	$25 – 28	660	Casserole & Lid, 6 qt.	$60 – 65
384	Ramekin, 6 oz.	$14 – 15	771-250	Platter, turkey, 16"	$60 – 65
385	Au Gratin, 9⅜"	$20 – 22	771-785	Platter, turkey, 19"	$75 – 80
387	Quiche Server, 10½"	$30 – 32	780	Lasagna Server, lg., 15"	$40 – 45
440	Canister & Lid, ex. lg., 2¾ qt.	$25 – 30	781	Lasagna Server, med., 13"	$35 – 40
450	Canister & Lid, lg., 2 qt.	$20 – 25	785	Platter, ex. lg., 19"	$45 – 05
460	Canister & Lid, med., 1 qt.	$18 – 20			

Canary Mixing Bowls, Canister Set, and Serving Platters: Metlox catalog sheet.

Country Time: Metlox catalog sheet.

Midnight Blue Mixing Bowls, Canister Set, and Serving Platters: Metlox catalog sheet.

Solid Color Serving Platters

033 Midnight Blue, 034 Sky Blue, 035 Yellow, 036 White, 061 Cranberry, 063 Aqua, 066 Black, 073 Rose, 076 Canary, 088 French Blue

250	Platter, lg., 16"	$40 – 45
771-250	Platter, turkey, 16" (White only)	$60 – 65
771-785	Platter, turkey, 19" (White only)	$75 – 80
774-785	Platter, steer, 19" (White only)	$75 – 80
785	Platter, ex. lg., 19"	$50 – 55

Solid Color Mixing Bowls

033 Midnight Blue, 034 Sky Blue, 035 Yellow, 036 White, 063 Aqua, 066 Black, 073 Rose, 076 Canary, 088 French Blue

101	Mixing Bowl, sm., 16 oz.	$25 – 30
102	Mixing Bowl, med., 44 oz.	$30 – 35
103	Mixing Bowl, lg., 84 oz.	$35 – 40

Pattern Mixing Bowls

709 Country Time, 760 Blue Stipple, 930 True Blue, 941 Laura

101	Mixing Bowl, sm., 16 oz.	$25 – 30
102	Mixing Bowl, med., 44 oz.	$30 – 35
103	Mixing Bowl, lg., 84 oz.	$35 – 40

145 Hand Forged Holders

105	Salad Susan (for 100)	$22 – 25
405	Coffee Service	$40 – 45
485	5 qt. Tureen Holder (for 480)	$20 – 22
625	2 qt. Casserole Holder (for 620)	$15 – 18
645	4 qt. Casserole Holder (for 640)	$18 – 20
665	6 qt. Casserole Holder (for 660)	$20 – 22
675	5 qt. Bean Pot Holder (for 670)	$20 – 22
785	Lasagna Server, lg. Holder (for 780)	$22 – 25
795	Lasagna Server, med. Holder (for 781)	$20 – 22

Songs of Christmas

Songs of Christmas, a series of nine limited edition collector plates, was issued one per year from 1971 to 1979. Each decorative plate depicted a scene based on a traditional carol or secular Christmas song. Because the Vernonware V 780 Della Robbia 8½" salad plate was used as the template, this was the only artware line assigned to the Vernonware Division. The border of the plate was a beautifully carved arrangement of fruit, foliage, and flowers styled after carvings by the renowned Della Robbia family of sculptors in Florence, Italy. Each plate resembled a Christmas wreath encircling a sculptured bas-relief scene in the center of the plate. The scenes were either hand painted in various colors or hand rubbed with one color. The border arrangement was either unpainted or hand rubbed. The word "CHRISTMAS" and the year of the plate were sculpted in the bottom of the border. Each plate was signed with the name of the plate, the plate's number in the series, the name of the series, the year of the plate, and the Vernonware backstamp — "Vernon ware" in an oval followed by "Division of Metlox Potteries, California, USA." Some backstamps included the item number of the plate. Each plate was gift-boxed. Molds were destroyed in December of each year when the limited run was complete.

Each plate is valued from $65 to $80. Use the high end of the scale for a plate in the original box.

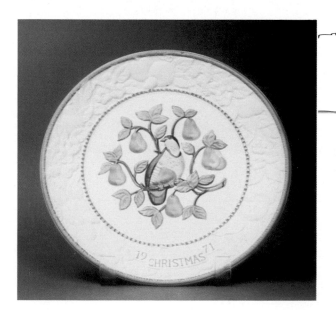

A full color partridge perches in a lush pear tree . . . the first gift 'my true love sent to me.'

Songs of Christmas:
#771-111, 1971 —
"A Partridge in a Pear Tree."

Songs of Christmas:
#772-111, 1972 —
"Jingle Bells."

Sculptured bas-relief of trees, sleigh and 'Grandma's house' is hand-painted in bright, life-like colors.

288

Gleaming halos, hand-painted with 14 Karat bright gold and fired for permanence, add rich beauty to the lovely sculptured cameo-effect of the Mother and Child, surrounded by lilies, field flowers and an adoring lamb. The border of fruit and foliage, carved in the Della Robbia tradition, is hand-rubbed with the green of the plate background.

Songs of Christmas: #773-111, 1973 — "The First Noel."

Songs of Christmas: #774-111, 1974 — "It Came Upon a Midnight Clear."

A peaceful pastoral scene, beautifully carved and hand-rubbed in subtle green-tones, creating a soft, antique, cameo effect.

An artistically carved picture of the Holy Family, hand-rubbed in a heavenly blue-tone that bathes the scene in a mystic light.

Songs of Christmas: #775-111, 1975 — "O Holy Night."

Songs of Christmas: #776-111, 1976 — "Hark! The Herald Angels Sing."

The famous angel Gabriel weathervane of Newburyport, carved in bas-relief, is the motif for this charming hand-rubbed blue-tone plate.

Songs of Christmas:
#777-111, 1977 — "Away in the Manger."

The Christ Child, with a golden halo, surrounded by adoring animals, is carved in bas-relief, hand-painted in muted colors.

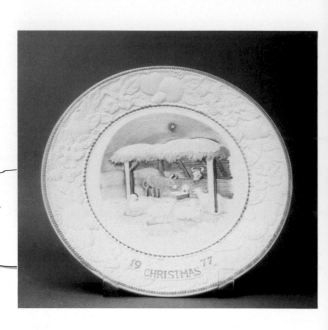

. . .all your fond memories, of a White Christmas, come to mind as you see this sculptured bas-relief full color, hand-painted scene of three young carolers, singing lustily in front of a snow covered home, decorated for the holidays.

Songs of Christmas:
#778-111, 1978 — "White Christmas."

Songs of Christmas:
#779-111, 1979 —
"The Little Drummer Boy."

The Little Drummer Boy accompanied by a lamb, a rabbit and a squirrel, marches through the snow, singing his praise to the Lord. The charming scene is sculptured in bas-relief, hand-painted in full color.

Laura

Canister Sets

A decorative canister set to suit every style, every color kitchen or pantry. Choose from Provincial — Contemporary — Traditional — Casual.

Metlox is noted for its large number of canister sets which became staple items for the company. Along with the typical four-piece canister set, two-piece and three-piece sets were also produced in a profusion of styles, shapes, and designs. Many of the sets were created by Allen and Shaw.

Most sets were issued as separate artware items. Others, however, were included in a related artware line, e.g. the Strawberry, Daisy, and Owl canister sets. Following Metlox's classification, these canisters are listed both in the canister master list and in the appropriate artware line chapter. The item numbers are identical for both listings. Canister sets were also included in certain dinnerware patterns. Each of these is listed with its pattern in the dinnerware section and, for convenience, in a cross-reference list in this chapter.

Since the large canisters resemble cookie jars in size and look, collectors often mistake the two. In several instances Metlox used the same item for both purposes. To clarify any confusion, Metlox's identification and designation of the canisters have been strictly observed in this text.

Canister Sets: Metlox brochure showing Tulips, Plain Red, Daisy, Owl, and Strawberry sets.

All known company item numbers are given for each artware canister. Many of the canisters have two or three item numbers because

Metlox occasionally changed the artware's numbering system. The item number serves to approximate the date of production as follows.

1. Early 1960s: Numbers 12 – 18, the single pantry canisters.

2. 1963 through the mid-1960s: "900" series numbers with each canister assigned an individual three-digit item number. Numbers are arranged in consecutive order by set.

3. 1967 through 1976: Each canister was assigned a six-digit number divided into pairs of three numbers each. The first three numbers, ranging from 040 to 120, represented the canister set's name. The second indicated the canister size — 440 for the extra large (flour), 450 for the large (sugar), 460 for the medium (coffee), and 470 for the small (tea). The Vegetable Line was numbered 230 – 234 followed by the three-digit size number.

4. 1976 through the early 1980s: The same six-digit numbering system with "400" series numbers for each canister set's name. The Vegetable Line was numbered 301 – 305. The 040 Strawberry, 050 Daisy, and 120 Owl canister sets were not renumbered.

5. Early 1980s though mid-1980s: The same six-digit numbering system with "600" and "700" series numbers for the canister set's name. The Vegetable Line was assigned numbers 702 – 706.

6. Mid-1980s until closing: The same six-digit numbering system with a variety of three-digit numbers for each canister set's name.

Measurements are repeated in the lists exactly as they appear in brochure material. Most indicate capacity in quarts and pints rather than weight in pounds and ounces or size in height and/or width.

Designers and modelers took extra care to ensure the stated capacity of each canister design because retailers considered that measurement more important and informative to customers than the others.

The various shapes of the canister sets provide as much interest as their colorful, hand-decorated patterns. In the discussion below, both the artware and the dinnerware canister sets are grouped by common shape. Company shape names are given when known.

1. The Provincial Shape Canister Set.

A. Provincial dinnerware patterns: P 120 Provincial Blue, P 140 Homestead Provincial, P 190 California Provincial, P 290 Happy Time, P 380 Colonial Heritage, P 390 Red Rooster (Decorated), P 391 Red Rooster (Red), P 480 Jamestown, P 490 Provincial Fruit, P 510 Golden Fruit, P 550 Provincial Rose.

B. Artware canister sets: 919 – 922 American Provincial (Boy/Girl), 923 – 926 American Contemporary (Clover), 099 Mushroom, 110 Spanish Floral, 111 Tulip-Orange, 112 Tulip-Blue, 113 La Casa.

Created in the early 1950s for the Provincial dinnerware patterns, this cylindrical shape was used most often. The dinnerware pattern canisters featured wood lids with ceramic finials. The artware canisters had ceramic lids.

2. The Can Shape Canister Set.

A. Dinnerware patterns: V 761 Country Floral (also assigned the number 670 as a separate artware canister set), V 762 Chesapeake.

B. Gourmetware line: V 757 Gourmet White.

C. Artware canister sets: 660 Country White, 709 Country Time, 930 True Blue, 941 Laura, Duck Blues, Gourmet Banded, the Can Shape canisters in various solid colors.

The Can Shape was a 1980s revival of the Provincial Shape canister set with a different company shape name. The artware canisters

113 470 Small

113 460 Medium

113 450 Large

113 440 Extra Large

Canister Set: Metlox La Casa catalog sheet.

930 True Blue and 941 Laura used the decoration and pattern number of their matching dinnerware pattern. Duck Blues copied the Duck Blues cookie jar.

Canister Set: Duck Blues Metlox catalog sheet.

Canister Set: Gourmet Banded Metlox catalog sheet.

3. The Traditional Shape Canister Set.

A. Traditional dinnerware patterns: P 240 Sculptured Grape, P 241 Sonoma, P 242 Mission, P 250 Antique Grape, P 560 Woodland Gold, P 590 California Strawberry.

Designed in the early 1960s, this lovely, bulbous shape was incorporated into the most popular Traditional dinnerware patterns. It was used again in 1988 for the Sonoma and Mission patterns. Two variations of this shape were used in the following unnamed artware canister groups.

B. 931 – 934 Eagle Provincial — First Series, 991 – 994 Tulip (with tulip lid finial), 080 Eagle Provincial — Second Series, 081 1776 Line, 091 Gourmet, 650 Gourmet (Banded) canister sets.

This version was slightly wider in the middle than toward the bottom. The Eagle Provincial sets and the 1776 Line utilized an American eagle decoration. The First Series of Eagle Provincial included groups of patriotic stars as additional decoration while the Second Series substituted the date "1776." The 1776 Line canisters were identical to the Second Series except that the lids were brown with white finials. 091 Gourmet varied designs of a wine bottle and glass, cheese, and fruit. 650 Gourmet (Banded) featured color bands.

C. 098 Gourmet II, 101 – 104 Mediteré canister sets.

This shape was a smaller, slimmer variation of the above shape. The two-toned color of Gourmet II, golden yellow and orange, coordinated with the P 140 Gourmet gourmetware line. The Mediteré set decorated each jar, numbered separately, with a different color.

4. The Tempo Shape Canister Set.

A. Dinnerware patterns: P 441 – 446 California Tempo patterns.

B. Artware canister set: 093 Four Seasons.

These were wide, cylindrical shapes with a smaller, footed base. The California Tempo canister set was offered in solid walnut only. The Four Seasons set boasted elaborate lids with a design of pinecones, nuts, pears, or blooms representing each season. The extra large canister was used for several cookie jars — the Daisy Cookie Canister, the Green with Daisy Lid, and the Yellow with Daisy Lid.

5. 101 Poppy, 117 La Mancha Gold, 118 La Mancha White, 119 La Mancha Green, 412 Plain Red Canister Sets.

These cylindrical shapes with footed bases of equal width were larger than the other canister shapes. The La Mancha and Poppy canister sets consisted of three canisters — the sugar, coffee, and tea. Plain Red added the flour canister which was identical to the sugar canister. Although similar in solid color or design, the La Mancha and Poppy canister sets were never included with the La Mancha or the Wild Poppy dinnerware patterns.

6. The Galaxy Shape Canister Set.

This short-lived design, which flared at the top, was produced in the mid-1980s. Two solid color series were released. The First Series used the colors and item numbers of the Galaxy (First Series) dinnerware patterns; the Second Series appeared in a variety of Colorstax dinnerware colors.

7. 090 Fruit Traditional, 095 Daisy Bouquet Canister Sets.

This ball shape was round and squat. The four-piece Daisy Bouquet set with a hand-decorated pattern should not be confused with the three-piece Daisy set which featured a sculptured design and belonged to the 050 Daisy Accessories artware line.

Canister Sets: Metlox brochure showing Four Seasons, Owl, Granada Gold, Granada Green, and Vegetable sets.

8. The Granada Shape Canister Set: 096 Granada Gold, 097 Granada Green.

These square jars presented a single flower stem design with flat lids.

9. Colorstax Dinnerware Canister.

This single canister was a slimmer, taller variation of the Granada shape with a squash-shaped lid finial. It was produced in the early Colorstax dinnerware colors.

10. The 915 – 918 Basket Shape Canister Sets.

The Basket Shape came in a white or natural coloring. Although this shape was identical to that of the Basket cookie jars, Metlox produced the Basket canisters in two sizes and always classified them as canisters. All of the Basket canisters featured a flowered finial.

11. The 901 – 906 and 935 – 940 California Geranium Canister Sets.

These delightful canisters had a flowerpot bottom and a geranium bloom cluster and leaves lid.

12. The 911 – 914 California Contemporary Canister Sets.

These sandstone and jadestone two-piece sets displayed the circular groove styling of studio wheel pottery.

13. The Numbers 12 – 18 Single Pantry Canisters.

Each single canister was a realistic representation of a fruit or a fish. The Watermelon, Grape, Grapefruit, Orange, and Pineapple canisters were later reclassified as cookie jars.

14. The Vegetable Canister Sets.

A. Dinnerware patterns: P 591 California Whitestone, California Harvest.

B. Artware lines: Vegetable Line, 005 "Terra Madre" for Metlox — Hecho en Mexico.

The realism of these shapes, intensified by intricately sculptured details, prompted their inclusion in several dinnerware patterns and artware lines. While P 591 California Whitestone offered the items in white, California Harvest and the Vegetable Line presented them in natural colors. The 1988 undecorated "Terra Madre" line featured a Southwest, sandstone look by using red instead of white clay. The Vegetable Line and California Whitestone offered only five canisters — the Corn, Squash, Broccoli, Eggplant, and Pepper. California Harvest included the Tomato and Pumpkin canisters. "Terra Madre" added the Artichoke and four cookie jar designs classified as canisters — Henrietta (chicken), the Egg Basket, the Pumpkin, and Margarita — to the five Vegetable Line canisters.

I5. Miscellaneous Artware Line Canister Sets: 040 Strawberry, 050 Daisy, I20 Owl, 680 Bear Canisters.

The Strawberry, Owl, and Daisy canisters were three-piece sets. The large Strawberry and Owl canisters were identical to the cookie jar from the same line. The Daisy set displayed a sculptured daisy bouquet design on a jar with a pedestal base. The Bear canisters imitated the Beau Bear cookie jar. Three-piece and four-piece sets of this series were released. The three-piece set consisted of the extra large canister (identical to the cookie jar), the large canister, and the medium canister. The four-piece set, issued in smaller quantities, added the small canister. All four canisters presented the Beau Bear, each with a different bow decoration. The extra large bear had a maroon bow, the large bear had a blue bow, and the medium bear a yellow bow. The scarce small bear is believed to have had a maroon bow.

Bear Canisters: extra large bear canister, large bear canister, and medium bear canister. Pictured with the bear salt and pepper shakers from the Beau Bear Giftware Group.

Canister Sets: Metlox brochure showing Gourmet, Eagle Provincial, Daisy Bouquet, Fruit Traditional, Spanish Floral, and Mediteree sets.

Fruit Traditional: small canister and lid.

Canister Sets: Metlox brochure showing Fruit Traditional, Gourmet, Daisy Bouquet, Spanish Floral, and Mushroom sets.

Daisy Bouquet: small canister and lid.

Canister Set:
Metlox Gourmet II catalog sheet.

Canister Sets

Single Pantry Canisters

13	Grape	$200 – 250
15	Grapefruit, 9 x 8"	$175 – 200
16	Orange, 9 x 8"	$60 – 70
17	Pineapple, 11¾ x 7"	$75 – 100
14	Red Fish, 9 x 11 x 6"	$90 – 100
18	Tomato, 7¼ x 8"	$50 – 60
12	Watermelon	$300 – 325
14W	White Fish, 9 x 11 x 6"	$90 – 100

Vegetable Line Canisters

230 440 301 440 702 440	Corn, 2½ qt.	$90 – 100
231 450 302 450 704 450	Broccoli, 1½ qt.	$120 – 135
232 460 303 460 705 460	Eggplant, 1¼ qt.	$125 – 150
233 470 304 470 706 470	Red Pepper, 1½ pt.	$100 – 125
234 450 305 450 703 440	Squash, 2½ qt.	$150 – 175

"Terra Madre" for Metlox
Hecho en Mexico Canisters

005-470	Artichoke	$55 – 65
005-571	Henrietta (Chicken)	$65 – 80
005-582	Egg Basket	$75 – 100
005-585	Pumpkin	$95 – 110
005-647	Margarita	$200 – 225
005-702	Corn	$70 – 80
005-703	Squash	$120 – 140
005-704	Broccoli	$95 – 110
005-705	Eggplant	$100 – 120
005-706	Bell Pepper	$80 – 100

American Contemporary (Clover)

923	Extra Large, 10"	$25 – 30
924	Large, 7½"	$20 – 25
925	Medium, 6"	$18 – 20
926	Small, 5¾"	$15 – 18

American Provincial (Boy/Girl)

919	Extra Large, 10"	$30 – 35

920	Large, 7½"	$25 – 30
921	Medium, 6"	$20 – 25
922	Small, 5¾"	$18 – 20

Basket, Natural, with Flower Lid

917	Large	$40 – 50
918	Medium	$35 – 40

Basket, White with Flower Lid

915	Large	$40 – 50
916	Medium	$35 – 40

Bear

680 440	Extra Large, 2½ qt.	$40 – 50
680 450	Large, 2 qt.	$70 – 80
680 460	Medium, 1½ qt.	$60 – 70
680 470	Small, 1 qt.	$150+

California Contemporary, Jadestone

913	Large, 10½"	$25 – 30
914	Medium, 8"	$20 – 25

California Contemporary, Sandstone

911	Large, 10½"	$25 – 30
912	Medium, 8"	$20 – 25

California Geranium, Blue

939	Large, 12"	$30 – 35
940	Medium, 10½"	$25 – 30

California Geranium, Orange

937	Large, 12"	$30 – 35
938	Medium, 10½"	$25 – 30

California Geranium, Pink

901	Large, 12"	$30 – 35
902	Medium, 10½"	$25 – 30

California Geranium, Red

903	Large, 12"	$30 – 35
904	Medium, 10½"	$25 – 30

California Geranium, White

935	Large, 12"	$30 – 35
936	Medium, 10½"	$25 – 30

(continued)

California Geranium, Yellow

905   Large, 12" . . . . $30 – 35
906   Medium, 10½" . . . . $25 – 30

Can Shape Canister Sets

(Four sizes available in various Colorstax colors)

440   Extra Large, 2¾ qt. . . . . $22 – 25
450   Large, 2 qt. . . . . $20 – 22
460   Medium, 1 qt. . . . . $18 – 20
470   Small, 1 pt. . . . . $15 – 18

Country Time

709 440   Extra Large, 2¾ qt. . . . . $22 – 25
709 450   Large, 2 qt. . . . . $20 – 22
709 460   Medium, 1 qt. . . . . $18 – 20
709 470   Small, 1 pt. . . . . $15 – 18

Country White

660 440   Extra Large, 2¾ qt. . . . . $22 – 25
660 450   Large, 2 qt. . . . . $20 – 22
660 460   Medium, 1 qt. . . . . $18 – 20
660 470   Small, 1 pt. . . . . $15 – 18

Daisy

050 450   Large, 3½ qt. . . . . $45 – 50
690 450

050 460   Medium, 3 qt. . . . . $40 – 45
690 460

050 470   Small, 2½ qt. . . . . $35 – 40
690 470

Daisy Bouquet

911   Extra Large, 3 qt. . . . . $30 – 35
095 440
404 440

912   Large, 2 qt. . . . . $25 – 30
095 450
404 450

913   Medium, 1½ qt. . . . . $20 – 25
095 460
404 460

914   Small, 1 qt. . . . . $18 – 20
095 470
404 470

Duck Blues

— 440   Extra Large, 2¾ qt. . . . . $45 – 50
— 450   Large, 2 qt. . . . . $40 – 45
— 460   Medium, 1 qt. . . . . $30 – 35

— 470   Small, 1 pt. . . . . $25 – 30

Eagle Provincial, First Series

931   Extra Large, 11" . . . . $30 – 35
932   Large, 10" . . . . $25 – 30
933   Medium, 9" . . . . $20 – 25
934   Small, 7" . . . . $18 – 20

Eagle Provincial, Second Series

080 440   Extra Large, 3 qt. . . . . $30 – 35
080 450   Large, 2½ qt. . . . . $25 – 30
080 460   Medium, 1½ qt. . . . . $20 – 25
080 470   Small, 1 qt. . . . . $18 – 20

Four Seasons

093 440   Winter, extra large, 3½ qt. . . . . . $30 – 35
093 450   Autumn, large, 2 qt. . . . . $25 – 30
093 460   Summer, medium, 1½ qt. . . . . . . $20 – 25
093 470   Spring, small, 1 qt. . . . . $18 – 20

Fruit Traditional

907   Extra Large, 3 qt., 10½" . . . . $30 – 35
090 440
402 440

908   Large, 2 qt., 8½" . . . . $25 – 30
090 450
402 450

909   Medium, 1½ qt., 7½" . . . . $20 – 25
090 460
402 460

910   Small, 1 qt., 6¾" . . . . $18 – 20
090 470
402 470

Galaxy Shape Canister Sets

(Four sizes available in each color)

First Series colors	Second Series colors
473 Black	034 Sky Blue
481 Midnight Blue	035 Yellow
483 Rose	036 White
486 Sky Blue	063 Aqua
487 White	073 Rose
488 Yellow	088 French Blue

440   Extra Large, 2¾ qt. . . . . $22 – 25
450   Large, 2 qt. . . . . $20 – 22
460   Medium, 1 qt. . . . . $18 – 20
470   Small, 1 pt. . . . . $15 – 18

(continued)

Gourmet

927	Extra Large, 3 qt., 11"	$30 – 35
091 440		
403 440		
928	Large, 2½ qt., 10"	$25 – 30
091 450		
403 450		
929	Medium, 1½ qt., 9"	$20 – 25
091 460		
403 460		
930	Small, 1 qt., 7"	$18 – 20
091 470		
403 470		

Gourmet II

098 440	Extra Large, 2½ qt.	$25 – 30
098 450	Large, 1½ qt.	$22 – 25
098 460	Medium, 1 qt.	$20 – 22
098 470	Small, 1½ pt.	$18 – 20

Gourmet (Banded)

650 440	Extra Large, 3 qt.	$25 – 30
650 450	Large, 2½ qt.	$22 – 25
650 460	Medium, 1½ qt.	$20 – 22
650 470	Small, 1 qt.	$18 – 20

Gourmet Banded

— 440	Extra Large, 2¾ qt.	$22 – 25
— 450	Large, 2 qt.	$20 – 22
— 460	Medium, 1 qt.	$18 – 20
— 470	Small, 1 pt.	$15 – 18

Granada Gold

096 450	Large, 3 qt.	$20 – 25
096 460	Medium, 2¼ qt.	$18 – 20
096 470	Small, 1¾ qt.	$15 – 18

Granada Green

097 450	Large, 3 qt.	$20 – 25
097 460	Medium, 2¼ qt.	$18 – 20
097 470	Small, 1¾ qt.	$15 – 18

La Casa

113 440	Extra Large	$25 – 30
113 450	Large	$20 – 25
113 460	Medium	$18 – 20
113 470	Small.	$15 – 18

La Mancha Gold

117 450	Sugar, large, 5 lb.	$25 – 30
117 460	Coffee, medium, 1½ lb.	$20 – 25
117 470	Tea, small, 16 oz.	$18 – 20

La Mancha Green

119 450	Sugar, large, 5 lb.	$25 – 30
119 460	Coffee, medium, 1½ lb.	$20 – 25
119 470	Tea, small, 16 oz.	$18 – 20

La Mancha White

118 450	Sugar, large, 5 lb.	$25 – 30
118 460	Coffee, medium, 1½ lb.	$20 – 25
118 470	Tea, small, 16 oz.	$18 – 20

Laura

941 440	Extra Large, 2¾ qt.	$25 – 30
941 450	Large, 2 qt.	$20 – 25
941 460	Medium, 1 qt.	$18 – 20
941 470	Small, 1 pt.	$15 – 18

Mediteree

101 450	Gold, extra large, 2 qt.	$25 – 30
102 460	Orange, large, 1½ qt.	$20 – 25
103 470	Beige, medium, 1 qt.	$18 – 20
104 475	Green, small, 1½ pt.	$15 – 18

Mushroom

099 440	Extra large, 2¾ qt.	$25 – 30
408 440		
099 450	Large, 2 qt.	$20 – 25
408 450		
099 460	Medium, 1 qt.	$18 – 20
408 460		
099 470	Small, 1 pt.	$15 – 18
408 470		

Owl

120 450	Large, 2½ qt.	$40 – 45
700 450		
120 460	Medium, 2 qt.	$35 – 40
700 460		
120 470	Small, 1½ qt.	$30 – 35
700 470		

Plain Red

412 440	Flour, extra large, 5 lb.	$25 – 30
412 450	Sugar, large, 5 lb.	$25 – 30
412 460	Coffee, medium, 1½ lb.	$20 – 25
412 470	Tea, small, 16 oz.	$18 – 20

(continued)

Poppy

101 450	Sugar, large, 5 lb.	$30 – 35
101 460	Coffee, medium, 1½ lb.	$25 – 30
101 470	Tea, small, 16 oz.	$20 – 25

1776 Line

081 440	Extra Large, 3 qt.	$30 – 35
081 450	Large, 2½ qt.	$25 – 30
081 460	Medium, 1½ qt.	$20 – 25
081 470	Small, 1 qt.	$18 – 20

Spanish Floral

919 110 440 405 440	Extra Large, 2¾ qt.	$25 – 30
920 110 450 405 450	Large, 2 qt.	$20 – 25
921 110 460 405 460	Medium, 1 qt.	$18 – 20
922 110 470 405 470	Small, 1 pt.	$15 – 18

Strawberry

040 450	Large, 3½ qt.	$60 – 70
040 460	Medium, 3 qt.	$45 – 55
040 470	Small, 2½ qt.	$30 – 40

True Blue

930 440	Extra Large, 2¾ qt.	$25 – 30
930 450	Large, 2 qt.	$20 – 25
930 460	Medium, 1 qt.	$18 – 20
930 470	Small, 1 pt.	$15 – 18

Tulip, Blue

112 440 410 440	Extra Large, 2¾ qt.	$25 – 30
112 450 410 450	Large, 2 qt.	$20 – 25
112 460 410 460	Medium, 1 qt.	$18 – 20
112 470 410 470	Small, 1 pt.	$15 – 18

Tulip, Orange

111 440 409 440	Extra Large, 2¾ qt.	$25 – 30
111 450 409 450	Large, 2 qt.	$20 – 25
111 460 409 460	Medium, 1 qt.	$18 – 20
111 470 409 470	Small, 1 pt.	$15 – 18

Tulip (with Tulip Lid Finial)

991	Extra Large	$30 – 35
992	Large	$25 – 30
993	Medium	$20 – 25
994	Small	$18 – 20

Cross-Reference List of Canister Sets

Dinnerware Shape Sets

Provincial Dinnerware Shape Canister Sets

P 190 California Provincial
P 380 Colonial Heritage
P 510 Golden Fruit
P 290 Happy Time
P 140 Homestead Provincial
P 480 Jamestown
P 120 Provincial Blue
P 490 Provincial Fruit
P 550 Provincial Rose
P 390 Red Rooster (Decorated)
P 391 Red Rooster (Red)

    440 Flour Canister & Lid
    450 Sugar Canister & Lid
    460 Coffee Canister & Lid
    470 Tea Canister & Lid

Traditional Dinnerware Shape Canister Sets

P 250 Antique Grape
P 590 California Strawberry
P 240 Sculptured Grape
P 560 Woodland Gold

    440 Flour Canister & Lid
    450 Sugar Canister & Lid
    460 Coffee Canister & Lid
    470 Tea Canister & Lid

P 241 Sonoma
P 242 Mission

    440 Flour Canister & Lid
    450 Sugar Canister & Lid
    460 Coffee Canister & Lid

Gourmetware Line

757 Gourmet White Canister Set

440 Extra Large, 2¾ qt.
450 Large, 2 qt.
460 Medium, 1 qt.
470 Small, 1 pt.

Dinnerware Pattern Sets

California Harvest Group
Dinnerware Pattern Canisters

430 Squash, 2½ qt.
435 Tomato, 2 qt.
440 Corn, 2½ qt.
450 Broccoli, 1½ qt.
460 Eggplant, 1½ qt.
470 Red Pepper, ¾ qt.
585 Pumpkin, 2½ qt.

P 440 California Tempo
Dinnerware Pattern Canister Set

P 441 Walnut with Sky Blue
P 442 Walnut with Yellow Gold
P 443 Walnut with Beige
P 444 Walnut with Terra Cotta
P 445 Walnut with Olive Green
P 446 Walnut with White

    440 Flour Canister & Lid
    450 Sugar Canister & Lid
    460 Coffee Canister & Lid
    470 Tea Canister & Lid

P 591 California Whitestone
Dinnerware Pattern Canister Set

440 Corn Canister & Lid, 2½ qt.
450 Squash Canister & Lid, 2½ qt.
450 Broccoli Canister & Lid, 1½ qt.
460 Eggplant Canister & Lid, 1¼ qt.
470 Pepper Canister & Lid, 1½ pt.

V 761 Country Floral and V 762 Chesapeake
Dinnerware Pattern Canister Sets

440 Extra Large, 2¾ qt.
450 Large, 2 qt.
460 Medium, 1 qt.
470 Small, 1 pt.

Colorstax Dinnerware Canister

450 Canister & Lid, 2 qt.

Cookie Jars

The reputation of the Poppytrail Artware Division was greatly enhanced by the extensive line of cookie jars produced from the late 1950s until the company's closing in 1989. Three-dimensional highlighting, rich and vivid underglaze colors, extraordinary attention to detail, and a variety of entertaining subjects characterize the line. Although cookie jar production was originally initiated just to add another colorful offering to the division's various lines, its importance increased gradually and continually until it became a mainstay during the financially troubled 1980s. The jars' success was due to a very talented, imaginative staff who were intensely dedicated to their craft. Evan K. Shaw's "spare no expense, time, or effort" philosophy inspired these designers and modelers always to achieve a perfected, ceramic realization of their initial designs. The originality, quality, and beauty of the jars are the reasons for their growing popularity with collectors today.

Designers

The gifted group of designers who created the Metlox cookie jars truly loved the cookie jar concept and approached it as an art form. Three of these individuals — Bob Allen, Mel Shaw, and Helen McIntosh — came to Metlox from animation backgrounds at Walt Disney, Harman Ising, and MGM. This is evident in the cartoon-like styling and poses of many of the cookie jar characters. Perhaps it is not a coincidence that the production of cookie jars began shortly after Metlox lost its lucrative Disney Figurine contract. Much of the creative energy and attention lavished on that line seems to have been channeled into cookie jar design. Allen and Shaw are credited for most of the early jars. Beginning in the mid-1960s, Helen McIntosh was allowed to display her special expertise as she became the primary designer of cookie jars. Modeler Vincent Martinez closely assisted McIntosh, Phyllis Ord, and Helen Slater with the practical, technical side of production, sometimes slightly altering their original designs to facilitate manufacture. From the mid-1970s, Martinez designed his own jars and was instrumental in the creation of the 1980s giftware groups with a cookie jar subject or theme. John Johnson also deserves special mention for his wonderful underglaze colors which added greatly to the quality look and lustrous beauty of the jars. Vincent Martinez provided the following list which credits, to the best of his memory, each artist with his or her designs.

Cookie Jars and their Designers

Unknown: Mammy, Scrub Woman
Frank Irwin: Debutante
Allen and Shaw: Apple, Golden Delicious
    Apple, Red
    Barrel Series
    Basket Series
    Blue Bird on Pinecone
    Blue Bird on Stump
    Calf – Says "Moo"
    Candy Girl
    Cookie Boy
    Eagle Provincial (1776 date)
    Eagle Provincial Cookie Canister (3 stars)
    Elephant
    Grape
    Grapefruit
    "Happy" the Clown
    Hen
    Hen and Chick
    Humpty Dumpty (no feet)
    Jolly Chef
    Kangaroo
    Kitten – Says "Meow"
    Lamb – Says "Baa"
    Mediteree Series
    Orange
    Pear, Green
    Pear, Yellow
    Pineapple
    Pinocchio
    Pumpkin (boy on lid)
    Rabbit on Cabbage
    Rabbit (with carrot)
    Rocking Horse
    Rooster
    Santa Head
    Schoolhouse
    Scout, Brownie
    Scout, Cub
    Space Rocket
    Squirrel on Pinecone
    Squirrel on Stump
    Squirrel (with acorn)
    Strawberry
    Watermelon
    Wells Fargo
    Woodpecker on Acorn
Helen McIntosh: Bear, Ballerina
    Bear, Beau
    Bear, Circus
    Bear, Roller — with Martinez

Bear, Uncle Sam
Cat, Calico
Cat, Katy
Clown, White
Clown, Yellow
Cow, Purple
Cow, Yellow
Dog (white)
Dog, Fido
Dog, Gingham
Dog, Scottie, Black
Dog, Scottie, White
Duck, Puddles
Flamingo
Goose, Lucy
Goose, Mother
Granada Green
Humpty Dumpty (seated with feet)
Lamb with Flowers
Lion
Little Red Riding Hood
Merry Go Round — with Martinez
Mouse, Chef Pierre
Mouse Mobile
Noah's Ark
Owl, Blue
Owl, Brown
Owl, White
Owls on Stump
Parrot
Pelican, Salty
Pig, Slenderella
Poodle, Black
Poodle, White
Pretty Anne
Rabbit, Easter Bunny
Rabbit, Mrs. Bunny (holding cookbook)
Raccoon, Cookie Bandit
Rag Doll, Boy
Rag Doll, Girl
Rose
Santa, Standing
Topsy
Tulip
Turtle, Flash
Walrus, Wally
Phyllis Ord: Bear, Koala
    Bear, Teddy
    Cookie Girl
    Daisy Cookie Canister
    Daisy Topiary Cookie Jar

Gingerbread
Green with Daisy Lid
Miller's Sack
Seal, Sammy
Yellow with Daisy Lid
Helen Slater: "Cookie Creations" Series
    Chickadee
    Children of the World
    Feathered Friends
    Sunflowers
    Tulip Time
    Embossed Yellow
    Intaglio
    Sun
Vincent Martinez: Barn, Mac's
    Bear, Panda
    Bear, Teddy (with red heart)
    Beaver, Bucky
    Calf, Ferdinand
    Cat, Ali
    Chicken, Mother Hen
    Dinosaur, Dina — Stegosaurus
    Dinosaur, Mona — Monoclonius
    Dinosaur, Rex — Tyrannosaurus Rex
    Duck Blues
    Duck, Francine
    Duck, Sir Francis Drake
    Dutch Boy
    Dutch Girl
    Egg Basket
    Frog, the Prince
    Hippo, Bubbles
    Hippo, Dottie
    Lamb, White
    Lighthouse
    Mammy, Cook
    Mushroom Cottage
    Nun
    Pig, Little
    Piggy, Little
    Pumpkin (stem on lid)
    Rabbit (clover bloom finial)
    Rabbit, Mrs. Bunny (holding carrot)
    Whale, Blue
    Whale, White
    Wheat Shock
Bob Chandler: Bear, Sombrero, Pancho
    Drummer Boy
George Newsome: Dog, Bassett
    Penguin, Frosty
Melinda Avery: Loveland

Process

An awareness and understanding of the complicated modeling process of a cookie jar mold leads to a greater appreciation of the finished product. The following is a simplified explanation furnished by Vincent Martinez, one of the chief modelers of the cookie jars.

    1. The basic shape of the jar, including the lid, is sculptured as a solid "lump" in plasteline, a clay mixed with oils and wax that does not harden, thus allowing the modeler to sculpt the jar's design and change details easily.

    2. A waste mold of plaster of Paris is made from the plasteline model.

    3. Plaster of Paris is poured into the waste mold to produce a solid plaster lump that, after finishing details are applied, resembles the jar's original design. Mold release gel, mixed with water to form a greasy soap, is coated on the waste mold interior. The gel prevents the plaster of Paris from hardening onto the mold.

    4. The plaster lump becomes the base model from which the jar's master molds are made. A cookie jar's hollow, convex shape with three-dimensional styling necessarily prohibits the use of just one mold. A minimum of two and usually several more master molds are required, including the lid as a separate piece. The modeler calculates the number of sections. Clay walls block off each section on the plaster lump. The sections are cast separately in plaster of Paris.

    5. A block and case of hydrastone (a very fine, hard cement) is made for each section. The one-piece square block contains the image of the part. The square case of four parts forms walls around the block that are held together with a metal belt.

    6. Plaster of Paris production molds are cast from each permanent master mold block and case.

    7. Slip (liquid clay) is poured into the production mold. When a calculated, evenly distributed amount of the slip has adhered to the mold, the excess slip is poured out. A good production mold lasts for 60 to 80 casts without losing its fine detailing.

    8. The resulting greenware parts are fitted and smoothed together with the worker's fingers, water, and a sponge to form the completed jar.

Relating this involved, tedious process to one jar's production, the very elaborate styling of the Noah's Ark cookie jar required 11 separate parts. Therefore, 11 block and case master molds had to be made. Although not every jar design needed this many master molds, a majority were very complicated. Vincent Martinez introduced two-section mold designs in 1985 in an effort to cut production costs and work time.

Classification

Only those jars classified as cookie jars in brochures or by Metlox employees are included in the comprehensive list below. Due to their similar size and character/subject shapes, the large and medium canisters of several canister sets are commonly mistaken for cookie jars. Indeed, these canisters can function as a cookie jar. Company brochure material, however, specifically distinguishes the two classifications, always listing cookie jars together as one group and canister sets as another. In a few cases, such as the Strawberry jar, Metlox marketed an identical shape as both a cookie jar and a large canister.

Often the same cookie jar design appeared as a member of a complementary artware line or as the subject/theme of a giftware group. This necessitated including the jar in two or more lists. An excellent example is the popular Brown Owl cookie jar by Helen McIntosh. In addition to the brown jar, blue and white versions of the same design were sold with the 120 Owl Line or by themselves. The brown jar also served as the large canister of the Owl canister set, which in turn was sold both by itself and as part of the Owl Line.

The comprehensive list catalogs and prices all the Metlox jars a collector can reasonably expect to find, including common color and design variations. Several additional criteria, besides Metlox's designation of an item as a cookie jar, were established for inclusion in the list. The jar had to be approved for mass production, manufactured in at least a small quantity, and preferably marketed nationwide. It is important to realize that the hand decorators meticulously had to follow a prescribed color scheme for each approved, mass-produced jar in all color variations. The criteria automatically excluded one-of-a-kind design and decoration variations as well as experimental designs that were never produced. When the company closed in 1989, these rarities were sold, along with the remaining inventory on hand, at very reduced prices. Limited, special order cookie jar designs with a unique, custom decoration produced for one individual, company, or organization were also not considered. All of the above exceptions account for nearly all of the unusual jars found by collectors. These items, which do not meet the established criteria, have surfaced in the marketplace. Because of their scarcity, the value of these jars is determined by the desire of the potential buyer. The authenticity of these unusual, rare jars was verified by company designers who determined whether or not each jar was produced in sufficient quantity to be included in the list.

Each jar is listed by its official company name and any known company aka name variant which was obtained from brochure material or designated by company employees. Incorrect collector nicknames are not included in the listings. To avoid mistaken identification and to clarify any uncertainty, distinguishing descriptions are given in parentheses if two or more decorative or design variations of the same jar were produced. Following Metlox's customary practice, the jars are arranged in alphabetical order by subject matter, i.e. apple, barn, barrel, basket, bear, etc. A few well-known jars are listed by their name, such as Candy Girl, Cookie Boy, "Happy" the Clown, etc. Whenever Metlox included a size or capacity measurement in brochure material, this information is added to the listing.

Numbering Systems

Metlox employed four different item numbering systems, each encompassing a definite time period, during the production years of the cookie jars. A popular, bestselling jar was renumbered with each change if it was continued in production. In the comprehensive list all known item numbers are given with each jar's listing in the order they were assigned. The item numbers indicate approximately when the jar was introduced and merchandised. The four numbering systems are discussed below. Skipped numbers within a given range do not indicate a missing jar.

1. The first system included jars from the late 1950s until 1963. These early jars, combined with other artware lines in a general artware numbering system ranging from one through 999, were randomly assigned numbers from 12 through 39. Design variations were assigned the same number with a different capital letter added to indicate each variation. For example, 30 was the Apple Barrel, 30C the Cookie Barrel, 30P the Pretzel Barrel, and 30N the Squirrel Nut Barrel. Several numbers were used twice for two separate jars, possibly indicating a limited production of one of the jars.

2. From the fall of 1963 until 1967, each jar was assigned a separate "600" series number ranging from 611 to 664. The number 807 Eagle Provincial cookie canister (listed as a cookie jar) was numbered with the Eagle Provincial — First Series artware line.

3. In 1967 a new numbering system assigned each jar a six-digit number divided into two groups of three numbers each. The first group, "100" or "200" series numbers, denoted the jar's name. The second set of digits was usually 550, Metlox's item number for a cookie jar. Very infrequently the number 440 for an extra large canister or 450 for a large canister was given to a jar that could be used either as a cookie jar or as a canister. A cookie jar included in an artware line was assigned the line's number, e.g. 040 for Strawberry Accessories, 050 for Daisy Accessories, 080 for Eagle Provincial — Second Series, and 120 for the Owl Line

4. The last numbering system first appeared in brochure materials dated 1976. Although it followed the six-digit scheme of the previous

system, "500" and "600" series numbers were adopted for the first set of numbers. A large amount of company material from 1976 though the 1980s was available. This material dates more precisely the introduction of new jars as shown below.

11/76: jars 501 550 – 557 550 (renumbered jars and new jars). Only the numbers and/or names of new jars from the following dated brochures are listed below. New decorated versions of earlier jars are included.

1978: jars 558 550 – 566 550
9/80: jars 567 550 – 575 550
5/82: jars 576 550 – 583 550
1983: jars 585 550 – 597 550
5/84: jars 599 550 – 602 550

6/85: —	Calf, Ferdinand
607 550	Dog, Scottie, Black
609 550	Dog, Scottie, White
—	Duck Blues
611 550	Goose, Lucy
—	Humpty Dumpty (seated with feet)
—	Lamb, White
—	Pig, Little
616 550	Rabbit, Mrs. Bunny (holding carrot)
—	Seal, Sammy
6/86: —	Cat, Ali
622 550	Duck, Francine
—	Dutch Boy
—	Dutch Girl
624 550	Mammy, Cook, Yellow
—	Rabbit, Easter Bunny (color glazed)
1987: 629 550	Barn, Mac's
633-36 550	Dinosaur, Dina
637-40 550	Dinosaur, Mona
641-44 550	Dinosaur, Rex
628 550	Flamingo
830 550	Loveland
632 550	Mammy, Cook, Blue
631 550	Topsy, Blue Polka Dots
4/88: 645 550	Mammy, Cook, Red
652 550	Topsy, Red Polka Dots
651 550	Topsy, Yellow Polka Dots

The Mammy (Scrub Woman) and Debutante date from the 1940s. Santa Head was an Allen and Shaw design from the 1950s. Embossed Yellow, Intaglio, and Sun are shown in a photograph of jars introduced in the mid-1970s. These remaining jars are from the mid- to late 1980s.

Bear, Circus	Rabbit, Easter Bunny (solid chocolate)
Bear, Teddy (with red heart)	Rabbit, Mrs. Bunny (holding cookbook)
Cow, Yellow (no flowers)	Santa, Standing (solid chocolate)
three Dinosaurs in lavender	Santa, Standing (black man)
Hippo, Dottie	Topsy (solid blue apron)
Nun	

Markings

Metlox used a variety of in-mold marks, paper labels, and ink stamps to sign the cookie jars. It is assumed that all jars without an in-mold mark or an ink stamp originally bore a paper label. Occasionally a jar was marked both with an in-mold mark or an ink stamp and a paper label. Ink stamps appear to have been the least used marking. The most common in-mold mark on pre-1980s jars was "MADE IN" — "Poppytrail" superimposed over an outline of California — "CALIF."

Frequent variations of this mark were:

1. "MADE IN" — "Poppytrail" superimposed over an outline of California — "CALIF." — "U.S.A."

2. "MADE IN" — "Poppytrail" superimposed over an outline of California — "METLOX" superimposed over the southern half of the outline of California — "CALIF." — "U.S.A."

Jars were often marked "MADE" — "IN" — "U.S.A." or just "U.S.A." Many jars introduced during or after 1983 read "METLOX" — "CALIF." — "U.S.A." Selected jars designed by Vincent Martinez were designated:

1. "METLOX" — "CALIF." — "U.S.A." with "By Vincent" in script — "© '87."

2. "METLOX" — "CALIF." — "U.S.A." — "©" with "By Vincent" in script.

Variations of all of the above in-mold marks (exact capitalization and number of lines uncertain) included:

1. Made in Calif., Poppytrail
2. Made in Calif., U.S.A.
3. Made in Poppytrail, U.S.A.
4. Poppytrail, Calif, U.S.A.
5. Metlox, Made in U.S.A.
6. Metlox, U.S.A.

Common ink stamps were:

1. "U.S.A."

2. and the 1980s "Original" underlined and in script — "CALIFORNIA" — "POTTERY" — "BY" — "Metlox."

Familiar paper labels were:

1. gold in the shape of a poppy that read "MADE IN" — "CALIFORNIA" — "Poppytrail" in script — "POTTERY" — "BY" — "METLOX."

2. a scalloped, circular shape with "METLOX MANUFACTURING CO." encircling a "©."

A cross-reference list of additional cookie jars contains cookie jars included in dinnerware patterns, the jars specifically designed for the Disney Figurine line, and canisters that are sometimes used as cookie jars. Each of these is discussed in the appropriate dinnerware or artware chapter.

Metlox catalog sheets, usually showing many cookie jars per page, are reprinted so that as many jars as possible can be shown. Readers and collectors are strongly urged to consult Fred and Joyce Roerig's *Collector's Encyclopedia of Cookie Jars, Book I and Book II*, excellent reference books with numerous photographs of cookie jars by Metlox and many other companies. A special thanks to Joyce Roerig who shared her extensive knowledge and love of the Metlox cookie jars and her time in establishing pricing.

Remarks on Selected Cookie Jars

Tom & Jerry Jar

The solid color Tom & Jerry Bowl cookie jar was the only jar produced by Metlox during the Prouty years (1927 – 46). Mentioned in 1939 advertising material, it was an item offered in the large "200" Series (aka Poppy Trail) dinnerware pattern. Except for the missing "Tom & Jerry" inscription, the jar was identical to the Tom & Jerry punch bowl in the dinnerware pattern. It came in the same assortment of vivid colors with a gloss glaze and pastel colors with a satin glaze.

Cookie Jar: Debutante (pink dress).

Debutante

The fascinating history of the Debutante jar began at a small ceramics pottery on San Fernando Boulevard owned and operated by the family of Metlox modeler Frank Irwin. The jar was designed by the young Irwin as part of his family's nursery rhyme line produced in the late 1930s. When the Irwins joined Evan K. Shaw at American Pottery, the line was continued in production. Shaw demonstrated his appreciation of the jar by manufacturing it through the late 1940s after his purchase of Metlox.

Mammy (Scrub Woman)

The Mammy (Scrub Woman) was first produced by Brad Keeler in workspace he rented at Evan K. Shaw's American Pottery during the early 1940s. The jar was designed by one of Keeler's employees. When Keeler moved his business after the disastrous fire at American Pottery in 1946, he sold the molds, blocks, and cases to Shaw who continued to produce the jar through the late 1940s at Metlox.

Provincial Shape Jar

The cookie jar included in the Provincial dinnerware shape was identical in size and shape to the extra large canister of the Provincial canister set. Introduced in the early 1950s, this cylindrical design, a ceramic jar and a wood lid with a ceramic finial, was produced in 11 Provincial dinnerware patterns. The word "Cookies" appeared under nine of the dinnerware patterns' design, by itself on the all-white P 480 Jamestown, and not at all on the all-red P 391 Red Rooster (Red).

Disney Jars

The four Walt Disney cookie jars — Donald Duck (holding his hat), Donald Duck (holding a cookie), Dumbo, and the gorgeous Cinderella's Coach — were created as members of the Disney Figurine Line. Produced in relatively small numbers, they are extremely rare. Prices are astronomical for these jars since Disney figurine collectors, as well as cookie jar enthusiasts, vie for them.

Fruit Jars

The Watermelon, Grape, Grapefruit, Orange, and Pineapple jars, originally designated as single pantry canisters, were intended as "go-alongs" for the Casual Serving Accessories, a line of table and food serving items in the form of realistic fruit, corn, and sombrero shapes. All of the fruit jars were reclassified as cookie jars in 1963.

"Story Book Cookie Jars"

The following jars were labeled "Story Book Cookie Jars" in brochure material from the late 1950s and the early 1960s.

21 Squirrel on Stump	29 Schoolhouse
21B Blue Bird on Stump	30 Apple Barrel
22 Kitten – Says "Meow"	30C Cookie Barrel
23 "Happy" the Clown	30N Squirrel Nut Barrel
25 Jolly Chef	30P Pretzel Barrel
26 Cookie Boy	31 Rocking Horse
27 Pinocchio	32 Humpty Dumpty
28 Candy Girl	33 Elephant

Cookie Jar: Orange.

Cookie Jar: Squirrel on Pinecone.

34 Rabbit on Cabbage
35 Wells Fargo
36 Squirrel on Pine Cone
36B Blue Bird on Pine Cone

37 Kangaroo
38 Hen and Chick
39 Lamb – Says "Baa"

A "California Ceramic Creations" artware catalog contains these entertaining blurbs about the line and some of its jars.

Story Book Cookie Jars
Straight from the Pages of Mother Goose

"These charming novelty cookie jars will enchant the youngsters and amuse grownups. Long after the wonderful world of childhood is gone, young fry will remember the great adventure of stealing cookies from Pinocchio's head, or dipping into goodies 'hidden' in the Little Country Schoolhouse! And what could be gayer in the kitchen than one of these Story Book cookie jars to add a colorful decorative note?

Tattle-Tale... #22

Meows when you tip her hat to warn Mother that a grubby little fist is reaching for a cookie! 10" high.

Candy Girl... #28

Blonde, sweet and demure, specially when her head is filled with sugar and spice 'n everything nice! 9" high.

Cookie Jar: "Happy" the Clown.

Pinocchio... #27

What could be more fitting than to stuff this famous Boy of fiction with spicy ginger cookies? 11" high.

Jolly Chef... #25

Keeps what he knows about cooking under his hat, where all good chefs keep their secrets! 11" high.

Happy, the Clown... #23

He's grinning all over because he knows where Mother hid the cookies! 11" high.

Cookie Boy... #26

There are no snails or puppy dog tails in this boy! He's sweet as can be with his head filled with goodies! 9" high.

The Little Country Schoolhouse... #29

...When little hands lift off the roof, the bell rings a warning for Mother! 11" high."

The Kitten — Says "Meow," Lamb — Says "Baa," and Calf — Says "Moo" jars were designed with criers (voice boxes) that were activated when the jar's lid was removed. Designers Allen and Shaw's inspiration for this concept was the Tat-L-Tale cookie jar which also had a crier in the lid. This jar was produced by Helen's Ware where Allen and Shaw worked for a short period in 1946 before joining Metlox. The round voice boxes, usually made of cardboard and sometimes plastic or tin, were glued into round casting holes designed into the underside of the jar's lid. The Schoolhouse came with a bell which hung in the tower on top of the roof lid.

Each of the Barrels had two copper bands encircling each jar.

Baskets

Eleven variations of the Basket cookie jar were produced, six with natural coloring and five in white. The difference between each jar was the lid's decoration. The white and natural baskets with a flower lid both came in a large and a medium size and were always classified as canisters, never cookie jars, by Metlox.

Daisy Jars

The Green with Daisy Lid and the Yellow with Daisy Lid jars were straight-sided, canister-like shapes identical to the extra large canister of the Tempo dinnerware shape. The same jar, decorated with carvings of daisies on the side of the jar as well as the lid, became the Daisy Cookie Canister.

Cookie Creations

During the mid-1970s, Helen Slater, a studio art potter hired by Metlox to design the Poppets and Toppets lines, created eight cookie jars with an atypical look. Her hand-thrown style is apparent in the jars' ultra-embossed patterns that seem to have been created by attaching separate clay parts to the jar body. This effect, however, was achieved by the modeling skill of Vincent Martinez. The Cookie Creations Series, promoted as "a new concept in cookie jars," featured five cylindrical jars with childlike images and flat lids with finials shaped as the jar's subject matter. Sun, Embossed Yellow, and Intaglio were canister-like jars with abstract designs. Merchandised on a limited basis only, the jars were discontinued after a brief production run.

Bisque Jars

Teddy Bear, Gingerbread, Cookie Girl, Little Piggy, Mouse Mobile, Cookie Bandit, Noah's Ark, and Owls on Stump were first introduced in bisque versions. A textured slip, colored with terra cotta, was sprayed onto each jar to give a rough finish. Selected details in the design were then highlighted with color glazes. This technique was very similar to the Poppets process. Glazed versions of each jar, hand decorated with underglaze colors, were released in 1978.

Cookie Jar: Gingerbread (bisque version).

Decorative Variations

Rag Doll, Girl and Pretty Anne were the same design. The Rag Doll, Girl was dressed in a plain white jumper over a blue blouse while Pretty Anne wore a white jumper decorated with orange flowers and an orange stripe over a yellow blouse.

Cookie Jar: Pretty Anne.

The white Dog and the cream Dog, Fido were identical, as were the brown Walrus and a slightly smaller cream Walrus, Wally. In both cases, the second versions were decorated differently and given a name.

Three versions of the Hippo were created. Bubbles came in a yellow and green or a light gray and green version. Dottie was white with yellow dots.

All other jars with decorative variations (unless specifically discussed below) kept the same name. The variations are described in parentheses after the jar's name in the comprehensive list.

Duck Jars

Duck Blues and Duck, Francine were variations of the popular Sir Francis Drake jar. Duck Blues featured Sir Francis Drake with blue instead of green decoration. Francine was the Sir Francis design sporting a hat.

Easter Bunnies

The original version of the Easter Bunny Rabbit was a solid chocolate color. This version was produced in a small, trial run. When it did not sell well, the second, and more common, decorated version was introduced.

Cookie Jar: Easter Bunny Rabbit.

A similar set of circumstances applied to Mrs. Bunny Rabbit. The first Mrs. Bunny held a cookbook saying "Mud Fudge." This was altered to the popular Mrs. Bunny holding a carrot design.

Santa

The Standing Santa was marketed in three versions. The first, resembling a solid chocolate candy figure, did not sell well. The second, more familiar version depicted a hand-decorated Santa as a white man. The third version, Santa as a black man, came later. Shortly before the company closed, a terra cotta experimental version was also produced in very limited numbers.

Mammy and Topsy

The color variations of the Mammy (Cook) and Topsy jars were released over a three-year period from 1986 – 88. Yellow Mammy was the first to appear. Initially, many retailers, feeling the subject matter of the jar might offend some African Americans, were reluctant to carry the jar. Their attitude changed when sales were excellent. Metlox added the Blue Mammy and Blue Topsy in 1987. The first version of Topsy featured her with a blue and white apron. This was quickly altered to the familiar blue polka dots design. The sustained popularity of these jars led to the introduction of the Red Mammy, Yellow Polka Dots Topsy, and Red Polka Dots Topsy in 1988, along with the creation of the Mammy & Me giftware groups in yellow, blue, or red which included the Mammy & Pappy shakers with the Mammy and Topsy cookie jars.

Vegetable Line

The four large, single canisters of the Vegetable Line — the Corn, Squash, Broccoli, and Eggplant — are often used as cookie jars. These realistic shapes in natural colors, however, were always classified as canisters by Metlox. An all-white version of these canisters was included in the P 591 California Whitestone dinnerware pattern.

"Terra Madre"

The 1988 "Terra Madre" for Metlox — Hecho en Mexico line included eight large jars designated as canisters by Metlox that are some-

Cookie Jars: Standing Santa in black man and white man versions.

times mistaken for cookie jars. This short-lived line, produced for Metlox by a small factory in Tecate, Mexico, used the molds, blocks, and cases of original Metlox designs. "Terra Madre" — Spanish for "Mother Earth" — featured a Southwest, sandstone look created by the use of red instead of white clay. Four of the Vegetable Line canisters — the Corn, Squash, Broccoli, and Eggplant — and three cookie jar designs — the Egg Basket, Pumpkin (stem on lid), and Henrietta (Chicken) — were manufactured. Vincent Martinez created Margarita, a Mexicanized version of his Dutch Girl cookie jar, specially for the line. If Metlox had not closed, a glazed, hand-decorated version of Margarita, produced in Manhattan Beach, was planned.

Artware Jars

The following pre-1980 artware lines contained these cookie jars:

1. Eagle Provincial — First Series: Eagle Provincial Cookie Canister (three stars);

2. 040 Strawberry Accessories: Strawberry;

3. 050 Daisy Accessories: Daisy Cookie Canister and Daisy Topiary Cookie Jar;

4. 080 Eagle Provincial — Second Series: Eagle Provincial Cookie Jar (1776 date); and

5. 120 Owl Line: Blue Owl, Brown Owl, and White Owl.

The 1980s giftware groups with a cookie jar character as the subject or theme are discussed in the next chapter.

Experimental Jars

Company employees could not give a completely accurate account of all of the cookie jars created experimentally or as special orders. Decoration variations may include antique finish, solid chocolate, glazed white bisque, or terra cotta versions of jars created during the 1980s. An Ali Cat, decorated with numerous flower stems, has been found. Solid versions of the three dinosaurs in Colorstax colors other than aqua, French blue, rose, yellow, and lavender may appear. An all-red Apple was a custom-ordered variation. The Cow continues to be reported in a variety of slightly different colorings. A second Poodle, not the crocheted-looking version in black or white (with front paws up and a bow on its head), was designed but never marketed. The second is sitting upright (like Fido) with blended colors from soft gray to charcoal, black eyes, a pink tongue, and a deep blue or a yellow collar. A few of Vincent Martinez's all-white Standing French Chefs (holding a mixing bowl and a spoon) and Christmas Tree cookie jars were made in very limited numbers.

The above are a few examples, and surely other "new jars," which have their own special value, will surface in the collecting world. Metlox's emphasis on the production of cookie jars naturally entailed much experimentation. To add these one-of-a-kind jars to a comprehensive list of commonly-found, mass-produced jars would be a detriment to both the exactness of the list and the uniqueness of the jars.

550 cookie jars POPPYTRAIL ARTWARE

196 550 Clown, White
200 550 Teddy Bear
202 550 Little Red Riding Hood
197 550 Pretty Ann
195 550 Grapefruit
198 550 Cow with Butterfly, Yellow
201 550 Ginger Bread
203 550 Green with Daisy Lid
204 550 Yellow with Daisy Lid

Cookie Jars: Metlox catalog sheet.

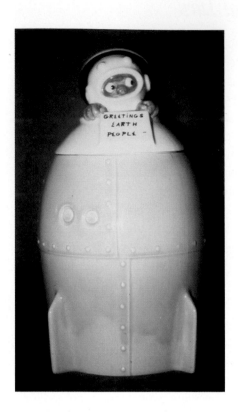

Cookie Jar: Space Rocket.

Cookie Jars: Metlox 1960 artware brochure.

Cookie Jars: Metlox catalog sheet.

#29 Schoolhouse - 11"   #33 Elephant - 11"   #30 Apple Barrel - 11"

#22 Kitten-Meows - 10"   #32 Humpty Dumpty - 11"   #27 Pinocchio - 11"   #31 Rocking Horse - 11"

#23 "Happy" the Clown - 11"   #25 Chef - 11"   #26 Cookie Boy - 9"   28# Candy Girl - 9"

Cookie Jars: Metlox catalog sheet.

Cookie Jar: Gingham Dog (blue).

Cookie Jar: Calf (Ferdinand).

Cookie Jar: rare version of the Purple Cow (with no flowers — just a rope and a bell — and a white head).

Cookie Jars: 1976 Metlox catalog.

Cookie Jar: Walrus (Wally).

Cookie Jar: Little Red Riding Hood.

Cookie Jar: Drummer Boy.

Cookie Jar: Nun.

Cookie Jar: Mona — Monoclonius (rose).

Cookie Jar: Cow-painted Rex — Tyrannosaurus Rex.

Cookie Jars: "The Year of the Dinosaur" Metlox catalog sheet.

Cookie Jar: Yellow Clown.

Cookie Jars: Metlox catalog sheet.

Cookie Jar: Bassett Dog.

Cookie Jar: Santa Head.

Cookie Jars: 1976 Metlox catalog.

Cookie Jar: Dutch Boy.

Cookie Jar: Katy Cat.

Cookie Jar: Flamingo.

Cookie Jar: Raccoon (Cookie Bandit).

Cookie Jars: Metlox catalog sheet.

Cookie Jar: Parrot.

Cookie Jar: Black Scottie Dog.

Cookie Jar: Chicken (Mother Hen).

Cookie Jar: Calf — says "Moo."

Cookie Jar: White Owl.

Apple | Bear, Koala | Bear, Panda | Bear, Roller | Bear, Teddy, Brown | Beaver, Bucky

Cat, Calico | Chicken (Mother Hen) | Clown, White | Cow, Yellow | Dog, Gingham | Duck (Puddles)

Duck (Sir Francis Drake) | Egg Basket | Frog (Prince) | Ginger Bread | Mouse Mobile | Noah's Ark

Orange | Parrot | Rabbit | Rabbit on Cabbage | Raccoon (Cookie Bandit) | Rag Doll Boy

Rag Doll Girl | Squirrel on Pinecone | Strawberry | Whale, White | Lighthouse

Cookie Jars: Metlox catalog sheet.

Cookie Jar: Circus Bear.

Cookie Jar: Uncle Sam Bear.

Cookie Jar: Teddy Bear (with red heart).

319

Cookie Jar: Pineapple.

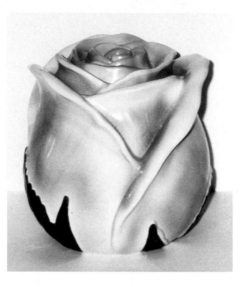

Cookie Jar: Rose.

Cookie Jar: Egg Basket.

Cookie Jars: Metlox catalog.

Cookie Jar: Blue Bird on Pinecone.

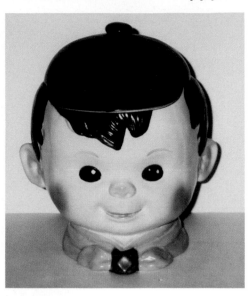

Cookie Jar: Cub Scout.

Cookie Jar: Lighthouse.

Cookie Jar: Experimental version of Ali Cat decorated with flowers.

Cookie Jar: Mac's Barn.

Cookie Jar: Brown Teddy Bear (color glazed).

Cookie Jars: 1976 catalog cover.

Cookie Jars: Metlox catalog sheet showing various cookie jars and some items from giftware lines.

Cookie Jars

20Y [623]	Apple, Golden Delicious, 9½"	$125 – 150
20 [620][167 550][503 550]	Apple, Red, 3½ qt., 9½"	$75 – 85
629 550	Barn, Mac's	$350+
30C	Barrel, with Cookie Lid, 11" (aka Cookie Barrel)	$100 – 125
660	Barrel, with Green Apple Lid	$100 – 125
30P	Barrel, with Pretzel Lid, 11" (aka Pretzel Barrel)	$100 – 125
30 [630][174 550][507 550]	Barrel, with Red Apple Lid, 3¾ qt., 11" (aka Apple Barrel)	$40 – 50
30N	Barrel, with Squirrel & Nuts Lid, 11" (aka Squirrel Nut Barrel)	$75 – 85
31 [638]	Basket, Natural, with Basket Lid, 10½" (aka Basket)	$35 – 45
31C	Basket, Natural, with Cookie Lid, 10½" (aka Cookie Basket)	$40 – 50
656 [180 550][512 550]	Basket, Natural, with Fruit Lid, 4 qt. (aka Fruit Basket)	$40 – 50
	[listed as 655 in one catalog; pictured with a white jar in a brochure]	
657	Basket, Natural, w/Green Apple Lid	$40 – 50
31A [640]	Basket, Natural, with Red Apple Lid, 11" (aka Apple Basket)	$40 – 50
31N	Basket, Natural, w/Squirrel & Nuts Lid, 11" (aka Squirrel and Nuts on a Basket)	$75 – 85
659	Basket, White, with Basket Lid	$35 – 45
655	Basket, White, w/Fruit Lid (natural colors)[listed as 656 in one catalog]	$40 – 50
191 550	Basket, White, w/Fruit Lid (light and dark brown colors), 4 qt. (aka Golden Fruit) [pictured with a natural jar in one catalog]	$40 – 50
658	Basket, White, w/Green Apple Lid	$40 – 50
641	Basket, White, w/Red Apple Lid	$40 – 50
597 550	Bear, Ballerina	$125 – 150
586 550	Bear, Beau	$40 – 50
—	Bear, Circus	$350+
549 550	Bear, Koala	$100 – 125
578 550	Bear, Panda (without lollipop)	$80 – 100
—	Bear, Panda (with lollipop)	$350+
568 550	Bear, Roller	$100 – 125
591 550	Bear, Sombrero, Pancho	$125 – 150
200 550 [527 550]	Bear, Teddy (bisque), 3 qt.	$40 – 45
558 550	Bear, Teddy, brown (color glazed)	$40 – 45
538 550	Bear, Teddy, white, 3 qt.	$40 – 45
—	Bear, Teddy (with red heart)	$175 – 200
601 550	Bear, Uncle Sam	$950+
581 550	Beaver, Bucky	$150 – 175
36B [642][178 550]	Blue Bird on Pinecone (glaze decorated), 3 qt.	$150 – 175
—	Blue Bird on Pinecone (stain finish), 3 qt.	$65 – 75
21B [633]	Blue Bird on Stump (glaze decorated)	$175 – 200
—	Blue Bird on Stump (stain finish)	$65 – 75
—	Calf, Ferdinand	$750+
28 [628][173 550][506 550]	Calf — Says "Moo," 3½ qt., 10½"	$350 – 375
28	Candy Girl, 9"	$325 – 350
—	Cat, Ali	$200 – 225
556 550	Cat, Calico (green w/pink ribbon)	$200 – 225
572 550	Cat, Calico (cream w/blue ribbon)	$140 – 150

(continued)

589 550	Cat, Katy	$75 – 95
571 550	Chicken, Mother Hen (white)	$125 – 150
196 550 [524 550]	Clown, White (blue accents), 3 qt.	$225 – 250
574 550	Clown, White (black accents)	$200 – 225
614 [163 550] [514 550]	Clown, Yellow, 3 qt.	$125 – 150
26	Cookie Boy, 9"	$325 – 350

"Cookie Creations" Series

215 550	Chickadee, 2 qt.	$65 – 85
217 550	Children of the World, 2 qt.	$125 – 150
214 550	Feathered Friends, 2 qt.	$65 – 85
216 550	Sunflowers, 2 qt.	$65 – 85
213 550	Tulip Time, 2 qt.	$65 – 85

537 550	Cookie Girl (bisque), 2½ qt.	$40 – 50
564 550	Cookie Girl (color glazed)	$70 – 80
184 550 [518 550]	Cow, Purple (w/pink flowers and butterfly; yellow bell), 2½ qt.	$600 – 700
570 550	Cow, Purple (w/white flowers; yellow butterfly and bell)	$600 – 700
198 550 [526 550]	Cow, Yellow (w/white flowers and butterfly; yellow bell), 2½ qt.	$350 – 375
—	Cow, Yellow (with no flowers; orange-white butterfly and orange bell)	$500+
050 440	Daisy Cookie Canister, 3½ qt.	$35 – 45
615 [050 550]	Daisy Topiary Cookie Jar, 2¾ qt.	$65 – 75
—	Debutante a. blue dress	$400+
	b. pink dress	$400+

"The Year of the Dinosaur"

Dina-Stegosaurus	633 550	Aqua	$150 – 175
	634 550	French Blue	$150 – 175
	635 550	Rose	$150 – 175
	636 550	Yellow	$150 – 175
	—	Lavender (experimental)	$200 – 225
Mona-Monoclonius	637 550	Aqua	$150 – 175
	638 550	French Blue	$150 – 175
	639 550	Rose	$150 – 175
	640 550	Yellow	$150 – 175
	—	Lavender (experimental)	$200 – 225
Rex-Tyrannosaurus Rex	641 550	Aqua	$150 – 175
	642 550	French Blue	$150 – 175
	643 550	Rose	$150 – 175
	644 550	Yellow	$150 – 175
	—	Lavender (experimental)	$200 – 225
	—	Cow-Painted Rex	$350+

553 550	Dog (white)	$200 – 225
592 550	Dog, Bassett	$650+
595 550	Dog, Fido (cream)	$200 – 225
557 550	Dog, Gingham (blue)	$200 – 225
573 550	Dog, Gingham (cream with blue collar)	$140 – 150

(continued)

607 550	Dog, Scottie, black	$125 – 150
609 550	Dog, Scottie, white	$175 – 200
192 550 [520 550]	Drummer Boy, 2½ qt.	$500+
—	Duck Blues.	$100 – 125
622 550	Duck, Francine.	$250 – 275
579 550	Duck, Puddles a. yellow raincoat	$50 – 60
	b. white raincoat w/yellow trim.	$50 – 60
569 550	Duck, Sir Francis Drake	$40 – 50
—	Dutch Boy	$300 – 325
—	Dutch Girl	$350+
807	Eagle Provincial — First Series Cookie Canister (blue; three stars). . .	$35 – 45
080 550	Eagle Provincial — Second Series (blue; 1776 date).	$35 – 45
582 550	Egg Basket	$175 – 200
33	Elephant, 11"	$750+
—	Embossed Yellow	$35 – 45
628 550	Flamingo	$750+
567 550	Frog, the Prince.	$225 – 250
201 550 [528 550]	Gingerbread (bisque), 3½ qt.	$100 – 125
559 550	Gingerbread (color glazed)	$150 – 175
611 550	Goose, Lucy	$150 – 175
186 550 [519 550]	Goose, Mother, 2 qt.	$300 – 325
623 [170 550]	Granada Green, 3 qt.	$35 – 45
13 [613][162 550]	Grape	$200 – 250
15 [615][195 550][523 550]	Grapefruit, 3 qt.	$175 – 200
203 550	Green with Daisy Lid	$35 – 45
23	"Happy" the Clown, 11"	$350+
183 550	Hen (blue)	$250 – 300
38	Hen and Chick	$350+
566 550	Hippo, Bubbles (yellow and green)	$350+
596 550	Hippo, Bubbles (light gray and green)	$350+
—	Hippo, Dottie (white w/yellow dots)	$350+
32	Humpty Dumpty (no feet), 11"	$500+
—	Humpty Dumpty (seated w/feet)	$250 – 275
—	Intaglio	$35 – 45
25	Jolly Chef, 11" a. blue eyes	$400 – 425
	b. black eyes	$400 – 425
37	Kangaroo, 11¼"	$1,000+
22 [622][169 550][504 550]	Kitten — Says "Meow," 2¾ qt., 10" (aka Tattle-Tale)	$100 – 125
39 [639][177 550][510 550]	Lamb — Says "Baa," 3½ qt.	$100 – 125
—	Lamb, White	$275 – 300
185 550	Lamb with Flowers, 2½ qt.	$300 – 325
583 550	Lighthouse	$350+
187 550	Lion, 2 qt. a. yellow	$150 – 175
	b. green.	$100 – 125
202 550	Little Red Riding Hood	$1,250+
830 550	Loveland	$65 – 75
632 550	Mammy, Cook, Blue	$550 – 575
645 550	Mammy, Cook, Red	$750 – 850

(continued)

624 550	Mammy, Cook, Yellow	$450 – 500
—	Mammy, Scrub Woman	$2,000+
103 450	Mediereé, Beige, 2½ qt.	$35 – 45
101 450	Mediereé, Gold, 2½ qt.	$35 – 45
104 450	Mediereé, Green, 2½ qt.	$35 – 45
102 450	Mediereé, Orange, 2½ qt.	$35 – 45
624	Merry Go Round (blue, white, green)	$200 – 225
171 550	Merry Go Round (orange, yellow, white)	$200 – 225
190 550	Merry Go Round (red, blue, yellow, white)	$200 – 225
551 550	Miller's Sack	$50 – 75
594 550	Mouse, Chef Pierre	$100 – 125
548 550	Mouse Mobile (bisque)	$100 – 125
565 550	Mouse Mobile (color glazed)	$175 – 200
550 550	Mushroom Cottage	$300 – 350
534 550	Noah's Ark (bisque), 2½ qt.	$125 – 150
562 550	Noah's Ark (color glazed)	$175 – 200
—	Nun	$1,000+
16 [616][164 550][501 550]	Orange, 3½ qt.	$60 – 70
121 450	Owl, Blue, 2½ qt.	$65 – 75
625 [120 450][120 550]	Owl, Brown, 2½ qt.	$40 – 45
122 450	Owl, White, 2½ qt.	$65 – 75
535 550	Owls on Stump (bisque), 2½ qt.	$45 – 55
563 550	Owls on Stump (color glazed)	$85 – 95
555 550	Parrot	$350+
611 [160 550]	Pear, Green	$100 – 125
614	Pear, Yellow	$125 – 150
588 550	Pelican, Salty	$175 – 200
593 550	Penguin, Frosty a. short coat	$100 – 125
	b. full-length coat	$100 – 125
—	Pig, Little	$300 – 325
600 550	Pig, Slenderella	$125 – 150
531 550	Piggy, Little (bisque), 3 qt.	$125 – 150
560 550	Piggy, Little (decorated)	$150 – 175
575 550	Piggy, Little (plain white)	$125 – 150
17 [617][165 550][502 550]	Pineapple, 3¾ qt.	$75 – 100
27 [627][172 550][505 550]	Pinocchio, 3 qt., 11"	$375 – 400
653	Poodle, Black	N/D
654	Poodle, White	N/D
197 550 [525 550]	Pretty Anne, 2½ qt.	$175 – 200
632	Pumpkin (boy on lid)	$500+
585 550	Pumpkin (stem on lid)	$150 – 175
576 550	Rabbit, (clover bloom finial)	$225 – 250
—	Rabbit, Easter Bunny (solid chocolate)	$350+
—	Rabbit, Easter Bunny (color glazed)	$300 – 325
—	Rabbit, Mrs. Bunny (holding cookbook saying "Mud Fudge")	$350+
616 550	Rabbit, Mrs. Bunny (holding carrot)	$100 – 125
34 [634][175 550][508 550]	Rabbit on Cabbage, 3 qt., 10"	$125 – 150
25 [625]	Rabbit (with carrot), glaze decorated	$450+

(continued)

645	Rabbit (with carrot), stain finish	$300 – 325
532 550	Raccoon, Cookie Bandit (bisque), 2¾ qt.	$75 – 100
561 550	Raccoon, Cookie Bandit (color glazed)	$125 – 150
621 [168 550][516 550]	Rag Doll, Boy, 1¾ qt.	$200 – 225
618 [166 550][515 550]	Rag Doll, Girl, 2½ qt.	$175 – 200
31	Rocking Horse, 11"	$425+
182 550	Rooster (blue), 2 qt.	$325 – 350
663 [181 550][513 550]	Rose, 2¾ qt.	$400 – 425
—	Santa Head	$400+
—	Santa, Standing (solid chocolate)	$900+
599 550	Santa, Standing (white man)	$675 – 750
—	Santa, Standing (black man)	$750+
29	Schoolhouse, 11" (aka The Little Country Schoolhouse)	$375+
661	Scout, Brownie	$750+
662	Scout, Cub	$750+
—	Seal, Sammy	$500+
23	Space Rocket, 12⅞"	$750+
36 [636][176 550][509 550]	Squirrel on Pinecone (glaze decorated), 3 qt., 11"	$80 – 90
—	Squirrel on Pinecone (stain finish), 3 qt., 11"	$65 – 75
21 [629]	Squirrel on Stump (glaze decorated)	$75 – 100
—	Squirrel on Stump (stain finish)	$65 – 75
24 [624]	Squirrel (with acorn), glaze decorated	$400 – 425
644	Squirrel (with acorn), stain finish	$300 – 325
19 [619][040 450][040 550] [587 550]	Strawberry, 3½ qt., 9½"	$60 – 70
—	Sun	$35 – 45
—	Topsy (solid blue apron)	$500 – 550
631 550	Topsy, Blue Polka Dots	$550 – 575
652 550	Topsy, Red Polka Dots	$800+
651 550	Topsy, Yellow Polka Dots	$550 – 575
664	Tulip	$500+
602 550	Turtle, Flash	$375+
552 550	Walrus (brown and white)	$350 – 375
590 550	Walrus, Wally (cream with blue tie and hat)	$200 – 225
12 [612][161 550]	Watermelon	$300 – 325
35	Wells Fargo, 11 x 9"	$500 – 550
554 550	Whale, Blue	$400 – 450
577 550	Whale, White	$300 – 350
194 550 [522 550]	Wheat Shock, 4 qt.	$100 – 125
193 550	Woodpecker on Acorn, 3 qt.	$375 – 400
204 550	Yellow with Daisy Lid	$50 – 60

Cross-Reference List of Additional Cookie Jars

"200" Series Dinnerware Pattern Cookie Jar & Lid

—   Tom & Jerry Bowl & Lid (without words; various colors)

Provincial Dinnerware Shape Cookie Jar & Lid

P 190 550 California Provincial
P 380 550 Colonial Heritage
P 510 550 Golden Fruit
P 290 550 Happy Time
P 140 550 Homestead Provincial
P 480 550 Jamestown
P 120 550 Provincial Blue
P 490 550 Provincial Fruit
P 550 550 Provincial Rose
P 390 550 Red Rooster (Decorated)
P 391 550 Red Rooster (Red)

Pescado Dinnerware Pattern Fish Cookie Jar & Lid

034 550 Sky Blue
035 550 Yellow
036 550 White
063 550 Aqua
073 550 Rose
199 550 Hand Decorated

Walt Disney Cookie Jars

215 Donald Duck   a: holding hat in front
                              b: holding cookie in front
277 Dumbo
— Cinderella's Coach

Vegetable Line Canisters Used as Cookie Jars

301 440 Corn, 2½ qt.
302 450 Broccoli, 1½ qt.
303 460 Eggplant, 1¼ qt.
305 450 Squash, 2½ qt.

"Terra Madre" Canisters Used as Cookie Jars

005 571 Henrietta (Chicken)
005 582 Egg Basket
005 585 Pumpkin
005 647 Margarita
005 702 Corn
005 703 Squash
005 704 Broccoli
005 705 Eggplant

1980s Giftware Groups

Giftware groups, offering theme- or subject-related accessory items, became a Metlox specialty during the 1980s. A cookie jar character served as the subject for many of these groups. This idea was not new. In the mid-1960s the successful 120 Owl Line was inspired by Helen McIntosh's Brown Owl cookie jar. Now, during this period of continual economic decline for the company, the idea was revived. Metlox hoped to capitalize further on the popularity of its cookie jars by producing matching giftware accessories. Several other groups — the Banks, Carousel Mugs, Chip 'N Dips, and Flower Pots — added variety to the overall selection. Groups that Metlox classified as "Gourmet Giftware" — 757 Gourmet White, Cabbage Line, Mixing Bowls, Serving Platters, and various canister sets — are discussed in the appropriate artware chapters.

All of the cookie jar groups did not include the same selection of items. Although most common groups contained a cookie jar,

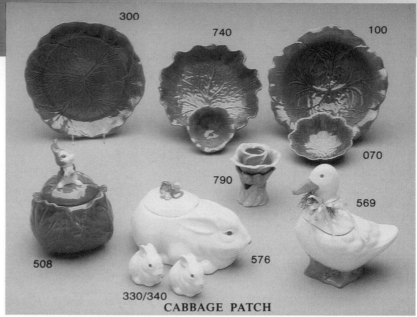

CABBAGE PATCH

platter, and salt and pepper set, many times a different mixture of additional items was offered in each group. The items copied the design and coloring of the cookie jar subject styled either as the same shape or as a hand-decorated pattern. The soup tureen was the cookie jar shape with an opening in the lid for a ladle. The salt and pepper set typically was an identical pair. Both clock designs were battery-operated.

The individual giftware groups are discussed in chronological order. Usually the cookie jar was introduced several years before the group. Each item in a group was assigned a six-digit number. The first three digits was the group's number, usually the same as the cookie jar's number. The second set of three digits was the item number — 550 for a cookie jar, 330 for a salt, 340 for a pepper, 170 for a platter, 760 for a mug, etc. — adopted from the dinnerware item numbering system. A special thanks to Vincent Martinez and Melinda Avery who supplied much valuable information about each group, including the designer's name.

1982

Duck Group: The original item selection included the Sir Francis Drake cookie jar, the duck platter, the three-piece duck tureen, and the duck salt and pepper set. The Francine cookie jar and the Ducks in Circle chip 'n dip were added in 1986. Designed by Vincent Martinez.

Duck Group: Duck (Francine) cookie jar, duck salt, and duck pepper.

Rabbit Group: The white rabbit with the clover bloom finial, designed by Vincent Martinez, was the subject.

Nautical Group: This theme-related group featured Vincent Martinez's Lighthouse cookie jar and sailboat platter. Helen McIntosh contributed the seal salt and pepper.

Chicken Group: A combination of old and new designs comprised this large group. Vincent Martinez created the Mother Hen cookie jar, chicken platter, and three-piece chicken tureen. The chicken individual server, chicken casserole, and chicken salt and pepper were respectively the original hen on nest, chicken covered casserole, and hen on nest salt designs from the early 1950s Provincial dinnerware shape by Allen and Shaw.

1983

Proud Bear Plate: The interesting history of this gift plate began when Melinda Avery conceived the idea while waiting in line at a carwash. The car in front of her had a bumper sticker reading "I'm Proud to be an American." She immediately visualized Beau Bear waving an American flag on a plate with this boast inscribed on the border. Robert McIntosh designed her concept and Bob Chandler modeled the plate. The Provincial shape dinner plate with rivet styling was chosen as the template. The center was a white background sporting a hand-decorated bas-relief of Beau Bear wearing a maroon bow and waving the flag. The border was tan, complementing the bear's coloring. "I'M PROUD TO BE AN AMERICAN" appeared on the border also in bas-relief. At first, Metlox distributed the plate with a Metlox backstamp. When the plate did not sell well, Metlox transferred the

merchandising rights to The Red Plate Company, a giftware plate specialist. These plates were backstamped "THE RED PLATE COMPANY" — "CALIFORNIA, USA 1983" — "PROUD BEAR PLATE."

1984

Sombrero Group: This large group of 13 items was modeled on two popular designs. The Sombrero bear shakers imitated the Sombrero Bear (Pancho) cookie jar. The other items were styled after Allen and Shaw's sombrero chip 'n dip, a perennial favorite since its introduction around 1960. Designed by Bob Chandler.

Sombrero Group: Sombrero Bear pepper and ashtray/candy dish.

Bear Group: Helen McIntosh's lovable Beau Bear cookie jar provided the model for the salt and pepper set. The Beau Bear canisters, produced as three-piece and four-piece sets, were never included as members.

Beau Bear Group: bear salt and bear pepper.

Mouse Group: Originally, this group was limited to the Chef Mouse (Pierre) cookie jar (blue neckband), the small mouse pepper (yellow neckband), and the large mouse salt (green neckband). The

Proud Bear plate.

Julius Cheeser cheese shaker (green neckband), the same design as the salt shaker, was added in 1986. Designed by Helen McIntosh.

Carousel Mugs: These straight-sided mugs in 13 solid colors were also offered in the Colorstax dinnerware pattern as an alternative to the regular, slightly concave mugs. Bob Chandler designed the Carousel mugs to be machine-made rather than hand-cast in molds.

1985

Duck Blues Group: This group featured the Sir Frances Drake cookie jar, the duck platter, and the duck salt and pepper set of the Duck Group decorated with blue instead of green. The quiche server and clock (a 1986 addition) both displayed a hand-decorated duck pattern rather than a duck shape. The four-piece Duck Blues canister set was not included in the group. Designed by Vincent Martinez.

Seal Group: Phyllis Ord's Sammy Seal cookie jar was combined with Helen McIntosh's seal shakers which also appeared in the Nautical Group.

Seal Group: Seal (Sammy) cookie jar, seal salt, and seal pepper.

1986

Cat Group: Vincent Martinez's Ali Cat cookie jar inspired the cat platter and cat salt and pepper.

Humpty Dumpty Group: Helen McIntosh created the cookie jar, and Bob Chandler designed the child's set which included a clock, plate, bowl, and comical two-handled mug, all decorated with hand-painted patterns.

Blue Bird Group: The V 760 Blue Bird dinnerware pattern, rather than a cookie jar, provided the hand-painted design for this unusual mixture by Bob Chandler. The 2-quart pitcher was adapted from the redesigned Provincial dinnerware shape. Other decorated versions of the three-piece mixing bowl set appeared in Colorstax and as a Gourmet Giftware item. Bob Chandler created the clock design which was also used in the Duck Blues, Humpty Dumpty, and Loveland groups.

Christmas Group: This distinctive set by Helen McIntosh was a theme-related group. Santa designs, decorated as a white man or a black man, were the Standing Santa cookie jar and the Santa candy dish/planter. The chip 'n dip and three candy dishes were Christmas tree shapes. The chip 'n dip is extremely rare. Unfortunately, a Christmas Tree cookie jar by Vincent Martinez was never mass produced.

Banks: Helen McIntosh designed the three animal banks. The black splotches on white coloring of the Cow and Piggy (IRA) were later imitated in the Holstein Herd dinnerware pattern.

Chip 'N Dips: The green cabbage, white cabbage, and sombrero chip 'n dips were 1960s designs by Allen and Shaw. Vincent Martinez created the others. The Ducks in Circle featured small Sir Francis Drake ducks on the bowl interior. The flowered Lady's Bonnet displayed a yellow bow tie with small blue flowers that encircled the dip while the other two Lady's Bonnets had a blue or a yellow band.

Cat Group: cat platter.

1987

1989

Loveland Group: This three-piece set was created by Melinda Avery. The clock's hand-painted pattern featured a two-story house in the center and a heart with two tulip stems on the top and the bottom. The canister from Colorstax served as the cookie jar with the word "COOKIES," the heart, and the two tulips as decoration. The two-quart pitcher from the Provincial dinnerware shape presented the house and flowers with heart-shaped blooms.

Flower Pots: Three sizes of flower pots, designed by Bob Chandler, were offered in an assortment of six colors. They were also included in Colorstax.

Round Clock: This impressive piece, designed by Vincent Martinez shortly before the company closed, was plagued with production problems. Because it tended to crack during normal firing with other pieces, the clock needed a separate firing at lower temperatures that was slower and more expensive. Production was halted early in its run by the company's abrupt close. Originally intended to be offered in the six colors of the flower pots, only aqua was produced in any quantity.

1988

Mammy & Me: This four-piece set, offered in yellow, blue, or red decoration, showcased the popular Mammy and Topsy cookie jars with the Mammy salt and Pappy pepper shakers. Vincent Martinez designed the Mammy and Pappy items, and Helen McIntosh created Topsy. This group is very collectible today, appealing to cookie jar as well as black memorabilia collectors.

Cabbage Patch Group: The most eclectic of all of the groups, this assortment combined four green cabbage items, three cookie jars (Rabbit on a Cabbage, Sir Francis Drake, and the white rabbit), and the rabbit shakers. The unique item was the Simmering Rose Potpourri Burner designed by Vincent Martinez. The complementary colors of the members added to the attractiveness of the group.

Giftware Groups: Metlox catalog sheet.

DUCK BLUES   DUCK, (SIR FRANCIS DRAKE)   GOOSE, LUCY

DUCK (PUDDLES)   APPLE   ORANGE   STRAWBERRY   PUMPKIN   RABBIT ON CABBAGE   RACCOON (COOKIE BANDIT)

RABBIT   PIG, LITTLE   PIG, SLENDERELLA   LAMB, WHITE   HUMPTY DUMPTY   RABBIT (MRS. BUNNY)

PIG, LITTLE   PIG, SLENDERELLA   RABBIT, EASTER BUNNY   RABBIT, MRS. BUNNY   RABBIT ON CABBAGE   STRAWBERRY   DUTCH BOY (NEW)   DUTCH GIRL (NEW)

BLUE BIRD   LADY'S BONNET CHIP 'N DIP   COW BANK (NEW)   RABBIT BANK (NEW)   PIGGY BANK (IRA) (NEW)   CABBAGE CHIP 'N DIP

CHRISTMAS   SHELL CHIP 'N DIP LOTUS COLORS   COLORSTAX COLORS

BBQ Plate 11"   Demitasse Cup & Saucer 5 oz.   Buffet Plate 12"   Jumbo Cup & Saucer 16 oz.   Coupe Plate 13"

Giftware Groups: Metlox catalog sheets.

Duck, Sir Francis Drake

Duck Platter, Salt & Pepper

Duck Tureen 3 pc. set

Rabbit

Rabbit Platter, Salt & Pepper

Rabbit Tureen 3 pc. set

Chicken Mother Hen, Salt & Pepper

Chicken Platter

Chicken Tureen 3 pc. set

Individual server and lid

Chicken Casserole 2 qt.

Sailboat Platter Salt & Pepper

Lighthouse Cookie Jar

Apricot, Black, Canary, Cranberry, Jade, Lilac, Midnight Blue, Plum, Rose, Sand, Sky Blue, White, Yellow

NEW FOR 1983 AND 1984

Beau Bear Salt & Pepper

Sombrero Bear, Pancho Salt & Pepper

Ballerina Bear

Chef Mouse, Pierre Salt & Pepper

Cat, Katy

Dog, Bassett

Dog, Fido

Pumpkin

Hippo, Bubbles

Pelican, Salty

Penguin, Frosty

Walrus, Wally

Giftware Groups: Metlox catalog sheet.

Flower Pots/Clock: Metlox catalog sheet.

Duck Group: Duck tureen, lid, and ladle.

Duck Group: Duck (Sir Francis Drake) cookie jar, duck salt, and duck pepper.

Giftware Groups

Banks
821 001 Cow	$150 – 175
822 001 Piggy, IRA	$120 – 140
823 001 Rabbit	$120 – 140

Bear or Beau Bear Group
586 550 Beau Bear Cookie Jar	$40 – 50
586 330 Bear Salt	$15 – 20
586 340 Bear Pepper	$15 – 20

Blue Bird Group
760 101 Mixing Bowl, sm., 16 oz.	$25 – 30
760 102 Mixing Bowl, med., 44 oz.	$30 – 35
760 103 Mixing Bowl, lg., 84 oz.	$35 – 40
760 370 Pitcher, lg., 2 qt.	$45 – 50
760 — Clock	$110 – 125

Cabbage Patch Group
508 550 Rabbit on a Cabbage Cookie Jar	$125 – 150
569 550 Duck Cookie Jar, Sir Francis Drake	$40 – 50
576 550 Rabbit Cookie Jar, white	$225 – 250
758 070 Cabbage Soup Bowl, 8"	$16 – 18
758 100 Cabbage Salad Bowl, 14"	$55 – 60
758 300 Cabbage Leaf Platter, 14"	$40 – 45
576 330 Rabbit Salt	$40 – 45
576 340 Rabbit Pepper	$40 – 45
758 740 Cabbage Chip 'N Dip, green, 12½"	$50 – 55
073 790 Simmering Rose Potpourri Burner, 6½"	$70 – 75

Carousel Mugs, 10 oz.
103 760 Apricot	$14 – 15
104 760 Black	$14 – 15
105 760 Canary	$14 – 15
106 760 Jade	$14 – 15
107 760 Lilac	$14 – 15
108 760 Plum	$14 – 15
109 760 Rose	$14 – 15
110 760 Sand	$14 – 15
111 760 Sky Blue	$14 – 15
112 760 White	$14 – 15
113 760 Cranberry	$14 – 15
114 760 Midnight Blue	$14 – 15
115 760 Yellow	$14 – 15

Cat Group
— Cat Cookie Jar, Ali	$200 – 225
— Cat Platter	$65 – 75
— Cat Salt	$40 – 45
— Cat Pepper	$40 – 45

Chicken or Mother Hen Group
571 550 Chicken Cookie Jar, Mother Hen	$125 – 150
571 121-2 Chicken Individual Server & Lid	$80 – 85
571 170 Chicken Platter	$60 – 70
571 330 Chicken Salt	$20 – 25
571 340 Chicken Pepper	$20 – 25
571 620 Chicken Casserole & Lid, 2 qt.	$115 – 125
571 784 Chicken Tureen, Lid, Ladle (3-pc. set)	$125 – 135

Chip 'N Dips
300 740 Cabbage, green, 12"	$50 – 55
303 740 Cabbage, white, 12"	$40 – 45
320 740 Sombrero	$40 – 45
330 740 Lady's Bonnet, Blue Band	$50 – 55
331 740 Lady's Bonnet, Yellow Band	$50 – 55
360 740 Lady's Bonnet, Flowers	$55 – 60
370 740 Ducks in Circle	$65 – 70

Christmas Group
599 550 Standing Santa Cookie Jar (white man)	$675 – 750
— Standing Santa Cookie Jar (black man)	$750+
— Santa Candy Dish/Planter (white man)	$100 – 125
— Santa Candy Dish/Planter (black man)	N/D
— Christmas Tree Chip 'N Dip	N/D
— Christmas Tree 3-Section Candy Dish, lg.	$65 – 70
— Christmas Tree Candy Dish, med.	$35 – 40
— Christmas Tree Candy Dish, sm.	$25 – 30

Duck Group
569 550 Duck Cookie Jar, Sir Francis Drake	$40 – 50
622 550 Duck Cookie Jar, Francine	$250 – 275
569 170 Duck Platter	$60 – 70
569 330 Duck Salt	$30 – 35
569 340 Duck Pepper	$30 – 35
370 740 Ducks in Circle Chip 'N Dip	$65 – 70
569 784 Duck Tureen, Lid, Ladle (3-pc. set)	$125 – 135

Duck Blues Group
— Duck Blues Cookie Jar	$100 – 125
— Duck Blues Platter	$60 – 70
— Duck Blues Salt	$50 – 60
— Duck Blues Pepper	$50 – 60

(continued)

—	Duck Blues Quiche Server	$30 – 35
—	Duck Clock	$115 – 125

Flower Pots

034 Sky Blue	063 Aqua
035 Yellow	073 Rose
036 White	077 Red

560	6" Flower Pot	$18 – 20
561	6" Flower Pot Saucer	$7 – 8
570	7" Flower Pot	$20 – 22
561	7" Flower Pot Saucer	$7 – 8
580	8" Flower Pot	$22 – 25
581	8" Flower Pot Saucer	$9 – 10

Humpty Dumpty Group

—	Humpty Dumpty Cookie Jar	$250 – 275
—	Humpty Dumpty Child's Plate	$20 – 25
—	Humpty Dumpty Child's Bowl	$25 – 30
—	Humpty Dumpty Child's Mug, 2-handled	$35 – 40
—	Humpty Dumpty Clock	$125 – 135

Loveland Group

830 550	Loveland Cookie Jar	$65 – 75
830 047	Loveland Clock	$110 – 120
830 370	Loveland Pitcher, 2 qt.	$40 – 45

"Mammy & Me" Group

624 550	Mammy Cookie Jar, Yellow	$450 – 500
624 330	Mammy Salt, Yellow	$80 – 90
624 341	Pappy Pepper, Yellow	$80 – 90
651 550	Topsy Cookie Jar, Yellow Polka Dots	$550 – 575
632 550	Mammy Cookie Jar, Blue	$550 – 575
632 330	Mammy Salt, Blue	$80 – 90
632 341	Pappy Pepper, Blue	$80 – 90
631 550	Topsy Cookie Jar, Blue Polka Dots	$550 – 575
645 550	Mammy Cookie Jar, Red	$750 – 850
645 330	Mammy Salt, Red	$100 – 125
645 341	Pappy Pepper, Red	$100 – 125
652 550	Topsy Cookie Jar, Red Polka Dots	$800+

Mouse or Chef Mouse Group

594 550	Mouse Cookie Jar, Chef Pierre	$100 – 125
594 330	Mouse Salt	$40 – 45
594 340	Mouse Pepper	$40 – 45
594 335	Julius Cheeser Cheese Shaker	$45 – 50

Nautical Group

583 550	Lighthouse Cookie Jar	$350+
583 170	Sailboat Platter	$60 – 65
583 330	Seal Salt	$65 – 75
583 340	Seal Pepper	$65 – 75

Rabbit Group

576 550	Rabbit Cookie Jar	$225 – 250
576 170	Rabbit Platter	$75 – 85
576 330	Rabbit Salt	$40 – 45
576 340	Rabbit Pepper	$40 – 45
576 784	Rabbit Tureen, Lid, Ladle (3-pc. set)	$135 – 150

Seal Group

—	Seal Cookie Jar, Sammy	$500+
—	Seal Salt	$65 – 75
—	Seal Pepper	$65 – 75

Sombrero Group

591 550	Sombrero Bear Cookie Jar, Pancho	$125 – 150
320 018	Hot Sauce Cup	$12 – 15
320 040	Salad/Taco Plate	$10 – 12
320 170	Platter, lg.	$30 – 35
320 330	Sombrero Bear Salt	$20 – 25
320 340	Sombrero Bear Pepper	$20 – 25
320 420	Sombrero Bowl	$12 – 15
320 620	Casserole & Lid, 2 qt.	$40 – 45
320 640	Casserole & Lid, 4 qt.	$60 – 65
320 740	Sombrero Chip 'N Dip	$40 – 45
320 760	Mug	$15 – 18
320 781	Lasagna Server, med.	$35 – 40
320 910	Ashtray/Candy Dish	$25 – 30

Miscellaneous

—	Proud Bear Plate	$65 – 75
515	"Metlox Est. 1927 California Pottery" Clock, rnd.	$400+

Contributors

Kathi Amerine

Joyce Becker

Mary Ann Brenner

Lilian Cardona

Paul Carollo

Betty Casey

Sherri and Tim Cole

David Collie

Joan Connor

Dick Deitz

Oletha Dobbs

Rhea and Gene Evanson

Marv Fogleman

Rose Mary and Charles Follett

Shirley Grace

John Grogan

Barbara Hilton

Tamara Hodge

Evelyn Jackowski

Mike Kelly

Ann Kerr

Stacy Lackey

Cynthia Lair

Roberta and Bill Lear

Charlie Liebentritt

Laurence Martin

Anne, Mary Lynn, and Larry McDonald

John McGinley

Katherine McGinnis

Kelly Middendorp

Max Miller

Pat Minton

Anne W. Nelson

Wayne Otway

Caroline Peacock

Don Peacock

Keith Robinson

Greg Rollie

Louise Rountree

Mary Ann Rydowski

John Savell

Lynda and Rick Saxton

Cal Schluter

Judy Scott

Craig Solomonson

Georgana Stabler

Bill Stern

Terry Telford

Richard Theiss

Judi and Dave Thompson

Beverly Varner

Magdalene Vulkovic

Linda Waters

Larry Weitkemper

B.A. Wellman

Fred Wilhelm

Brenda Williams

Photograph Contributors

Most of the photography in this book is credited to the following individuals and lab:

Juan Fernandez, photographer
Georgian Cordell, consultant
NPL Incorporated
1926 West Gray
Houston, TX 77019
713-527-9300

Other special contributions were provided by the following collectors and photographers:

Cookie Jars
Harvey Takasugi
Tom Clyde

Prouty Artware and Dinnerware
James Elliot-Bishop
Reba Schneider
Shel Izen Photography
7345 35th Ave., NE
Seattle, WA 98115
206-527-4755

Metlox Miniatures
David Dudley

Prouty Artware
Thomas Derrah
Chris Dearborn
Keith Robinson

Disney Figurines
Stan Pawlowski

Directory of Metlox Dealers

The following contributors regularly stock and mail order Metlox items.

Joel Albert
10406 Montpelier Cir.
Orlando, FL 32821
407-352-1957

Samantha Burdick
Burdick Antiques and Collectibles
646 Mt. Hermon Station Rd.
Northfield, MA 01360
413-498-5552

Lorna and Mick Chase
Fiesta Plus
380 Hawkins Crawford Rd.
Cookeville, TN 38501
615-372-8333

Jack Chipman
P.O. Box 1079
Venice, CA 90291
(artware only)

Deborah Dykstra
Cookie Jar Junction
1025 E. Armetta Dr.
Camp Verde, AZ 86322
520-567-3688

James Elliot-Bishop
Elliot's 20th Century California Pottery
8412 5th Ave., NE
Seattle, WA 98115
206-527-7038

Lois Finnerty
9167 Pekin Rd.
Novelty, OH 44072
216-338-4528

Doris Frizzell
5687 Oakdale Dr.
Springfield, IL 62707
217-529-3873

Carl Gibbs Jr.
The California Connection Dinnerware Shop
1716 Westheimer
Houston, TX 77098
713-521-9661 (home)
713-529-8340 (shop)

Laura Kaspar
9260 McLean
Beaumont, TX 77707
409-866-1567

David Lackey
David Lackey Antiques and China Matching Service
2311 Westheimer
Houston, TX 77098
713-942-7171

Marlene LaTurco
The China Hutch
3719 Redthorne Dr.
Amelia, OH 45102
513-752-1057

Larry and Linda Love
Dinnerware Classics!
4125 Sperry St.
Dallas, TX 75214
214-821-6852

Stan Pawlowski
Ski Sculptures and Fine Jewelry
3028 E. Broadway
Long Beach, CA 90803
310-433-9999
(Disney figurines only)

Lisa Rastello
Milkweed Antiques
5 N 531 Ancient Oak Ln.
St. Charles, IL 60175
708-377-4612

David Reardon
P.O. Box 460157
San Francisco, CA 94114
(Freeform dinnerware patterns only)

Veronica Sanford
Veronica and Del's Antiques
415-355-5617
(artware only)

Reba Schneider
Reba's Classic Ceramics
222 Westlake Ave., N.
Seattle, WA 98109
206-622-2459

Elizabeth Scott
3655 Camellia Dr.
San Bernardino, CA 92404
909-883-0601

Clarence Souza
Front Porch Collectibles
154 Massasoit Dr.
Warwick, RI 02888
401-461-8094

Bibliography

Chipman, Jack. *Collector's Encyclopedia of California Pottery*. Paducah, KY: Collector Books, 1992.

Cunningham, Jo. *The Collector's Encyclopedia of American Dinnerware*. Paducah, KY: Collector Books, 1982.

Dennis, Jan. *A Walk Beside the Sea: A History of Manhattan Beach*. Manhattan Beach, CA: Janstan Studio, 1987.

Duke, Harvey. *Official Price Guide to Pottery and Porcelain, Eighth Edition, Revised and Expanded*. New York, NY: The House of Collectibles, 1995.

Lehner, Lois. *Lehner's Encyclopedia of U.S. Marks on Pottery, Porcelain and Clay*. Paducah, KY: Collector Books, 1988.

Nelson, Maxine. *Versatile Vernon Kilns Book II*. Paducah, KY: Collector Books, 1983.

Nelson, Maxine. *Collectible Vernon Kilns*. Paducah, KY: Collector Books, 1994.

Roerig, Fred and Joyce Herndon Roerig. *The Collector's Encyclopedia of Cookie Jars*. Paducah, KY: Collector Books, 1991.

Roerig, Fred and Joyce Herndon Roerig. *The Collector's Encyclopedia of Cookie Jars Book II*. Paducah, KY: Collector Books, 1994.

Schroeder's
ANTIQUES
Price Guide

. . . is the #1 best-selling antiques & collectibles value guide on the market today, and here's why . . .

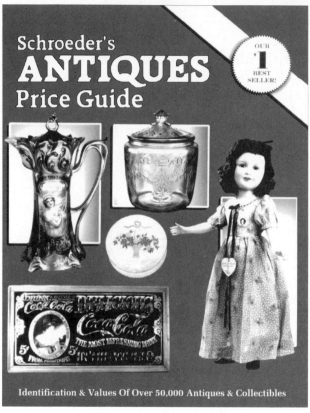

Schroeder's **ANTIQUES** Price Guide

OUR #1 BEST SELLER!

Identification & Values Of Over 50,000 Antiques & Collectibles

8½ x 11, 608 Pages, $14.95

COLLECTOR BOOKS
A Division of Schroeder Publishing Co., Inc.